"A rich and diverse collection of essays, this book is a fine testimony to the capacity of David Ford as a Christian theologian. It not only connects church and the university, worship and theology, the academic study of religion and the Abrahamic faiths, but it also encourages others to share that vocation and fulfill its vision."

—David Fergusson

University of Edinburgh

The Vocation of Theology Today

The Vocation of Theology Today

A Festschrift for David Ford

Edited by
TOM GREGGS,
RACHEL MUERS,
and SIMEON ZAHL

CASCADE *Books* • Eugene, Oregon

THE VOCATION OF THEOLOGY TODAY
A Festschrift for David Ford

Cascade Books
An Imprint of Wipf and Stock Publishers
199 W. 8th Ave., Suite 3
Eugene, OR 97401

www.wipfandstock.com

ISBN 13: 978-1-61097-625-1

Cataloguing-in-Publication data:

The vocation of theology today : a Festschrift for David Ford / edited by Tom Greggs, Rachel Muers, and Simeon Zahl.

xiv + 410 pp. ; 23 cm. Includes bibliographical references and index.

ISBN 13: 978-1-61097-625-1

1. Ford, David, 1948–. 2. Theology. 3. Theology—Methodology. I. Greggs, Tom. II. Muers, Rachel. III. Zahl, Simeon. IV. Title.

BR118 G73 2013

Manufactured in the U.S.A.

Contents

Acknowledgments / xi

Contributors / xiii

1 Introduction—*Tom Greggs, Rachel Muers, and Simeon Zahl* / 1

PART ONE: Conversing with Theologians

2 Being a Wise Apprentice to the Communion of Modern Saints: On the Need for Conversation with a Plurality of Theological Interlocutors—*Tom Greggs* / 21

3 The Wisdom and Love of God: Starting a Conversation between Schleiermacher and Ford—*Paul T. Nimmo* / 35

4 The Many Moods of Revelation—*Jason Fout* / 48

5 What Has the "Lutheran" Paul to Do with John? Passive Righteousness and Abiding in the Vine—*Simeon Zahl* / 61

PART TWO: Attending to Scripture

6 Transforming the Grammar of Human Jealousy: Israel's Jealousy in Romans 9–11—*Susannah Ticciati* / 77

7 A Disharmony of the Gospels—*Nicholas Adams* / 92

8 Attending to Scripture: The Homiletic Imperative —*Frances Young* / 108

9 Wisdom and Rapture—*Janet Martin Soskice* / 122

PART THREE: In and For the Church

10 Beyond "Belief": Liturgy and the Cognitive Apprehension of God—*Sarah Coakley* / 131

11 Wonder-Voyaging: The Pneumatological Character of David Ford's Theology—*Ben Quash* / 146

12 "A Secular and Religious World": David Ford's Contribution to the Secularization Debate—*Timothy Jenkins* / 163

13 Theology among the Humanities—*Rowan Williams* / 178

PART FOUR: Reasoning between Faiths

14 What Kinds of Thinking Complement What Kinds of Societal Action?—*Peter Ochs* / 193

15 Theology as a Vocation: A Weberian Perspective —*Basit Bilal Koshul* / 211

16 Dialogue in the Dust: On the Wisdom of Inter-religious Encounter—*Michael Barnes SJ* / 228

PART FIVE: Speaking and Listening in Public

17 Tales of the Unexpected: Theology in Public Space —*Rachel Muers* / 245

18 The Habitus of the Theologian: Thinking through Theological Vocation in Conversation with David Ford —*Alistair I. McFadyen* / 259

19 Between the Constraints of Freedom and the Aspirations of Love: On Bergson, Levinas, and Theology in the Service of Politics—*Paul D. Janz* / 273

PART SIX: Theology and the University

20 For Its Own Sake, For God's Sake: Wisdom and Delight in the University—*Mike Higton* / 289

21 The Place and Significance of Theology in the Contemporary University—*Joseph D. Galgalo* / 303

22 Ecclesial Theology in the University—*C. C. Pecknold* / 314

23 The Shaping of Catholic Theology in the UK Public Academy—*Paul D. Murray* / 330

PART SEVEN: Theology and the Face

24 The Transforming Power of People with Disabilities —*Jean Vanier* / 345

25 Facing Each Other: Friendship, Meaning, and Shaping a World—*Micheal O'Siadhail* / 359

26 "Playing Face to Face"—*Deborah Hardy Ford* / 374

Bibliography of David Ford's Published Works / 393

Index / 401

Acknowledgments

The editors of this book would like to acknowledge a number of people who have been significant in its development. Early conversations about the idea of creating a Festschrift for David Ford also involved Mike Higton, Paul Nimmo, and Ben Quash; each played important roles in helping to determine the form such a project should take. Iain Torrance and Richard Hays have provided ongoing support for the book. Frances Clemson, David Ford's research assistant, generously prepared the bibliography of David's works. Robin Parry, the commissioning editor for this book, has been helpful, gracious, and flexible in the book's production. And Deborah Hardy Ford has not only had to write her own chapter underneath her husband's nose (and keep the secret from him), but has encouraged the editors throughout, as she has done for generations of David's students and former students.

Contributors

Nicholas Adams is Senior Lecturer in Systematic Theology and Theological Ethics at New College, University of Edinburgh.

Michael Barnes is Reader and Senior Tutor in Inter-religious Relations at Heythrop College, University of London.

Sarah Coakley is Norris-Hulse Professor of Divinity at the University of Cambridge.

Deborah Hardy Ford is an Anglican priest, Chaplain at Addenbrookes Hospital, and a psychoanalytical psychotherapist.

Jason Fout is Assistant Professor of Anglican Theology at Bexley Hall, Ohio, USA.

Joseph Galgalo is the Vice-Chancellor of St Paul's University, Limuru, Kenya.

Tom Greggs is Professor of Historical and Doctrinal Theology at King's College, University of Aberdeen.

Mike Higton is Academic Co-Director of the Cambridge Inter-faith Programme, University of Cambridge, and Senior Lecturer in the Department of Theology and Religion at Exeter University.

Paul D. Janz is Professor of Philosophical Theology and Head of the Department of Theology and Religious Studies at King's College London.

Timothy Jenkins is Reader in the Study of Religion at the University of Cambridge.

Basit Koshul is Associate Professor in the Department of Humanities and Social Sciences at the Lahore University of Management Sciences.

Alistair McFadyen is Senior Lecturer in Systematic Theology at the University of Leeds.

Rachel Muers is Senior Lecturer in Christian Studies at the University of Leeds.

Paul Murray is Professor of Systematic Theology and Director of the Centre for Catholic Studies at the University of Durham.

Paul T. Nimmo is Meldrum Lecturer in Theology at New College, University of Edinburgh.

Peter Ochs is Edgar M. Bronfman Professor of Modern Judaic Studies at the University of Virginia.

Micheal O'Siadhail is an Irish poet and former research professor in the Dublin Institute for Advanced Studies.

C. C. Pecknold is Assistant Professor of Systematic Theology at the Catholic University of America.

Ben Quash is Professor of Christianity and the Arts at King's College London.

Janet Martin Soskice is Professor of Philosophical Theology at Jesus College, University of Cambridge.

Susannah Ticciati is Lecturer in Systematic Theology at King's College London.

Jean Vanier is a Canadian Catholic philosopher and humanitarian, and is the founder of L'Arche.

Rowan Williams is Master of Magdalene College, University of Cambridge, and is the former archbishop of Canterbury.

Frances Young is Cadbury Professor of Theology Emerita at the University of Birmingham.

Simeon Zahl is Junior Research Fellow in Theology at St. John's College, University of Oxford.

1

Introduction

Tom Greggs, Rachel Muers, Simeon Zahl

Living a Theological Vocation

David Ford's illustrious academic career is, by his own publicly stated account, an indefinitely extended interruption of his path toward a career in business management. This might mark him out as an unusual theologian. Yet for many professional and amateur theologians throughout the world, as well as for the wider audience that engages with his work on public issues, he is in important respects a definitive theologian; in person or through his writings, he shows them what theology is about. Perhaps the serendipitous nature of David's move into theology has something to say about the vocation of theology itself—called in unpredictable ways out of, and into, the complexities of everyday life. It probably also has something to say about the particular gifts he has brought to theological communities and institutions.

Several of the chapters in this collection, particularly in the final section, focus on aspects of David Ford's life within and beyond the academy that have been particularly significant for his theological work and vocation. He has also, in recent years, given interviews and written short pieces reflecting on his theological journey and identifying formative experiences and encounters,[1] and in this introduction we simply offer a sketch of his theological voyage.

David Ford was born in Dublin in 1948. His undergraduate degree at Trinity College Dublin was in Classics; following graduation, and as a prelude to taking up a management position in industry, he accepted a scholarship to study theology at St. John's College, Cambridge. From there he went to Yale for a master's degree, and returned to Cambridge to study for his doctorate (later published as *Barth and God's Story*) under the supervision of Donald MacKinnon and Stephen Sykes. In 1976 he was appointed as a lecturer in theology at Birmingham, where he stayed until he became, in 1991, the first lay theologian to hold the Regius Chair of Divinity at Cambridge. He is the director of the Cambridge Inter-faith Programme, which was established under his leadership in 2002. Other academic institutions with which he has been closely associated include the Center for Theological Inquiry at Princeton, the Cambridge Theological Federation, the Society for Scriptural Reasoning (of which he was a co-founder), and the Society for the Study of Theology. From 2003 to 2008 he was an academic member of the "Davos" World Economic Forum Council of 100 Leaders. He has been a consultant to the international L'Arche movement since 1993. His theological work with the Church of England and the Anglican Communion includes many years' service on the Doctrine Commission, and serving as a consultant to the global Anglican Primates' Meeting.

This outline biography already reflects many of the themes that recur in this book and that are judged by its authors to be key to Ford's distinctive contributions to theology—the interrelations of church, academy, and public life; the importance of building sustainable institutions, and the creativity and energy that is required for such institution-building; and global and local conversations with and around Scripture and tradition.

One long-running conversation that had a decisive influence on Ford's theological vocation requires particular attention here. Ford's friendship and collaboration with Daniel W. Hardy began when Ford was appointed as lecturer in theology at the University of Birmingham. The chapter in this volume by Deborah Hardy Ford includes her recollections of her father's excitement at David Ford's arrival as a new dialogue partner and colleague. For the younger theologian, the connection with Hardy was to be central to his network of theological friendships and conversations for over thirty years. Their collaboration was far more than a sharing of

1. See Cunningham, "Practical Theology"; Ford, "Journey into Interfaith."

occasional tasks; it was a sustained co-labouring in the service of a shared, though differentiated, theological vocation, of which their co-authored work—*Jubilate: Theology in Praise*—tells only a small part of the story.

Another part of that story emerges in the work edited and written by David Ford, Deborah Hardy Ford, and Peter Ochs after Hardy's death, *Wording a Radiance*. Here both the intensity and the profound hospitality of the theological friendship between Ford and Hardy becomes apparent, as reflections on and from Hardy's final months emerge in Ford's voice, alongside the voices of the other authors and the voices of numerous friends and colleagues whom they drew into their conversations. Still another part of the story of this collaboration could, perhaps, be told through the work of numerous graduate students. Without starting a "school" or a unified movement, Ford and Hardy created the space for continuing and growing networks of theological dialogue, sustained by a shared sense of the joy and the importance of theology.

This collaboration also became the site for a seminal three-way dialogue and friendship between Ford, Hardy, and Peter Ochs. Their dialogue and friendship, across faith traditions (later drawing in Muslim scholars), was central to the development of the distinctive modes of practising and thinking about interfaith engagement found in and around Scriptural Reasoning. Ochs and Ford have continued to accompany, nourish, and shape each other's academic and institutional work over two decades.

Ford's own evolving understanding of the theologian's vocation is reflected in a sequence of programmatic statements about theology's place in the university, in the churches, and in the contemporary world. His inaugural lecture as Regius Professor of Divinity at Cambridge, *A Long Rumour of Wisdom*, on the form and public vocation of theology and religious studies, was followed by numerous articles and occasional pieces on the task of theology,[2] and the major collection of essays, *Shaping Theology*. Most recently, he wrote *The Future of Christian Theology*, setting out a manifesto for a practice rooted deeply in Scripture, tradition, and communities of faith, but also formed by and attentive to a rapidly changing contemporary context.

A more wide-reaching contribution to the future of the discipline is seen in Ford's ongoing commitment to inviting others into the space of theology and making it possible for them to join in the theological task. As mentioned earlier, his name is probably familiar to most undergraduate

2. See, for example, "Theological Wisdom, British Style" and the articles that followed it.

students of theology, in the English-speaking world and beyond, as one of the people from whom they have learned about what theology is, how it has been done in the past, and how to start thinking about their own place within it. Publications throughout his career have made significant contributions to the teaching of theology. The *Very Short Introduction* to theology, three editions of *The Modern Theologians*, and the *Jesus* and *Modern Theologians* readers, all embody the wish, not to encompass or define the field in a restricting way, but to offer a realistic and attractive picture of an activity in which readers can learn to participate.

David Ford is widely recognised for his contribution to the creation and sustaining of academic institutions, and not only for the study of theology. The account he gives in a number of his published works of the mutual benefit to be gained from the genuine integration of theology *and* religious studies in research and teaching of the highest quality, has been carried through in his work with colleagues to extend, strengthen—and rehouse—the Cambridge Faculty of Divinity. He has also served, over many years, several institutions that seek to embody the fruitful relationship between academic theology and faith communities. His commitment to institution-building is reflected not least in his extraordinary efforts—and extraordinary successes—in raising funds to support academic theology and to secure its future in numerous contexts.

Most recently, he became the founding director of the Cambridge Inter-faith Programme. The early work of the Programme includes a major project on the place of religion in the research university—that is, the place of religion beyond the academic discipline of theology and religious studies. The message, which is echoed strongly in many of Ford's writings, is that the university matters not only as a place where theology (and religious studies) can be pursued, but for its own sake—and ultimately, to pre-empt a discussion in Mike Higton's contribution to this book, for God's sake. Ford's developing theological preoccupation with the nature and reality of wisdom is played out in his commitment to the university as a place where wisdom can be sought and found in the service of the common good. The title of one of his widely distributed lectures suggests the magnitude of what he takes to be at stake in the future of the university: "Knowledge, Meaning and the World's Great Challenges."

Characteristics of a Theological Oeuvre

David Ford has been highly prolific over the course of his academic career. At the time of writing, he is the author or co-author of ten books, and the editor or co-editor of a further eight—and that is not to mention the extensive list of articles and book chapters to be found in the bibliography at the end of this volume, or indeed the many hundreds of papers, addresses, and sermons, in academic, ecclesial, and other public contexts, that do not appear in print. Sheer volume alone does not, however, explain why it is difficult to produce a brief summary and introduction to key themes in Ford's theological work and development over the past four decades. Rather, as Alistair McFadyen's essay in this volume explores in more detail, Ford's work reflects a degree of scepticism about grand narratives and neat package summaries in theology. He generally prefers to enter deeply into the particularities of a given work, a given figure, or a given context, avoiding as far as possible the pressures to determine in advance what will be found. At the same time, there are certain themes that have particularly preoccupied him at different periods, and general features of his work over the years that can be helpfully noted—especially for those getting to know his theological approach for the first time.

Those with the patience to engage Ford's theological work deeply will be rewarded with a profound vision of Christian theology. Firstly, for Ford, theology is related integrally to the praise of God and to worship (see, in particular, *Jubilate*). Theology is grounded in the things we do for God's sake, and in the orientation of the self toward God in worship, prayer, and singing (*Self and Salvation*). In later work, Ford develops this theme further as he reflects on worship as the blessing of God's name, and blessing as the fundamental relational dynamic between God, humanity, and all of creation.[3] Theological attention to blessing enables a resolute focus on living and acting "for God's sake" to be combined with attention to creaturely particularity, to the many creatures who live from and toward divine blessing.

Despite certain reservations on his part, Ford has often been read in close connection with the so-called Yale School in theology (sometimes known as postliberalism), centred on the figures of Hans Frei, George Lindbeck, and others associated with Yale in the later part of the twentieth century, and their many students.[4] The association, although contestable,

3. Ford, *Shaping Theology*, 208.

4. See Fodor, "Postliberal Theology." Peter Ochs, one of David's closest collaborators

is helpful as a starting point for understanding Ford's theological orientation, for several reasons. First, Ford counts the work of his Yale teacher and mentor Hans Frei as among his most important theological influences. Second, his work over the years has evinced what could be called a postliberal concern to take the best of contemporary academic thought and criticism seriously while at the same time finding new ways, and rediscovering old ways, to remain deeply loyal to traditional Christian teachings and traditions—in the confident conviction that this is possible! Third, his theological approach is centred upon the Bible as the baseline, dialogue partner, and ongoing creative source for theology, while seeking at the same time to be fully alert to the contributions of historical and other forms of criticism—as well as myriad sources outside of the traditional remit of Christian theology (including Jewish and Muslim sources). Fourth, Ford deeply appreciates, and has himself taken forward in creative new ways, the postliberal insight that theology is as shaped by practices and contexts as it is by conceptualities and doctrines. Finally, there has been a long-standing interest in the theme of narrative (and genre) as a theological category—a category, of great interest to Frei as well,[5] and to which we now turn.

Ford's first book—a revision of his doctoral dissertation, published as *Barth and God's Story*—brought together three lifelong interests: the Bible, the theology of Karl Barth, and the usefulness of narrative and narrative-related categories as a fresh and stimulating resource for biblical interpretation. *Barth and God's Story* brought to light a key feature of Barth's work, the role of biblical narrative in his theology, and argued for the usefulness for theology of seeing the Bible not simply as a set of propositions or a work of pure history, but as a collection of stories (and other genres), carefully crafted to be inhabited and drawn into instead of simply reduced to principles or to sheer information.

More recently, Ford has turned from narrative alone toward a related theme, that of *drama*.[6] Drawing on the typology from literature and poetry of "epic," "lyric," and "dramatic," he has argued that while there is certainly a crucial place for "epic" overviews and overarching narratives in theology and beyond, as well as for introspective, "lyrical" theologizing, the most

and friends over many years, devotes a chapter to Ford's work in his recent book on postliberal Christianity and Judaism, *Another Reformation*, 195–221.

5. Frei, *Eclipse*.

6. Ford, *Future of Christian Theology*, chapters 2 and 3. Key dialogue partners here have been Hans Urs von Balthasar, and Ford's student and long-time colleague Ben Quash. See Quash, *Theology and the Drama of History*.

fruitful category of all for understanding "the Bible, Theology, and Life"[7] is "drama." Drama is particularly effective at conveying "the dynamic particularity of human existence, with its physicality, surprises, initiatives, contingencies, necessities, tensions, and multi-leveled complexity. . . . As it unfolds, a drama invites us to become engaged."[8] To understand "drama" in this sense—including not least the accompanying scepticism Ford has about the tyranny of non-dramatic, "epic" claims in theology that reject alternative approaches, narratives, and confessions out of hand—is to go a long way toward understanding David Ford's approach to theology and the Bible, as well as to academic and institutional work more generally.[9]

If there is a *cantus firmus* in Ford's work, it is creative theological engagement with the Bible. *Barth and God's Story* is explicitly about the concept of biblical narrative. *Meaning and Truth in 2 Corinthians* was co-written with a biblical scholar, his Birmingham colleague Frances Young. *Christian Wisdom* is in large sections an extended reflection on the book of Job, above all on the extraordinary question, "Does Job fear God for nothing?" (Job 1:9). And in more recent years, Ford's attention has turned to the Gospel of John, in a multi-year project due to culminate in a full theological commentary on the Gospel.

Ford summarizes key features of his theological approach to the Bible in the concluding chapter of *The Future of Christian Theology*, aptly titled "The Bible: Creative Source of Theology."[10] First, his approach treats the Bible, without apology, as the canonical Christian Scripture. For Ford this *includes* reading the Bible as a work of literature or history, and in relation to (for example) linguistics, gender studies, sociology, or comparative religion. Second, his approach starts from the view that "there is no necessary conflict or tension between theological interpretation and good scholarship," nor between theological interpretation and hermeneutics. Finally, the core activity for a theologian in relation to the Bible is "thinking through the theological wisdom of Scripture."[11] These are not empty words for Ford: he has spent his career thinking deeply, wisely, and

7. Ford, *Future of Christian Theology*, 23.

8. Ibid.

9. Indeed, chapter 2 in *The Future of Christian Theology*, on drama, may be the best single introduction to Ford's theological approach.

10. Ford, *Future of Christian Theology*, chapter 10. See also especially Ford, "Reading Scripture with Intensity."

11. Ford, *Future of Christian Theology*, 193–95.

theologically through Christian Scripture, and perhaps the best way to learn what he means is to watch him *do* it in his writing.

Much of Ford's theological work over the years has entailed careful, multifaceted unpacking of slightly unexpected "mediating" categories and symbols from the Bible and from life, such as "the face," "cries," and "wisdom." These categories are "mediating" because they often sidestep traditional theological binaries and antagonisms, while being generative for theologians from a wide variety of confessional, theological, and contextual backgrounds. These categories also tend to be rooted deeply in the Bible, in theological tradition, and in pastoral and ecclesial realities.

One important example is the image of "the face," which served as the unifying theme of Ford's first major monograph after arriving at Cambridge as Regius Professor of Divinity, *Self and Salvation*.[12] "Each [human] face is uniquely individual" and therefore highlights the inescapability of human particularity; but each face at the same time is "a primary locus for relating to others and the world" (above all through emotional expression and speech).[13] A human face is fully itself, yet utterly open to the world. An anthropology that begins with the image of the face entails a fundamentally "other-oriented concept of self,"[14] and in this and other senses the face of Jesus Christ is therefore the archetypical "face."[15] The Bible is full of faces, and of face-to-face encounters, from Jesus' shining face at the transfiguration (Matt 17:2), to God's refusal to show his face to Moses (Exod 33:20), to St Paul's meditation on eschatological standing with "unveiled faces" before the Lord (2 Cor 3:18). Altogether, the "face" image brings into fruitful interaction a variety of key theological and biblical themes (especially related to anthropology, soteriology, and Christology), without easily mapping onto a particular confession or dogmatic stance. It serves to open up key sections of the Bible theologically in new, unexpected, and multilayered ways.

In a later monograph, *Christian Wisdom*, Ford explores a different and related theme: *cries*. Like faces, "cries" convey particularity and emotion, but also range very widely in significance, from cries of joy, to cries of surprise, to babies' cries, to cries of pain. Perhaps the most significant

12. Ford, *Self and Salvation*.

13. Ibid., 19.

14. Ibid., 166. Here Ford draws on the thought of Paul Ricoeur, one of his chief theological influences and dialogue partners over many years.

15. As Ford notes, the question of Jesus' face also serves as a bridge between theology and visual art, even as it connects to debates about icons and iconoclasm in the history of the church. Ibid., 181–83.

use of the "cries" theme in this book is the latter, as Ford addresses questions of theodicy through reflection on cries of suffering, reading the book of Job and attending at length to the unanswered cries of the victims of the Shoah.[16] These are cries that "cannot be summarised, synthesized, or done justice to" by mere prose or by neat intellectual systems.[17] Ford's attention to the unassimilable cries of the Shoah is one of the many aspects of his work that has been deeply influenced by his lifelong friendship and intellectual partnership with the poet Micheal O'Siadhail (see O'Siadhail's chapter in this volume), and by his extensive theological engagement with poetry.[18]

As important as any category for Ford has been what he calls "Christian Wisdom." It was the subject of his inaugural lecture as Regius Professor of Divinity as early as 1992,[19] and his work on the theme ultimately culminated in the monograph *Christian Wisdom: Desiring God and Learning in Love*. Above all, for Ford, wisdom is about making judgments and decisions, about engaging with difficult questions and responsibilities in the world in a way that leads to flourishing and avoids "foolishness." Wisdom, as Ford understands it, starts with the realization that many problems—practical, intellectual, theological—do not have an easy solution that can be deduced straightforwardly from some prior principle or other. Wisdom combines "knowledge, understanding, good judgment, and far-sighted decision-making," and can involve both cool rationality and dynamic passion; it includes "the challenges and dilemmas of prudence, justice, and compassion" and the "shaping over time of communities and their institutions"; and it deals with the "discernment of meaning, truth, and right conduct in religion."[20] The great advantage of the term is that it "unites understanding with practice and is concerned to engage with the whole of life."[21] It is a "dramatic" category in Ford's sense, always dynamically engaged with the particulars of life before God.

One helpful way of understanding what Ford means is to consider the many and complex responsibilities and competing priorities faced by, for example, a university professor like himself. Such a person is constantly

16. Ford, *Christian Wisdom*, chapter 4. On this theme, see also Ford, "Apophasis and the Shoah."

17. Ford, *Christian Wisdom*, 121.

18. O'Siadhail, *The Gossamer Wall*.

19. Ford, *Long Rumour of Wisdom*.

20. Ford, *Christian Wisdom*.

21. Ford, *Future of Christian Theology*.

engaged in difficult tasks: choosing between many excellent candidates for studentships or faculty posts; helping to determine the allocation of funds in a cash-strapped university setting, where many causes are both deserving and sorely in need; all the complexities of the professional judgments involved in peer review and examining; choosing what to write about, which books to read, which concepts to focus on in one's own research; and so on. There are few easy or pat answers to such questions. The dynamic virtue by which one seeks to answer them well, taking all relevant factors into consideration, is wisdom. For Christians, as Ford's theology seeks to demonstrate, this means not least seeking *God's* wisdom through the Spirit.

Ford has not yet written a monograph on the Holy Spirit (his students live in hope!),[22] but key categories like wisdom, desire, and praise are deeply undergirded by pneumatology, as is his basic orientation toward practice and particularity over theoretical abstraction and "epic" claims. Peter Ochs has demonstrated plausibly that the Spirit is a (the?) unifying theme in Ford's work, characterizing his thought (especially in *Christian Wisdom*) as a "reparative pneumatology."[23] Ford has also engaged with Pentecostal theology, perhaps the most thoroughly Spirit-oriented contemporary approach, for far longer and in more depth than have most non-Pentecostal academic theologians.[24]

In Ford's view, the "vagueness" and multiple, superabundant character of the Spirit can serve as a helpful counterbalance to the equally important definiteness with which Jesus can be identified. The Spirit's particular work is characterized by generativity, by boundary crossing and boundary breaking, by the call to play a part in God's drama, by gifts and power, by stretching comfort zones, by its irreducible character as a gift we must always ask for and never possess, and by the giving of signs, among many other characteristics.[25] Above all, pneumatology informs, for Ford, a kind of hope-filled, Spirit-seeking pragmatism about the world, in which every opportunity that arises, every event and circumstance that is experienced, and every person that is encountered, is potentially a gift and opportunity

22. There are, however, a number of essays on the subject. See especially Ford, "In the Spirit"; Ford, *Christian Wisdom*, chapter 6 ("Learning to Live in the Spirit"); Ford, "Holy Spirit and Christian Spirituality."

23. Ochs, *Another Reformation*, 195.

24. Due both to his enthusiasm for the subject and the serendipitous presence of his colleague Walter Hollenweger at Birmingham, Ford has supervised and examined a large number of doctorates on charismatic and Pentecostal themes over the years.

25. Ford, "In the Spirit."

of the Spirit. In this it has informed not just his theology but his academic, institutional, and personal practice as well.

Since the late 1990s, Ford has been deeply involved in the interfaith practice of Scriptural Reasoning, of which he (with Peter Ochs and Daniel W. Hardy) is a founder. Scriptural Reasoning is a practice of Jews, Muslims, and Christians reading each other's Scriptures together. It has gained increasing influence as a form of substantive interfaith engagement that does not require one's particular faith and tradition to be left at the door. It is no surprise that Ford has been drawn to Scriptural Reasoning, even apart from his personal history with it: it is utterly focused on Scripture, including the Bible; it prioritizes practice over theory while still taking theory extremely seriously; it both allows for deep particularity (in Ford's case, the particularity of his own Christian tradition) and is open to seeing the Spirit at work across boundaries, including religious boundaries; and it entails face-to-face encounter and is deeply oriented toward friendship and collegiality. Not only has Ford practiced Scriptural Reasoning for many years, he has also written extensively on it and on interfaith engagement.[26]

The Conversations in This Book

Given the wide range of David Ford's theological interests, it is hardly surprising that his interlocutors and students have engaged in a vast array of theological projects and followed a series of different theological paths, creating a series of conversations across differences of theological taste, concern, method, mood, and focus. Ford's writing and teaching does not produce or engage with "Fordians," but has repeatedly shaped theologians and theology: that is one of his great virtues as a theological educator, dialogue partner, and friend. It is for that reason that this book seeks to honour David Ford, not simply by reflecting upon his work, or upon a single theme that he has considered, but by offering programmatic suggestions across a range of areas and sub-disciplines for the vocation of theology today.

Ford's own restlessness with the contemporary state of the discipline is replicated in those he has taught, and those with whom he has worked closely. Rather than harking back to a golden theological age in some

26. See especially Ford, *Christian Wisdom*, chapter 8 ("An Inter-Faith Wisdom"); Ford, "Developing Scriptural Reasoning Further"; Ford, *Future of Christian Theology*, chapter 7 ("Inter-Faith Blessing"); Ford and Pecknold, *Promise of Scriptural Reasoning*.

romanticized past, there is in Ford's work a sense of urgency for theology in the present as it presses into the future. That one of his recent books is entitled *The Future of Theology* is no accident, nor is his use of "manifestos" and "maxims" in his writings and lectures. Through his publications and his successive generations of doctoral students, Ford has shaped the future of theology and challenged theology to think about its calling, purpose, and vocation.

The book begins by examining, and entering into, conversations with major theological thinkers. Ford's doctoral studies on Karl Barth, only a few years after Barth's death, pay testimony to his concern to engage with key figures in theology, particularly from the modern period; but the very mode of that engagement demonstrates that the task of examining these figures is determinately *theological*—conversing with them, rather than engaging in forming some manner of contemporary scholasticism. In his essay on the need for a plurality of theological interlocutors, Tom Greggs picks up this theme and examines the nature of historical theology as a theological discipline, through examination of the communion of saints and through David Ford's motif of "conversation." This plurality of conversation partners is then reflected in the subsequent chapters of this section. In his essay on Schleiermacher, Paul Nimmo examines the focus in the theology of both Ford and Schleiermacher on the wisdom and the love of God, and the transformative and retransformative effect of this on theological thinking and on practical concerns. Jason Fout's essay on Karl Barth and Rowan Williams explores Ford's category of the "moods" of faith and theology, to suggest that we might think in terms of an encompassing "ecology" of moods of revelation, in order better to fulfil the vocation of theology by doing fuller justice to the One who God is. In the final essay of this section, Simeon Zahl engages with Luther on central issues in the interpretation of the New Testament, finding that pneumatology creates unexpected possibilities for "bridge-building" in theological conversation.

Ford's conversations with theological tradition are also, and crucially, conversations around Scripture and through attention to Scripture. Susannah Ticciati's essay on jealousy in Romans demonstrates the theological fruitfulness of patiently "searching the depths" of Scripture in order to discover healing and transformative patterns of reasoning. This particular searching of the depths discovers, in Romans 9–11, a transformation of the grammar of human jealousy and a salvific reshaping of identity "rooted in the capaciousness of God." Nicholas Adams' reflections on different theological approaches to the disharmony of the Gospels around the genealogies of Jesus point us toward the complexity that is faced in the reading of Scripture, and toward the need to see this complexity and variance as a resource for continued depths of engagement with the Bible, rather than a problem to be elided or solved. The essays by Frances Young and Janet Soskice, emerging from sermons, display the vocation of theology to engage in fresh, creative, and fruitful ways with Scripture in all of its multivocity and with all of its potential for never-ending engagement.

As the use of sermons in Young's and Soskice's essays recalls, David Ford's reading of Scripture has been rooted throughout his academic life in his personal devotion and in ecclesial communities. The first lay person to hold the post of Regius Professor of Divinity at Cambridge, Ford has tirelessly given his energy to the church, and has worked to connect academy and *ecclesia* in both his academic and institutional work.[27] In her chapter, David Ford's colleague, Sarah Coakley, offers suggestive ways of thinking about the relation of liturgical sense experience to the question of theological "truth" in a way that fits none of the mainstream philosophical accounts of cognition with exactitude. For Coakley, liturgy provides access to a certain kind of "truth" that it alone can supply; it gives that access because a particular epistemic *apparatus* and form of cognition is being trained in the engagement in the liturgy. This is a fitting tribute to David Ford's own love of liturgy and the saying of the daily office. For all of his commitment to the church, the mode of Ford's theology is not overly "churchy," however, and it is certainly never sectarian. Ben Quash identifies Ford's ecclesial vision as arising from the "ambient pneumatology" which it possesses at its heart. This is a theology that, Quash asserts, does not close down, but has what he terms "ample room." Ford's ecclesial vision includes the God-given importance of "enjoyment," and a desire to make these good things as "wholly present" to everyone it possibly can. These concerns are in some ways hardly surprising, since Ford's work exists very much within the broader ecology of academic and societal life; and the need for theology to attend to these should never be in competition with its ecclesial concerns. Tim Jenkins in his essay examines David Ford's description of society as "complexly religious and secular," suggesting that it is time for theologians to consider the complex sociological conditions in which they perform theology. This theme is picked up more directly in relation to the discipline of theology in the essay by Rowan Williams

27. *The Shape of Living*, written originally for the archbishop of Canterbury's Lent course, is one of many examples of Ford's work that places theology explicitly at the service of church communities and institutions.

on "Theology among the Humanities," in which Williams advocates the importance of theology attending to the question of how we come to know something of "how to be human before God."

Ford's non-sectarian, ecclesial openness has expressed itself in his simultaneous concern for entering more deeply into one's own faith, more deeply into the world, and more deeply into knowledge of and engagement with other faiths. The development of serious interfaith (especially, but not only, Abrahamic) theological work has been one of the most significant changes to the context of theology in recent years, and David Ford's contribution has been pivotal. It is appropriate, therefore, that Ford is honoured with essays on the vocation of interfaith engagement, and with essays by Jewish and Muslim colleagues. Peter Ochs reflects on the theology and public work of Don Isaac Abravanel, in order to pattern relations between the theological commitments of a figure and the institutional practices they engage in. Ochs argues that the time has come to search out within the work of thinkers what he terms "the virtues and measures of performative thinking as a theological vocation." Basit Koshul, in some sense, fulfils in relation to Ford the agenda set by Ochs in his chapter. Examining Ford's work in relation to Weber, Koshul explores the claim that "renewal comes through the stranger," and asserts that strangers and strangeness are so much a part of the contemporary cultural condition that for any theology to be relevant at this juncture in history it must face and address the reality of the stranger's condition directly. Theological commitment and public theological virtues, for Koshul, are symbiotic. That symbiosis is also found in Michael Barnes' essay, which takes as its premise the idea that theology is shaped by its performance as much as by its content. For Barnes, interfaith dialogue is not simply about identifying some textually inscribed wisdom, but about learning how to *live* wisely in a pluralist world; and it is that to which a theology of the religions must address itself.

The relation of practices to theological commitments in interfaith relations leads on to a consideration of the public vocation of theology, beyond—though always in relation to—the churches. In the section titled "Speaking and Listening in Public," Rachel Muers suggests that theology's public vocation in a postsecular (or "religious and secular") context includes telling and reflecting on "miracles," which she defines as stories, relationships, and events that are not expected or allowed for by dominant narratives, paradigms, and patterns of life. Linking these themes to scriptural resources, Muers explores these themes in relation to Acts 3, and the story of the healing of the lame man. Alistair McFadyen, engaging at length with Ford's theological career, reflects on the way theological work is self-consciously shaped and energized by the particular and multiple contexts, conversations, and concerns of the theologian's life in the world. For McFadyen, this indicates *inter alia* the distinctive importance of the lay theological vocation. Identifying a specific contemporary public vocation for theology, Paul D. Janz, drawing on Henri Bergson and Emmanuel Lévinas, argues for theological engagement with an urgent and fundamental question in contemporary Western politics and ethics—the question of how to relate the political obligations of freedom and the ethical obligations of love. Janz argues that theology has a vocation to stand in the breach, to make possible a "hospitable interdisciplinarity" comparable to Ford's "hospitable wisdom-seeking."

David Ford's theological work has been done in universities. For him, this has not simply been a relationship of convenience—a place in which one might as well do theology as anywhere else. A committed institution builder and advocate of interdisciplinary approaches to theology, Ford has reflected, especially in the later years of his work, on the nature of the university as an institution, and on the place of Theology and Religious Studies within the university. It is appropriate, therefore, that four of Ford's former doctoral students reflect on the vocation of theology in the section on "Theology and the University." Mike Higton explores in his chapter the relationship between studying "for its own sake" and studying "for God's sake"; themes which are often brought close together in Ford's writings about universities. Arguing that "learning for its own sake" is problematic on its own (because there are no criteria for what sort of learning is worth pursuing), Higton asserts that it is more useful (and not just theologically useful) when learning is brought into closer connection with learning "for God's sake." Joseph Galgalo suggests that theology in a university offers a space in which reflection and conversation about pressing challenges—social and political as well as intellectual—can take place across intellectual disciplines. He draws on experience at St. Paul's Limuru, which incorporates reflective practice into the theological curriculum, to explore theology's calling to develop contextual responses to the pressing questions that arise within communities of faith. The interrelation of communities of faith and university theology is also addressed in the chapter by Chad Pecknold. Pecknold argues that theologians' claims to "intellectual freedom" make no sense without attention to ecclesial as well as university context. He argues that Christian truth is "impartial" because catholic, and thereby more inclusive and more appropriate for founding rationality than the particular cultural norms of a "secular" university. Another Roman Catholic contributor, Paul Murray, provides a somewhat different account in his chapter. Offering a theological and historical account of institution building in Durham University, Murray suggests that the postmodern public academy can help preserve within a properly ecclesial theology the critical and creative functions authentic to it in mutually critical engagement with other traditions.

A consideration of the contexts of David Ford's theology would be incomplete without recognizing the personal and interpersonal character of theology. The three essays that conclude this book draw attention to this aspect of Ford's work and its significance for the vocation of theology. Jean Vanier's chapter presents reflections on the theological lessons learned in the L'Arche communities, seeking to understand the vocation of theology in relation to theological resources outside academic contexts. Vanier offers for theological reflection the transformative power of relationships of care and friendship with people with disabilities; the primacy of face-to-face relationships over time; and the serendipitous and graced character of friendship in these contexts. Ford's oldest friend, the poet and writer Micheal O'Siadhail, explores the setting of theology, considering theology as conversational, as developed through cross-fertilisation, and as based in friendship. In the concluding chapter of this volume, Ford's wife, Deborah Hardy Ford, draws on her pastoral experience and on C. S. Lewis's *Till We Have Faces* to consider the psychological and theological significance of "facing"—centrally, the transformative significance of knowing oneself to be loved, and flourishing in loving face-to-face relationships.

Although these chapters are disparate in terms of the focuses and themes that they offer and consider, they are united in the concern to consider the practice of theology in the contemporary church, university, and world. What emerges from this volume is, we hope, a kaleidoscopic vision of the task and calling of theology—refracting the light of God through different contexts, conversation partners, and themes, and patterning a complex but centred theological vision. That complexity and centred diversity is in many ways appropriate to the theological vision and embodied vocation of David Ford.

Bibliography

Cunningham, David S. "The Practical Theology of David Ford." *The Christian Century* 120.9 (May 3, 2003) 30–37.

Fodor, James. "Postliberal Theology." In *The Modern Theologians: An Introduction to Christian Theology since* 1918, edited by David F. Ford with Rachel Muers, 229–48. 3rd ed. Oxford: Blackwell, 2005.

Ford, David F. "Apophasis and the Shoah: Where was Jesus Christ at Auschwitz?" In *Silence and the Word: Apophasis and Incarnation*, edited by Oliver Davies and Denys Turner, 185–200. Cambridge: Cambridge University Press, 2002.

———. *Barth and God's Story: Biblical Narrative and the Theological Method of Karl Barth in the Church Dogmatics*. Frankfurt am Main: Lang, 1981.

———. *Christian Wisdom: Desiring God and Learning in Love*. Cambridge Studies in Christian Doctrine. Cambridge: Cambridge University Press, 2007.

———. "Developing Scriptural Reasoning Further." In *Scripture, Reason, and the Contemporary Islam-West Encounter: Studying the "Other," Understanding the "Self,"* edited by Basit Bilal Koshul and Steven Kepnes, 201–19. New York: Palgrave Macmillan, 2007.

———. *The Future of Christian Theology*. Blackwell Manifestos. Oxford: Wiley-Blackwell, 2011.

———. "Holy Spirit and Christian Spirituality." In *The Cambridge Companion to Postmodern Theology*, edited by Kevin J. Vanhoozer, 269–90. Cambridge: Cambridge University Press, 2003.

———. "In the Spirit: Learning Wisdom, Giving Signs." In *The Holy Spirit in the World Today*, edited by Jane Williams, 42–63. London: Alpha International, 2011.

———, and Mike Higton, editors. *Jesus: An Oxford Reader*. Oxford: Oxford University Press, 2002.

———. "A Journey into Interfaith Engagement." *Huffington Post*, 2 April, 2011. Online: http://www.huffingtonpost.com/david-ford/a-journey-into-interfaith_b_843057.html.

———. "Knowledge, Meaning and the World's Great Challenges: Reinventing Cambridge University in the Twenty-first Century." The Gomes Lecture, delivered at Emmanuel College on 14 February 2003. *Emmanuel College Magazine* LXXXV (2002–2003) 38–63; and *Scottish Journal of Theology* 57 (2004) 182–202.

———. *A Long Rumour of Wisdom: Redescribing Theology: Inaugural Lecture as Regius Professor of Divinity*. Cambridge: Cambridge University Press, 1992.

——— and Frances M. Young. *Meaning and Truth in 2 Corinthians*. London: SPCK, 1987.

———, editor. *The Modern Theologians: An Introduction to Christian Theology in the Twentieth Century*. Oxford: Blackwell, 1989.

———, and Mike Higton, with Simeon Zahl, editors. *The Modern Theologians Reader*. Malden, MA: Wiley-Blackwell, 2012.

———, and C. C. Pecknold, editors. *The Promise of Scriptural Reasoning*. Directions in Modern Theology. Oxford: Wiley-Blackwell, 2006.

———. "Reading Scripture with Intensity: Academic, Ecclesial, Inter-faith, and Divine." *The Princeton Seminary Bulletin* 26.1 (2005) 22–35.

———. *Self and Salvation: Being Transformed*. Cambridge Studies in Christian Doctrine. Cambridge: Cambridge University Press, 1999.

———. *The Shape of Living: Spiritual Directions for Everyday Life*. London: Fount, 1997.

———. *Shaping Theology: Engagements in a Religious and Secular World*. Challenges in Contemporary Theology. Oxford: Blackwell, 2007.

———. "Theological Wisdom, British Style." *The Christian Century* 117 (April 5, 2000) 388–91.

———. *Theology: A Very Short Introduction*. Oxford: Oxford University Press, 1999.

Frei, Hans. *The Eclipse of Biblical Narrative: A Study in Eighteenth and Nineteenth Century Hermeneutics*. New Haven: Yale University Press, 1974.

Hardy, Daniel W., and David F. Ford. *Jubilate: Theology in Praise*. London: Darton, Longman & Todd, 1984.

———, with Deborah Hardy Ford, Peter Ochs, and David F. Ford. *Wording a Radiance: Parting Conversations on God and the Church*. London: SCM, 2010.

O'Siadhail, Micheal. *The Gossamer Wall: Poems in Witness to the Holocaust*. Tarset: Bloodaxe, 2002.

Ochs, Peter. *Another Reformation: Postliberal Christianity and the Jews*. Grand Rapids: Baker Academic, 2011.

Quash, Ben. *Theology and the Drama of History*. Cambridge Studies in Christian Doctrine. Cambridge: Cambridge University Press, 2008.

PART ONE

Conversing with Theologians

2

Being a Wise Apprentice to the Communion of Modern Saints

On the Need for Conversation with a Plurality of Theological Interlocutors

Tom Greggs

King's College, University of Aberdeen

During a conversation at Society for the Study of Theology some years ago, David Ford asked a question of a group of people in the bar: "Who is your most significant theological conversation partner?" As one might expect, the usual suspects were variously mentioned—Barth, Augustine, Luther, Aquinas, Schleiermacher, Bonhoeffer, Frei. Ford himself, however, could name no single theologian who had been more influential and significant than another, citing Scripture as his own primary interlocutor. Part of this inability to locate his theology within any one school or at the feet of any one figure surely arises in part from David Ford's theological restlessness: his theology is one that is never wholly satisfied with where theology has arrived at, and seeks to push theology on further as it moves into the future. This restlessness is not, however, an easy restlessness, somehow dissatisfied with the central tenets of the Christian faith. It is, instead, a restlessness that is related to the desire to press on into the future *from* somewhere, moving with the great cloud of witnesses. Ford has recently put the matter thus: "In every generation . . . theology has had to come to terms with its past in fresh situations, trying to discern how best to be faithful, loving, and hopeful, and praying for the Holy Spirit as it does so. To cry out for the Spirit is to seek wisdom for God's sake and to be open to following both trodden and untrodden ways. So twenty-first-century Christian theology inherits vast riches from the past but can never simply repeat them."[1] This desire to press beyond the boundaries of current theological thought determines that a multiplicity of conversation partners is needed,[2] since that desire itself arises from a belief that no theology (and no individual theologian's theology) has yet arrived. But it does not mean that we are to ignore the "vast riches from the past"; it merely means that we can "never simply repeat them." Thus, for all of Ford's engagement with the history of modern theology,[3] the reason for those historical engagements has not been simply to justify one modern theologian's perspective as the yardstick by which all else might be measured, or for the sake of singular engagement in historical *Erklärung*; it has, instead, been for the sake of learning from recent masters the art of theological thinking.

In this chapter, I will identify the need for contemporary theology to engage in the study of historical theology. However, in doing this, I will also identify certain dangerous ways in which historical theology can be used by contemporary theology, revolving around locating oneself unwisely in relation to three axes: history versus contemporaneity, continuity versus difference, and tradition versus context. In response to these problems, I seek to locate David Ford's historical theological method in the church's affirmation of the communion of saints. This creedal belief determines that engagements with historical figures in the history of Christian thought are genuine, living conversations across time. Each of these conversations is, moreover, for the sake of the contemporary church, which is already a part of the eternal communion of saints. Such an approach to historical (even modern historical) theology is considered wise for a theological enterprise that seeks neither to ignore the tradition and discourses of the past, nor anachronistically to adopt them unquestioningly in the present.

1. Ford, *Future of Christian Theology*, 6–7.

2. Cf. Ford, *Future of Christian Theology*, 97.

3. Ford's three editions of *Modern Theologians* being the prime example of this, as well as his book on Barth, *Barth and God's Story*.

A Living Engagement with a Breadth of Figures: Beyond History versus Contemporaneity

Theological wisdom seeks to do justice to many contexts, levels, voices, moods, genres, systems, and responsibilities.[4]

The article of the creed "*sanctorum communionem*" finds its origins in late fourth-century Gaul. Although its original meaning was probably little more than a further description of the preceding article ("Holy Catholic Church") and its insertion into the creed perhaps came only in protest against the Donatist schism, it is clear that very soon the phrase was interpreted as meaning the fellowship of all believers with the holy of all ages (both living and in heaven).[5] The idea of a participation of the contemporary church in the eternal communion of saints joins the church in the present to the church in every age, seeing the *ecclesia* as not simply the gathered community of a given place and time, but a part of the one universal church, not only geographically but also historically. When the present expressions of church seek to understand themselves in continuity with the past, they do so, therefore, as part of the one communion of saints.

Theologically speaking, then, we might imagine that in connecting the contemporary church of any age to the great company of saints who have gone before, the creed's affirmation of the communion of saints is the basis of the theological grounds for the engagement with historical theology. But what is that engagement to look like? How does it avoid either idolizing the past and history at the expense of the present, or making a god of the contemporary at the expense of the wisdom history offers us in understanding our present?

First of all, historical theology must involve a serious acquisition of the thought of the past, alert to the dangers of the cult of the modern and the propensity to fad or vogue in theological speech. In theology, as in all academic discourse, whoever is married to the spirit of the age becomes a widow in the next.[6] In theology's case, however, this is not because of some

4. Maxim 7, "Epilogue," in Ford, *Modern Theologians*, 761.

5. Kelly, *Early Christian Creeds*, 389–91.

6. This is surely why those theologies that aim to be most modern date more easily than those that do not: Tillich and Bultmann, for example, now feel very dated in comparison to Barth, not least because the philosophical assumptions to which they wedded themselves are no longer vogue or contemporary.

notion of progress in knowledge or the like, on the one hand (though that certainly may have its place), nor because of the identification of anachronistic antiquarian eccentricities, on the other. Instead, the critical rejection of historical theology's claims on the basis of any given external norm[7] that clashes with the traditional claims of the church, is primarily a denial and rejection of the creedal affirmation of the communion of saints. While those who do reject historical theology's claims will no doubt rush to defend their connection to the church of all ages on the basis of various linguistic expressions of extralinguistic categories, it is clear that for them, even so, the learning of the present is the master that judges the learning of the past, and to which the learning of the past must always be subject. Modern thought, in its desire for universal rational categories (with a very limited definition of the *ratio*), judges that which is premodern as unscientific and insufficient, seeing true knowledge as always lying ahead in future human capacity, and nervous of tradition and any claim it makes to authority.[8] However, a belief in the communion of saints must surely affirm the equidistance of the church of any age to the kingdom of God, and to God's eschaton: what we have in the church of any given "today" is a (lesser) witness to that universal and eternal communion of all ages. The learning of the past must be treated with seriousness and the respect that it deserves, as part of God's revelatory work by the power of the Holy Spirit in communities of faith throughout all ages and times. Furthermore, this very belief itself pushes theology to recognize the contingency of all of its present speech and its limitedness, not ultimately before the horizons of human knowledge, but before God's ultimacy and infinity. Paul's statement that for now we "see dimly as through a mirror" is not a statement about the future progression of human knowledge,[9] but a statement about the ultimate future life with God of the faithful. Faithful retrieval of important theological figures of the past (and the engagement with some of those whose importance has been underestimated) is integral to the theology of a church that understands itself to be a part of the communion of saints. As Ford himself puts it: "There is . . . immense scope for *creative retrievals* along the lines of the twentieth century's new interpretations and applications of theologies of the past, such as those of Gregory of Nyssa,

7. Frei, *Types of Christian Theology*, Type 1, 28–30.

8. We might see this as arising from Kant's desire for us to be liberated from our "self-incurred tutelage"; something which invites a challenge to tradition in Enlightenment thinking.

9. 1 Cor 13:12; cf. Greggs, "Eschatological Tension."

Maximus the Confessor, Augustine, Thomas Aquinas, Martin Luther, John Calvin, Ignatius Loyola, Richard Hooker, and Jonathan Edwards. Without ignoring those, it may be time to hear more about Origen, Aphrahat and Ephrem, Bonaventure, Dante, Erasmus, Traherne, Milton, Coleridge, and Christoph Blumhardt."[10]

This need to engage with figures of the past is not only to learn from what past theological thinkers might offer, but also to ensure that theology speaks with an appropriate level of humility: an awareness of the limitations and the learning of past thinkers will help theology to speak with the knowledge of its own current limits, not simply within the academy, but more profoundly in relation to the object of theological study—God. The hubris of modern thought is reminded not only of its own passing nature, in light of past vogues, but is ultimately humbled in light of the object of theological science—the eternal and infinite God.

Second, as Ford himself notes, the engagement with theologies and theologians of the past cannot be a simple repetition of the past, for the sake of historical interest only. Such engagements need to be *creative*.[11] The confession of a belief in the communion of saints not only affirms the importance of the saints of the past, but also affirms the connectedness of the church today to the church of all ages: the church today is as important as any other historical instantiation of God's community. This has two implications. First of all, historical study cannot *theologically* simply be for its own sake. This is not to say that ecclesiastical thinking and historians of dogma have no place in the Theology Department. Rather, it is to say that the place that such work has *theologically* is in relation to enabling contemporary theologians to learn from the saints of old. To learn from these figures certainly involves careful exegesis of their work, linguistic tools, and contextual appreciation. But those skills are there in order that an engagement in understanding these theologians *today* might take place: *Erklärung* is essential for the purpose of *Verstehen*. Reading and rereading classical theological texts is a mode of establishing for the contemporary theologian "relationships of cohabitation"[12] with the communion of saints in order to stimulate formative theology today (that is, a theology that seeks to form and shape the theology it has learnt from, not simply to crystallize or harden it). Reading historical figures

10. Ford, *Future of Christian Theology*, 101, emphasis added.

11. Ibid.

12. Ibid., 99.

should be a means of communing with them, rather than simply observing them in some laboratory setting. As Karl Barth puts it, regarding the Reformation (though the point applies to any period of theology):

> If we concern ourselves *today* with Christian doctrine, there is no point in staring spellbound at the sixteenth century and holding on to what was said then and there as unmoveably and unchangeably as possible. Such a procedure would be inconsistent with the Reformation. It is always a misunderstanding of the communion of saints and a misunderstanding also of the fathers when their confession is later understood as chains, so that Christian doctrine today could only be a repetition of their confession. In the communion of the saints there should be *reverence* and *thankfulness* for the fathers of the church, those who have gone before us and in their time have reflected on the gospel. But there is also *freedom* in the communion of the saints. Real respect and real thanksgiving are free.[13]

Related to this, the second implication of this need for creative retrieval is that theology (and, one might say, the church) today cannot pick some arbitrary point in history or a single historical figure to be the yardstick by which the benefits and validity of all other theology is understood and measured. This is a propensity in much contemporary theology.[14] However, to use one single point as the basis for all theological judgements fails to appreciate the theologian's task in seeking to form theology for the contemporary church, and fails to appreciate the plurality of saints with whom the theologian is to be in dialogue. This means that theologians cannot simply master one theological perspective and reject all others. Far better is to follow Ford's advice: "Enter into the complexities of arguments, let your assumptions and frameworks be challenged, and sustain ongoing debate even with those who seem to have it very wrong."[15] Ongoing and lively engagement with multiple figures from the past sustains and nourishes contemporary theology, rather than replacing contemporary theology with claims from one single point of the history of the world and of the church.

13. Barth, *Learning Jesus Christ*, 21.

14. Nicholas Healy sees this as associated primarily with the church rather than theology (Healy, "What is Systematic Theology?" 25). Surely his point about *status quo ante* could be applied to Radical Orthodoxy; or in a somewhat different way to systematic theology which engages a single historical figure as the basis for all contemporary theological claims.

15. Ford, *Christian Wisdom*, 198.

Engaging with different historical theologians is a wise way to realize the contemporaneity of theological speech, the contextual nature of all theological claims, and the limits of all theology (and each theologian, even the greatest). This is not, however, to ignore the authority of past theologians. To quote Barth once again:

> [I]t is impossible to speak without having first heard. All speaking is a response to these fathers and brethren. Therefore these fathers and brethren have a definite authority, the authority of prior witnesses of the Word of God, who have to be respected as such. Just because the Evangelical confession is a confession of the vitality and the presence of God's Word actualised again and again, it is also a confession of the communion of saints and therefore of what is, in a sense, an authoritative tradition of the Word of God, that is, of a human form in which that Word comes to all those who are summoned by it to faith and witness in the sphere of the Church and by its mouth—of a human form which is proper to it in the witness of these fathers and brethren . . .[16]

Furthermore, we cannot elide the difficulties and problems that exist in seeking to listen to these saints of old. The process of hearing them will involve careful and detailed historical work, which will point out how different these figures and their thoughts are from our own and those of our contemporary society. But the recognition of that very strangeness is in and of itself part of the formation of theology. In the theological epilogue of his book *Arius*, Rowan Williams puts the matter thus:

> The loyal and uncritical repetition of formulae is seen to be inadequate as a means of securing continuity at anything more than a formal level; Scripture and tradition require to be read in a way that brings out their strangeness, their non-obvious and non-contemporary qualities, in order that they may be read both freshly and truthfully from one generation to another. They need to be made more *difficult* before we can actually grasp their simplicities. Otherwise, we read with eyes not our own and think them through with minds not our own; the "deposit of faith" does not really come into contact with *ourselves*.[17]

The very process of careful (and respectful) historical exegesis brings out the strangeness of tradition, and the need to think carefully about

16. Barth, *Church Dogmatics* I/2, 573.

17. Williams, *Arius*, 236.

utilizing past theological claims today. This in itself raises the danger of transposing any one theologian's or any one theological school's thoughts into today's theological community uncritically.

How then is it that we are to imagine this need to move between two poles—learning from past theology, but not simply repeating past theology? Here, we may look to employ a very Fordian concept—conversation. Learning from the past does not involve simply repeating it, but dialoguing with it, conversing with, and (crucially) innovating in relation to it.

Genuine Conversation: Working through Continuity and Difference, Tradition and Context

Theology is practised collegially, in conversation and, best of all, in friendship; and, through the communion of saints, it is simultaneously premodern, modern, and postmodern.[18]

David Ford's enjoyment of conversation is well known to all who have worked closely with him. Learning for him is not just (note the qualifier "just" here) hours spent silently reading in libraries; it is hours spent reading in libraries *and* hours spent conversing with others about the texts. These conversations are not themselves simply directed at understanding the texts in their own right (though certainly this is an element); they are also conversations *with* the texts in order to think more generally about theology in the fuller sense. Ford has recently advocated the need for this conversation and learning through joint study, describing it as an "apprenticeship": "*Be apprenticed to wise readers.* Good readers are formed mainly through learning from other good readers, and hours spent with texts together are among the most fruitful in a theological education. Joint reading and interpretation of texts is at the heart of theological collegiality."[19] In this context, Ford clearly envisages round-table discussions about texts.[20] There is clearly an important place for this: as any teacher of theology knows, the text-based seminar is crucial to learning. However, an even deeper sense of conversation penetrates the approach to

18. Maxim 8, Ford, *Modern Theologians*, 761.

19. Ford, *Future of Christian Theology*, 174, emphasis original.

20. One can associate this with Scriptural and Biblical Reasoning groups, but also Ford's continual dialogue partners throughout his career and his joint projects, as well as such regular events as his "home seminar."

theological engagement *not only around texts but with texts* that Ford has. For him, historical theological texts themselves are dialogue and conversation partners: they are interlocutors, as much as those sat in the room. Not precious objects of antiquity to be viewed from afar, they are sources to learn alongside.

Study of an historical text can be a reasonably one-dimensional process: it speaks and we (with the aid of various exegetical tools) listen. However, theological engagement with important historical texts is innately multidimensional: it speaks—we listen—we respond critically or creatively—it forces us to listen once again in case we have not learned fully from it or misunderstood—and so on. This conversational encounter with an historical theological text is a wise way to resource contemporary theological thought. This has been the case throughout the history of the church, and—as Rowan Williams recognizes—is a marked element of twentieth-century theology as well: "If we look at the three great confessional traditions of Orthodoxy, Roman Catholicism and Protestantism between the thirties and the fifties of the last century, it is clear that the movements of greatest theological vitality are all movements of 'recovery,' *ressourcement*, rather than simple innovation or simple repetition."[21] While understanding deeply the dangers of eliding the differences between the present and the past, Williams also realizes that these modes of *ressourcement* (by the likes of Barth, Lossky, and Blondel) are very different in approach to the modes of engagement of the "more strictly professional historians of ideas."[22] The problem of getting the balance right between concern for continuity and concern for difference in study of the past is one that is not lost in treating historical texts as conversation and dialogue partners.[23] Listening carefully to what an historical text is saying in its own terms is the only way in which genuine conversation with it can take place: the need to listen carefully is true for any good conversation. There has to be a recognition of the text's otherness in order that the reader converses with it, rather than simply engaging in a monologue of her own thoughts. This means that careful exegesis with all available scholarly tools is necessary: texts should not simply be sublated to the concerns of the reader or the reader's theology. Original languages, contextual settings, background thoughts, and assumptions of texts must be explored to ensure that in listening to the text, we are *hearing* what is actually being said,

21. Williams, *Why Study the Past*, 97–98.

22. Ibid., 98.

23. Cf. ibid., 10.

and not presupposing that we can read these historical figures without the necessary tools.[24] But listening to the text, the theological reader should *respond*. This response should have learned from what the text has to offer, and it should also involve repeated revisiting of the text in question so as to check that the response has understood sufficiently what the text is saying. Like any good conversation, a theological engagement with historical theology is one that involves listening and speaking (and listening and speaking again and again). We will be able to identify good conversation when we see the highest standards of rigour in the approach to exegeting a text in its own context, and when that exegesis of a text does not end at simply clarifying and repeating, but instead understanding and engaging with the text *in the present context*: the response in light of the contemporary setting to what the text might say today is the point of the careful exegesis. Neither careful listening and scholarly practice, nor creative engagement and response in the present should stand in opposition: the former is necessary for the latter; the latter is, for historical theology, the reason for the existence of the former.

Although an approach to historical theological texts that uses conversation as its model might seem less historical than some form of "pure" history, studied in its "somewhat chilly light,"[25] the approach of conversation might be more true to the figures of the past than any cold "objective" historicism (if such a thing were possible or exists).[26] Let us take, for example, Barth's comments on Calvin. Although perhaps Calvin's greatest student in the twentieth century, Barth's radical departure from Calvin over the doctrine of election in *Church Dogmatics* II/2 is testimony to what it meant for Barth to be engaged with Calvin in conversation, and the struggles of that conversation are clear throughout Barth's reworking of election. Barth's words are not the creative writings of a theologian uninterested in the theological heritage of the church of the Reformation (and especially in its Reformed form), but are words in dialogue with that tradition as part of it. Indeed, long before the shift in his thinking about

24. Of course, this point also has implications for conversations with contemporary theologians: there cannot be any presumption that we have straightforward and easy access to their thoughts (or that we have "got" them), any more than there can be a presumption that we have easy and ready access to historical figures. The need for careful listening is also present for our engagements with our peers.

25. Williams, *Why Study the Past*, 98.

26. Most recent historiographies recognize that there is no such thing as purely objective history. This is a deeply complex field involving a large series of discussions and themes. For the best recent overview of this topic, see Iggers, *Historiography*.

the doctrine of election beginning in 1936,[27] Barth laid the foundations for such a use of Calvin (as he did elsewhere and at other points for use of other theologians similarly):

> Those who simply echo Calvin are not good Calvinists, that is, they are not really taught by Calvin. Being taught by Calvin means entering into dialogue with him, with Calvin as the teacher and ourselves as the students, he speaking, we doing our best to follow him and then—this is crux of the matter—making our own response to what he says. If that does not happen we might as well be listening to Chinese; the historical Calvin is not present. For that Calvin wants to teach and not just to say something that we will repeat.[28]

Learning from Calvin involved understanding what he had said enough to respond to rather than simply to repeat him. (One could say in parenthesis that the same approach needs to be applied to Barth himself by those who study him today.) Barth was aware that in approaching historical theological figures as a theologian, one needs to remain a theologian. Ford's advice on this is wise: "Beware of just repeating a tradition in new situations; be suspicious of simplifications and formulae."[29] This means that there will always be a certain degree of development, and even innovation, in theological speech.

Realizing that the God who will be who he will be (Exod 3:14) is ever ahead of us,[30] and realizing that theology must speak about the God of our ancestors (Exod 3:6) in the conditions in which it finds itself in the present, determines that theology will have to speak its truth differently at different points in history and time. This is not a manoeuvre that involves some degree of duplicity or elasticity with truth claims. It arises, rather, from the realization that, for the Christian, truth exists eschatologically and that the universality of the Christian faith involves some degree of development in and contextualization of its truth claims. As John Henry Newman puts it: "if Christianity be an universal religion, suited not to one locality or period, but to all times and places, it cannot but vary in its relations and dealings towards the world around it, that is,

27. See McCormack, *Karl Barth's Critically Realistic Dialectical Theology*, 454–55.

28. Barth, *Theology of John Calvin*, 4.

29. Ford, *Christian Wisdom*, 198.

30. On the future and causative nature of the verb form in relation to the name of God, see, for example, Brichto, *Names of God*, 19–25, and Bright, *History of Israel*, 157–58.

it will develop."[31] The Christian tradition is one of development from the past. Development implies both continuity and innovation with regard to the past. And for theology, that development comes through dialogical (conversational) engagement with theological figures of the past who are made contemporaries through the affirmation of the communion of the saints.

However, the very process of thinking about the way in which we might understand the theological wisdom of the past through the communion of saints in the present implies that the thoughts of those historical figures need to be related to the present, with all of its various contextual concerns and demands. Here, again, a tension exists in terms of how to understand the relationship between tradition and contemporary context, recognizing that traditions themselves exist within their own contextual settings. Theological engagements in historical theology have once again to exist between two poles (in addition to those of the contemporary and the historical, and continuity and difference): rejecting tradition for context or rejecting context for tradition. Theological approaches to historical theology require that the contemporary theological context be recognized in terms of their contextual effect on the understanding and reading of an historical text. As Ford points out, there is a need to appreciate "different regimes of reading" across premodern, modern, and late modern/postmodern periods. He writes: "The dialogue between *lectio divina*, scholasticism, humanism, historical critical and other approaches (literary, sociological, psychological, political, feminist, poststructuralist, and so on) and hermeneutics is a vital arena for wisdom-seeking with regard to other elements of the tradition besides Scripture. There is no one 'answer' to multiple modern critiques of Christian tradition: the critical questions need to be taken one by one and assessed."[32]

Tradition(s) and various contemporary contextual discourses need to be brought into dialogue with each other. This is a deeply complex task. Not only does one always need to be aware of the complex hermeneutical questions this raises,[33] but the very multiplicity of contextual discourses (and tools of study of the past) are also overwhelmingly vast,

31. Newman, *Essay on the Development of Christian Doctrine*, 150.

32. Ford, *Christian Wisdom*, 206–7.

33. Space does not allow a detailed engagement with this question; it is one to be addressed at another time.

"threatening a dissipation of energies."[34] This requires a degree of discernment about who would be the best and most suitable contextual dialogue partners to bring to the conversation with the communion of saints in which theological historical theology seeks to engage.[35] However, that desire for discernment cannot come at the expense of the benefits of unexpected fruitful dialogue partners, outside of the classical traditions of the church. In this age in which the need to think fruitfully about Christianity's existence in secular and pluralistic countries (what Ford speaks of as the "complexly religious and secular" world), those others from the context in which the church finds itself, and to which and from which theology must speak, will inevitably include secular philosophers as well as those of other faiths.

Conclusion

The best theological approaches to historical theology reject the binary choices between history and contemporaneity; continuity and difference; and tradition and context. Understanding theology as a conversation that takes place with and within the communion of saints, the stark choices of a contemporary or an historical approach to theology cease to be fully meaningful. In viewing the engagement of theology today with historical theology as a *conversation* within and with the community of saints, there is a need to attend to both continuity and difference between the historical source and the contemporary world, and to the context of the present reader (and the reader being read) and tradition. David Ford's engagements with modern theologians have been engagements in multiple conversations with members of the communion of saints of the modern period. What Ford has learned from these figures, however, is not just how they were theologians, but how to be a theologian in the context in which God in God's providence has placed us—today in the here and now. The plurality of Ford's engagements with modern theologians has determined that his theological formation is not simply one which has closed itself to all but one expression of the Christian tradition, rendering all others lesser by virtue of their lack of conformity to a single theological

34. Ford, *Christian Wisdom*, 87.

35. David Ford himself has engaged with various of these: literary theory (in *Barth and God's Story*), ethnography, poetry, historical biblical criticism, philosophy, Jewish and Islamic thought, etc.

figure, but one which is open to continual and future conversations with multiple others for the sake of theological speech today, and ultimately for the sake of the God who is always before us. Seeking to apprentice ourselves to the master practitioners of the past, and to learn all that we can from them, is surely a wise way to become a theologian today: "Let us become apprentices of saints!"[36]

Bibliography

Barth, Karl. *Church Dogmatics* I/2: *The Doctrine of the Word of God*. Translated by G. T. Thompson and H. Knight. Edited by G. W. Bromiley and T. F. Torrance. 2nd ed. Edinburgh: T. & T. Clark, 1956.

———. *Learning Jesus Christ through the Heidelberg Catechism*. Grand Rapids: Eerdmans, 1964.

———. *The Theology of John Calvin*. Grand Rapids: Eerdmans, 1995.

Brichto, H. C. *The Names of God*. Oxford: Oxford University Press, 1998.

Bright, John. *A History of Israel*. 3rd ed. London: SCM, 1981.

Ford, David F. *Barth and God's Story: Biblical Narrative and the Theological Method of Karl Barth in the* Church Dogmatics. Frankfurt am Main: Lang, 1981.

———. *Christian Wisdom: Desiring God and Learning in Love*. Cambridge: Cambridge University Press, 2007.

———. *The Future of Christian Theology*. Oxford: Wiley-Blackwell, 2011.

———, with Rachel Muers, editors. *The Modern Theologians: An Introduction to Christian Theology since* 1918. 3rd ed. Oxford: Blackwell, 2005.

Frei, Hans. *Types of Christian Theology*. New Haven: Yale University Press, 1994.

Greggs, Tom. "The Eschatological Tension of Theological Method: Some Reflections after Reading Daniel W. Hardy's 'Creation and Eschatology.'" *Theology* 113 (2010) 339–47.

Healy, Nicholas M. "What is Systematic Theology?" *International Journal of Systematic Theology* 11 (2009) 24–39.

Iggers, Georg G. *Historiography in the Twentieth Century: From Scientific Objectivity to the Postmodern Challenge*. Hanover, NH: Wesleyan University Press, 1997.

Kelly, J. N. D. *Early Christian Creeds*. London: Longmans, 1960.

McCormack, Bruce L. *Karl Barth's Critically Realistic Dialectical Theology: Its Genesis and Development*, 1909–1936. Oxford: Oxford University Press, 1995.

Newman, John Henry. *An Essay on the Development of Christian Doctrine*. London: Penguin, 1974.

Williams, Rowan. *Arius: Heresy and Tradition*. London: SCM, 2001.

———. *Why Study the Past? The Quest for the Historical Church*. London: Darton, Longman & Todd, 2005.

36. Ford, *Christian Wisdom*, 86.

3

The Wisdom and Love of God

Starting a Conversation between Schleiermacher and Ford

Paul T. Nimmo

New College, University of Edinburgh

Introduction

In his work *Christian Wisdom: Desiring God and Learning in Love*, David Ford advances for consideration a coordinating set of three divine perfections which together offer one way of identifying the Christian God. The perfections are love, wisdom, and blessedness, and they are brought together in Ford's summary phrase "the God of blessing who loves in wisdom."[1] Ford notes that love and wisdom appear in many catalogues of the divine attributes, in which they often occupy pivotal positions (CW, 239), and explains with approval that "as one works with the whole of Scripture and the tradition, these two perfections prove their worth again and again as headings under which to think of God and God's relation to the world, and they also resonate with the most important dimensions of human existence today" (CW, 240). To these two regularly prioritized

1. Ford, *Christian Wisdom*, 236–50. References hereafter appear inline with the prefix CW.

perfections, Ford proposes the addition of blessedness, asserting that this addition captures something of the divine "beauty, power (in blessing and cursing), happiness, joy, and holiness," and—of particular importance—"glory" (CW, 242).

One work of theology in which at least the first two of these attributes occupy a similarly significant role is *The Christian Faith* of Friedrich Schleiermacher. Both the treatment of the divine attributes in that work and the second and major section of the work as a whole culminate in the passionate assertion that, of all the divine attributes, love and wisdom *alone* "can claim to be not mere attributes but also expressions of the very essence of God."[2] For Schleiermacher, it is not merely the case that these two attributes offer a fitting climax to his dogmatic enterprise;[3] it is also the case that the divine love and wisdom offer an integrating vector that retrospectively illuminates the entire theological course traversed in his work. The concept of blessedness, meanwhile, though not specifically listed by Schleiermacher among the divine attributes,[4] is a central concept for his work in Christology and soteriology (§101, 431–38), and thus stands—albeit in a different register—directly in relation to the divine being.

This short essay seeks to bring the understanding of the divine love and wisdom in these two works into a conversation, and correspondingly has two sections. First, on the assumption that readers of this volume may be more familiar with Ford's conception of the divine love and wisdom in *Christian Wisdom*, it offers a brief account of Schleiermacher's construal of these divine attributes in *The Christian Faith*. And second, it makes an initial foray into elucidating resonances and discordances between these treatments by probing a little further their respective approaches to experience and to Scripture.[5] A brief conclusion suggests where the most significant parallel between the two thinkers on this matter might lie.

2. Schleiermacher, *Christian Faith*, §167.2, 731–32. Further references appear inline by section number and page number.

3. Schleiermacher, *On the Glaubenslehre*, 59.

4. Schleiermacher does assert in passing that blessedness is an isolated attribute that is often added to catalogues of the divine attributes by inference (§50.3, 199). It would seem plausible that Schleiermacher might rank the attribution to God of blessedness along with that of mercy, as something "more appropriate to the language of preaching and poetry than to that of dogmatic theology" (§85 heading, 353). It is also plausible that Ford would contest this strongly.

5. It does so in the hope of capturing something of the spirit of Ford's own work, which draws creatively on a multiplicity of conversations with radically different theological dialogue partners in the anticipation of generating constructive and fruitful insights.

The Divine Love and Wisdom in Schleiermacher's *The Christian Faith*

Schleiermacher's doctrine of God is undoubtedly one of the most remarkable writings on the topic in the history of Christian theology. Before turning to his treatment of divine love and wisdom in particular, it is helpful to consider its daring methodology and its innovative structure.

First, its methodology: Schleiermacher defines Christian doctrines as "accounts of the Christian religious affections set forth in speech" (§15 thesis, 76). His entire dogmatic enterprise thereby rests fundamentally neither on Scripture, nor on reason *per se*, nor even on tradition (in any conventional sense), but on the lived experience of the Christian community. According to Schleiermacher's quasi-transcendental analysis in the introduction to *The Christian Faith*, all religious piety is fundamentally grounded on the (in)famous "feeling of absolute dependence" (§4, 12–18). This feeling is "the consciousness that the whole of our spontaneous activity comes from a source outside of us" (§4.3, 16), and Schleiermacher explicitly designates the "Whence" of this absolute feeling of dependence by the term "God" (§4.4, 16). In lived human experience, however, Schleiermacher insists that the feeling of absolute dependence is never found in such abstraction; instead, it only ever occurs in conjunction with the feelings and experiences of day-to-day life and thus in concrete form (§5 thesis, 18). Correspondingly, as he moves towards the dogmatic sections of *The Christian Faith*, Schleiermacher offers a more precise construal of specifically Christian piety. He posits that in Christianity "everything is related to the redemption accomplished by Jesus of Nazareth" (§11 thesis, 52), which assertion indicates both a realization of redemption (grace) and something antithetical from which redemption is necessary (sin). Indeed, *all* religious moments in the Christian community, as free expressions of the underlying feeling of absolute dependence, come into existence through the same redemption of Jesus (§11.3, 56). It is upon the basis of these very moments, as experienced, reflected, and communicated in the Christian community, that Schleiermacher constructs his dogmatic formulations in general, and his doctrine of God in particular.[6] This daring foundation was as controversial in its day as it has been ever since.[7]

6. See further on this paragraph McCormack, "What Has Basel to Do with Berlin?" 152–62.

7. In *On the Glaubenslehre*, Schleiermacher attempts to address many of his contemporary critics; later critical works famously include Karl Barth, *The Theology of Schleiermacher*, and Emil Brunner, *Die Mystik and das Wort*. That such critics were

Second, its structure: the primary conceptual device that Schleiermacher uses to arrange *The Christian Faith* is the antithesis of sin and grace. This dialectic, mentioned above, is present—in Schleiermacher's view—universally in the Christian religious affections. In the *second* major section of his work, Schleiermacher presents his dogmatic material pertaining to this antithesis in two subdivisions: there is, first, an explication of the consciousness of sin, and, second, an explication of the consciousness of grace. Meanwhile, in the *first* major section of his work, he treats of the religious self-consciousness "presupposed by and contained in every Christian Religious Affection" (heading to "First Part," 131). This is at first sight a rather unusual procedure: having just begun his dogmatics proper, this first section represents an explicit transcendental move, *abstracting* from the feeling of redemption in Jesus Christ. Schleiermacher is deeply aware that this is rather controversial, but staunchly defends his procedure, arguing carefully that it avoids any "natural theology" (§29.2, 124). In each of these three parts of *The Christian Faith*—the presuppositions, the consciousness of sin, and the consciousness of grace—Schleiermacher offers three types of dogmatic propositions. The first aspect of each part offers propositions as descriptions of the *Christian religious self-consciousness*; the second aspect offers utterances regarding *the constitution of the world*, and the third aspect offers a conception of *the divine attributes*.[8] What this means is that the doctrine of God *per se* does not appear in one section of *The Christian Faith* or even in three sections *seriatim*, but is distributed over these three subdivisions of the work as a whole. Schleiermacher is hopeful that this is a helpful and positive way to avoid some of the problems of other presentations of the doctrine (§31.2, 128). However, this unique presentation has also been controversial both in its day and ever since.[9]

Schleiermacher's handling of the divine attributes of love and wisdom is rendered far clearer by these explanations of methodology and structure. First, Schleiermacher seeks to derive their meaning—as he did that of the other divine attributes—on the basis of the Christian religious

---

often guilty of seriously misrepresenting and grievously misinterpreting Schleiermacher on many points has been well established.

8. The order of the second and third aspects is, however, reversed in the very first section.

9. Again, see *On the Glaubenslehre* for Schleiermacher's own response to some of his contemporary critics. For some more recent attention to these matters, see the contributions in *Journal for Theology and Church 7: Schleiermacher as Contemporary*, as well as other works cited below.

affections alone: "nothing can be taken as fundamental save that in the Divine Essence which explains the feeling of absolute dependence" (§50.3.199).[10] And second, Schleiermacher presents their meaning under his third and final treatment of the divine attributes, of those relating to redemption, and thereby provides a fitting climax to the whole given that love and wisdom are the only attributes that he considers to express the very essence of God (§168.2, 732–33).

Materially, the exposition of divine love and wisdom in *The Christian Faith* is strongly connected with the divine government of the world. For Schleiermacher, the tracing of the consciousness of redemption to the divine causality leads us to posit that the divine purpose is set on "the union of the Divine Essence with human nature in the Person of Christ, and . . . with the community of believers through the Holy Spirit as the one object of the divine world-government" (§164.2, 724). Hence the whole purpose of creation, providence, and incarnation—indeed, of all things—is this uniting activity of God.

The divine attributes underlying this uniting activity are the divine love and wisdom. Love, Schleiermacher writes in an initial definition, is "the impulse to unite self with neighbour and to will to be in neighbour" (§165.1, 726). It is by virtue of this attribute, then, that God imparts Godself to humanity in the activity of redemption in the two unions noted above. Wisdom, according to Schleiermacher's initial definition, is "the right outlining of plans and purposes . . . in their manifold characteristics and in the whole round of reciprocal relations" (§166.1, 727). It is by virtue of this attribute, then, that God organizes the whole sphere of redemption in order to realize the purpose of the divine love. Crucially, Schleiermacher immediately qualifies this initial exposition by insisting that while these two attributes are separable in human life, "in the Divine Essence . . . the two attributes are never separate in any way; they are so entirely one that each may be regarded as being intrinsically connected to the other" (§166.2, 727).

At this point, Schleiermacher considers the text of 1 John 4:16: "God is Love" (§167, 730–32). According to Schleiermacher, there is no distinction in God between essence and attributes, thus the predication of *any* attribute to God must refer to the divine essence. However, Schleiermacher observes, in Scripture only love is explicitly identified with the essence

10. It should correspondingly come as no surprise that Schleiermacher (in broad terms) prefers the *via causalitatis* to the *via eminentiae* and the *via negationis*. This tendency is captured in his statement that "all divine attributes . . . must somehow go back to the divine causality" (§50.3, 198).

of God; correspondingly, then, Schleiermacher proposes that "love alone and no other attribute can be equated . . . with God" (§167.1, 730). Notably, this statement functions for Schleiermacher to *include* the divine wisdom, as attested by his statement that alone love and wisdom can *both* "claim to be not mere attributes but also expressions of the very essence of God" (§167.2, 731–32) and by his conclusion that "where almighty love is, there must also absolute wisdom be" (§167.2, 732). Schleiermacher's justification for endorsing this scriptural claim is that the divine love and wisdom are uniquely present to the Christian religious consciousness. Yet there remains a difference. That love is a divine attribute enters the God-consciousness *directly*: Schleiermacher explains that "We have the sense of divine love directly in the consciousness of redemption . . . [; it] is the basis on which all the rest of our God-consciousness is built up" (§167.2, 732). That wisdom is a divine attribute, however, enters the God-consciousness only *indirectly*, as we sense how the divine government arranges all things for the impartation of the divine love (§167.2, 732).

Ultimately, what this treatment of the divine love and wisdom means is that Schleiermacher's presentations of the divine attributes in the previous sections—on the basis of the Christian consciousness of sin and on the basis of the presupposition of the Christian religious consciousness—are now seen to be incomplete. In view of the consciousness of redemption, in which it is recognized that love and wisdom can be uniquely predicated of God, these earlier attributes must be reconsidered. Schleiermacher recalls that those attributes treated under the first division—eternity and omnipresence, omnipotence and omniscience—were developed explicitly "by abstraction from the definite feeling of our God-consciousness" (§167.2, 731). Consequently, he writes, *taken on their own*, they reflect a belief in God (as almighty and eternal) that is "nothing more than the shadow of faith which even the devils may have" (§167.2, 731). And he recalls that those attributes treated under the second division—holiness and justice—were there defined by Schleiermacher in relation to evil, and thus, *taken as such*, pertain to a limited sphere and have no independent existence. All the attributes considered prior to this point in *The Christian Faith* therefore belong to a preparatory stage of dogmatic enquiry. Consequently, they only gain full Christian significance as they are projected or resolved into the full consciousness of redemption in Jesus Christ.

Schleiermacher's understanding of the divine love and wisdom thus stands at the formal and material apex of his doctrine of the divine attributes. It offers a presentation of the doctrine of God that is radically christomorphic, and utterly grounded in the Christian experience of redemption.[11] Moreover, it presents for Christian dogmatics a conception of God that indicates the sheer incarnational gratuity of the love of God for all of creation and of the wisdom of God in bringing creation towards redemption.

Ford and Schleiermacher Talking Love and Wisdom

As theologians, and for all their differences, David Ford and Friedrich Schleiermacher share much in common. Both are deeply committed to the flourishing of the church; both are deeply committed to the flourishing of the academy; and both are deeply committed to the flourishing of theology.[12] In what follows, then, there follows a theological experiment that seeks to initiate a conversation between them. This conversation proceeds on the basis of Ford's *Christian Wisdom* and Schleiermacher's *The Christian Faith*, two very different texts with very different aims. It nevertheless seeks to delineate potential resonances and discordances between these theological works in respect of their treatments of the divine love and wisdom. In so doing, it hopes to go a little beyond surface similarities and differences to interrogate deeper underlying relationships. In what follows, two aspects of these texts will be briefly considered: their respective approaches to experience and their respective approaches to Scripture.

On Experience

The book *Christian Wisdom*, Ford writes, is explicitly "my attempt as a Christian thinker to search out a wisdom for living in the twenty-first century" (CW, 2). Its principal aim is thus to offer practical guidance for wise ways of being a Christian today. To this end, it draws heavily on Ford's own involvements with the Scriptural Reasoning movement (CW, chapter 8) and L'Arche communities (CW, chapter 10) as well as on his interests in

11. Important treatments in recent English-language scholarship of the divine attributes in the work of Schleiermacher include Williams, *Schleiermacher the Theologian*, 123–35, and Lamm, *Schleiermacher's Theological Appropriation of Spinoza*, 212–25.

12. For evidence in respect of Schleiermacher, see Redeker, *Schleiermacher*, or Nowak, *Schleiermacher*. For evidence in respect of David Ford, and pending one of his Research Associates over the years writing a full intellectual biography, spend five minutes in conversation with him.

the concrete contexts of Christian wisdom after the Holocaust (CW, chapter 4) and Christian wisdom in the university (CW, chapter 9). Between these major engagements and the many anecdotal and autobiographical interludes which are also presented, *Christian Wisdom* is a book in which theology takes the category of human experience seriously, precisely in order to be able to offer a wisdom that is "involved in history and its traumas" (CW, 103).

The prominence of human experience in *Christian Wisdom* is particularly evident in its consideration of "the importance for wisdom of cries and of the diverse moods that express the significance of cries" (CW, 120). Ford explores in detail such "cries" in the life of Job (CW, chapters 3 and 4) and in the life of Jesus (CW, chapter 5), though in the background of Ford's thinking lie also the cries of so many others—of the heavenly host in Revelation, of the victims of the Holocaust, of the disabled, of the world at large. His treatment of cries reaches its climax where Ford considers "the cries of God" (CW, 248). At this point, Ford explicitly invokes the divine wisdom. He refers to measuring God's wisdom by God's discernment of cries in the world (CW, 248–49), and to the cry of Jesus from the cross as acknowledging and being the "touchstone for wisdom in God" (CW, 249). This divine wisdom is "committed to human existence whatever the consequences," against the background of God desiring "one who in love gives a perfect 'for nothing' response" (CW, 249).[13] In resonating with the cry of the martyr Stephen of Acts 6–7, posits Ford, "we learn the love and wisdom of God together" (CW, 249).

This description of the divine wisdom is by no means intended by Ford to be exhaustive of the matter, nor is it intended to be a systematic treatment. Nevertheless, a number of resonances with the work of Schleiermacher are already discernible. First, and most basically, there is a real emphasis in the work of both thinkers on the lived experience of Christian communities as being a constructive—and often provocative—resource in Christian theology. Second, there is a clear sense in both *Christian Wisdom* and *The Christian Faith* of the immensity of the love and wisdom of God. For Ford, this is manifest in the divine commitment to humanity, centred in the incarnation, which knows no limits in its gracious overabundance. For Schleiermacher, this is manifest in the divine government of creation, again centred in the incarnation, which renders absolute the

13. Or, to use Ford's alternative expression, one who realizes that "*God is to be loved for God's sake*" (CW, 225, emphasis original). These expressions both allude to the idea of Job fearing God "for nothing" (CW, 132), an idea elucidated in Ford's exegesis of Job and invoked repeatedly as a significant theme elsewhere in the text.

gracious Self-impartation of God. Third, there is arguably a discernible connection between the way in which these theologians perceive the *telos* of the love and wisdom of God. For Ford, that which is desired by the God who acts "for my name's sake" and without sparing the Son is a loving response on the part of humanity "for nothing," in the sense of "relating to God not for what he receives, but for nothing, for the sake of God's name, for God's own sake" (CW, 100). For Schleiermacher, that which is desired by the God who enters without compulsion into a loving union of God with humanity is the human recognition that the relationship to God, by virtue of which one can conform to the divine will, is owed entirely to Christ (§166.2, 730).

At the same time, there is one point at which the conceptions of the divine love and wisdom in these works seem to diverge radically—the centrality, or otherwise, of the cross and its ramifications for understanding these divine attributes. Significantly, at no point in the treatment of the divine attributes in *The Christian Faith* is the crucifixion foregrounded. Instead, as we have seen, it is the incarnation—the union of the Divine Essence with human nature in the person of Jesus Christ—that is rendered central. For Ford, by contrast, it is the cry of dereliction from the cross—which Schleiermacher implicitly understands in light of the remainder of Psalm 22 and which thus, for him, does not indicate a disturbance in Jesus' God-consciousness (§101.4, 436)—that is pivotal to a correct understanding of the divine love and wisdom, as well as to a genuine Christian participation in these attributes by way of God's "for my sake" and the human "for God's sake" (CW, 249).

There can be no question of simple adjudication here, particularly in light of the different exegetical possibilities available. However, two points of interest might be registered. First, in highlighting the constancy of Jesus' consciousness of God in the extreme of the suffering of the crucifixion (§101.4, 436), Schleiermacher in his Christology seems to be positing—with Ford—*precisely* a climax of the kind of reconciliatory "for nothing" love of God for humanity.[14] And second, conversely, in his desire that we are brought by grace to emulate Jesus' undisturbed consciousness of God, Schleiermacher seems clearly to desire—with Ford—that we might have that "mind of Christ," which "involves wholehearted participation in the radical transformation begun in Christ" (CW, 184). If these claims hold,

14. The consciousness of God, after all, is never a *datum*, but is always a *dandum* (§4.4, 18).

then the conclusions of Ford and Schleiermacher at this point may be rather more convergent than first expected.

On Scripture

Throughout *Christian Wisdom*, Ford writes, "the focus is especially on the Christian Scriptures and their interpretation today" (CW, 2). As indicated already, the volume offers a lengthy engagement with the book of Job (CW, chapters 3 and 4), but it also contains extensive exegetical sections exploring—most prominently—Luke, John, Acts, and 1 Corinthians.

Part of Ford's aim in *Christian Wisdom*, exemplified in this exegetical work, is to offer a "wisdom interpretation of Scripture," a hermeneutic that seeks—among other goals—to advance beyond considering the indicative and imperative moods of Scripture in isolation and to attend also to the insights of the interrogative, subjunctive, and optative moods of the text (CW, chapter 2). Yet underlying this hermeneutical impulse there lies a very robust doctrine of Scripture indeed; one that is given expression by way of a series of theses (CW, 79–89). Correspondingly, Ford's engagement with Scripture goes beyond the level of plain narrative and engages with the details of each text. He writes, for example, with respect to the narratives in Luke and Acts, that "much of the wisdom is in the way the story is told . . . [such that] the narrative pattern and detail, the encounters and images, and the key events and statements, yield their meaning by being savored in their specificity" (CW, 43). In practice, this leads in *Christian Wisdom* to certain verses of Scripture carrying extraordinary significance. In respect of the divine wisdom, for example, the cry from the cross noted above, along with the text of Job 28:27 (which leads Ford to exclaim that, "God himself searched out wisdom!" [CW, 137][15]), bear immense explanatory power for Ford.

It is evident without much reflection that the treatment of Scripture in *Christian Wisdom* is radically different to that found in *The Christian Faith*. As was outlined above, Schleiermacher's entire dogmatic enterprise—including his understanding of the divine attributes—is grounded directly on the Christian religious affections, and not directly on Scripture. Moreover, the discipline within which a genuine and profound engagement with the text of Scripture takes place, for Schleiermacher, is exegetical theology, which is to be distinguished from dogmatic theology

15. It is likely that Schleiermacher would simply reject this statement as nonsensical, yet it forms an important dimension of Ford's understanding of divine wisdom.

and thus does not appear in *The Christian Faith*.[16] Ford, throughout the pages of *Christian Wisdom*, is, by contrast, far more keen to integrate explicitly the insights of Scripture with the discourse of theology. Moreover, where Ford is keen to focus on the instructive theological power of the finest details of the scriptural texts, Schleiermacher prefers a more holistic, "large-viewed use of Scripture" in theology (§27.3, 116), directed instead to the recreation of the religious feelings of the original authors.[17]

For all that it is founded on Christian experience, however, *The Christian Faith*—with *Christian Wisdom*—takes Scripture with immense seriousness, indeed as possessing both "constitutive" and "critical" normative influence for Christian piety (§131.2, 606).[18] The justice that Schleiermacher feels that he must do to 1 John 4:16 in his treatment of the divine love is worthy of mention here, as is his (albeit meagre) quotation of other Scriptural passages in this subdivision.[19] For Schleiermacher, this high regard for Scripture goes together with the demand for full and ongoing critical engagement with the text of Scripture (§131.1, 605). In this way, Schleiermacher clearly escapes Ford's concern that one might unwisely "formulate doctrines or other theological conclusions with reference to Scripture and then forget that reference, failing to keep open the engagement with Scripture that is needed if the theology is to avoid becoming fossilised" (CW, 43). Indeed, Schleiermacher considers "the changing transformation of the Christian fellowship as living piety enters . . . into combination with this or that new aspect of human experience"—which, it could be argued, a dynamic engagement with Scripture directly facilitates—as being directly "the proper work of divine wisdom" (§168.2, 735). It seems that Ford could only agree.

Conclusion

The understandings of the divine love and wisdom in the works of Ford and Schleiermacher explored above, for all their many differences, share many similarities. In both texts, the conception of these attributes is relentlessly christomorphic, and is informed not only by the canonical text of Scripture but also by the lived experience of faith. In a longer conversation, there would be more to be said on the points made, and further points

16. Schleiermacher, *Brief Outline of Theology*, §31, 14, and §§81–102, 35–43.

17. See further Nimmo, "[E]in ins Große gehender Schriftgebrauch."

18. Nimmo, "[E]in ins Große gehender Schriftgebrauch."

19. The other passages quoted are Col 1:16, Jas 2:19, and Acts 17:24–25.

to be explored,[20] but (hopefully) some perhaps unexpected resonances are already perceptible. What is certainly evident in the work of both thinkers is that the divine love and wisdom together effect not only the redemption of humanity and of the creation, but also transform and transform again Christian thinking about God.

Ultimately, however, perhaps the most significant resonance between the work of Ford and Schleiermacher is their mutual perception that the divine love and wisdom have immediate practical implications. As cited above, Ford contends that the divine wisdom is "a divine quality that must be humanly embodied" (CW, 134). Schleiermacher, similarly, insists that the divine wisdom, "as the unfolding of the divine love, conducts us . . . to the realm of Christian Ethics" (§169.3, 736). For both thinkers, then, there arises the important and inescapable challenge of how to relate the wisdom of God to the wisdom and activity of humanity.

This challenge of discerning wisdom faces Christians of every generation as they engage the question of how to engage faithfully both with the God who is love and wisdom and with the complex cries of a fallen world. The works of Schleiermacher and Ford suggest and exemplify the view that such engagement is only possible on the basis of a lived relationship with God in Jesus Christ "for nothing." And they additionally propose and practise that such engagement must proceed on the basis of sustained attention to and dynamic interrogation of experience and Scripture. For these reasons, the works of Ford and Schleiermacher provide those facing the same challenge today not only with wise examples to imitate but also with exemplary wisdom to attend.

Bibliography

Barth, Karl. *The Theology of Schleiermacher: Lectures at Göttingen, Winter Semester of 1923/24*. Translated by Geoffrey W. Bromiley. Edited by Dietrich Ritschl. Edinburgh: T. & T. Clark, 1982.

Brunner, Heinrich Emil. *Die Mystik and das Wort: Der Gegensatz zwischen moderner Religionsauffassung und christlichem Glauben dargestellt an der Theologie Schleiermachers*. Tübingen: Mohr, 1924.

Ford, David F. *Christian Wisdom: Desiring God and Learning in Love*. Cambridge: Cambridge University Press, 2007.

Lamm, Julia A. *The Living God: Schleiermacher's Theological Appropriation of Spinoza*. University Park: Pennsylvania State University Press, 1996.

20. Such further points of fruitful conversation might include the role of the Spirit in the divine love and wisdom, the divine love and wisdom in the community, and the relationship between the divine love and wisdom and the Old Testament.

McCormack, Bruce. "What Has Basel to Do with Berlin? Continuities in the Theologies of Barth and Schleiermacher." *Princeton Seminary Bulletin* 23.2 (2002) 146–73.

Nimmo, Paul T. "'[E]in ins Große gehender Schriftgebrauch': Friedrich Schleiermacher and the Doctrine of Scripture." Paper delivered at the University of Notre Dame, June 2011, forthcoming in print.

Nowak, Kurt. *Schleiermacher: Leben, Werk und Wirkung.* Göttingen: Vandenhoeck & Ruprecht, 2001.

Redeker, Martin. *Schleiermacher: Life and Thought.* Translated by John Wallhausser. Philadelphia: Fortress, 1973.

Schleiermacher, Friedrich. *Brief Outline of Theology as a Field of Study.* Translated by Terrence N. Tice. Louisville: Westminster John Knox, 2011.

———. *The Christian Faith.* Translated by various. Edited by H. R. Mackintosh and J. S. Stewart. Edinburgh: T. & T. Clark, 1999.

———. *On the Glaubenslehre.* Translated by James Duke and Francis Fiorenza. AAR Texts and Translations 3. Atlanta: Scholars, 1981.

Williams, Robert R. *Schleiermacher the Theologian: The Construction of the Doctrine of God.* Philadelphia: Fortress, 1978.

4

The Many Moods of Revelation

Jason Fout

Bexley Hall

David Ford is well known for the collaborative, conversational quality of his theology, an observation that this volume verifies and extends.[1] A part of this conversational engagement is bringing together far-flung and disparate thinkers for the sake of what might be called heuristic exploration. In this he reads texts and engages others, being alert to continuities and discontinuities, working to think expansively while shunning claims of theorizing exhaustively, neither rushing to foreclose questions nor eschewing definition, being attentive to the potential for "surprise."

Many of his students and colleagues can attest to face-to-face conversations with him in which, while discussing their work, he raised a question, unexpected at first, exposing surprising, generative connections. Sometimes these questions flow out of his own work—in recent years, connections with wisdom, the university, reading Scripture, inter-Abrahamic engagements, the Gospel of John—but they are motivated by a desire to think expansively and synthetically, to do justice to the One who God is. In his own work, this heuristic exploration allows him to approach topics through multiple lenses and in unconventional ways. In all of this there is an effort, in conversation with the tradition and contemporary thought, to

1. As for my own conversations, I am grateful to Paul Nimmo and Craig Hovey for their helpful remarks on an earlier draft of this chapter.

make a contribution to the church, its doctrine and life, by seeking most adequately to describe the encompassing reality of God, in whom "we live and move and have our being."[2]

In what follows below I carry out such a "Fordian" heuristic exploration in which I take a set of concepts from his work and transpose them slightly in order to raise questions in another conversation. More specifically, I present revelation as discussed by Karl Barth in the *Church Dogmatics*, specifically in relation to God's covenant with humanity, and Barth's insistence that such revelation is in the indicative and imperative. In order to provide a contrast to this account, I turn to Rowan Williams' account of revelation in his essay "Trinity and Revelation." Williams draws on several other thinkers in this essay, particularly Paul Ricoeur; partly owing to his dependence on Ricoeur, Williams seems to imply that revelation is primarily in the subjunctive. Interleaved with this, I present Ford's discussion of the "moods" of faith and theology to suggest that we might think in terms of an encompassing "ecology" of "moods" of revelation—and in doing so, better fulfil the vocation of theology by doing fuller justice to the One who God is.

Revelation in the Indicative and Imperative

The importance and centrality of revelation in the *Dogmatics* can hardly be understated, and Barth gives the doctrine a distinct character. To summarize briefly, for Barth, God reveals Godself apart from human questing for knowledge of God. In this, revelation is above all God's revealing of Godself: it is about God's priority, freedom, and pre-eminence. And God reveals Godself as the One who loves the creation, and elects humanity in Jesus Christ to be God's beloved covenant-partner.[3] Thus, this revealing is not of God's bare presence or existence, but the shape of the One God is, in Jesus Christ. Closely related to this revealing is God's command to the human creature, in which the human is freed to correspond to the grace of God in Christ, to live as one elect by God, and become God's covenant-partner.[4] Dogmatics and ethics are intrinsic to each other for Barth, and, bound up in revelation, both share a fundamentally declarative or

2. Acts 17:28, in which, according to the story, Paul uses this phrase from a preexisting Athenian poem to proclaim to the Athenians the "Lord of heaven and earth" (17:24).

3. Barth, *Church Dogmatics* II/2, 411.

4. Ibid., 575.

indicative[5] character to which human response is elicited (in the imperative) albeit in a subsequent and confirmatory manner.

This connection of indicative and imperative may be seen clearly in several places in the *Dogmatics*. In setting out the covenant of God with humanity, Barth insists that there are two elements: God's election and God's command to humanity as those who are chosen to be God's covenant-partners.[6] Thus the covenant involves both law and gospel, not as two parts but as the one Word of God.[7] Barth elaborates, saying "The truth of the evangelical indicative means that the full stop with which it concludes becomes an exclamation mark. It becomes itself an imperative."[8] What God has done in election (indicative, gospel) issues forth in a command to humanity (imperative, law), bearing fruit in human obedience.

Later in the *Dogmatics*, Barth turns to the question of the possibility of providing grounds for the presupposition and assertion of Jesus Christ as the Mediator and prophet. Barth asserts that the "starting point" for answering this question is "the fact" that in Jesus Christ we are dealing indisputably not with humanity but with "the presence and action of God."[9] Barth makes this claim on the basis that "in this life God Himself is present as acting Subject," and where "God is present as active Subject; where he lives, as is the case in the life of Jesus Christ, life is . . . definitely and primarily declaration, and therefore light, truth, Word and glory."[10] Moreover, Barth goes on to specify that Jesus as the one Word of God "means first that he is the total and complete declaration of God concerning Himself and the men whom he addresses in His Word."[11] Barth is unambiguous that the presence of God in revelation and reconciliation gives a purely declarative, or indicative quality to the prophetic office of the Mediator; it is a shining forth of God's self-declaration. Moreover, this indicative issues forth in an imperative, in God's awakening the human to fellowship with God and calling the human to be witness to God's work.[12]

5. Various linguistic models categorize moods differently. As my primary concern is not linguistic, I shall not weigh in on this matter, but, in order to proceed, I adopt the five moods used by Ford: indicative, imperative, interrogative, subjunctive, and optative.

6. Barth, *Church Dogmatics* II/2, 510.

7. Ibid., 511.

8. Ibid., 512.

9. Barth, *Church Dogmatics* IV/3.1, 79.

10. Ibid.

11. Ibid., 99.

12. Barth, *Church Dogmatics* IV/3.2, 481.

If there were any doubt about this indicative character, Barth makes it abundantly clear in a section in which he discusses the three resisting elements in humanity that futilely oppose the completed victory of Christ. He describes them in terms of a progressively insidious sequence, starting with humanity's penchant to ignore God's Word, moving on to the making of God's grace innocuous through reducing it to a "world view," and concluding with the most subtle opposition of all, which makes of grace something "religious" and hence domesticated.[13] This latter form, the most pernicious of all, has the greatest likeness to genuine Christian faith. Barth continues: "[E]verything will still sound great and august and holy. But it will no longer be the indicative and imperative which impinge incisively upon the present. It will no longer give offence. It will no longer be engaged in attack. It will wound no one, and therefore it will not really help anyone. It will no longer spread unrest, and therefore no longer give rest."[14] This form of opposition of humanity to God is the "most cunning," as it domesticates the Word of grace. And so, for Barth, a principal mark of God's revelation is not merely its character as declaration, but that it takes this form in the indicative and imperative and seemingly nothing else. Any other form would be, *ipso facto*, strong evidence of humanity's perverse penchant to replace God's Word with its own.

This is a serious point and I would insist that God may and does make declarations, and God's Word may be and is in the indicative and imperative—and, indeed, that humanity is often quite occupied with evasion, making God into something domesticated or merely "religious." Moreover, I would agree that there is no ambiguity about whether Jesus Christ is the mediator and reconciler between God and humanity. But I wonder if this treatment of revelation might also be too restricting of God's freedom and competence, seeming to rule out revelation in anything other than the indicative and imperative.[15]

13. Barth, *Church Dogmatics* IV/3.1, 253–60.

14. Ibid., 259.

15. I speak here of the "competence" of God simply to indicate God's sufficiency in God's self freely to achieve God's aims and ends as God chooses in God's wisdom, consistent with the one whom God is. Very often "omnipotence" is used to speak in this way about God, but I am not sure the term is most helpful. Taken in itself, it seems to tie God's agency to power, perhaps overwhelming power. Yet the Christian God is seen most clearly and paradigmatically in Jesus Christ, who is on any account not an example of conventional power, dominating or otherwise. And yet, Jesus Christ is "the power of God for salvation" (Rom 1:16). Thus, I speak of God's "competency" to indicate that God achieves God's purposes in God's way, without struggle or hindrance, yet may do so in ways that appear humble or weak in conventional terms, and that are not adequately rendered by "omnipotence," being "all-powerful."

The Many Moods of Revelation

The indicative and imperative are grammatical moods that allow the speaker to express an attitude towards what she is saying, but they are not the only ones. In English, other grammatical moods include the interrogative, the optative, and the subjunctive, as well as others. As terms for understanding God's revealing these are strictly metaphorical and analogous (as they are for Barth), inasmuch as revelation is not to be understood only as a linguistic or speech act. Moreover, my use of it is heuristic, given that other languages specify grammatical moods differently: one should not suppose that God's revealing is in strict accord with the conventions of the English or German languages! Nevertheless, Barth sees fit to use such terms in speaking of revelation, which then raises the question: why just these two moods?

David Ford considers the meaningful interconnectedness of "moods" as an analogy in two separate contexts, one discussing "the moods of faith," another "the moods of theology." Ford develops this notion first in the context of considering Christian wisdom, and particularly the shape of a wisdom-influenced theology that responds to various "cries."[16] In a section of a later work on Christian theology in the twenty-first century, he expands from talking about the moods of faith to the moods of theology.

Eschewing the model of theology as a set of ready-made answers, Ford suggests that there is a "dynamic ecology of theological thinking."[17] This ecology is comprised by multiple "moods," perhaps chiefly the indicative and imperative (declaring the truth, enjoining obedience—both particularly fitting for dogmatic theology), but doing justice to it also requires the interrogative (questioning, letting ourselves be questioned), the subjunctive (being open to contingency, possibilities, surprise), and the optative (expressing wishes, desires, hopes). Each of these last three moods seem to imply something like an openness and interactivity, which Ford suggests are fitting for theology: they may be combined variously, according to the need and situation.[18] Each of these five elements are crucial to such an ecology, but finding the proper balance is a matter of wisdom.

If we were to query the suggestion from Barth that revelation is properly considered in the indicative and imperative forms, transposing Ford's suggestion of a broader ecology of grammatical "moods" for theology into

16. Ford, *Christian Wisdom*, 45.

17. Ford, *Future of Christian Theology*, 69.

18. Ibid.

talk of revelation shows promise. We might then explore the three other "moods" Ford draws from grammatical discourse to fill out the "modes of expression" of revelation, without denying that revelation is widely present in indicative and imperative forms as well. Ford implies something like this transposition himself, as he suggests that the "wisdom" of Job's friends, inattentive as it is to the cries of trauma, falsely "represents God as operating mainly in indicatives (especially judgements) and imperatives."[19]

If we transpose these moods from theology, human thinking about God and God's ways with the world, to revelation, God's act to declare Godself to the world, this naturally raises some questions. First, it might appear that God's ultimacy, freedom, or finality are jeopardized by the openness or interactivity of the interrogative, optative, or subjunctive. If God knows or sees all, then why would a mood expressing potential such as the optative or subjunctive, or a mood of questioning such as the interrogative be needed? Does this suggest process or incompleteness in God? Yet my suggestion is not that God might *need* to reveal in these moods, any more than God might need to reveal in the indicative and imperative. Revelation implies an "audience," a "hearer": creation. And so this does not say anything about God's aseity, but rather specifies the way in which God relates to the creation in revealing. This God is competent to reveal in multiple moods in accord with God's wisdom: God's use of one mood or another is not according to God's needs, but creation's.

Also, Ford writes about the moods of theology as an ecology whose balance may vary by context, needing human practical wisdom to get it right. Yet if revelation is God's act, at God's initiative, the ecology of moods in revelation is not a matter of human wisdom according to context, but must be considered a function of God's wisdom realized through God's acts. Yet this, in principle, does not limit God's revealing to the indicative and imperative.

So what might it mean for revelation to be in a "mood" other than the indicative and imperative? In what follows, I focus primarily on the possibility of revelation in the subjunctive and leave analysis of other moods to one side, simply owing to space.

Revelation in the Subjunctive

In the essay "Trinity and Revelation," Rowan Williams explores the way in which theological language is authorized by discussing how theologians

19. Ford, *Christian Wisdom*, 103.

may speak of revelation.[20] Although he does not engage the question of moods explicitly, his proposal situates revelation almost entirely within the subjunctive mood, as we shall see.

Williams' overall concern in the essay is to give an account of how we may speak of God on the basis of revelation without revelation simply being an "appeal to unchallengeable authority," theological language thus being opaque, heteronomous, "determined from an elusive 'elsewhere.'"[21] To put it positively, he is concerned for "learning about learning," that is, for the practice of theology being aware of the process of formation of its talk about God, and accountable for its present shape, rather than simply accepting such talk as delivered final and complete.[22] On the face of it, he might seem concerned to rule out revelation in the indicative and imperative *tout court*, because of its seeming completeness. But his primary focus is not God's act of revealing, but rather the (largely experiential) basis on which people might claim that something in particular is revelatory. In this, he and Barth embark on rather different projects, although not without some overlap as we shall see. But in the process of inquiring after "learning about learning," Williams does set out an understanding of revelation.

Williams draws on the work of Paul Ricoeur to suggest the revelation is about opening possibilities. Linking revelation and poetics, Ricoeur holds that the truth of poetic texts is a matter of manifesting a "'possible world,' a reality in which my human reality can also find itself: and in inviting me into its world, the text breaks open and extends my own possibilities."[23] In light of this, Williams states that revelation is "essentially to do with what is *generative* in our experience—events or transactions in our language that break existing frames of reference and initiate new possibilities of life."[24] Revelation is not a self-evident concept, but rather an idea "which emerges from a questioning attention to our present life in the light of a particular past—a past seen as 'generative.'"[25] On this account, revelation is a matter of the opening of new human possibilities in light of the experience of generativity. This is very much revelation in

20. Williams, "Trinity and Revelation," 131–47.

21. Ibid., 131.

22. Ibid., 130.

23. Ibid., 133, italics original. Williams particularly draws on Ricoeur's essay "Toward a Hermeneutic of the Idea of Revelation."

24. Williams, "Trinity and Revelation," 134.

25. Ibid.

the subjunctive: not only declared or commanded, but open to changing contingencies and new, perhaps surprising possibilities that are present.

It is revelation in the subjunctive: but one might wonder whether there is any room left for the indicative and imperative? As set out, this notion of revelation is entirely formal and abstract: it is about a human experience that may in principle be filled with any content (and, indeed, the same content may not prove "revelatory" to different people). Williams does go on through the rest of the essay to explore this notion through the specific lens of the Christian story, showing that the Trinity itself makes best sense of the revelation of God encountered in Jesus and the Holy Spirit. Yet there is nothing distinctly and specifically *Christian* about this notion of revelation: it is not itself a reflection on God's act in Christ, but a general hermeneutical consideration. Williams does attempt to introduce something like an (implicitly) indicative character to the account in saying that, in light of Ricoeur's perspective, revelation both "is and is not completed, 'over'; *what* we are interpreting is unquestionably this historical narrative and not another; we are not waiting for a more comprehensive and adequate story, because precisely of the comprehensiveness of the questioning provoked by this story."[26] Revelation has to do both with the originating events as well as the ongoing grappling with them. Yet since revelation is tethered so strongly to the human experience of generativity—it is what is generative *in human experience*, not an event (such as the incarnation) in itself—that it is hard to see what one would claim about this narrative if another simply did not find it generative: is the gospel of Jesus Christ, in itself, God's revelation? Or is it simply one story which some have found helpfully troubling?

Certainly one of the great gifts of the gospel is the way in which the Holy Spirit continues to use it to trouble us, to keep us awake at night, to open new possibilities and new life to us and the world: there is an unmistakable subjunctive character to it. Yet certainly that is because we find that it is, in fact, the revelation of God for the creation. Our dwelling with this narrative is not simply because as a community we have chosen a story which strikes us, but because it bears witness to the act of God in Jesus Christ, and there is therefore no more basic or encompassing perspective. The intrinsic logic of the gospel is not that it is *a* story, but *the* story—without thereby constituting us as masters of history.

Although Williams differentiates himself from Barth at a couple of points in the essay, there are nevertheless some convergences as well;

26. Ibid., 142.

namely, they agree that revelation does not originate with us. Even though Williams focuses on the human effects of revelation, these are not so far distant from Barth's case as it might seem. After all, as I have indicated above, to speak of God "revealing" implies a receiver, an "audience." Barth does not begin with human experience, nor seeks to be limited to a phenomenological account of it. But he does insist that God has elected to be God with us and not apart from us in Jesus Christ. God is with human creatures, and reveals to human creatures—and therefore "indicative" and "imperative" revelation is intrinsically related to human experience, the experience of creatures adopted in Christ and made covenant partners with God. Barth does not begin his analysis of revelation by turning to human experience as Williams does, but (formally at least) he ends in a place not so far distant from Williams.

Materially, though, he is differentiated from Williams in insisting that revelation is in the indicative and imperative: God's election and God's command, the gospel and the law. Williams, on the other hand, in speaking almost entirely about the opening of possibilities through the revelation of Christ and the work of the Holy Spirit, implicitly maintains that revelation is in the subjunctive, while neglecting the indicative and imperative moods.

Neither of these proposals is fully convincing. Williams unsatisfactorily connects revelation to a phenomenon of human experience, while also doing justice to the subjunctive. Barth shows the value of the indicative and imperative but in a way that seems to do less than full justice to the freedom and competence of God. In order to do fuller justice to all the moods of revelation, we return to Ford—and Scripture.

Scripture, Revelation, and Human Response

In discussing the moods of theology, Ford explains that such moods do not exist in isolation, but form an "ecology": a differentiated, connected, mutually informing whole. If we transpose this image into revelation, then we ought to say the same: the subjunctive cannot stand on its own. Moreover, it is not merely that the indicatives and imperatives are connected, but that the other moods are present in and connected with God's revealing as well. To show how this might be, we turn to Scripture, and the subjunctive mood.

As Ford indicates, the subjunctive, "in which possibilities are imagined and decisions made," is less often explicitly present in the biblical text, but the dynamic (particularly as he puts it, of surprise by the kingdom and agency of God) is not far from much of what is present, particularly in the form of Jesus' parables, or, for example, the Song of Mary.[27] It might also be detected implicitly in those responses of excess or overflow in response to God; for example, Paul's recounting the "abundant joy" and "wealth of generosity" of the Macedonians, even during a "severe ordeal of affliction" and "extreme poverty" (2 Cor 8:2).

One particularly striking example of the subjunctive in Scripture, as an opening of a possibility, is found in the resurrection appearances in the Gospel of John. Reports of an empty tomb and even an appearance to Mary Magdalene are circulating (20:1–18). The disciples were gathered in a house, and Jesus "came and stood among them." (v. 19) He bids them peace, shows them the marks of his suffering—which now seem to serve to identify him—and then commissions the disciples, "breathing" on them the Holy Spirit (vv. 19–22). John presents Jesus as saying to the disciples "if you forgive the sins of any, they are forgiven them; if you retain the sins of any, they are retained" (v. 23). In this commission, there is a new possibility opened for the disciples in the mission of the Spirit, a possibility left undefined in the commissioning and realized only in the life of the disciples, that sins may be forgiven or may be retained. This is a possibility, not merely a proposition or a command. We see here that, as Ford says in reference to a different text, the resurrection of Jesus "and the outpouring of the Holy Spirit, generate a superabundance of new possibilities that are global in scope."[28] Thus might revelation be considered not merely indicative and imperative, but subjunctive as well.

Yet this is not pure subjunctivity, for it dwells in an ecology of mutually implied moods. The possibility of forgiving sins would be a meaningless flight of fancy if, for example, there were not the indicatives and imperatives of God's covenant with Israel and the giving of the law on Sinai. Or the possibility of forgiving sins would be an idolatrous blasphemy apart from the indicatives and imperatives of the revelation of Jesus Christ as Word of God. Moreover, when taken as of a piece with Jesus' teaching and parables, the charge to forgive or retain sins is seen as not simply a neutral choice between two options: Jesus' teaching elsewhere (as in the Lord's prayer) suggests that God forgives us as we forgive others. Yet it is also still a possibility, not simply a veiled command to forgive. That both possibilities are named is surely significant. This commission is to be

27. Ford, *Christian Wisdom*, 48.

28. Ibid.

inhabited and lived out by the disciples in the Spirit: it is not determined in advance that sins (or which sins) must be or will be forgiven through their ministry, only that they may be.

In principle, this proposal and its turn to Scripture would be welcome in Williams' Ricoeurian ruminations, inasmuch as he speaks of poetic engagement with the text. It is differentiated from Williams, however, by maintaining that this story is significant in itself, beyond the possibilities it may open for its hearers. As part of an ecology of moods, it affirms the salutary possibility of Spirit-generated upheaval, but does so on the basis of Scripture's invocation of past events (above all, Jesus Christ) which are considered determinative.

But while Barth is fully occupied with Scripture in his work, and considers Christ determinative in a way similar to this, when he speaks of revelation he does not specifically have the text of the Bible in mind. Yet it seems like special pleading to stipulate that revelation takes place *through* Scripture, but as such stands entirely free from the actual concrete form of Scripture, as if biblical expressions in various moods were only "masks" for a revelation that is only actually found in the indicative and imperative. Scripture is not unrelated to revelation and Scripture itself speaks with multiple genres and voices; these genres and voices not being reduced to inessential forms which cloak a single genre "behind" the text, consisting of propositions and commands only.

I hope by now it is clear that this is not to deny the truth of what Barth has said about these two "moods" in terms of revelation: God may and does reveal in indicative and imperative "moods." However, his account seems attenuated. For Barth, God is the One who loves in freedom; why might not God then reveal in various moods, analogous to language, so that revelation might be, say, an opening up of a possibility, in a subjunctive mood? God's freedom to be who God is is perfect, and thus God is free to use whatever means God elects for the loving ends God has determined; God's revealing in multiple "moods" need not imply imperfection or indeterminacy on God's part, but might simply reveal God's competence to achieve God's ends in a way consistent with God's wisdom.

It might not even be too much to suggest the possibility not only of an ecology of moods in revelation, but even a certain kind of "conversational" aspect to it. I do not mean to suggest that this would be a conversation between autonomous equals. I mean rather that God's "speaking" or "revealing" in going beyond just the form of indicative statements or imperative commands might even invite response (and not only the response of obedience or confirmation which Barth would suggest).

Could it be that God uses not only God's own interrogation of humanity, but even human questioning of God? Biblical stories such as Abraham's discussion with God of the fate of Sodom (Gen 18:16–33), Moses' request to see God's glory (Exod 33:12—34:9), or Mary's asking "How can this be, since I am a virgin?" (Luke 1:34) suggest that there may well exist, in accord with God's wisdom, a conversation or questioning on our part which God uses as revelatory. While revelation is God's act, at God's initiative, God may incorporate human questioning and responsiveness in God's revelation in a way that dwelling solely in the indicative and imperative risks missing.

This does not sacrifice God's priority or freedom. But it might be said that God's ability and willingness to "converse" with creation, as the infinite approaches the finite and radically contingent and establishes it as a "conversation partner," is a "glorifying" of creation by God, and that this itself is an expression of God's glory.

This issue of multiple "moods" of revelation is significant for discerning the revelation, act, and call of God in the world: if certain forms of revelation are ruled out beforehand, then we risk foreshortening our work of discernment and obedience. Recognizing the possibility of these various moods helps us to see in a more encompassing fashion the shape of God and God's act, and may serve to prepare us for greater responsiveness. If theology can help the church in this way, it will have gone some distance towards fulfilling its vocation.

Affirming this possibility is not to shrink from the reliability and steadfastness of the God who is revealed in Jesus Christ, as if affirming the moods of revelation compromise other basic Christian affirmations. All the forms of revelation in whatever moods are the one act of the one God, and so the "possibility" (subjunctive) being opened up may be surprising, but will not be apart from the (indicative) revelation of Jesus Christ as Lord, and neither of them apart from God's "desire" (optative) for all to be brought to health, wholeness, salvation through Christ and his mission, or the Father's command to "listen to him!" (Luke 9:35—imperative). Indeed, as Ford suggests, our theology may operate in these many moods because God takes the initiative, with the "divine voice" speaking in all of these moods.[29]

29. Ford, *Future of Christian Theology*, 82.

What I am suggesting then is that God has "eloquence" and competence to "speak," revealing in various moods, and that these do not overwhelm and bracket out human agency to respond, even as any such human response is itself a gift of God. It is God's glory—God's praiseworthiness, honour, and even the streaming light of God's declaration—that God also glorifies the creation, constituting and establishing human agency. As such, in human reception, God's revelation is (to echo a phrase Williams draws from Paul Ricoeur) "as much a matter of an imagination called upon to open itself as it is a will called upon to submit," as we may respond to the free yet faithful, trustworthy yet surprising triune Lord revealed in Jesus Christ.[30]

Bibliography

Barth, Karl. *The Church Dogmatics* II/2: *The Doctrine of God*. Translated by G. W. Bromiley et al. Edited by G. W. Bromiley and T. F. Torrance. Edinburgh: T. & T. Clark, 1957.

———. *Church Dogmatics* IV.3.1: *The Doctrine of Creation*. Translated by J. W. Edwards. Edited by G. W. Bromiley and T. F. Torrance. Edinburgh: T. & T. Clark, 1958.

———. *Church Dogmatics* IV.3.2: *The Doctrine of Creation*. Translated by H. Knight. Edited by G. W. Bromiley and T. F. Torrance. Edinburgh: T. & T. Clark, 1960.

Ford, David F. *Christian Wisdom: Desiring God and Learning in Love*. Cambridge: Cambridge University Press, 2007.

———. *The Future of Christian Theology*. Oxford: Wiley-Blackwell, 2010.

Ricoeur, Paul. "Toward a Hermeneutic of the Idea of Revelation." In *Essays on Biblical Interpretation*, 73–118. Philadelphia: Fortress, 1980.

Williams, Rowan. "Trinity and Revelation." In *On Christian Theology*, 131–47. Oxford: Blackwell, 2000.

30. Ricoeur, "Toward a Hermeneutic," 117.

5

What Has the "Lutheran" Paul to Do with John?

Passive Righteousness and Abiding in the Vine[1]

Simeon Zahl

St. John's College, University of Oxford

In this essay I seek to outline one small but real bridge between more "Pauline" and more "Johannine" visions of salvation—broadly speaking, between soteriological outlooks that focus on righteousness and forgiveness issues, on the one hand, and participation in the divine life, on the other. Standing in as a representative interpreter of a more "Pauline" tradition here—perhaps somewhat controversially, I am aware[2]—will be sixteenth-century Reformer Martin Luther. My thesis is simple: that there is a surprising and generative degree of thematic and theological

1. The term "the 'Lutheran' Paul" is taken from the title of Stephen Westerholm's *Perspectives Old and New on Paul: The "Lutheran" Paul and His Critics.*

2. Though perhaps this is somewhat less the case today as, after several decades of fruitful discussion, many of the insights of the "new perspective on Paul" have been plumbed and some of its overstatements have been tempered. For an excellent overview, with particular reference to Luther, see Westerholm, *Perspectives Old and New on Paul*; cf. Dunn, *New Perspective on Paul*, 1–98.

correlation between Luther's soteriological concept of "passive righteousness," which in his *magnum opus* on Galatians he describes as the key to Paul, and the concept of "abiding"—*menein*—"in the vine" in John's Gospel.

In hosting a "conversation" here between Luther and the Johannine author (henceforth "John"), I am engaging in one small attempt at a wisdom learned from David Ford: of what could be called "bridge-building in the Spirit," which attempts to takes particulars deeply seriously while at the same time always hoping for unexpected connections and resources (he might say: blessings!) to arise in the Spirit. In a plural and complex world, such bridge-building, whether between ideas, between thinkers, between cultures, or between religions, is one of the most valuable and creative vocations of theology today, and it is one that Ford himself has modelled so compellingly for generations of students.

An old and important question in theology, which has taken on increasing significance in recent years, is whether and in what ways the fundamental soteriological visions of St. Paul and St. John come together. Although few issues in biblical interpretation have seen as much ink spilled over the centuries as Pauline soteriology, it is perhaps not overly controversial to observe a recurring preoccupation in Paul's epistles with issues of righteousness, the fulfilment of the law, and the forgiveness of sin, that finds relatively little immediate parallel in the Gospel of John. For John, by contrast, the fundamental soteriological image is a particular mode of being drawn into the life of the divine Trinity: being "in" Christ as Christ is "in" the Father (John 6:56; 10:38; 14:10–11, 20, 23; 15:4, 17:21–23; cf. 14:17b; 1 John 2:24). For Paul, although there is certainly language of being "in Christ" and other forms of "Christ mysticism,"[3] the problem of the law and of righteousness in God's sight is rarely distant. In John, there is the key nod to Pauline categories in John 1:17 ("The law indeed was given through Moses; grace and truth came through Jesus Christ"),[4] but the centre of gravity remains a mystical and underdetermined indwelling of Christ, referred to repeatedly above all in the Farewell Discourse.[5] There

3. For an overview, see Dunn, *Theology of Paul*, 390–404.

4. Additionally, if one includes 1 John as part of the Johannine canon, there is some further reference to sin and atonement in Pauline-type terms (e.g., 1 John 1:7—2:2), but there is not space here to get into the various controversies over Johannine authorship.

5. Noting the reference to Jesus as the Lamb of God in John 1:29, Barrett observes that "although [here and] in the passion John is at pains to draw out the analogy between Jesus and the paschal sacrifice (18:28; 19:36), he does not explain the death of

are many points of connection between these broad soteriological "visions," and it would be a mistake to draw too sharp of a contrast between them. But the difficulties in fully reconciling Paul and John on this theme should not be underestimated either. A highly significant recurring debate in Christian soteriology since the Reformation has been whether there is a *dominant* biblical conceptuality of salvation, a primary lens through which other models should be interpreted, and if so whether that lens is structured through the categories of (a) atonement, law, and forgiveness of sin or (b) participation in the triune divine life. This debate is as active today as it has ever been,[6] and Paul and John have respectively provided proof-texts for different sides in the discussion.

My claim in this essay is not to resolve these great questions. Instead, in conversation with Martin Luther and his interpretation of righteousness in Paul, my aim is to draw constructive theological attention to an under-recognized, biblically grounded point of contact between the two broad soteriological approaches. In doing this, I hope to help soften in some small way the academic and theological divide between participatory and forensic approaches to salvation, creating further space for constructive dialogue on these at times bitterly contested issues[7]—and if in the process we gain a better understanding of the larger biblical soteriological picture, all the better. I also seek to draw further attention to the positive, rather than just the negative, resources of Luther's approach to salvation, which has, by and large, been quite unfashionable in recent decades. Luther's constructive appeal to passive righteousness as a useful category for interpreting Paul and for making pastoral sense of the Christian life more broadly has perhaps been rejected or elided over too swiftly, especially in recent Anglophone theology and biblical studies. Its remarkable and unexpected connection with Johannine "abiding" is one of several reasons theologians might wish to reengage the category of *iustitia passiva* with due seriousness.

To say that I proceed in the spirit of David Ford's theology would be to understate. What follows grew directly out of an ongoing theological dialogue with Ford during the three years I was privileged to serve as his research associate at Cambridge. During those years our favourite

Jesus in sacrificial terms, and [such terms are] not characteristic of his thought." See Barrett, *Gospel according to St. John*, 81.

6. For discussion of this debate and its resurgence in recent decades, see Zahl, "Atonement."

7. For a recent example of how heated this debate can be, see Stephen Finlan's scholarly polemic, *Problems with Atonement*.

theological theme together was the Holy Spirit (a topic I first took up under his urging while a PhD student), and it was the Spirit that served as a kind of "bridge" between our respective theological preoccupations at the time: my own research on Martin Luther, and Ford's work on his theological commentary on the Gospel of John. The argument below, about the unexpected connections between *iustitia passiva* and "*menein*," "abiding," first came up during one of these conversations, while teaching a course together on the theological interpretation of John's Gospel.

"Passive Righteousness" in Luther's Galatians Introduction

Iustitia passiva is central to Luther's interpretation of justification in general and to his understanding of Pauline soteriology in particular. In Luther's 1535 *Lectures on Galatians*, the distinction between "passive" and "active" righteousness becomes the interpretive key to the letter. For him, the distinction is not less than "the argument and . . . summary of this Epistle to the Galatians."[8] Indeed so close, in Luther's thinking, is the concept of *iustitia passiva* to the centre of Pauline, and Christian, teaching about salvation that he is able to gloss "this most excellent and Christian [passive] righteousness" as "the doctrine of justification" itself[9]; without this distinction, "the whole of Christian doctrine is lost."[10]

What is *iustitia passiva* for Luther? His most important and influential discussion of the theme is in the *Lectures on Galatians* introduction.[11] Here Luther explains that "righteousness is of many kinds." There is "political righteousness," achieved by obeying the laws of the land. There is "ceremonial righteousness," "which human traditions teach," and which

8. Luther, *Lectures on Galatians*, 26:13.

9. Ibid., 9.

10. Ibid. A discussion of whether or to what degree Luther is correct in his assessment of this concept's role in Paul's thought is beyond the scope of this essay. At the very least, his is a useful theological category that captures some element or aspect of what is happening in Paul, and has been deeply influential for many later interpreters of Paul through the centuries. See Westerholm, *Perspectives Old and New on Paul*, 366–84. For a critical overview of the Lutheran tradition of Paul interpretation, see Watson, *Paul, Judaism, and the Gentiles*, chapter 1.

11. This point is evident not least in the fact that in, e.g., Bayer, Althaus, and Joest, discussion of *iustitia passiva* focuses around quotations from this introduction. See Bayer, *Martin Luthers Theologie*, 39–40; Althaus, *Theology of Martin Luther*, 228–29; Joest, *Gesetz und Freiheit*, 24–27. For a useful overview of Luther on righteousness and justification, see Althaus, *Theology of Martin Luther*, 224–50; cf. McGrath, *Iustitia Dei*, 218–35.

for him has to do with those sorts of religious behaviour that are good for religious order and "moral discipline" but have no "power to make satisfaction for sin, to placate God, and to earn grace." And there is "the righteousness of the Law or of the Decalog," which is exceedingly important in his view, but—crucially—quite distinct from "Christian" or "passive" righteousness.[12] Finally: "Over and above all these there is the righteousness of faith or Christian righteousness, which is to be distinguished most carefully from all the others."

What sets this final form of righteousness—variously called "the righteousness of faith," "Christian righteousness," and "passive righteousness"—apart for Luther is that while the first three varieties can in some sense be "achieved by us," or at least aimed at by us, and are thus "active" forms of righteousness, the latter type is something "which God imputes to us through Christ without works," and is therefore "a merely passive righteousness."[13] It comes from outside, and its defining characteristic is the fact that it is not dependent in any way on human agency. It "happens to" a person rather than being something that the person "does."

Connected to this kind of righteousness, of course, is a robust soteriological apparatus, what to later generations has often been summed up, slightly anachronistically, with the term "forensic justification."[14] In forensic models of justification, the crucial fact about "Christian righteousness" is that it is Christ's perfect righteousness, imputed or transferred to the sinner, resulting in a change of status in the sight of God the Father and Judge, due to Christ's satisfaction of a divine legal requirement on behalf of the individual. In this it is understood to be the mechanism of God's eternal salvation of sinners.

But, perhaps unexpectedly, this image—of God choosing to "see" Christ, in his perfect righteousness, instead of the individual, for purposes of salvation in the divine law court—is not in fact Luther's primary interest in the *Galatians* introduction and its elaboration of *iustitia passiva*. It is

12. Luther, *Lectures on Galatians*, 26:4.

13. Ibid., 4–5.

14. McGrath, *Iustitia Dei*, 238–41. Although "forensic" justification reaches its initial mature form slightly later, in the work of Philipp Melanchthon, the term unquestionably captures a highly significant feature of Luther's Reformation-era soteriology. The attempt by Tuomo Mannermaa and his students in recent decades to problematize this view—an important claim of the "Finnish interpretation of Luther"—has proven highly stimulating in a variety of respects, but ultimately is not very persuasive as a historical judgment about Luther's thought, for a host reasons I do not have space to go into here. See especially McInroy, "Rechtfertigung als Theosis"; Hailer, "Gottes Gnade als Teilgewährung"; Laato, "Justification."

certainly presupposed to one degree or another, and the presupposition is made explicit in a key paragraph,[15] but what seems to interest Luther most in this text is the element of *passivity* in particular, rather than its eternal implications in the first instance. What he elaborates at length and with great passion are (a) the non-contribution of human agency in salvation, and (b) the pastoral consequences for individuals that follow from this fundamental passivity at the heart of the justification of human beings. Perhaps quite a bit more than is usually the case among classical Protestant theologians on this subject, Luther is concerned with *iustitia passiva* as a way of life, as a mode of living *coram mundo* and *coram hominibus*, rather than just as a formal mechanism of eternal salvation *coram deo*. While the two are at one level utterly linked for him, they are also distinct enough to be spoken of separately. What is unexpected is that, in this particular text, his passion is for the former aspect.

In the *Lectures on Galatians* introduction, Luther identifies again and again the non-contribution of human agency as the crucial defining feature to be communicated about Christian righteousness. "For here we work nothing, render nothing to God; we only receive and permit someone else to work in us, namely, God. Therefore it is appropriate to call the righteousness of faith or Christian righteousness 'passive.'"[16] It is a righteousness "which we do not perform but receive, which we do not have but accept."[17] Again: "[D]o we do nothing and work nothing in order to obtain this righteousness? I reply: Nothing at all."[18] In part, the reason he hammers this point home again and again is that he believes it to be counterintuitive. That is, this approach is the opposite of what human beings by nature believe about themselves and about their relationship with God: "human reason cannot refrain from looking at active righteousness, that is, its own righteousness; nor can it shift its gaze to passive . . . righteousness. . . . So deeply is this evil rooted in us, and so completely have we acquired this unhappy habit!"[19] What Luther is trying to describe, and what he believes is the essence of Paul and indeed pastorally the heart of the lived Christian faith, is an approach to life in which one's worth and value, before God eternally but also before oneself and others from day to day, is radically independent of particular human activities and behaviours.

15. Luther, *Lectures on Galatians*, 26:8–9.

16. Ibid., 5.

17. Ibid., 6.

18. Ibid., 8.

19. Ibid., 5.

The implications of this as Luther sees them, to which he returns repeatedly, are feelings of abiding peace, joy, and rest,[20] and a certain kind of divinely grounded freedom in relation to the world. The correct outlook on the world for the one justified "passively" is to see the world (and oneself in the world) as suffused with the possibility of being an object of creative and animating divine activity, to which one must simply live in anticipation. As Wilfried Joest describes it in one of the most perceptive discussions of *iustitia passiva* in Luther, "God begins his work with us when our own activity goes quiet . . . both inwardly and outwardly. The zero point of human effective power is the place where God does his work."[21]

The "passive" life, then, as Luther characterizes it, is not the dour and robotic existence of forensic caricature,[22] but an existence pregnant with creative possibility through the Spirit. Importantly, the dominant metaphor for Christian life in the *Galatians* introduction is the deeply organic one of dry earth awaiting divine rain:[23] "As the earth itself does not produce rain and is unable to acquire it by its own strength, worship, and power but receives it only by heavenly gift from above, so this heavenly righteousness is given to us by God without our work or merit."[24] Again, just "as the earth does not bring forth fruit unless it has first been watered and made fruitful from above," good works and active involvement in the world are the product of divine action on a passive object.[25] Luther returns to the metaphor a third time in the conclusion of the piece: "When I have this [passive] righteousness within me, I descend from heaven like the rain that makes the earth fertile. That is, I come forth into another kingdom, and I perform good works whenever the opportunity arises."[26] Again and again, Luther characterizes human passivity in relation to divine agency in terms of an organic metaphor that simultaneously conveys fecundity, dynamism, and life *and* uncompromised dependence on God. As we shall now see, this parallels remarkably with the concept of "abiding in the vine" in John's Gospel.

20. Ibid., 11.

21. Joest, *Gesetz und Freiheit*, 25.

22. For a recent example of such caricature, see Finlan, *Problems with Atonement*, 75–79.

23. This imagery is almost certainly drawn in part from Isa 55:10–11. Cf. Ps 1:3.

24. Luther, *Lectures on Galatians*, 26:6.

25. Ibid., 8.

26. Ibid., 11.

Abiding in the Vine in John 15

The verb "*menein*" has a rich semantic range in John's Gospel. The NRSV translates it in John variously as "continue" (John 8:31), "remain" (7:9), and, most commonly and evocatively, "abide" (15:4–7, 9–10, etc.).[27] According to the Bauer-Danker lexicon, the phrase "*menein en tini*" in its various forms "is a favourite of John to denote an inward, enduring personal communion,"[28] between the Father and the Son (14:10), as well as, correspondingly, between Christ and believers (6:56; 15:4–10). In all of the possible meanings listed in Bauer-Danker, "remaining," "dwelling," and "abiding" are understood primarily or significantly *in contrast to a more active behaviour that would change circumstances rather than let them stay the way they are.* Where it means that "a person or thing remains where he, she, or it is"[29] this is understood as opposed to leaving, as opposed to actively changing location. More abstractly, it can mean to "not leave a certain realm or sphere,"[30] e.g., to "continue in what you have learned" (2 Tim 3:14), to "continue in my love" (John 15:9f.), or to "remain" in a state in which you are an object of God's wrath (3:36). A third major use is to "remain alive" or "continue to exist" (e.g., Phil 1:25) as opposed to dying or ceasing to exist, like "the food that *endures* [*menousan*] for eternal life," unlike "the food that perishes" (John 6:27).[31]

In each of these cases, along with connotations like stability, deeply involved intimacy, home, and a kind of living faithfulness, there is always an implied or explicit contrast with more active alternatives. That is, *menein* is about staying in some sense the same as opposed to being subject to a change in circumstances. It is about resting as opposed to working, about the wisdom in letting things remain as they are rather than always seeking to change or improve them. It is not a stretch, then, to say that while *menein* is not identical with "being passive," it does seem to have a significant "passive" element (where "passive" is understood simply as opposed to active, as it is for Luther, rather than in the pejorative contemporary sense of inactivity due to weakness or paralysis).

The most theologically significant use of *menein* in John's Gospel is in Jesus' image of himself as "the true vine" in John 15: "I am the true vine,

27. The RSV adds "dwell" in 14:17—in the NRSV it is "abide."

28. *BDAG*, 631.

29. Ibid., 630.

30. Ibid., 631.

31. Ibid.

and my Father is the vinegrower. . . . Abide [*meinate*] in me as I abide in you. Just as the branch cannot bear fruit by itself unless it abides [*mene*] in the vine, neither can you unless you abide in me. I am the vine, you are the branches. Those who abide in me [*o menwn en eimi*] and I in them bear much fruit, because apart from me you can do nothing" (John 15:1, 4–5). In the most comprehensive English-language commentary on John to date, Craig Keener describes this picture of abiding in the vine, in which Christ is the vine and believers are the vine's branches, as an "image of organic union" which communicates above all "complete and continued dependence for the Christian life on the indwelling of Christ."[32]

Part of what the vine image does is to take the "passive" element already present in *menein* and amplify it in two major ways. First, and most obviously, there is Jesus' own gloss on the image as emphasizing God's agency over and against human agency, when he interprets it as meaning that "apart from me you can do nothing," and, later in chapter 15, when he explains that "You did not choose me but I chose you. And I appointed you to go and bear fruit . . ." (15:16).

Second, plant metaphors of this type, which understand the human being as a plant or part of a plant and God as in various ways the caretaker or life-source of the plant—and there are many in the Bible[33]—are passive, in Luther's sense, by definition. Plants do not have agency the way that human beings do. They are alive and they do grow and change and "bear fruit" and have an impact on the world around them, but they do so in a way that completely bypasses human questions of will, reason, and choice. A plant's thriving is dependent entirely on factors beyond its "control": its soil and where it is planted, its water source, its access to sunlight, and, in this particular image, whether and in what way branches are pruned or cut (15:2). In John 15 this organic imagery of dependence is further built upon to create a double-dependence: Jesus, the vine, is dependent on the Father, and we, the branches, are completely dependent on the "vine." Our dependence is so deep that we are dependent on one who is himself radically dependent, just as a branch is doubly dependent (on the vine, which in turn is dependent on soil, water, and so on).

32. Keener, *Gospel of John*, 999. Keener himself notes, relevant to my larger argument, that in its emphasis on radical human dependence on divine intiative this "recalls an emphasis in Pauline theology" (ibid.). On Johannine abiding, see also Barrett, *Gospel according to St. John*, 84, 87, 474.

33. Cf. Ps 1:3; Isa 55:10–11; Matt 6:28–30; and Mark 4:3–20, 30–32, among others. Note also the multilayered reference to Jesus as a gardener in John 20:15.

Overall, John here is painting a picture of Christian existence as utterly intertwined with the divine life. The branch, after all, is literally an extension of the one plant, the Vine. In this sense the image fits beautifully with language of "participation" in God, and with the many other discussions of being "in" Christ as Christ is "in" the Father in John's Gospel. But equally, the image deliberately and without qualification intensifies connotations of passivity and dependence relative to divine agency. The major point being made in 15:1–10 is about dependence: "the branch is not able to bear fruit unless it remains on the vine," and, even more starkly, branches that are not connected to the vine die (they "wither," "are gathered, thrown into the fire, and burned" [15:6]). There is no moment of human agency or initiative here, and no gradualistic growing into increased dependence on the vine. In this sense, then, language of passivity, even *iustitia passiva*, is perhaps even more appropriate than "participation"—the latter usually implies at least some minimal active reciprocity that undermines, however slightly, the radical dependence and element of "non-contribution" (especially when participation is construed in terms of *theosis*,[34] as it often is). We might summarize this by saying that "abiding in the vine" describes a *passive* participation, while *iustitia passiva*, as a mode of living, is understood most accurately not robotically or "simply" forensically, but as implicating the whole person into a living relationship of dependence upon the agency of the Spirit, in all its creativity and fecundity.

Parallels and Differences

There are a number of further parallels between Lutheran "passive righteousness" and Johannine "abiding" worth noting briefly here, as well as some key differences. First, as has been implied, both descriptions leave the implicated person (the believer) in a state of freedom and creative expectation in relation to the world, waiting upon the activity of the Spirit. This is, once again, clearest in the organic metaphors: all the possibilities of a seed cared for in good soil are present for the one passively justified

34. Louth reminds us that *theosis* in the Orthodox tradition entails for human beings, among other things, "a real change that requires a serious ascetic commitment on our part" (Louth, "Place of *Theosis*," 43). By contrast, emphasis on at least a minimal contribution of human agency of the type Louth describes is Luther's *primary critical target* in developing the category of *iustitia passiva*. The pneumatic and soteriological breakthrough for Luther always comes precisely in the recognition of powerlessness and the bondage of the will, and the giving up of hope for even ostensibly divinely aided or transformed human willing and human powers.

through *iustitia aliena*, and all the fruit-bearing potential of a healthy vine—not least the production of wine!—stretches before the branch that "abides."

A second connection is that both draw explicitly upon the categories of righteousness and "good works." For the Lutheran term this is, of course, obvious—it is called *iustitia passiva* after all—but in John 15 we are also told that "abiding in [Christ's] love" is descriptively connected with keeping Christ's commandments, and Christ in turn abides in love by keeping the commandments of his Father (15:10; cf. 13:34–35; 14:21–23; 15:12). Although the connections to issues of righteousness and commandment-following are stronger and more central with the Lutheran category, we fail to understand Johannine "abiding," especially "in the vine," if we do not understand its connection to "fruit" and Christ's commandments, usually summarized in John in terms of love.[35]

Third, both *iustitia passiva* and "abiding" are described as having concrete affective consequences. For Luther, understanding that one is saved on the basis of passive righteousness means that you are free to feel "no terror or remorse of conscience," and "no sadness."[36] Positively, the consequence is that "there must be full and perfect joy in the Lord and peace of heart, where the heart declares: 'I do not die, because Christ lives who is my righteousness and my eternal and heavenly life.'"[37] *Iustitia passiva* has implications for eternity, but also for our bodily and emotional life. It is a pastoral, "horizontal" principle that is correlated with concrete internal feelings and states, as well as a "forensic" mechanism of eternal salvation. John, likewise, concludes his initial discussion of the vine metaphor by talking about how it relates to the affection of joy: "I have said these things to you so that my joy may be in you, and that your joy may be complete" (15:11). The consequence of abiding, of living in this way out of dependence on Jesus, the True Vine, is positive affect, namely, "abiding in love" (15:10) and experiencing completeness of joy. The Johannine category "eternal life"[38] is always in view where the connection between

35. Hoskyns, *Fourth Gospel*, 476–79; Barrett, *Gospel according to St. John*, 476.

36. Luther, *Lectures on Galatians*, 26:8.

37. Ibid., 9. See also ibid., 6, 7, and 11.

38. "Eternal life" is a more complex and broad-reaching category in John than simply eternal habitation with God after a future eschatological judgment, but insofar as it is characterized as chronologically without limit, and there is understood to be a group who have not received it or will not receive it, it at least *includes* something like what Luther would have understood by salvation. See Barrett, *Gospel according to St. John*, 78–81.

Christ and the believer is discussed in John, but, as with Luther, this includes day-to-day affections, not just future eschatological states. For both Luther and John, what is at stake is a "horizontal," day-to-day pastoral reality, rather than just a formal, proleptic soteriological mechanism.

For all of these several layers of connections and parallels, however, *iustita passiva* and "abiding in the vine" are not synonyms. Neither should one simply be reduced to the other. Instead, their relationship is best understood as overlapping, complementary, and mutually reinforcing.

One important difference is that "abiding" is a first-order biblical category, where "passive righteousness," though drawn with plausibility and care from particular discussions of "righteousness" in the Epistle to the Galatians and elsewhere, is ultimately a second-order interpretive category. Related to this is the fact that the distinction between passive and active righteousness is a precise and durable theological concept in Luther's soteriology, whereas "abiding in the vine" is one of many salvation categories and metaphors in a Gospel known for its many layers and multiple meanings (other salvation metaphors in John include, e.g., being drawn to the one who is "lifted up" like Moses' serpent in chapter 3, eating of the bread from heaven in chapter 6, and drinking "living water" "gushing up to eternal life" in chapter 4). Third, as has been noted throughout, Luther and John are ultimately drawing on broadly different—though, we might hope, ultimately complementary—soteriological apparatuses and emphases ("forensic" justification vs. being "in" Christ as Christ is "in" the Father).

One particularly helpful way of understanding the differences here is to assess *iustitia passiva* and "abiding in the vine," in good Lutheran fashion,[39] in terms of how they "preach"—that is, in terms of what message is likely to be heard and what pastoral problems are helpfully addressed when these categories are spoken of from the pulpit or otherwise publicly proclaimed. From this point of view, we might say that the call to "abide" in Christ, the true vine, would be especially likely to speak to the "weary and heavy laden" (Matt 11:28), those exhausted by religious and secular striving. The call to "abide" is a call to rest, and to expect and hope for life and love to derive from a source outside oneself, rather than from within or on the basis of one's own limited moral and spiritual resources.

Iustitia passiva, on the other hand, addresses more directly or acutely problems of conscience and guilt, feelings of unworthiness and the fear of

39. And in a fashion appropriate to honour David Ford's lifetime of thoughtful and pastorally minded preaching.

judgment. Here one's worth or value in the sight of a God who is, among other things, a judge, is given from without, as passive righteousness imputed from Christ, precisely as opposed to the quest to create it for oneself through moral effort. Both categories emphasize the deep importance of trusting in divine agency over and against human agency; given this, however, "abiding" is especially a word for the weary and the lifeless, and the call to trust in righteousness from outside oneself is particularly a word for the guilty and the damned.

Once again, the rhetorical directions here, like the categories themselves, are complementary and overlapping but not identical. Together, passive righteousness and "abiding in the vine" present a vision of Christian life that emphasizes restful, organic trust in the agency of God, and the freedom not to worry so much about the limits and failures of one's own agency. But they do so in what we might, following David Ford, call a "dramatic"[40] fashion. Abiding in God's own righteousness and life means being thrown forth into the world by the Spirit, freely drawn to engage with the world as it presents itself instead of worrying about oneself; and free, like David, to view each encounter—whether with a person, a place, an idea, an institution, an experience, a culture, a poem, or an endless variety of other things—as a moment pregnant with creative possibility in the Spirit.

Bibliography

Althaus, Paul. *The Theology of Martin Luther*. Translated by Robert C. Schultz. Philadelphia: Fortress, 1966.

Barrett, C. K. *The Gospel according to St. John: An Introduction with Commentary and Notes on the Greek Text*. 2nd ed. London: SPCK, 1978.

Bauer, Walter, and Frederick William Danker. *A Greek-English Lexicon of the New Testament and Other Early Christian Literature*. 3rd ed. Chicago: University of Chicago Press, 2000.

Bayer, Oswald. *Martin Luthers Theologie*. 2nd ed. Tübingen: Mohr Siebeck, 2004.

Dunn, James D. G. *The New Perspective on Paul*. Rev. ed. Grand Rapids: Eerdmans, 2007.

———. *The Theology of Paul the Apostle*. London: T. & T. Clark, 1998.

Finlan, Stephen. *Problems with Atonement: The Origins of, and Controversy about, the Atonement Doctrine*. Collegeville, MN: Liturgical, 2005.

Ford, David F. *The Future of Christian Theology*. Oxford: Wiley-Blackwell, 2011.

Hailer, M. "Gottes Gnade als Teilgewährung an ihm. Überlegungen zur finnischen Luther-Interpretation." *Evangelische Theologie* 71 (2011) 35–49.

40. Ford, *Future of Christian Theology*, 23–42.

Hoskyns, Edwyn Clement. *The Fourth Gospel*. Edited by Francis Noel Davey. London: Faber & Faber, 1947.

Joest, Wilfried. *Gesetz und Freiheit: Das Problem des* Tertius usus legis *bei Luther und die neutestamentliche Parainese*. 3rd ed. Göttingen: Vandenhoeck & Ruprecht, 1961.

Keener, Craig S. *The Gospel of John: A Commentary*. 2 vols. Peabody, MA: Hendrickson, 2003.

Laato, T. "Justification: The Stumbling Block of the Finnish Luther School." *Concordia Theological Quarterly* 72 (2008) 327–46.

Louth, Andrew. "The Place of *Theosis* in Orthodox Theology." In *Partakers of the Divine Nature: The History and Development of Deification in the Christian Traditions*, edited by Michael J. Christensen and Jeffery A. Wittung, 32–44. Grand Rapids: Baker Academic, 2007.

Luther, Martin. *Lectures on Galatians* 1535: *Chapters* 1–4. Luther's Works, vol. 26. Edited by Jaroslav Pelikan and Walter A. Hansen. St. Louis: Concordia, 1963.

McGrath, Alister E. *Iustitia Dei: A History of the Christian Doctrine of Justification*. 3rd ed. Cambridge: Cambridge University Press, 2005.

McInroy, Mark J. "Rechtfertigung als Theosis. Zur neueren Diskussion über die Lutherdeutung der Finnischen Schule." *Catholica* (Münster) 66.1 (2012) 1–27.

Watson, Francis. *Paul, Judaism, and the Gentiles: A Sociological Approach*. Cambridge: Cambridge University Press, 1989.

Westerholm, Stephen. *Perspectives Old and New on Paul: The "Lutheran" Paul and His Critics*. Grand Rapids: Eerdmans, 2004.

Zahl, Simeon. "Atonement." In *The Oxford Handbook of Theology and Modern European Thought*, edited by Nicholas Adams, George Pattison, and Graham Ward, 611–32. Oxford: Oxford University Press, 2013.

PART TWO

Attending to Scripture

6

Transforming the Grammar of Human Jealousy

Israel's Jealousy in Romans 9–11[1]

Susannah Ticciati

King's College London

Egō parazēloso humas ep' ouk ethnei,
ep' ethnei asunetōi parorgiō humas

I will make you jealous of those who are not a nation;
with a foolish nation I will make you angry.[2]

(Rom 10:19, citing Deut 32:21 LXX,
but with Israel in the second rather than third person)

alla tōi autōn paraptōmati hē sōtēria tois ethnesin,
eis to parazēlōsai autous.

But through their trespass salvation has come to the Gentiles,
so as to make Israel jealous.

(Rom 11:11)

1. This essay is an extended version of the middle section of my "The Non-Divisive Difference of Election: A Reading of Romans 9–11." *Journal of Theological Interpretation* 6.2 (2012) 257–78. Adapted with permission.

2. In this chapter I will use the RSV translation unless otherwise stated.

eph' hoson men oun eimi egō ethnōn apostolos, tēn diakonian mou doxazō, ei pōs parazēlōsō mou tēn sarka kai sōsō tinas ex autōn.

Inasmuch then as I am an apostle to the Gentiles, I magnify my ministry in order to make my fellow Jews jealous, and thus save some of them.

(Rom 11:13–14)

In this essay I will undertake a theological consideration of Israel's jealousy in Romans 9–11. The distinctively theological assumption that will underpin the exegesis is that God is not just another character within the drama of salvation history, but the source, impetus, and telos of this salvation history. Thus Israel's relationship with God is not just one relationship among others, but is constitutive of Israel in the extent and depths of its identity. Therefore, to ask what role Israel's jealousy plays within Israel's relationship with this God is to ask how it contributes to a transformative dynamic which goes to the core of its being. Paul places Israel's jealousy at a pivotal juncture in his theological landscape: at the intersection between the salvation of Israel and the salvation of the Gentiles. This suggests that it plays a crucial role within God's purposes. If so, as this essay will wager, it warrants a properly theological analysis which stops short of nothing less in its interrogation than the depths of what it is to be human in relationship with the God of Paul, the God of Israel, and the God of creation and salvation.

As we will discover below, the jealousy motif in Romans 9–11 is much puzzled over, being variously interpreted and being given various levels of significance within Paul's theology of salvation. None of the modern treatments I shall engage with (all coming from within the historical-critical tradition broadly conceived, and taking account of the New Perspective on Paul), however, goes beyond a thin description of the dynamic of Israel's jealousy and the way in which it plays into God's larger purposes. None, in other words, envisages it as a way in which God engages and transforms the depths of Israel in its humanity. The radical thesis for which I will argue in what follows is that God's provoking of Israel to jealousy is his transformation of the grammar of human jealousy.

In relation to the theme of this volume, I hope to display in this theological exegesis one aspect of what I see as being the vocation of theology today. If theology, in relating everything to God as the source and telos of all being, engages people in their greatest depths, it does so, when drawing on Scripture, by searching the depths of Scripture: by articulating its deeply embedded patterns of reasoning in their healing and transformative power. The essay is thus significantly informed by the practice of Scriptural Reasoning, which is premised upon a belief that the Scriptures of the three Abrahamic traditions are sources, respectively, of their deepest patterns of reasoning, and the hope that engaging with and articulating them will heal relations within and between the three traditions. As a Christian attempt to draw out deep reasonings within the Christian Scriptures, this essay does not have the intertraditional purview of Scriptural Reasoning. While it will have significant implications for interfaith relations, and especially Christian-Jewish relations given the theme of Romans 9–11, these are beyond the scope of the essay.

More specifically still, in relation to the purpose of this volume, the essay is heavily indebted to the work and thought of David Ford, not only in his distinctive contribution to Scriptural Reasoning or his numerous publications, but also as communicated in his doctoral supervising and more widely in the theological culture fostered by him in Cambridge. In particular, the essay reflects Ford's desire always to turn back to the scriptural source, and his trust that every time it will yield abundant and surprising fruit. This is concomitant with his non-reductive approach to Scripture and willingness to learn from all other interpretations, with no limits being placed on Scripture's richness. And it is rooted in his belief in the infinite richness of the God to which Scripture witnesses.

I

As the citations at the head of this essay show, Paul makes three references to Israel's jealousy within the course of his argument in Romans 9–11. These chapters concern the problem thrown up for Paul by the fact that the majority of his fellows Jews have not come to faith in Christ. If Christ is God's means of fulfilling his promises to Israel, and most of Israel is excluded from this fulfilment, how can God be said to have been faithful to his promises, and what can the continuing significance of God's election of Israel be? Israel's jealousy is (arguably) a significant aspect of Paul's solution to this problem. Israel's hardening is the occasion for the inclusion of the Gentiles, which in turn provokes Israel's jealousy, which is itself God's way of bringing about Israel's reinclusion. This narrative gains condensed expression in 11:11–12:

> *Legō oun, mē eptaisan hina pesōsin? Mē genoito! Alla tōi autōn paraptōmati hē sōtēria tois ethnesin, eis to parazēlōsai autous. Ei de to paraptōma autōn ploutos kosmou kai to hēttēma autōn ploutos ethnōn, posōi mallon to plērōma autōn.*
>
> So I ask, have they stumbled so as to fall? By no means! But through their trespass salvation has come to the Gentiles, so as to make Israel jealous. Now if their trespass means riches for the world, and if their failure means riches for the Gentiles, how much more will their full inclusion mean!

Israel's jealousy has been interpreted both positively and negatively, but either way is almost always interpreted competitively. Thus Stanley Stowers, who interprets it in the context of the footrace metaphor he finds operating from the end of chapter 9 through into chapter 11,[3] argues that Israel, when overtaken by the Gentiles in the race, is filled with a competitive zeal to catch up. Its "jealousy," in this positive sense, is its competitive vying with the Gentiles.[4] James Dunn gives it more negative content, but still in a way which leads to good results: "In the mysterious workings of divine providence God uses human reactions one to another, even when motivated by protective self-interest, to further his own larger outreach of grace."[5] Specifically, Jews are provoked to jealousy by the success of the gospel, torn between their "covenant nationalism" and evident gentile blessing.[6]

Richard Bell, who devotes a whole monograph to the question, distinguishes several senses of the Greek root *zēl-* (which translates the Hebrew root *qn'*), both positive and negative. He argues that the meaning of *parazēloun* in 10:19 in the citation of Deut 32:21 is negative: "provoke to jealous anger"; while in 11:11 and 14 it takes on the positive sense of "provoke to emulation." For in the latter context it is a means by which Israel is brought to salvation.[7] A key theological reason for Israel's jealousy, according to Bell, is that its covenant privileges have been extended to the Gentiles. When Israel sees this, "she will be provoked to jealousy (manifested as emulation), and this prepares Israel for her salvation when

3. Stowers, *Rereading of Romans*, 312–15.

4. Ibid., 316.

5. Dunn, *Romans*, 668.

6. Ibid., 669.

7. See Bell, *Provoked to Jealousy*, 39–42, for an initial summary of this position, which is developed further in the later exegetical chapters.

she hears the gospel."[8] Pablo Gadenz questions Bell's reading, arguing that 10:19 and 11:11, 14 must be understood consistently and thus that the jealousy must in each case be negative, specifically interpreting it in chapter 11 as "the human face of Israel's hardening." He explains away the link with salvation in 11:14 by arguing that the *kai* is conjunctive not consecutive, some of Israel being made jealous, and others of Israel being saved.[9] Finally, Mark Nanos offers an unusual reading according to which Israel's jealousy has to do not with gentile salvation, but with Paul's gentile mission: that Paul is "fulfilling Israel's eschatological privilege of bringing light to the gentiles," while they are missing out. They will thus be induced to reconsider his proclamation.[10]

II

With the exception of Gadenz, who dissociates Israel's jealousy from Israel's salvation, each of these interpreters argues for a competitive jealousy, which God uses to the benefit of the competing parties. While this is an entirely natural reading, I will argue that a consideration of the theological context should make us pause before assuming the natural. More specifically, an alternative reading is invited by the presence of an important intertext for the jealousy motif: Deuteronomy 32, the Song of Moses. Paul's first invocation of Israel's jealousy is by way of citation of Deuteronomy 32:21, as we have seen. The full verse from which Paul cites reads:

> *Autoi parazēlōsan me ep' ou theōi, parōxunan me en tois eidōlois autōn; kagō parazēlōsō autous ep' ouk ethnei, epi ethnei asunetōi parorgiō autous.*
>
> They made me jealous with what is no God, provoked me with their idols. So I will make them jealous with what is no nation, provoke them with a nation lacking understanding.
>
> (Deut 32:21 LXX, translation from NETS)

Israel's jealousy is here paralleled with *God's* jealousy. Should we not be open, therefore, to its taking on a different dynamic from human jealousy more generally, insofar as it comes to reflect God's own distinctive

8. Ibid., 166; cf. 181–83.

9. Gadenz, *Jews and Gentiles*, 245–46, 249–50.

10. Nanos, *Mystery of Romans*, 248–50.

jealousy? Before exploring this possibility, it needs to be set in the context of the wider intertextual relationship between Romans 9–11 and Deuteronomy 32. The following account has strong resonance with the analysis of Bell, who argues that Deuteronomy 32 is a significant intertext for Romans 9–11 and a key source for Paul's jealousy motif.[11] However, I will reach beyond Bell in the theological conclusions drawn.

In Deuteronomy 32[12] Moses recites a song to the assembly of Israel in view of Israel's future rebellion, both as a witness against them and in order to forestall their foreseen rebellion. The verse Paul cites comes at the culmination of a description of Israel's abandonment of God for other gods. That Paul has in mind the whole Song when he cites part of this verse is suggested by the way in which Romans 9–11 recapitulates its broader narrative pattern, such that Paul's discussion of Israel's jealousy can be seen precisely as his own bold interpretive twist within this recapitulation. The Song, having depicted God's loving kindness towards Israel (32:4–14), recounts Israel's abandonment of God in pursuit of other gods (32:15–18). It continues by detailing God's envisaged punishment of Israel (32:19–25) before it comes finally and in dramatic reversal to the compassion he will have on Israel (32:36), vindicating his people by bringing its enemies to their downfall (32:34–35), and thereby vindicating his own name (32:39–42). As Moses' God moves from killing to making alive, from wounding to healing (Deut. 32:39), so Paul's God moves from hardening to saving (Rom. 11:7–16; 11:25–27). Bell highlights the fact that the same tension can be found in both Romans 9–11 and the Song: "between God's judgement on Israel and his love for Israel and therefore his desire to save Israel."[13] The resultant salvific pattern, narrated in the Song, is echoed in Romans: Israel's election, trespass[14] and judgment are followed by its final salvation.

But what is arguably just a minor note in Deuteronomy—God's making Israel jealous with another nation—in Romans is no longer just part of Israel's punishment, but is blown up into a central theme. The "no

11. Bell, *Provoked to Jealousy*, 200–201, 269–81.

12. As we have seen, Paul cites the LXX. The MT and LXX of the Song generally correspond to one another. However, there is one significant divergence for the purposes of the present argument, which will be highlighted below.

13. Bell, *Provoked to Jealousy*, 280.

14. Bell argues that *paraptōma* in 11:12 should be translated "trespass," given that the Song lies in the background, where Moses indicts Israel for her disobedience (ibid., 271).

nation" is no longer just a pawn in God's game with Israel, ultimately to be overthrown as Israel's, and therefore God's, enemy, but is that for the sake of which Israel is hardened, and therefore becomes in its own right part of God's salvific plan. Bell argues that Paul is drawing in this interpretive development on Deut 32:43 LXX, one place at which the LXX differs significantly from the MT, speaking not of the Gentiles praising Israel in response to YHWH's avenging of their blood, but rather of the Gentiles rejoicing *with* Israel: *euphranthēte, ethnē, meta tou laou autou.* Paul cites the same verse to this effect in Romans 15:10. Bell claims that Paul interpreted this verse to refer to the inclusion of the Gentiles in the people of God.[15]

God's jealousy is a strong note within the Song (being implied in verse 16 and made explicit for the first time in verse 19, before its occurrence in the verse cited by Paul[16]), suggesting that it is a significant context for Israel's jealousy. But what is the nature of divine jealousy, and what does it suggest for the nature of the jealousy of Israel that it brings about? In this as in several other cases the cause of God's jealousy is Israel's idolatry. The question is whether it has anything in common with the jealousy of human love relationships, such as Rachel's jealousy of Leah in Genesis 30:1.[17] Bell defines such jealousy as triangular, involving the subject, a good which the subject fears losing, and that which threatens the subject's possession of the good.[18] In this case the three corners are Rachel, Jacob, and Leah. This translates easily into the situation of God and idolatrous Israel, the three corners being God, Israel, and the foreign gods. However, the question is whether such a translation can be made without undue anthropomorphism. Bell is keen not to treat God's jealousy reductively, by removing what is essential to and distinctive of (human) jealousy, as happens, for example, when it is translated instead as "anger" or "zeal."[19] Indeed, by contrast with those who "shy away from the idea of Yahweh being the husband of Israel who is provoked to jealousy

15. Ibid., 272.

16. In the LXX. The MT has the root *qn'* in verse 16 but not verse 19.

17. Bell gives this as an example of jealousy (rather than envy), along with Genesis 37:11, given the three-sidedness of the relationships in each case. See Bell, *Provoked to Jealousy*, 10–11 (and nn. 47–49). This is in the context of a thorough cataloguing of the different meanings of "jealousy" in English, of the root *qn'* throughout the Hebrew Bible and rabbinic literature, and of the *zēl-* word field in the New Testament, LXX, and beyond. See ibid., 5–42.

18. Ibid., 5–6.

19. He argues against "zeal" in Deuteronomy 29:19 [KJV 29:20] and against "zealous" or simply "angry" when *qn'* is used adjectivally of *El* or *YHWH*. See ibid., 14–16.

when Israel turns to other gods," he upholds a robust sense of jealousy here involving the same triangle as human jealousy, fully recognizing and embracing the anthropomorphic nature of the idea.[20]

By contrast, H. G. L. Peels (in the entry on *qn'* in the *New International Dictionary of Old Testament Theology and Exegesis*) is clearly wary of anthropomorphism and cautious in defining uses of *qn'* with respect to God. Thus he claims, "Any association with self-centered pettiness, fear of losing property, envy, or jealousy is absent in the context of the manifestation of the *qin'â* of God. The translation 'jealous' is, therefore, inadequate." And he goes on implicitly to reject the triangular reading of Bell even in the context of Israel's idolatry: "God's 'jealousy' is not directed against the idols, but against the disloyal covenant partner. His *qin'â* is not like that of the deceived husband against his rival, but rather like that of the lord/sovereign who does not tolerate anyone else next to him in the covenant with his subjects. . . . Idolatry is pre-eminently a violation of covenant."[21]

At this point, I would argue, it is not so much a question of philology as one of hermeneutics. How is the God of the Old Testament to be understood—through what hermeneutical lens? I have already declared my hand in this respect, claiming (in the first paragraph of the essay) that "God is not just another character within the drama of salvation history, but the source, impetus, and telos of this salvation history." Thus, while anthropomorphic language cannot be avoided (indeed it is all we have to work with), it cannot be understood anthropomorphically. I would suggest, further, that a word such as "jealous" should not be jettisoned in favour of "zealous," for example, since while the latter may conceal its anthropomorphic nature, it is in fact no less human or creaturely than "jealous." The advantage of "jealous" is that it makes the interpreter work harder. I situate myself in this way in the tradition of exegesis of the likes of Tertullian and Origen, acknowledging the necessary humanness of our language about God, but also the fact that when it is used in the divine context it accrues meaning appropriate to the divine.

In order to understand any meaning accrued by "jealous," we will need a fuller doctrine of God. The doctrine of creation *ex nihilo* is a good starting point, and I will follow Rowan Williams's interpretation of it in

20. Bell, *Provoked to Jealousy*, 15–17.

21. VanGemeren, *New International Dictionary*, 939.

"On Being Creatures."[22] What it implies is a relationship between God and creation in which God is the whole context and presupposition of creation, such that creation has no independent standpoint from which it can struggle against God, even in its rebellion. Psalm 139 evokes this picture in a powerful way, suggesting that there is no stepping outside of God's purposes: "Whither shall I go from thy Spirit? Or whither shall I flee from thy presence" (v. 7). Likewise Job 38–41 portrays a sovereign God who precedes any human propensity to righteousness or wickedness, transcending these human categories and placing them in a context beyond the human being's imagining. The opening of Genesis, too, implies a God who creates not by struggle with chaotic forces, but by sovereign word. Evil will thus have to be interpreted in a very particular way, not as an independent principle, or as the rebellion of the autonomous creature; indeed, any autonomy gained in contradistinction to God's can only be an illusion. Evil only corrupts the creature and thus is better described (if it can be at all) as a struggle of the creature against itself.

However, if this is so, then human jealousy of the triangular kind described above loses its sense when predicated of God, since it would presume an autonomy of creaturely agency, which sets the creature over against God in such a way that the creature can choose to take or leave God, running off with foreign gods. But if God is the whole context of creaturely being, then there is no taking leave of God. God cannot be threatened by such desertion, or by the third party that tempts to desertion. On the other hand, this must not be taken to imply the equal and opposite: that God is indifferent towards Israel's comings and goings. God's "jealousy" transcends both creaturely passion and creaturely impassivity. Given this, God's jealousy is most appropriately reinterpreted as God's radical orientation towards Israel's well-being. God harnesses everything for the good of Israel, even when God does so in ways that are incomprehensible to it, bringing into question the devices and desires of its own heart. But the result will always be Israel's liberation, and specifically, its liberation from idolatry. It is just such liberation in which Deuteronomy 32 culminates (interpreted through this hermeneutical lens):

> For the Lord will judge his people and be comforted over his slaves.
> For he saw them paralyzed, both failed under attack and enfeebled.
> And the Lord said: Where are their gods,
> they in whom they trusted,

22. Williams, "On Being Creatures," 63–78.

the fat of whose sacrifices you were eating
and were drinking the wine of their libations?
Let them rise up and help you,
and let them be protectors for you!
See, see that I am, and there is no god except me.
I will kill, and I will make alive; I will strike, and I will heal,
and there is no one who will deliver from my hands. . . .
Be glad, O skies, with him, and let all the divine sons
do obeisance to him.
Be glad, O nations, with his people,
and let all the angels of God prevail for him.
For he will avenge the blood of his sons and take revenge
and repay the enemies with a sentence,
and he will repay those who hate,
and the Lord shall cleanse the land of his people.
(Deut 32:36–39; 43 LXX, NETS)

Israel is paralyzed by its allegiance to idols, and God's jealousy is directed towards its healing and strengthening, by setting it back in right relationship with its true God. On the route to this liberation, however, is *Israel's* jealousy. While in Deuteronomy 32 this is not dwelt on, perhaps as a moment in which God's goodness to Israel has become opaque, in Romans 9–11 it looms large as the means by which God brings about Israel's ultimate salvation. And it is to this context that we must return if we are going to get a handle on the nature of Israel's jealousy in relation to the no-nation, bearing in mind the wider context of God's jealousy discovered in Deuteronomy 32.

III

Just as we asked of God what it would mean to be jealous when nothing can be a threat to God's sovereignty, so we can ask of Israel what it can mean for it to be jealous of a God whom it cannot lose to another, who cannot be unfaithful to it, and whose elect and beloved people it irrevocably remains. But it is just such claims that are in question for Paul in Romans 9–11, having apparently been brought into jeopardy by God's turning towards the Gentiles—the no-nation. The nature of Israel's jealousy fundamentally depends on the stance taken towards such claims. Paul clearly argues for their endorsement, but in doing so he undermines the possibility of any competitive or rivalrous jealousy on the part of Israel along the lines of the triangular relationship described above. Approaching the question from a doctrinal angle, for Israel to desire exclusive ownership of God would be to misunderstand the nature of God's allegiance to Israel. Israel is not an independent entity that God chooses to come into relationship with where he might have chosen another relationship instead, one that would pull him in another direction. Israel is God's creation and therefore has its very being in God. God's capaciousness for other relationships is due to his being the context of them all, rather than a point within a nexus of relations, pulled this way and that by them.

If a competitive jealousy is a natural response to God's turning to the Gentiles in Christ, it is not one that will go unchallenged. Insofar as Paul understands Israel's jealousy as a precursor to, and even means of, its salvation (Rom 11:14), he invites a reinterpretation of this jealousy as non-competitive, in keeping rather with the God of his proclamation.[23] As such, it cannot be a possessive jealousy that seeks to wrest God away from the nations, for this would be to misunderstand the God who saves. A clue to the nature of Paul's reinterpreted jealousy lies in the salvific pattern outlined in 11:11–12 (cited above) and reiterated in 11:25–26a:

> *Ou gar thelō humas agnoien, adelphoi, to mustērion touto, hina mē ētc [par'] heautois phronimoi, hoti pōrōsis apo merous tōi Israēl gegonen archis hou to plērōma tōn ethnōn eiselthēi, kai houtōs pas Israēl sōthēsetai . . .*
>
> Lest you be wise in your own conceits, I want you to understand this mystery, brethren: a hardening has come upon part of Israel, until the full number of the Gentiles come in, and so all Israel will be saved . . .

If Israel's hardening and exclusion are understood to be an integral part of the path to its ultimate salvation, its salvation cannot consist simply in an inclusion that is just the reversal of its exclusion. Rather, Israel's exclusion is a clue to its identity as the people of *this* God: a God who cannot be anyone's possession, who thus cannot be "my God" as opposed to "yours." In its exclusion Israel does not lose its God but finds its God as the God who is also the God of others. It is not enough, here, to say that God is and remains Israel's God *and*, as limitless, is the God of others as

23. Given the scope of Paul's vision and its eschatological purview, this reinterpreted jealousy may be regarded as the transformative telos of Israel, as it comes to new understanding of its God in the light of Christ and of Paul's ministry—rather than necessarily an immediate result of the Gentile gospel.

well. This could be mistaken to be an "and" of distribution, in which God is shared out among Israel and the nations, so that effectively Israel gets only a part of God. What it misses is that God is Israel's God precisely *as* the God of others. Israel's relationship with God is not diluted but intensified in God's relating to others: God belongs wholly to Israel as the God of others. To sharpen the paradox, God belongs to Israel as the God who does not belong to Israel (for God transcends the creaturely dynamics of belonging). Its jealousy, we can conclude, is its desire to relinquish the God who is (exclusively) its God and embrace the God whom it cannot possess. As desire for *this* God, its jealousy is fundamentally non-possessive.[24]

As such, Israel's jealousy corresponds precisely with God's jealousy as displayed in Deuteronomy 32, as the parallelism in 32:21 allowed us to imagine. As we saw, God's jealousy had as its goal the freeing of Israel from its debilitating dependency on impotent creatures, giving it an identity beyond such creaturely negotiations as rooted in the God who transcends them. Unlike Israel's idols, God's existence and worth do not depend on Israel's regard for him. Thus God's jealousy does not turn Israel into a means for God's own ends, but is wholly for Israel's sake. Correspondingly, Israel in its jealousy does not seek a God who is reciprocally dependent on it, but the God who in his self-sufficiency is free to be wholly there for Israel—and as such free to be there for others also. In short, because God does not instrumentalize Israel, thereby becoming dependent on Israel for his identity, God cannot be reduced to his relationship with Israel. Thus Israel's liberation goes hand in hand with God's freedom to liberate others.

To sum up, Paul has in his creative recapitulation of Deuteronomy 32 also creatively reinterpreted human jealousy. Indeed, we might say more precisely that Paul has *altered the grammar of human jealousy.*

24. The dynamic articulated here has strong resonances with Rowan Williams's understanding of the identity of Israel as this gains (re-)definition and (re-)direction in Christ, set forth in "The Finality of Christ." However, Williams goes as far as to imply that Israel's loss of the God that is "its" God is its dissolution as a people. He cites Timothy Radcliffe as follows: "the vocation of Israel was to become truly the people of God in ceasing to be a people at all" (ibid., 99). He recognizes the dangers of saying this as a Christian, but only insofar as the church itself has characteristically become an ersatz people. He thus retains the universal vision of a peopleless people of God. By contrast, in the reading of Romans offered here Israel remains (implicitly) the concrete and fleshly people of God, forever differentiated from the Gentiles. Its relinquishment of its God is not its disbanding as a people.

Israel's jealousy is a *non-possessive jealousy*. It finds its God just as it relinquishes its God, receiving back the God who is also the God of others. Israel is thus the people of a God who is not "its" God (as opposed to "theirs"). Again, paradoxically, its God is not its God. This paradox is the index of a transformation in the grammar of possession. It indicates the possibility of a sharing that does not involve dividing up. More strongly, it reveals a kind of sharing, to the point of giving up, which is proportional to one's own gain. God, unlike finite creaturely goods, is not a limited resource. Israel's identity is rooted, beyond creaturely finitude and frailty and the possessiveness this gives rise to, in the divine infinitude in all its capaciousness. But as such, Israel is also free to re-conceive creaturely goods as gifts of God which are non-necessary to its identity, but which point to the abundance of God that cannot be lost. Thus its relationship with God leads to a transformed relationship with all creaturely goods as free to be shared.

This is the radical nature of the salvific transformation Paul envisages for Israel. As we hypothesized at the outset of this essay, Israel's jealousy—poised significantly at the intersection between the salvation of the Gentiles and the salvation of Israel—does indeed go to the core of its being, drawing it up into a fundamental transformation of its humanness, no longer dependent for its identity on creaturely goods, but rooted in the capaciousness of God. This truth was already there in Deuteronomy 32, but it is sounded at a new and heightened pitch in Christ, as God expands his covenant to include the Gentiles.

IV

The question left hanging from all this is the status of the Gentiles in this transformative process. My attempt to address this question will form an epilogue to the essay.

God's election of Israel sets Israel apart from other nations. However, if Israel's *jealousy* in any way characterizes its difference, this difference will be one that unites across the difference. For as we have seen, Israel is freed in its non-possessive jealousy to reconceive of all creaturely goods as for sharing, and more fundamentally still, to reconceive of its God as the God of others also. What separates Israel from other nations—its God—is also what unites it with them. However, an immediate danger lurks. Paul is convinced that the election and calling of Israel are irrevocable (Rom 11:28–29), and by implication that the distinctiveness and uniqueness of Israel amongst the nations persists. In other words, there can be no ironing out of the distinction between Jews and Gentiles. But it could easily be thought to follow from the uniting of Israel and the nations under one God (as described above) that Israel's God has become simply "everyone's God." Such universalism reduces difference to sameness, undermining the uniqueness of Israel. What, then, might safeguard Israel's inclusiveness against its degeneration into a uniform universalism?

It is precisely at this juncture, I would argue, that the Gentiles come into their own. I can only indicate briefly here how this is so, for it takes us into a new and complex passage within Romans 9–11: the olive tree analogy of Romans 11:17–24. Paul develops this analogy to remind Gentiles that their existence is a *derivative existence*. By it he indicates that Gentile identity is dependent on and secondary to Israel (esp. 11:18: "remember it is not you that support the root, but the root that supports you"); and second, that Gentile identity and existence ultimately derive from God, as a gift of grace (esp. 11:20–22: "you stand fast only through faith. So do not become proud, but stand in awe . . ." [v. 20b]). If Israel exhibits an alteration of the grammar of jealousy, and so of possession, then Gentiles are invited to embody an alteration in the grammar of identity and of agency. On the one hand, they do not define themselves but gain their identity from another to whom they are secondary. As secondary, however, they are not inferior: their derivativeness is a sharing in the rich root (11:17), and is thus the source of the richness of their identity. On the other hand, their achievement of righteousness, while genuinely their own, is not their own but is granted them by God. Their agency is rooted in God's agency: "Note then the kindness and the severity of God: severity towards those who have fallen, but God's kindness to you, provided you continue in his kindness; otherwise you too will be cut off" (11:22). This verse holds together without compromise and without explanation God's agency and human agency. By evoking these two aspects of Gentile existence, the olive tree analogy displays a logic of non-competition: non-competitive identity on the one hand and non-competitive agency on the other.

The Gentiles share in Israel's God, but they do so derivatively and therefore differently. This corrects the potential degenerate universalism of Israel's inclusiveness, since it marks the differentiation within this inclusiveness. In other words, Gentile derivativeness is a sign of others who come first. While Israel's distinctiveness was inherently inclusive, the distinctiveness of the Gentiles instantiates the irreducibility of otherness. Hence, if Israel's difference was a difference that unites, we might say that the Gentile difference is a unity that differentiates: their sharing in the rich root precisely holds open the difference between Israel and the nations.

To conclude, while the prerogative of Israel in its non-possessive jealousy is to include others, the prerogative of those included is to witness to the continuing uniqueness of Israel, as those who have come first. This further frees Israel from the burden of maintaining its uniqueness. Its non-possessive jealousy of God serves, as we have now seen, precisely to underline this.

Bibliography

Bell, Richard H. *Provoked to Jealousy: The Origin and the Purpose of the Jealousy Motif in Romans 9–11*. Tübingen: Mohr, 1994.

Dunn, James D. G. *Romans 9–16*. Word Biblical Commentary 38b. Dallas: Word, 1988.

Gadenz, Pablo T. *Called from the Jews and from the Gentiles: Pauline Ecclesiology in Romans 9–11*. Tübingen: Mohr Siebeck, 2009.

Nanos, Mark D. *The Mystery of Romans: The Jewish Context of Paul's Letter*. Minneapolis: Fortress, 1996.

Stowers, Stanley K. *A Rereading of Romans: Justice, Jews, and Gentiles*. New Haven: Yale University Press, 1994.

VanGemeren, Willem. *New International Dictionary of Old Testament Theology and Exegesis*. Vol. 3. Grand Rapids: Zondervan, 1996.

Williams, Rowan. "The Finality of Christ." In *On Christian Theology*, 93–106. Oxford: Blackwell, 2000.

———. "On Being Creatures." In *On Christian Theology*, 63–78. Oxford: Blackwell, 2000.

7

A Disharmony of the Gospels

Nicholas Adams

University of Edinburgh

One of the constant features of the theology of David Ford, whose work this volume honours, is its focus on Scripture. In particular, Ford has insisted (and shown in his own writing) that engagements with traditions other than his own Anglican Christianity are most fruitfully undertaken through joint attention to Scripture.

A second constant feature is an insistence on adopting a "both-and" approach to apparent oppositions whenever possible; that is, whenever such a generous approach does not cause damage to the integrity of theological practices or the identities of those who sustain them. This "both-and" approach is easily misunderstood. It is not a dogmatic position advanced for its own sake, but a habit that consciously compensates for what Ford sees as the excessively agonistic tendencies of some contemporary Christian theologies which needlessly (and counterproductively) advance themselves at the expense of their opponents. I read Ford's "both-and" approach as a corrective tendency, rather than a substantial position, and I interpret it as undertaken for the sake of the church and its neighbours, rather than for the sake of a particular theological school.

More substantially, a "both-and" approach implies a distinct logic for handling apparent contradictions. Where contradictions are signs of positions that really are opposed to each other, Ford advocates a straightforward logic of opposition and distinguishes right from wrong approaches.[1] Where contradictions are merely apparent, however, and where a deeper investigation is called for—one where distinctions are maintained, but placed in relation to each other—Ford adopts a logic of relation, which one might also call a "wisdom logic."[2] A wisdom logic refuses false oppositions, and finds ways to show that apparently rival positions become more generative when seen in relation to each other, often in relation to a common object.

One of the best ways to display the fruits of a "both-and" approach—this "wisdom logic"—is to consider Scripture. This essay considers the genealogies of Jesus in Matthew and Luke. These genealogies are different, a fact which prompted early opponents of Christianity to want to pit them against each other, in an "either-or" fashion, and thus to expose the alleged inconsistency of Christian religion. I compare two responses to this threat. Both responses reject the explicit "either-or" challenge. One is a "both-and" approach that acknowledges the differences, and holds them to be theologically generative (Augustine). The other is a "harmonizing" approach that plays down the differences, and holds them to be insignificant (Calvin).

The texts interpreted by the theologians are from Matthew and Luke.

1. This can be seen clearly in the discussion "Against idolatries" in Ford, *Self and Salvation*, 46ff.

2. This is most obvious in his handling of the different patterns of reasoning displayed in "Scriptural Reasoning" where Jews, Christians, and Muslims read their Scriptures together. Ford adopts a "both-and" approach that does not abolish differences in a soup of sameness, but maintains distinctions in a way that constantly places them in relation to each other. See Ford, *Christian Wisdom*, 273ff.

Matthew chapter 1

1 An account of the genealogy[a] of Jesus the Messiah,[b] the son of David, the son of Abraham.

2 Abraham was the father of Isaac, and Isaac the father of Jacob, and Jacob the father of Judah and his brothers, 3 and Judah the father of Perez and Zerah by Tamar, and Perez the father of Hezron, and Hezron the father of Aram, 4 and Aram the father of Aminadab, and Aminadab the father of Nahshon, and Nahshon the father of Salmon, 5 and Salmon the father of Boaz by Rahab, and Boaz the father of Obed by Ruth, and Obed the father of Jesse, 6 and Jesse the father of King David. And David was the father of Solomon by the wife of Uriah, 7 and Solomon the father of Rehoboam, and Rehoboam the father of Abijah, and Abijah the father of Asaph,[c] 8 and Asaph[d] the father of Jehoshaphat, and Jehoshaphat the father of Joram, and Joram the father of Uzziah, 9 and Uzziah the father of Jotham, and Jotham the father of Ahaz, and Ahaz the father of Hezekiah, 10 and Hezekiah the father of Manasseh, and Manasseh the father of Amos,[e] and Amos[f] the father of Josiah, 11 and Josiah the father of Jechoniah and his brothers, at the time of the deportation to Babylon. 12 And after the deportation to Babylon: Jechoniah was the father of Salathiel, and Salathiel the father of Zerubbabel, 13 and Zerubbabel the father of Abiud, and Abiud the father of Eliakim, and Eliakim the father of Azor, 14 and Azor the father of Zadok, and Zadok the father of Achim, and Achim the father of Eliud, 15 and Eliud the father of Eleazar, and Eleazar the father of Matthan, and Matthan the father of Jacob, 16 and Jacob the father of Joseph the husband of Mary, of whom Jesus was born, who is called the Messiah.[g] 17 So all the generations from Abraham to David are fourteen generations; and from David to the deportation to Babylon, fourteen generations; and from the deportation to Babylon to the Messiah,[h] fourteen generations.

a Or *birth.* b Or *Jesus Christ.* c Other ancient authorities read *Asa.* d Other ancient authorities read *Asa.* e Other ancient authorities read *Amon.* f Other ancient authorities read *Amon.* g Or *the Christ.* h Or *the Christ.* i Or *Jesus Christ.* j Other ancient authorities read *her firstborn son.*

Luke chapter 3

[23]Jesus was about thirty years old when he began his work.

He was the son (as was thought) of Joseph son of Heli, [24]son of Matthat, son
of Levi, son of Melchi, son of Jannai, son of Joseph, [25]son of Mattathias, son
of Amos, son of Nahum, son of Esli, son of Naggai, [26]son of Maath, son of
Mattathias, son of Semein, son of Josech, son of Joda, [27]son of Joanan, son
of Rhesa, son of Zerubbabel, son of Shealtiel,[i] son of Neri, [28]son of Melchi,
son of Addi, son of Cosam, son of Elmadam, son of Er, [29]son of Joshua, son
of Eliezer, son of Jorim, son of Matthat, son of Levi, [30]son of Simeon, son of
Judah, son of Joseph, son of Jonam, son of Eliakim, [31]son of Melea, son of
Menna, son of Mattatha, son of Nathan, son of David, [32]son of Jesse, son of
Obed, son of Boaz, son of Sala,[j] son of Nahshon, [33]son of Amminadab, son of
Admin, son of Arni,[k] son of Hezron, son of Perez, son of Judah, [34]son of Jacob, son of Isaac, son of Abraham, son of Terah, son of Nahor, [35]son of Serug,
son of Reu, son of Peleg, son of Eber, son of Shelah, [36]son of Cainan, son of
Arphaxad, son of Shem, son of Noah, son of Lamech, [37]son of Methuselah,
son of Enoch, son of Jared, son of Mahalaleel, son of Cainan, [38]son of Enos,
son of Seth, son of Adam, son of God.

i Gk *Salathiel.* j Other ancient authorities read *Salmon.* k Other ancient authorities read *Amminadab, son of Aram*; others vary widely.

Augustine's *De Consensu Evangelistarum* was probably composed around 400 AD, while he was working on *De Trinitate*. This "consensus" of all four Gospels is thus a mature work.[3]

The first question to ask is: why are there four Gospels? Augustine does not insist there should be four Gospels, rather than three or five. Neither does he volunteer any speculations about who knew which sources, or how these might have been handled. His view is more relaxed:

> however they may appear to have kept each of them a certain order of narration proper to himself, this certainly is not to be taken as if each individual writer chose to write in ignorance of what his predecessor had done or left out, as matters about which there was no information, things which another nevertheless is discovered to have recorded. But the fact is, that just as they received each of them the gift of inspiration, they abstained from adding to their several labours any superfluous conjoint compositions.[4]

For Augustine, the differences of repetition and variation are differences of divine gifts of inspiration. The Gospel writers repeat what is needed for their tasks, and omit what is superfluous to those needs.

We should view Augustine's handling of the variation in the genealogies found in Matthew and Luke against this broader sense of the meaning of variation, as gift, in the Gospels. Augustine's purpose overall is to "look into the accounts which the four evangelists have given us of Christ, [to show] how they agree internally and [with] each other."[5] He lays out the differences between these two accounts, notices apparent contradictions and interprets the differences. It is a reading that tries to account for repetitive variations, which shows minimally that differences between Matthew and the other evangelists are not an indication of mutual contradiction.[6]

Augustine's *Consensus* is not a demonstration that the four Gospels all agree: the differences between them matter and are not harmonized away. Augustine presupposes that each Gospel writer after Matthew knows the work of the previous writer or writers, and this means that there must be some purpose to their task other than strict repetition.

3. Augustine, *De Consensus*; Augustine, *Harmony*. Where I have amended Salmond's translation, this is signified by the presence of square brackets in the quotation.

4. Augustine, *Consensus*, bk. 1, ch. 2.

5. Ibid., bk. 2, prologue.

6. Schellong, *Calvins*, 47.

Mark is the "*breviator*" of Matthew's royal account; Luke attends to the "priestly person" of Christ; John emphasizes the divinity of Christ. This non-reductive approach can be seen plainly in Augustine's handling of the different genealogies. There are three principal differences: Matthew and Luke trace their genealogies through different sons of David, Matthew via Solomon, Luke via Nathan; Matthew *descends* from Abraham, Luke *ascends* to God; Matthew lists forty generations, Luke lists seventy-seven. These differences matter to Augustine and are found to be theologically significant. As will be clear from the account Augustine develops, the Gospels would be greatly impoverished if there were only one genealogy: each communicates a distinct theology, and both are needed. It nicely displays a "both-and" approach to an "either-or" problem.

All of the three principal differences serve a single theological claim for Augustine: "it is the taking of our sins upon Himself by the Lord Christ that is signified in the genealogy of Matthew, while in the genealogy of Luke it is the abolition of our sins by the Lord Christ that is expressed."[7] Matthew's account is of mortality, royalty, and the burden of sin. Luke's account is of divinity, priesthood, and the expiation of sin. Matthew focuses on mortality by beginning with Abraham and descending through the generations; Luke evokes divinity (although not as much as John) by beginning with Jesus and ascending to God. Matthew shows a royal interest in descending from David via Solomon the king; Luke draws attention to the priestly lineage by ascending to David via Nathan the prophet.[8] This has a double function: Solomon's mother was the one with whom David sinned, thus showing Matthew's emphasis on the weight of sin that bears down onto Christ through the generations; Nathan was the prophet through whom God took away David's sin, thus demonstrating the remission of sins that Jesus effects in an ascension towards God.

Augustine identifies three questions: (1) Jesus' parenthood and the corollary problem of tracing Jesus' genealogy through Joseph; (2) the differing names of Joseph's father in the two accounts; (3) the number of generations in the lists. In all three cases, Augustine offers a properly theological account of the differences.

7. Augustine, *Consensus*, bk. 2, ch. 4.

8. In the *Consensus* Augustine identifies David's son Nathan (2 Sam 5:14) with the prophet Nathan (2 Sam 12:13). Even before the advent of modern biblical scholarship, this was a howler, and Augustine himself corrects it in *Retractions*, II.16.

(1) Parenthood. Matthew traces Jesus' lineage from Abraham via David to Joseph. This "account of the generation of Christ according to the flesh" is desirable because it makes sense of Jesus as "son of man"; however it appears to be a problem because Joseph was obviously not Jesus' father according to the flesh. Augustine explores this via a brief explanation of marriage. Augustine insists that even when for two persons "there is no connection between the sexes of the body," "the relation [of marriage] can still remain." In a slightly later passage, he makes this claim even more strongly, going so far as to distinguish "the real union of marriage" from "the intercourse of the flesh." In conclusion, "therefore it is not true that Joseph should not be called the father of Jesus because he did not beget him by lying together [*concumbendo*], when indeed he may quite properly [*recte*] be the father of one who was not begotten by his own wife but whom he may have adopted from someone else."[9]

Augustine considers Joseph to be Jesus' legitimate father by reason of adoption. Augustine will return to the matter of adoption for the second problem, as we shall see. He considers and refuses the conclusion that Jesus is thus son of David "only" by adoption because of the opening of Paul's letter to the Romans. Because Paul identifies Jesus as "descended from David *according to the flesh*" (Rom 1:3, my emphasis), and because this cannot, biologically, refer to Joseph, it follows that Paul must be referring to someone else. Who? Mary. Augustine phrases it as a question: "how much more ought we to accept without any hesitation the position that Mary herself also was descended in some way, according to the laws of blood, from the lineage of David?" He also supports his argument by bringing in the "priestly" concerns of Luke: "Moreover, since the priestly lineage of this woman is not passed over in silence [*tacetur*], inasmuch as Luke makes known [*insinuante*] that Elisabeth, whom he records to be of the daughters of Aaron, was her cousin, we ought most firmly to hold that the flesh of Christ sprang from both lines; namely, from the line of the kings, and of the priests . . ."[10]

(2) Joseph's father. In Matthew, Joseph's father is Jacob the son of Matthan (Matt 1:15). In Luke, Joseph's father is Heli the son of Matthat (Luke 3:23). Who is really Joseph's father? Augustine has an answer. Joseph himself was adopted. He thus has two fathers: one of the names denotes

9. Augustine, *Consensus*, bk. 2, ch. 1. I have retranslated this to bring out Augustine's sexual language, for which Salmond offers euphemisms.

10. Ibid., bk. 2, ch. 2.

Joseph's biological father; the other denotes the father who adopted him. Augustine suggests (thinking in Latin) that because Matthew uses the phrase "Jacob begat Joseph," and Luke uses the phrase "Joseph who was the son of Heli," it is easy (Augustine's word: *facile*) to infer that Jacob fathered Joseph, and Heli adopted him. Augustine offers no further evidence for this (there is none) and, given the simplicity of his solution, it is noteworthy that he spends so long elaborating it: the reasoning is repetitive and insistent. This may be an indication of the importance of the problem and the need to deal with it decisively, or it may be that Augustine compensates for lack of evidence with assertion. Augustine argues that adoption was a practice with no less a venerable heritage than Jacob's adoption of Ephraim and Manasseh (Gen 48:5). He also draws a theological association between adoption and baptism. Taken together, his suggestion that Joseph was adopted "might easily suggest itself . . . to a man of piety decided enough to make him consider it right to seek some worthier explanation than that of simply crediting the evangelist with stating what is false."[11] This is a nice summary of Augustine's approach to scriptural problems: they demand theological investigation rather than the pretence that they do not exist.

(3) The number of generations. Matthew enumerates forty generations; Luke has seventy-seven. For Augustine, this is an opportunity to reflect on the symbolism of the different numbers. The forty generations in Matthew are the forty days of fasting by Moses on Mount Sinai (Exod 34:28), the forty days of Elijah's travel to Horeb (1 Kgs 19:8), the forty days of Jesus' fasting in the Wilderness (Matt 4:2), the forty days Jesus appeared after the resurrection (Acts 1:3). There are four seasons of the year; there are four winds; forty is four times ten, and ten can be made up by adding together numbers between one and four together successively. Forty is, for Augustine, "a sign of that laborious period in which, under the discipline of Christ the King, we have to fight against the devil," an earthly and mortal period made necessary by sin. "In this way, then, as Matthew undertook [to show] Christ as the King who came into this world, and into this earthly and mortal life of men, for the purpose of exercising rule over us who have to struggle with temptation, he began with Abraham, and enumerated forty men."[12]

11. Ibid., bk. 2, ch. 3.

12. Ibid., bk. 2, ch. 4.

Where forty is the number of discipline under sin, and in which sinful number the sinless Christ is not included in Matthew's account, the seventy-seven counted by Luke "denotes the thorough remission and abolition of all sins," as in the injunction to forgive one's brother seventy-seven times (Matt 18:22). For Augustine it is significant that, whereas Jesus is not included by Matthew in the number forty, which signifies sin, he is included, by Luke, in the number seventy-seven, which signifies the remission of sin. Seventy-seven is such a sign for Augustine because it is the product of seven and eleven. The number ten is the number of righteousness (ten commandments) and the transgression of ten is eleven. In Exodus 26:7, there are eleven curtains of hair for the tabernacle and, Augustine asks, "who can doubt that the haircloth has a bearing upon the expression of sin?" There are seven days in a week, and eleven signifies the transgression of righteousness: "we are brought with all due propriety to the number seventy-seven as the sign of sin in its totality." Augustine sums up: "the reckoning of this number is here brought to its conclusion by the Holy Spirit, who appeared in the form of a dove on the occasion of that baptism, in connection with which the number in question is called to mind [*commemoratur*]."[13]

Augustine's reasoning is elaborate. The contrast between Solomon and Nathan is forced because Augustine fails to distinguish Nathan the prophet and Nathan the son of David. Matthew himself draws attention to the repetition of fourteens, but shows no interest at all in the number forty at all: it is the reader who must count them. Luke lists, but only the reader explicitly "calls to mind," the number of generations. If one chooses not to count Jesus, one has seventy-six generations; if one chooses to include God (as the text does), one has seventy-eight. The number seventy-seven seems to signify sin just as much as forty, even in Augustine's account: it is the number of times one must forgive wrongdoing. And if one concedes that one of these signifies the expiation of sin, the number forty is just as strong a candidate through its association with ascetic practices whose goal is purification.

One may dispute with Augustine. But the crucial point is that Augustine argues theologically, in a "both-and" way, from the differences in Matthew and Luke, rather than attempting to level them into a unity. Augustine's *Consensus* shows itself to be an attempt to see differences not as cracks, exploited by pagans and needing to be plastered over by

13. Ibid., bk. 2, ch. 4. I have amended Salmond's translation.

Christians, but as importantly different retellings of one truth. The genealogies of Matthew and Luke are not identical; they repeat with variation, and the differences are an occasion for theological reflection. One must readily admit that Augustine does not always do this. Much of the *Consensus* is devoted to showing that at no point are there contradictions between the Gospel accounts. It is nonetheless significant that in the case of the genealogies his strategy is not minimization of the differences, but even the exaggeration of them, and the direction of those differences to theological ends.

We turn now to a much later treatment. Calvin's *Harmony of the Gospels* is a harmony of Matthew, Mark, and Luke, not of all the Gospels. Its genre of scriptural interpretation is quite distinct from Augustine's *Consensus*. Augustine's implied readership includes not only Christians who earnestly desire a demonstration that the texts do not confound each other, but also non-Christians who find in the differences between the Gospels proof that Christian religion is founded on false teaching. This is not Calvin's readership. It is evident from the "epistle dedicatory" to his 1555 edition (the first) that the *Harmony* is intended as a teaching aid, rather than as a polemical tool intended to defend the church against external attack. Calvin addresses questions that are debated within the church, including questions where previously suggested answers mirror confessional rivalries and disagreements. For Calvin the differences between the Gospels do not place the truth of the Christian religion in jeopardy. Rather, they pose educational challenges that call for sober theological pedagogy.

Calvin produces a new text. It furnishes the reader with a single narrative, in which the different Gospels are blended together. The whole proceeds passage by passage, either from a single evangelist or of all three Synoptics, followed by commentary. It might thus be best considered a study edition of the Synoptic Gospels, complete with notes. Our interest is in the account he gives of the genealogies in Matthew and Luke.

Like Augustine, Calvin groups Matthew, Mark, and Luke over against John: "John differs . . . quite considerably from the other three in that he devotes himself very much to describing the character and influence of Christ as it comes from Him to us, while they concentrate more on the one point, that our Christ was that Son of God, the Redeemer promised to mankind."[14] The grounds on which he does so, however, depart from

14. Calvin, *Harmony*, xii.

Augustine, for whom the Synoptic evangelists emphasize Christ's human nature, whereas John emphasizes the divine nature. Calvin, by contrast, sees the Synoptic evangelists as emphasizing Christ as promised Messiah, and John emphasizing Christ's power. Calvin differs further from Augustine in denying that the Gospel writers knew each other's work. Whereas, for Augustine, the three Synoptic evangelists (and John) know, in turn, the previous Gospels and write as members of the body of Christ, for Calvin the evangelists do not know each other's work, and their harmony is correspondingly more "astonishing," and is itself evidence of the direction of divine providence *qua* Holy Spirit. One might say that Augustine reads the text as a christological artefact, whereas for Calvin it is more pneumatological.

Calvin reproduces the genealogies, with Matthew first and Luke second, and then begins his commentary.[15] I identify the following questions answered by Calvin: (1) Whose genealogy appears in Luke? (2) Who was David's son? A third is not answered: Who is Joseph's father?

(1) Whose genealogy? Calvin begins by noting that "there is not complete agreement on these two genealogies," and suggests that the nub of the disagreement concerns whether both Matthew and Luke trace the genealogy of Joseph, or whether Matthew traces Joseph's line, and Luke Mary's. Augustine had reasoned that Mary was descended from David, but he concluded this on the basis of Romans 1:3: "who was descended from David according to the flesh," not on the basis of Luke's genealogy. Calvin presents the view that Joseph must have taken a wife from his own tribe, according to the law (Num 26:5), from which it follows that his genealogy is also Mary's to a degree. Calvin entertains the possibility that Joseph and Mary might not have observed the law and rejects it. The evangelists "took it for granted that Joseph, being a man of upright and sincere character, would only have married a wife, as the Law prescribed, from his own kin."[16] Mary's genealogy is thus included in Joseph's.

The next problem to be considered by Calvin is whether Matthew reproduces Joseph's line, and Luke reproduces Mary's. For Calvin this is "easily refuted." Some may allege that when Luke says "son of Heli" he means "son-in-law of Heli," thus implying Mary to be Heli's daughter. Calvin dismisses this as unattested anywhere else in Scripture, as well as

15. Ibid., 52–61.

16. Ibid., 54.

being contrary to "the course of nature," a nature whose course he does not illuminate further.

(2) David's Son. Like Augustine, Calvin is interested in how the descent from David is understood. Augustine had found significance in Solomon's royalty (Matthew) and Nathan's prophethood (Luke), and used this as inspiration for meditation on the different theological characters of the two Gospels. Calvin's interest is also theologically motivated, but it concerns the Messianic promise. He reads 2 Samuel 7:12–14, Psalm 132:11 (and presumably 1 Chr 28:5) as confirming that for Christ to be Christ, he must be descended from Solomon. If Matthew's genealogy is from Solomon, and Luke's Marian genealogy is from Nathan, then Jesus' biological genealogy from Solomon is "deleted." This cannot be. Mary must be a descendent of Solomon, or the promise is in vain. Calvin's implied reasoning is that the promise is not in vain, and that therefore his readers can be certain Mary was descended from Solomon.

This still leaves the interesting question of Luke's genealogy: why does it appear different from Matthew's, and does Luke's naming of David's son Nathan indeed strike Christ out from Solomon's line? Augustine had argued for two lines for Joseph, a biological line (Solomon to Jacob) and an adopted line (Nathan to Heli). Calvin shows no knowledge of this argument. Because Calvin insists that both Matthew and Luke offer biological genealogies for Joseph (and therefore Mary), he must account for the different sons of David found in Matthew and Luke.

Calvin has an explanation that, while simple in conclusion, is fascinatingly contorted in reasoning. Calvin argues that Matthew offers a *legal* descent, while Luke offers a *natural* descent. This is a line of argument followed, says Calvin, by "good and experienced interpreters." The argument is this: The murder of Ahaziah (2 Kgs 9:27) probably marked the end of Solomon's biological line; this is suggested by the murder of all the royal seed by his mother Athaliah (2 Kgs 11:1). Calvin reasons that if an heir to Ahaziah had been alive at the time, he would have been grandson to Athaliah, and she "would have been willing to reign as his grandmother under the pretext of guardianship."[17] Therefore, there was no surviving heir, and Solomon's line ended. This reading encounters some obstacles, as Calvin admits. For example, Joash is called "the son of Ahaziah" (2 Chr 22:11). Calvin speculates that this is not a literal son; it means merely that Joash was the next legitimate heir. The ending of

17. Ibid., 57.

Solomon's line poses an obvious problem: if it ended, how then is Christ a descendant of Solomon? Here Calvin invokes the notion of a "legal" descent: Christ is descended "naturally," i.e., biologically, from Nathan; yet "he may be reckoned [Solomon's] son in legal order, as He took His origin from the kings."[18] Calvin's problems are not quite over: even if one accepts a distinction between legal and natural descent, there is still the difference between Jacob and Heli. If Calvin is right that the two genealogies are identical (albeit natural and legal respectively), then these two must be the same person. Calvin is emphatic: "there can be no doubt, that from the time of the Babylonian exile, they are speaking of the same men in some cases by different names." He also speculates that Matthew "felt free to overlook some names" because his is a legal genealogy, whereas Luke did not, because he gave a natural genealogy.

(3) Joseph's Father. Calvin adopts an aggressive stance towards readers who might want to investigate the difference between Jacob and Heli more closely: "I have discussed the genealogy of Christ, all in all, as far as appeared to be useful. If any are diverted by a greater curiosity, I recollect Paul's warning and prefer a level-headed restraint to trifling and worthless sophistry. We know the passage in Titus 3.9 where he tells us to shun foolish questionings and genealogies."[19] This closes the chain of reasoning, or at least brings it screeching to a halt. The question of Joseph's father is effectively forbidden.

Like Augustine's speculation of the adoption by Heli, with which it is incompatible, Calvin's argument is unsupported by further evidence, and commends itself solely by reason of being internally consistent, if strained. It certainly is strained: if the "biological" link guaranteed by Mary secures only a "legal" descent from Solomon, why is it not sufficient for Jesus to have a "legal" descent from Joseph? If the biology breaks off at Ahaziah, what is to be gained by insisting upon the biological link through Mary? It is not obvious that a legal descent needs to be buttressed by a natural descent, to use Calvin's terminology. It is all the more remarkable that—like Augustine, who says his solution is "easy to infer"—Calvin assures his reader that "the solution is ready to hand" (*in promptu est solutio*).[20] This ends Calvin's essay on the genealogies. It is followed by line-by-line commentary on aspects of the Matthaean text only, with no reference to Luke.

18. Ibid.
19. Ibid., 5.
20. Ibid., 57.

Both Augustine and Calvin wrestle with problems of interpretation raised by the repetition of the genealogy, and by the significant variation this repetition displays. Both offer elaborate reasoning to address the problem. Augustine uses the difficulties creatively as a spur to theological meditation. His reading is theologically creative and helps to reader to read with new eyes and ears. Augustine uses the difference between Solomon and Nathan to host a discussion about the royal character of Matthew's Gospel and the priestly interest of Luke's; he finds in the difference between downward and upward genealogies an opportunity to launch a contrast between the downward weight of sin (Matthew) and the upward flight of expiation (Luke); he reads into the different numbers of generations an entire number symbolism of sin and redemption. Problems are converted into opportunities to preach the gospel. For Calvin the variation is played down. Calvin levels the difference between Solomon and Nathan by asserting an identical lineage described "legally" and "naturally." Of the difference between downward and upward genealogies he says: "as it contains no difficulty, there is no need to say any more."[21] As to the different numbers of generations he voices two views. At first he says simply, "Matthew thinks in terms of legality, and . . . to aid the reader's memory he simply lists three groups of fourteen."[22] Later on Calvin qualifies this as a "half truth" and suggests that there is a "threefold condition" of the people that is mirrored in the three groupings of fourteen: first, there is the period "before princedon"; second, there is "the majesty of kingship"; third, there is the period of expectation of the Messiah.[23] Calvin clearly reads theologically. His description of the significance of sin in the Davidic line and his attentiveness to messianic titles both discharge important theological functions. But Calvin finds no theological significance in the *variations* present in the repetitions of the genealogies in the way that Augustine does. His account is not "both-and," but rather a denial of difference.

Where Augustine sees and hears differences, and puts them to work, Calvin sees and hears identity and sameness. Where Augustine exaggerates the differences and improvises in a gloriously wild and bizarre fashion, Calvin tends to shut down debate. After rehearsing strained arguments, he threatens readers with being intellectually "unprofitable and vain" if they have further questions. When it comes down to details of interpretation, Calvin simply puts Luke to one side, without explanation,

21. Ibid., 55.

22. Ibid.

23. Ibid., 58.

and concentrates solely on Matthew: this has the effect of ensuring that the reader encounters no repetition or variation.

The theological point of departure for this paper is the possibility that the plurality of the Gospel might be read as something *theologically* significant. The theological task, displayed in Ford's "both-and" theology and here seen in Augustine's interpretive practice, is to value repetition as a mode of divine expression. The Gospels themselves are already harmonies. Repetition and variation are not merely features of later interpretation, but are already modelled in Scripture, which teaches its readers how to read and reread. The Gospels need not be straightened out and cured of their repetition and variation. Ignoring variation impoverishes the gospel. Calvin's tendency to "correct" variation through an insistence on strict repetition persists in modern approaches to Scripture. There is a website, "The Skeptic's Annotated Bible," whose purpose is to identify the variations (or "contradictions") in Scripture and treat them, like Celsus, as proof of the falsity of its teaching.[24] It is not surprising that many Christians respond to such challenges as Calvin does, and deny that there is any variation (or at least any meaningful variation). This has the unfortunate consequence that one pays less close attention to Scripture. Augustine, by contrast, does not hear variation as contradiction, but as differently repeated "consensus," where the variation is real, but the apparent contradiction is evidence of an endless task of interpretation. Augustine commends *both* Matthew *and* Luke. The task is genuinely endless, not least because each new interpretation does not reduce but adds to the variations, creating yet more tasks for each succeeding generation. Even Calvin is an inspiration here, constantly bringing diverse parts of Scripture into dialogue with each other, urging the reader to read ever more widely and deeply. To hear difference as a task, rather than as a threat, is to hear Scripture as Scripture, as generative, rather than merely as information, or as a stream of data with pieces missing.

This is the promise of David Ford's "both-and" approach, which is focused on Scripture, for theology. The task is a musical task: to hear variation, and to put it to work, and in that work to vary the variations themselves, giving the world something already heard yet endlessly new to hear.

24. See http://www.skepticsannotatedbible.com/contra/.

Bibliography

Augustine. *De Consensu Evangelistarum libri quatuor*. In *Sancti Aurelii Augustini . . . opera omnia multis sermonibus ineditis aucta et locupleta*. Volume 34. Rome: Nuova Biblioteca Agostiniana. Online: http://www.augustinus.it/latino/consenso_evangelisti/index2.htm.

———. *Harmony of the Gospels*. In *Nicene and Post-Nicene Fathers*, First Series, vol. VI. Translated by S. D. F. Salmond. Edited by Philip Schaff. New York: Christian Literature, 1886.

Calvin, Jean. *A Harmony of the Gospels Matthew, Mark and Luke*. Translated by A. W. Morrison. Edited by D. W. Torrance and T. F. Torrance. Edinburgh: Saint Andrew, 1972. The Latin text of the 1582 edition is available courtesy of openlibrary.org: http://openlibrary.org/books/OL23361470M/Harmonia_ex_Evangelistis_tribus_composita_Matthaeo_Marco_Luca.

Ford, David. *Christian Wisdom: Desiring God and Learning in Love*. Cambridge: Cambridge University Press, 2007.

———. *Self and Salvation: Being Transformed*. Cambridge: Cambridge University Press, 1999.

Schellong, Dieter. *Calvins Auslegung der synoptischen Evangelien*. Munich: Kaiser, 1969.

8

Attending to Scripture

The Homiletic Imperative

Frances Young

University of Birmingham

Popularly there is a widespread perception that theology is an intellectual, "ivory tower" pursuit, remote from the lives of "ordinary people," and more likely to threaten faith than enhance it. No doubt the pressures for survival as a respectable discipline in the context of the modern secularised University has had a good deal to do with this, but one suspects that the shifting of various tectonic plates beneath modern/postmodern societies have contributed to a series of chasms opening up over which the laborious building of bridges may gradually come to be seen as the vocation of Christian theology. In this endeavour, David Ford can surely be identified as a pioneer; one who has attended to split between the public and the private, the religious and the secular, the Christian and the "Other." This offering in his honour focuses on yet other rifts that have concerned him—those between academy and church, and between the Bible as the object of historical research and Scripture as the subject of theology.

Theological interpretation of Scripture has become something of a growth industry, but the work of David Ford may be seen as ahead of its time in opening up this endeavour, not least in the joint project that he initiated, *Meaning and Truth in 2 Corinthians*. Equally significant is the way in which his theology has been earthed in worship since his early work, *Jubilate*, co-authored with Dan Hardy. For, historically speaking, liturgy has been the prime context in which Scripture has been read, and its interpretation has principally been rhetorical exposition to energise the faith and life of a particular ecclesial community in specific circumstances at a precise place and time. Indeed, it could be asserted that preaching is not only the most pervasive locus of exegesis but also the most appropriate form of theological discourse. So perhaps it is not surprising that David has been equally at home in pulpits as in lecture halls. My intention here, then, is to exemplify the kind of bridge-building possible if we focus on the homiletic location of theology and scriptural interpretation, and to do this by offering, with brief comment, two actual sermons delivered by the author on specific occasions to theologically engaged congregations.

I

The first example was preached in Leuven at the end of a conference of systematic theologians on the subject, *Godhead Here in Hiding*.[1] The context of that conference, and its incarnational theme, is significant for the sermon's content, as is the ecumenical nature of the congregation and the assumption that the hearers would be familiar with key scriptural material. The lections, from which the homily took its genesis and to which it refers, were Philippians 2:5–11 and John 12:31–36.

Sermon on Philippians 2:5–11 and John 12:31–36

Immediately after the passage from John 12 we find the words, "Jesus left and hid himself."

The profound paradoxes of John's Gospel can easily be flattened by a docetic reading. The fact is that all through the Gospel the glory of Jesus is hidden in the reality of his ordinary human existence, if not for readers who are "in the know," at least for most of the participants. They demand signs, yet cannot see the signs that are given. Some see and believe; some are to be blessed because they believe without seeing. Some give testimony to his glory; yet some see yet do not see, like Nicodemus, while many see

1. Proceedings published in Merrigan, *Godhead Here in Hiding*.

but do not believe, flocking after him because of the signs, but not beginning to discern the reality that confronts them—they just ate the loaves and had their fill.

So Jesus divides people, and people are judged by their response. He said, "'For judgement I have come into this world, so that the blind will see and those who see will become blind.' Some Pharisees who were with him heard him say this, and asked, 'What? Are we also blind?' Jesus said, 'If you were blind you wouldn't have sin; but now you claim that you see, your sin remains.'"

Their judgement lay in their unconscious inability to see—just after the passage we read, the evangelist reflects that this fulfils Isaiah's prophecy: "He has blinded their eyes, and deadened their hearts, so that they can neither see with their eyes, nor understand with their hearts, nor turn—and I would heal them." Isaiah said this because he saw his glory and spoke of him, and many did believe in him—and yet . . . and yet . . . so many did not. But "I did not come to judge the world but to save it," Jesus had said. Those with eyes to see perceive that the Word became flesh and dwelt among us, and we have seen his glory. But that perception takes discernment—for he hid himself.

These profound paradoxes come to a head in chapter 12, along with another persistent refrain—for "Now is the time of judgement" and "the hour has come for the Son of Man to be glorified." The "hour" has been postponed, time and again: at Cana, "My hour has not yet come" (2:4); before going to the Feast of Tabernacles, "My *kairos* isn't yet" (7:8). No one arrests him in the temple, because his time has not yet come (8:20). They try to stone him, but he hid himself (8:59).

Now, however, is the moment: chapter 12 prepares us for the passion story—for the biggest sign of all—indeed, the supreme sign! For the horror of the cross is itself the moment of glory, the moment when Jesus bears the judgement, the moment when, far from wafting away the darkness with a magic wand, he enters into its very depths and transforms it. Only by setting these difficult verses of chapter 12 into the whole drama of the Gospel can we begin to discern what they are about—the glory of the incarnation, the glory of the passion, the glory of the Lord hidden in the ordinariness, the darkness and the horror of the world.

About twenty years ago I was ordained as "a presbyter of the universal Church and one of John Wesley's preachers." One of our Methodist traditions is testimony, and I ask you to indulge me as I testify to seeing the glory in the darkness.

In 1991 I went to Lourdes with the Faith and Light pilgrimage. Faith and Light is a sister organisation to the L'Arche communities, and gathered in Lourdes were some twenty thousand pilgrims from all over the world, people with learning disabilities, their friends and families. Jean Vanier had invited me to give a *conférence* for parents. I could tell many stories from that time in Lourdes. Let me just share one.

Following the Stations of the Cross is not a Protestant custom, but on Good Friday afternoon I set out to do so, with my own extempore reflections. In Lourdes the Stations are set on a hill—quite literally—and you struggle up the steep slope from one more than life-size tableau to the next. I passed the *Ecce Homo*, and then eventually came to the moment when I met Mary. I was immediately taken back over the years to an earlier occasion when I met her. The nuns of the local convent had invited all their neighbours for a carol service, and I had gone along, taking my severely disabled son with me. For the first time in my life I had been in a chapel dominated by a huge statue of Mary. As I pushed my son's buggy back up the road, this poem appeared from nowhere:

Mary, my child's lovely.
Is yours lovely, too?
Little hands, little feet,
Curly hair, smiles sweet.

Mary, my child's broken.
Is yours broken, too?
Crushed by affliction,
Hurt by rejection,
Disfigured, stricken,
Silent submission.

Mary, my heart's bursting.
Is yours bursting, too?
Bursting with labour, travail, and pain.
Bursting with agony, ecstasy, gain.
Bursting with sympathy, anger, compassion.
Bursting with praising Love's transfiguration.

Mary, my heart's joyful.
Is yours joyful, too?

So in Lourdes I again met Mary and the weeping began. I went on round the corner and met the women of Jerusalem bringing their children to Christ as he carried his cross, seeking a blessing. As a Protestant I might have thought, "No such story in the Gospels!" But on this occasion such a response was far from my mind. I identified with the women, and in imagination brought my child for a blessing. Then I struggled on up, my eyes by now filled with tears. When I reached the Calvary at the top of the hill, the low afternoon sun was right behind it, dazzling, and I could see nothing—until I lined up the cross over the sun to cut the glare. Then I saw the cross in deep darkness, a silhouette, surrounded by the blaze of glory.

Afterwards I followed the path round, up over the hill and behind the cross, and from behind, it was illuminated. Philippians chapter 2 illuminates John's dark mystery, and in its own way it also points to hiddenness—in *kenosis*, another theme of which we have heard much in the last few days. Whatever the climax may say about being highly exalted, about receiving God's name, and God's worship, from all God's creatures, the passage is introduced in such a way as to emphasize the hiddenness, the descent, the self-effacement, the emptying—for it is presented as a type of what life in the Christian community should be, as our human grasping at glory gives way to mutual consideration and the mind of love that was in Christ Jesus.

Mutuality is the key—the way to avoid exploiting the poor; for you accord dignity to someone by receiving from them. Nothing is harder than being on the receiving end of help—doing good is easy by comparison! To find your deepest needs met by some of the poorest and most marginalized of all human beings—those with learning disabilities or brain damage, those who cannot compete in our success-oriented societies and whose situation is unchangeable—to discover the humility to receive peace and love and all the other fruits of the Spirit through relationship with the weakest of all—that is truly to discern the Risen Christ among us. This I have learned through L'Arche and Faith and Light.

Yet I discerned something of it long before—allow me another testimony: I was invited to lead studies for the Othona community; founded after the Second World War with a commitment to reconciliation, this community is based in the site of an old army camp on the East coast, is ecumenical, and every year invites German students to join in their summer activities. Each morning and evening they worship in the oldest place of Christian worship in England, St. Peter's-on-the-Wall at Bradwell, built out of the stones of the old Roman camp of Othona.

One evening the prayers were being led by Martin, the student-leader from Germany; he said he had planned for us simply to be in silence, but, he went on, "you cannot have silence with Arthur present." My disabled son, you see, gets more and more excited when there's an echo, and his inarticulate shouts get louder and louder . . . "So," said Martin, "we will create silence by singing Psalms." Arthur loves music and is quiet as long as people are singing! The Othona community—like others, Iona, Taizé—has created its own songs and psalms, and we sang one after another. Eventually we came to the Othona version of Psalm 131—a simple repeated chant, with these words:

> I am too little, Lord,
> to look down on others.
>
> I've not chased great affairs,
> nor matters beyond me.
>
> I've tamed my wild desires,
> and settled my soul.
>
> My soul's a new-fed child
> at rest on the breast.
>
> My brothers seek the Lord,
> both now and for ever.

As we sang, Arthur became the Christ figure among us.

All this points to the fact that the very notion of glory is gloriously subverted as the glory hour of Jesus proves to be his death—the hiding in darkness, the planting of the grain of wheat that cannot produce fruit unless it die, the bearing of the judgement that makes possible our release from suffering, blindness, and death.

So glory be to the Father, and to the Son, and to the Holy Spirit, Amen.

Comment

This example illustrates the homiletic imperative to collapse the distance between the Scriptures and the present, such that listeners find themselves taken up into the overarching story of God's dealings with all creation. Specific lections are suggestively explored through exegesis of their contexts, then grounded in the incarnational framework of Christian systematic theology and illuminated by contemporary experience offered in testimony, while the whole reflection is informed by the particular context of the specific occasion of the preaching.

II

The second example was preached at Hinde Street Methodist church in London's West End on the occasion of seventy-fifth anniversary of the Methodist Sacramental Fellowship (MSF),[2] a group born out of concern for the appropriate adoption within Methodism of the sacramental and liturgical traditions of the wider church. The sermon unashamedly draws on patristic scholarship to rub home the deeply historical grounding of the doctrinal tradition being explored, but is also informed by contemporary issues in society and the life of the church.

The Materiality of the Christian Tradition: Sermon on the Seventy-fifth Anniversary of the Methodist Sacramental Fellowship

Many things are supposed to have happened when Helena, the mother of the Emperor Constantine, made her pilgrimage to the Holy Land, but let me just highlight one: she took a load of soil back to Rome to be spread on the floor of her private chapel so that she could pray on ground on which the feet of the Saviour had trod. Why do I emphasize this? Because on this occasion of the seventy-fifth birthday of MSF I feel prompted to share some reflections on the sheer *materialism* of the Christian tradition.[3]

Materialism is today decried from pulpits all over the affluent Western world. It bespeaks a consumerist society where getting and spending dominates, where value is measured in cash terms, where comfort, success, and achievement trump commitment, concern for others, and even civilization. In reaction, some search for spirituality—any kind of spiritual escape from it all. But suppose it turns out to be the case that *ordinary, everyday material things constitute precisely what is holy.* As a teenager my

2. This sermon, "The Materialism of the Christian Tradition," was published in the *Methodist Sacramental Fellowship Bulletin*, and is reproduced in a slightly abbreviated form by permission.

3. I largely eschew footnotes to this sermon, but acknowledge some influence and quotations from Harvey, *Scenting Salvation*.

brother got the point: he said that Methodists should celebrate communion with a cup of tea and a bun!

The notion that matter might be sacred was profoundly alien to the religious philosophy of the ancient world: the soul was prized over the body; deplored was the corruption of spiritual realities by the grossness of matter, and of rationality by coarse emotions. And yes—Christianity was itself profoundly influenced by these attitudes.

One reason sometimes given for negative attitudes to bodies and matter was the disgust provoked by excrement and other discharged fluids. There is a revealing conversation in the Coptic *Life of Abba Apphou*, an Egyptian monk. He was arguing with his Patriarch, Theophilus, about whether we are made in God's image. Forced into a corner by Apphou's quotations from Scripture, Theophilus protested that God is impassible and self-sufficient—how ever could you think an ailing man squatting to perform his necessities is in God's image? Apphou appealed to the ordinariness of eucharistic bread—yet it is the body of Christ; Theophilus pointed out that it only becomes the body of Christ in the context of liturgy. Apphou indicated that it takes faith to accept that, and so it does to accept that humankind has been created in the image and likeness of God. He points out that the medium in which the Emperor's portrait or image is executed is quite different from the actual living Emperor, yet the image is honoured because the Emperor endorses it as his image. So God affirms that we are in his image, whatever our physical make-up. We might say God chooses to put his name there (Deut 12:5 et al.)

Not long before, the Cappadocian Fathers, in what we now call Turkey, were founding a hospice for lepers and outcasts on the grounds that however abhorrent—even non-human—their bodies seemed, they were still made in God's image. This approach arose from an old tradition in Christianity that sharply modified that negative outlook towards material things, only to be constantly in danger of suppression, not least at the Protestant Reformation. The goodness of creation and the sacramental presence of God within the mundane stuff of the material world are themes that have to be reclaimed time and time again in Christian history. The significance of MSF in the evangelical Methodist tradition perhaps lies precisely here.

The struggle began already in New Testament times, but came to a head in the second century. So-called Gnostic sects proclaimed a gospel of salvation *from* this material universe, in which spiritual beings had been trapped by the Demiurge or fallen Creator God. This understanding of salvation may well have been dominant in some areas touched by Christianity; and it is perhaps not all that far removed from otherworldly versions of the evangelical gospel, which proclaim escape from the world, the flesh, and the devil, and eternal life in heaven as salvation for the soul—pie-in-the-sky-when-you-die! What the struggle with the Gnostics did was to ensure that Christians would affirm that the utterly transcendent God, containing all things yet not contained, was not ashamed to get the divine hands dirty creating the material world—which meant that what was created was not dirty at all, but sacred, since it was declared good by the Creator, and the hands that made it were God's own Word and Spirit. Not for nothing were the eucharistic elements described as fruits of the earth, offered in thanksgiving to the Creator of all.[4] This ordinary stuff of the earth was sacred.

So a tradition of finding God *through the very material creation itself* was established, and this would produce:

- in the fourth century that wonderful celebration of creation found in Basil's *Homilies on the Hexaemeron* (= the *Six Days of Creation*);
- in the eighteenth century the glorious and joyous music of Haydn's *Creation*;
- and in the twentieth century Gerald Manley Hopkins wonderful poem "God's Grandeur" ("The world is charged with the grandeur of God . . .").

The struggle to defend this materialist emphasis continued over the nature of the resurrection. I remember my mother telling me the story of how in the twenties she went as a teenager on a Girl Guide camp in the Cotswolds. On the Sunday morning they went to the local parish church, and the preacher produced a vivid description of how, at the resurrection, all the lost limbs of the fallen in the First World War would float up in the air and join onto the right torsos. She found it all quite laughable, and we may well react by finding it much too literal, but that reaction was clearly around already in Paul's Corinth.

One of the more surprising pieces of research I have found myself doing recently has concerned the intimate connection between creation and resurrection in early Christian writings.[5] For 2 Maccabees and Paul, creation provided encouragement to faith in God even in the face of death:

4. Some may recognise implicit references to Irenaeus, here and in the previous sentence.

5. Young, "Naked or Clothed?"

if God can create in the first place, then of course God can re-create and restore. In the second century this argument was turned around into a philosophical defence of the whole notion of resurrection: if the lesser work—the making of a corruptible and passible body—is not unworthy of God, how much more is that the case with the greater work—the making of an incorruptible and impassible body!

Within the life of the church, however, the temptation has always been to identify the real person with some inner soul or spirit that is released from fetters at death. But faced with this, the earliest Christians affirmed that a human person is a composite of soul and body, and both body and soul would receive the appropriate changes for that transformation for the better, which is the resurrection. Indeed, in the second century we find utter rejection of the immortality of the soul; the apologist Tatian claimed that even if all trace of a person's physical existence were to be obliterated by fire or dispersed through waters, or torn in pieces by wild beasts, there is absolutely nothing to stop the creative power of God restoring that person to their pristine original condition.

By the fourth century we can observe Augustine shifting from his initial, highly spiritualizing understanding towards grappling with all kinds of questions about what this material, physical resurrection implied: Would babies be resurrected as adults? Would the elderly and infirm have their worn and wrinkled bodies, or the glow of youth? What about aborted foetuses? What about those who had been excessively fat or thin? There was not only the problem of dismemberment of those who had been martyred, but also other lost bodily traces—hair clippings, toe and fingernails, limbs lost to disease. Augustine insisted on the continuation of gender; and that martyrs would still have their scars.

A former student of mine, Susan Ashbrook Harvey, attributes this scrupulous attention to each and every one of these problems to the fact that his primary concern was "to ensure a continuity of the self as an individual person with an individual history." But the effect is not unlike that sermon my mother heard—a crudely literal, possibly laughable, set of speculations. Yet as we wryly smile, let us recognize how extraordinary it is that someone like Augustine could have reached this point.

And meanwhile in the East that other Christian Platonist, Gregory of Nyssa, likewise insists that creation and resurrection are acts of a kind, and the dissolved particles of the body, imprinted with a particular identity, will be reconstituted, then changed and re-formed so as to lose that heavy materiality and be set free for blessedness; while the Syrian poet Ephrem wrote:

> . . . I considered
> how the soul cannot
> have perception of Paradise
> without its mate, the body,
> its instrument and lyre.

Of course, above all, it was the incarnation that cemented this materialism, this affirmation of the bodily dimensions of human existence. Indeed, the reality of the human nature of Christ was another thing long since defended against spiritualizing tendencies—that far easier route of claiming that Jesus was like Tobit's angel in human disguise, and that the suffering and death of the Saviour was not real, rather than handling the paradox of the immortal dying.

It was in the same century as Helena took her heap of soil from the Holy Land to Rome that the church finally affirmed that here was no intermediary angel-like being but one who was the very divine self, whose self-emptying enabled his own birth, life, and death as a bodily human being in touch with material things, eating, drinking, weeping, suffering, dying. The incarnation put right at the heart of Christianity an essentially sacramental understanding of everything: the material world pointing beyond itself to the Creator, the human words of Scripture to the Word of God, the human reality of Jesus to his incarnated divinity, ordinary human beings to their transformation from sinners to saints, the physical bread and wine of the eucharist to the Body and Blood of Christ. Christianity's materialism is a necessary corollary of the claims made about Jesus Christ.

So it was also in that same fourth century that changes took place in Christian worship. In the early centuries, surrounded by a religious culture saturated with the stench of bloody sacrifices, the odours of incense, and the material representation of the gods in the forms of idols, Christianity had affirmed that its sacrifices were spiritual, its offerings consisted in fasting and prayers and doing good works. But now, with paganism on the retreat, the inherent materialism of Christianity was able to find its full expression, as sacred sites were identified and pilgrimage took off, as incense and icons were adopted and took on new meanings, as the relics of martyrs and saints became tokens of holiness, and old sacred sites were baptized into Christ—it is an extraordinary experience to walk through the eighteenth-century facade of the cathedral in Sicily's Syracuse to find yourself in a Greek temple!

Much of this was contentious, of course—there were ongoing protests against pictorial representation, against turning Mary into a goddess, anticipations of iconoclasts in the East and in the West Protestants and Puritans. For spiritualizing tendencies are perennial: the salvation of the soul, the immaterial Word of God, the *mere symbol* of the eucharist—these typically Protestant emphases drive out true sacramentalism. Yet that deep *materialist* structure in Christian thinking keeps resurfacing.

Now, though, we live in an offensively materialist society, where this-worldly success and plenty are presumed, sought after, and consumed, where the cult of sport has exposed perfect bodies and encouraged their nurture through physical discipline, where there has been a reaction against bodily inhibitions and sexual repression. So it is perhaps not surprising that materialism is routinely condemned from so many pulpits, and much of current culture is seen as a reaction against Christianity. Yet *Christianity surely is properly regarded as materialist through and through.*

Maybe the point is that, as always, the worst thing is the corruption of the best—*corruptio optimi pessima*, as the old Latin tag has it. If we really knew the sacredness of all the ordinary, material things of our lives perhaps we would treat them differently, value them more highly, want less and waste less—greed and exploitation could hardly survive if we truly treated things as holy. And abuse could hardly survive if we truly treated bodies as holy—the debates triggered by feminist and gay perspectives, not to mention those living with disability, have highlighted again the inalienable necessity of the body, its value and its sacredness.

Like Apphou and the Cappadocians, the L'Arche communities, where people commit to living in community with those who have, often profound, learning disabilities, have perceived beauty in damaged bodies, treasure in vulnerable and fragile persons. In the everydayness of attending to bodily functions, feeding and defecating, washing and dressing, the sanctity of bodies has been acknowledged, in a context in which their transformation is not through some kind of miracle, but through the recognition of God's love and power in mutual need. I thank God that this has become my experience too in daily attention to the needs of Arthur, my profoundly disabled adult son. The ecumenical character of the L'Arche communities often makes eucharistic communion impossible; so washing one another's feet has been developed as a paraliturgy at L'Arche. Yet this is surely no accident—for here bodily dependence on one another is sanctified. In the ordinary everyday business of living together, the divine image is discerned, treasure secreted in the ordinariness of clay pots (2 Cor 4:7) that are breakable, but in their brokenness expose the treasure within.

I guess old Apphou nailed it: the human body is not offensive—for despite weakness, despite dirt, greed, and sex, God has chosen to put God's name right there, in creating humanity, in becoming human; and in breaking bread, the utter materialism of Christianity is signified.

> Jesus said to them, "Very truly I tell you, unless you eat the flesh of the Son of Man and drink his blood, you have no life in you. Whoever eats my flesh and drinks my blood has eternal life, and I will raise them up at the last day. For my flesh is real food and my blood is real drink. Whoever eats my flesh and drinks my blood abide in me, and I in them." (John 6:53–55)

Thanks be to God. Amen.

Comment

At first sight this sermon may seem to have little explicit grounding in Scripture, and yet it implicitly portrays the profoundly countercultural stance that early Christians derived from the biblical accounts of creation and incarnation. The text quoted as its climax underlies the doctrinal history that has been sketched as characteristic of Christian theology. The sermon implies both analogies with the past and distance from it, while offering insights into Scripture and tradition that have a bearing on the liturgical and ecumenical issues faced by the gathered congregation on this specific occasion. So once again the homiletic imperative to circumvent the gap between the Scriptures and the present is paramount, and shapes the way of attending to Scripture through the lens of tradition.

Conclusion

In this chapter I have sought to exemplify the perennial homiletic imperative to read Scripture theologically and to collapse the distance between biblical text and living in the present in a way that energises the faith and action of a particular ecclesial community in specific circumstances at a precise place and time. Both examples demonstrate the potential fruitfulness of bridging the gap between academy and church through preaching; and, as it happens, they both refer to that other commitment I have shared with David Ford, namely to the theological importance of the

L'Arche communities and the insights of Jean Vanier, their founder. I offer these reflections as a mark of my profound gratitude for the way in which David has accompanied me in finding my vocation as a bridge between academy and church, and to mark the fact that he himself has probably done more than most to embody an understanding of the vocation of theology to bring Scripture to bear on all of life and its complexities.

Bibliography

Hardy, Daniel W., and David F. Ford. *Jubilate: Theology in Praise*. London: Darton, Longman & Todd, 1984.

Harvey, Susan Ashbrook. *Scenting Salvation: Ancient Christianity and the Olfactory Imagination*. Berkeley: University of California Press, 2006.

Merrigan, Terrence, editor. *Godhead Here in Hiding*. Leuven: Peeters, 2011.

Young, Frances. "The Materialism of the Christian Tradition." *Methodist Sacramental Fellowship Bulletin* 138 (Epiphany 2011) 4–10.

———. "Naked or Clothed? Eschatology and the Doctrine of Creation." In *The Church, the Afterlife and the Fate of the Soul*, edited by Peter Clarke and Tony Claydon. Woodbridge, UK: Boydell & Brewer, 2009.

———, and David F. Ford. *Meaning and Truth in 2 Corinthians*. London: SPCK, 1987.

9

Wisdom and Rapture

Janet Martin Soskice

Jesus College, University of Cambridge

Theologians are formed by their time, their texts, their community—by pursuing their own researches but also by needs and requests that comes unbidden (though not for that necessarily unwelcome). David Ford and I have been colleagues for many years and, while it would be unwise to think of a Cambridge "school" of theology, there are shared concerns that we take for granted. Let me enumerate a few: first, that theology is a practice and not just a subject matter. One could say being a theologian is a "discipline" somewhat as playing a musical instrument is a discipline. The practice of theology is a continuous training in faith seeking understanding. Secondly we share the conviction that theology done this way should work closely with scriptural texts and Scripture scholars. Thirdly we think that in the study and execution of theology form and content come together. (In these last two convictions I detect the influence of Paul Ricoeur on both of us.)

It follows that there are many theological tasks and practices that an active Christian theologian find herself engaged upon—in David's case (just to cite a few) in prisons, in L'Arche communities, and, pre-eminently with Dan Hardy, Peter Ochs, and many others, in Scriptural Reasoning. Theologians talk to painters and poets, deliver sermons, and do dry but important things like sit on boards, committees, and church commissions.

They raise money for good causes. All of these, even the least romantic, are relevant to the theological task and to one's own formation in the life of the church. Indeed it is a curious aspect of being a lay theologian (and David and I are amongst the first generation of such at Cambridge) that you find you are still called upon by the church. There is a lay vocation to theology and it is also a church vocation.

In this spirit, please find here a sermon. One can say different things in short span, in a sermon, than in a lecture or academic paper. The genre itself means that you are using Scripture and concerned with address. This was a sermon delivered at Westcott House, one of the Anglican theological colleges in Cambridge where David, as Regius Professor, sits on the Board. The first reading of the day was, appropriately enough given David's interests, from the Book of Wisdom and the second from Luke.

The Texts

Wisdom 7:22—8:1

> There is in her a spirit that is intelligent, holy,
> unique, manifold, subtle,
> mobile, clear, unpolluted,
> distinct, invulnerable, loving the good, keen,
> irresistible, beneficent, humane,
> steadfast, sure, free from anxiety,
> all-powerful, overseeing all,
> and penetrating through all spirits
> that are intelligent, pure, and altogether subtle.
> For wisdom is more mobile than any motion;
> because of her pureness she pervades and penetrates all things.
> For she is a breath of the power of God,
> and a pure emanation of the glory of the Almighty;
> therefore nothing defiled gains entrance into her.
> For she is a reflection of eternal light,
> a spotless mirror of the working of God,
> and an image of his goodness.
> Although she is but one, she can do all things,
> and while remaining in herself, she renews all things;
> in every generation she passes into holy souls
> and makes them friends of God, and prophets;
> for God loves nothing so much as the person who lives with wisdom.
> She is more beautiful than the sun,

and excels every constellation of the stars.
Compared with the light she is found to be superior,
for it is succeeded by the night,
but against wisdom evil does not prevail.

She reaches mightily from one end of the earth to the other,
and she orders all things well.

Luke 17:20–29

Once Jesus was asked by the Pharisees when the kingdom of God was coming, and he answered, "The kingdom of God is not coming with things that can be observed; nor will they say, 'Look, here it is!' or 'There it is!' For, in fact, the kingdom of God is among you."

Then he said to the disciples, "The days are coming when you will long to see one of the days of the Son of Man, and you will not see it. They will say to you, 'Look there!' or 'Look here!' Do not go, do not set off in pursuit. For as the lightning flashes and lights up the sky from one side to the other, so will the Son of Man be in his day. But first he must endure much suffering and be rejected by this generation. Just as it was in the days of Noah, so too it will be in the days of the Son of Man. They were eating and drinking, and marrying and being given in marriage, until the day Noah entered the ark, and the flood came and destroyed all of them. Likewise, just as it was in the days of Lot: they were eating and drinking, buying and selling, planting and building, but on the day that Lot left Sodom, it rained fire and sulphur from heaven and destroyed all of them."

The Sermon

"The kingdom of God is not coming with things that can be observed." This is the reply Jesus makes to the Pharisees who ask when the kingdom of God is coming. You will not be able to say, he tells them, "'Look, here it is!' or 'There it is!' For look, the kingdom of God is among you" (Luke 17:21).

Jesus goes on to say, this time to his disciples, that the days are coming when you will long to see the days of the Son of Man *and you will not see it.* "For as the lightning flashes and lights up the sky from one side to the other, so will the Son of Man be in his day." It will be like the time of Noah and the flood, or Lot and Sodom—wholly encompassing yet wholly unanticipated. This is a hard saying. To a degree it is in tension with what he has just said to the Pharisees: when speaking to his disciples Jesus seems to be looking forward to some "day," some future described in apocalyptic terms, whereas to the Pharisees, who apparently asked after just such a future event, he says that "the kingdom of God is among you." The kingdom of God is already here but the Pharisees cannot see it, and nor yet, it seems, do Jesus' own disciples whom he must caution not to look here, run there.

The metaphor Jesus uses suggest that this "day" will break out like a flash of lightning in the night, illuminating everything for a fraction of a second, before the darkness returns again. This is not consoling. We would like to find, if not the whole kingdom, at least solid and reliable evidence of it; for example, in works of charity—surely the kingdom of God is present in the work of Mother Teresa's sisters or in a congregation's work with refugees and asylum seekers? The kingdom of God must be amongst us in some palpable, visible ways—after all are we not building it?

Yet Luke's text seems to caution us against claiming too much. Or perhaps, its intimation of a sudden, unbiddable beauty and light, it consoles us in our weary perplexity as to when or even whether the kingdom of heaven is to be found.

The Old Testament reading of Solomon's extended praise for Wisdom follows from his account in Wisdom 6 of his early desire to seek Wisdom and, it seems, his success in finding it. Not only did God grant him understanding of the variety of plants and of the medical properties of roots, but also of the structure of the world, the beginning, end, and middle of times. Now I understand, he concludes immodestly, *everything* "for wisdom, the fashioner of all things, taught me" (Wis 7:21).

In the New Testament, notably in the Gospel of John but also in Paul, Christ is the true power and wisdom of God (1 Cor 1:24). It is Christ who, in John's Prologue, is the Word through whom all was made, who was in *the beginning* with God—the very bright utterer of creation. This same light was "the world came into being through him; yet the world did not know him. John says, "we have seen his glory" (John 1).

Word, Wisdom, Glory—all titles for the divine made manifest in the Apocryphal books, texts that were written at a time of persecution and of growing messianic expectations amongst the Jews. These Jewish divine names—Word, Wisdom, Glory—will also be applied in the New Testament to Jesus as the Christ.

There is a debate about the referent (or referents) for these names in the literature of Second Temple Judaism. Are they just a way to speak of God's acts? Are they names of angelic messengers or, more controversially, is there a sense in which the Jews are not straightforwardly monotheistic during this period? Are they demigods or daemons? I tend to be persuaded by Richard Bauckham's argument that these are not residues of polytheism but privileged titles for the one God, because all involve the power of creating, and this only God (and not angels or emissaries) can do.[1]

Wisdom is God's very agency in creating. And creating is not something that happened a long time ago but what is happening now, for the world is not free-standing but has, at every instant, its being as a gift from God. If God did not hold the whole world in being it would not, even for a microsecond, "be." So creation is now, and Wisdom is now, pervading all things and as Solomon says—"intelligent, holy, unique, manifold, subtle, mobile, incisive, unsullied, lucid, . . .beneficent, friendly, . . . all-surveying . . ." (Wis 7:22–23).

But how do we "see" Wisdom, this "Light" that John says is the true light coming into the world and which is the light through which all things were made? Light is everywhere but can only be seen by us when it hits something, a surface. Then we see a pale yellow rose or the dark glistening of a wet street in moonlight. Light needs to be captured. And here I must draw on an example I heard from Stephen Ortiger, OSB.[2] Father Ortiger pointed out that the early church, especially in the East, honoured Christ in its liturgy as the Wisdom of the Father but had this problem: how do you represent Christ as Wisdom in art and iconography? Father Ortiger pointed out that the architects of Justinian's basilica in Constantinople achieved a brilliant resolution in making the interior of the *Hagia Sophia* itself the icon. The building is constructed to be shot through with light, glancing and crossing in continuously changing bands and confluences—even the dark, Father Ortiger pointed out, describes the light—manifest, subtle, mobile, penetrating.

This is Christ, the Wisdom of God; this is the Light of creation, which is around us all the time yet hard to see, sometimes only glimpsed as when one flash of lightening illumines the sky from east to west. Might it be that the kingdom of God is there in place but we cannot see it?

1. See Bauckham, *Jesus and the God of Israel.*

2. Sermon delivered on the occasion of a wedding on 1 November 2011, in Cambridge.

Let's return to Luke and to a later mention of the kingdom in his Gospel, in chapter 22, a text sometimes used for the Feast of Christ the King. Jesus is on the cross between two thieves and over him is the mocking inscription, "This is the King of the Jews." One thief, famously, taunts Jesus and is rebuked by the other—"we are paying for what we did. But this man has done nothing wrong." And then, to the stricken Jesus, "Jesus, remember me when you come into your kingdom." "Indeed, I promise you' says Jesus, "today you will be with me in Paradise" (Luke 22:42–43).

This is an astonishing tableau when we think of its place in a Gospel that has been so much to do with following and discipleship, and with hopes for the coming kingdom of God. These all now seem to have evaporated. Jesus has been abandoned by his disciples and denied by Peter. In Luke's Gospel we are told that his friends stand, not at the foot of the cross but "at a distance." With friends keeping their distance it is left to a robber, a criminal, to console Jesus. We have no reason to believe this thief was, or ever had been, a follower of Jesus. He does not address Jesus as "Lord" but by name, saying "Jesus, remember me when you come into your kingdom." Yet it is this man, not the disciples who have toiled and troubled, who is told "today you will be with me in Paradise."

Why, we may ask, did the thief say to Jesus "remember me when you come into your kingdom"? Did he have more faith than the disciples, more than Peter? How much did he even know about Jesus, or believe? What if, as the text suggests, he simply thought Jesus was innocent and a good man—maybe deluded but a good man nonetheless?

What if the thief, from sheer human kindness, is *humouring* Jesus who he sees to be a good man dying alone with expectations dashed?[3] But Luke is ambivalent. He also suggests faith—perhaps just a lightning flash of hope against hope—that glancing illumination which for a fraction of a second lights the whole sky and compels the thought "what if it were true?" What if this man is the king of the Jews? It is a moment of the presence of the kingdom which Jesus warns his disciples and the Pharisees not to seek on the scaffoldings of piety. It is already among us, disguised by our preoccupations. It comes against expectations—now in the words of one ruined man to another—"today you will be with me in paradise"—and existence is lit up from end to end.

What if, even for a second, we were to glimpse of the kingdom of God? What if, for the thief, even a fingernail of faith was enough to glimpse

3. It is surprising that this cry to Jesus comes from a ruined fragment of the angry, preoccupied secular world.

the bounty of divine love, that Wisdom by which all is made? That would be enough to say truly "the kingdom of God is among us," enough for us to pursue those acts of mercy that bring it forward. It would be then not we who had captured the Light, but the Light who had captured us.

Bibliography

Bauckham, Richard. *Jesus and the God of Israel.* Milton Keynes, UK: Paternoster, 2008.

PART THREE

In and For the Church

10

Beyond "Belief"

Liturgy and the Cognitive Apprehension of God

Sarah Coakley

University of Cambridge

David Ford's theology has been characterized from an early point in his career by an impressive concern to integrate theology and praise—or rather, to articulate a theology *out of* praise and worship.[1] In more recent years, this interest has transmuted into his commitment to "Scriptural Reasoning" as a means of bringing Judaism, Christianity, and Islam into a genuinely shared quest for God, a means again founded in worship and disciplined attention, and yet in no way prescinding from the most cherished commitments of each tradition.[2] In this essay I offer my sincere *Gratulieren* to David Ford for his theological insights into the nature of worship by pressing a *philosophical* issue that arises when one seeks to parse the truth-significance of praise in its liturgical context. It might seem an odd question, but I shall nonetheless ask it at the outset: how, if at all, can liturgy be "true?" In order to begin to answer this, I start with a memorable little *vignette*.

1. See Ford and Hardy, *Living in Praise*.
2. See especially Ford and Pecknold, *The Promise of Scriptural Reasoning*.

Introduction: How Can Liturgy be "True?"

The Dominican Fergus Kerr records at one point the story of a precocious four-year-old boy, who commented thus after attending a solemn Christian liturgy that had greatly impressed him: "I know why churches are true," he said to his father. "It is because the people in them like singing and walking about in patterns."[3]

Now admittedly this particular child was the son of the British sociologist of religion, David Martin, and had doubtless absorbed more than just musical sensitivity from the ambience of his family and from their Anglo-Catholic eucharistic worship. But the child's intuition is striking, suggestive, and yet *prima facie* more than a little puzzling. The analytic philosopher might well baulk immediately at his comment; for does it not seem peculiar that a liturgy *per se* ("church," in the child's parlance) might—precisely through its music, its poetic hymnody, and its intentional bodily comportments (and not, at least according to this child's account, very obviously through any propositional content)—deliver, and even guarantee, "*truth*"? Is not this a category mistake? Is it not, literally, "beyond belief?"

Such an apparently weird suggestion, one might think, should come up more naturally in the world of the anthropologist (where, after all, "weird" things are precisely what are studied!) than in that of the philosopher. It reminds us, for instance, of Catherine Bell's insistence—building creatively on Bourdieu's understanding of "practice"—that ritual is *not* an optional frill that accompanies a rational commitment founded somewhere else (and previously), but is rather the irreducible purveying of such a commitment.[4] Or again, it recalls Talal Asad's memorable comment that contemporary secularized Northern Europeans lack faith not as a result of a failure in religious education, but on account of "untaught bodies."[5] But what can the *philosophy of religion* do with the idea that liturgy does not merely rehearse, or inculcate, the propositional beliefs of Christian faith that may have already been acknowledged rationally sometime previously, but that liturgy in and of itself purveys a particular kind of "truth" not necessarily limited to the propositional? It is the purpose of this chapter to muse speculatively on this puzzle and on its accompanying epistemological implications.

3. Kerr, *Theology*, 198, citing Martin, *Tracts*, 179.
4. Bell, *Ritual*, especially 1–12, 182–96; see Bourdieu, *Outline*.
5. Asad, "Remarks," 48.

To undertake this task, I am going to draw on three strands of thought that may not seem obviously to fit together. It will be my task to show that they can do so, and indeed that their braided force will together be stronger than their individual impact. The first strand relates to the sophisticated discussion of the category of "religious experience," and its putative veridical force, that developed within analytic philosophy of religion in the last part of the twentieth century. Here I shall utilize William P. Alston's *Perceiving God*, already established as a classic within this discussion, and both criticize and stretch its arguments for my own purposes. By setting Alston up as my straw man, I shall at the same time attempt to rescue and extend one aspect of his thinking—that of "doxastic practice"—for my own purposes. Secondly, I shall turn to some rich insights from recent *feminist* epistemology to bolster the force of those considerations I have taken forward from Alston. (This second move may also strike the reader as odd: surely secular feminist philosophy and analytic philosophy of religion are hardly compatible bedfellows? Yet I hope to be able to demonstrate that the interests of the former can well assist the extension of arguments of the latter towards a positive consideration of the veridical force of *embodied* religious practice.) Thirdly, and finally, I shall refer the discussion as developed so far to a rich, but neglected, strand of thought in patristic writing about the so-called spiritual senses. If I am right, this tradition may help us to develop a way of thinking about the relation of liturgical sense experience and noetic response to the question of theological "truth" in a way that fits none of the current analytic accounts of cognition with exactitude. It nonetheless holds promise for an alternative that could explain how liturgy purveys theological truth in a distinctive and irreducible way. If I am right, then well-conducted liturgy gives us a particular kind of access to "truth" that only liturgy can supply; and moreover, it gives us that access because a particular epistemic apparatus and form of cognition is being trained precisely in the performance of liturgy itself.

But before I go any further I need to rehearse a few important distinctions. I have so far been wielding the language of "liturgy" and "truth" (not to speak of their relation) with a certain carelessness. But it could be that liturgy and truth are related to one another in a number of different possible ways, and that "truth" is then differently construed according to the relevant scenario. One possibility, for instance, is that ordinary propositional truth *is* at stake after all (as self-evidently, e.g., in the recitation of the propositions of the Nicene Creed at the Mass), but that the bodily movements and accompanying affective responses of the liturgy enable those truths to be personally assimilated or internalized in ways that mere noetic assent could not achieve.[6] Or, secondly, it could be that liturgy actually *delivers* some theological truths in a particular and distinctive way, through performative utterances that are unique to its undertakings, and thus irreducible (e.g., "This is my body"; or, "I pronounce you man and wife").[7] Or, thirdly, it could in principle also be that liturgy, in virtue of certain repetitive belief-forming practices, could actually mount some kind of "justification" thereby for beliefs. Or, finally, and more subtly (as I was hinting just now), it could in addition be that the deeper "truth" at stake in the liturgy is not propositional at all, but "truth" in the particular sense intended by Christ when he said, according to John's Gospel, that *he* was himself "the way, the truth, and the life" (John 14:6). The intersection of liturgy and "truth" would then consist in the liturgy's capacity to train one's sensibility to the presence of Christ in the same liturgy, and to knit one more deeply into his "true body" through sacramental ingestion, attention to his Word, and the sharing of his communal love in the Spirit. Truth acquisition in this last case would involve something akin to knowledge-by-acquaintance or knowledge-by-relationship; but given that classic Christianity has found no philosophical oddity in insisting that God *is* truth, this is an option that should not be eschewed at the outset. Note too that these four possibilities are not, as far as I can see, mutually exclusive; and that the last, if defensible, could supply a certain undergirding incubus for the others.[8]

But let us now see how far into this nexus of possibilities Alston's existing epistemological project can take us. His is a project certainly not without immense philosophical sophistication.

Perceiving God: "Doxastic Practices" and the Senses

Alston's *Perceiving God*, which has already, and justly, achieved the status of a classic, seems to me to have two basic prongs to its epistemological

6. A line of thought somewhat parallel to this first possibility has been explored illuminatingly in Wynn, *Emotional Experience*.

7. See the well-known discussion by J. L. Austin of such "illocutionary" speech acts in *How to Do Things*. Austin's own insistence that such performatives cannot be "true" or "false," but rather merely "felicitious" or "infelicitous," has remained controversial.

8. Of course, the precise relationship of such truth-*qua*-divinity to propositional truth would then need to be clarified. I come back to this matter briefly at the close of this chapter.

argument that are somewhat problematically related. The first is the prong that sets out to do a complete end run around Kant (and indeed the entire hermeneutical tradition that later succeeded him), and insist on the possibility of *direct* and "unmediated" perceptions of God, unbesmirched by any cultural *addita*. The success of this first prong's strategy has always seemed to me dubious, and this for several reasons. First, it has to rely on assertion, rather than empirical demonstration, to insist that certain epistemic moments abscind from all linguistic and hermeneutical shaping (let alone ritualized performance).[9] Second, it implicitly valorizes thereby a Jamesian reading of "religious experience," which is sporadic, elevated, and supposedly self-authenticating. Yet this sort of reading (let us call it the "zapping" factor) actually fits very ill with the patient, repetitive, even humdrum practices of liturgy, prayer, and service with which most Christian lives are taken up. Further, the interpretation Alston gives here of the great Christian mystics (such as Teresa of Ávila and John of the Cross) to support his "zapping" interest, has to distort their intentions by excerpting supposedly "unitive" moments from their wider ascetical narrative of progression. Thirdly, Alston himself has to admit that in any case high-point experiences such as he understands to constitute "Mystical Perception" (MP) are not the lot of all. Finally, and more gravely, there is a danger in Alston's appeal to a "Theory of Appearing" that God will be treated as another, albeit unusual, item in the universe so to be "perceived," rather than appropriately conceived as the *sui generis* Creator and means *of* all perceptions. Let us then, for the meantime, leave this prong of the argument to one side: it may be that Alston's "Theory of Appearing" is an unnecessary distraction from the epistemic project enshrined in *liturgical* practice that I am explicating here.

The second prong of Alston's book, however, is much more interesting for our current purposes. It is one influenced—by Alston's own admission—by Wittgenstein's understanding of a "form of life," and by Reid's account of necessary "credulity"; and it is undergirded, in Alston's case, by a trenchant appeal to "reliabilism." Here, the notion of a "doxastic practice" is introduced to emphasize the epistemic importance of *repeated* acts of sensory cognition. It is argued that sensory experience involves both "input" and "output," with a consistency of success in accurate perception that pragmatically "justifies" our reliance on the deliverances of sense experience, all "defeaters" notwithstanding. (Of course, if I have a high temperature, a brain tumour, or have just consumed half a bottle of

9. Alston, *Perceiving God*, 37.

Scotch at speed, I should be wary of such reliance.) The circularity here is undeniable, but not *vicious*; I have flouted no epistemic duties in my "justified" belief that, under normal circumstances, my senses give me accurate information about the world.[10]

For Alston, of course, the argument then leads to a conjoining of the two prongs so described. If a non-vicious circularity is found fruitful, indeed fully reliable, in the case of our normal sense perceptions, what is to prevent an analogous argument being mounted for "justified belief" in what is delivered to us by "Mystical Perception" (MP)? Here (putatively) there is also a form of "input" and "output "; here there is an outside source of information (in this case, God) to be "perceived "; and here, too, there are "doxastic practices" by means of which such reliable information is processed.

What, however, if we lay aside the particular difficulties of Alston's "Theory of Appearing" as applied to putatively *unmediated* perceptions of God (and enshrined in the first prong of his argument), and instead do more creative work than he himself does with the notion of a "doxastic practice"?[11] For it is surely a disappointment that Alston, in *Perceiving God*, does nothing much to extend his use of this idea beyond the regular "input" and "output" of the five senses (and especially of sight); whereas the Wittgensteinian (and Reidian) background to what he proposes by way of "*socially mediated*" practices surely promises much more than Alston himself develops. One might be forgiven for coming away from his text with a picture of *individuals* (or rather, individual philosophers!) nervously checking the consistency and reliability of their visual "input" and "output" in relation to a web of established social networks and

10. The sense of "justification" at stake here is, of course, quite a weak one—as is pointed out by a number of critics, including Norman Kretzmann in "Mystical Perception," who distinguishes between forms of justification that would convince an atheistical outsider, and those that almost certainly would not (including Alston's essayed form). Nonetheless, Alston's clarification of the non-vicious nature of the circularity in such epistemic appeals rules out hostile and *immediate* rejections of the veracity of such perceptual claims. For a nuanced account of varieties of justification in current discussion in analytic epistemology, see Swinburne, *Epistemic Justification*, in which the notion of "diachronic" justification is added to take account of justification that is arrived at over time, in contrast to the more commonly discussed "synchronic" justification.

11. I have recently attempted an investigation along these lines in more detail than I pursue here in my long essay "Dark Contemplation and Epistemic Transformation." There, rather than examining the complexity of liturgical performance as such, I look at contemplation as a ramified "doxastic practice" and indicate how Alston's project could be creatively stretched to take account of it.

linguistically formed relations, and then, with a sigh of relief, pronouncing themselves "justified" in their belief that their perceptions are indeed "reliable"; and Alston even criticizes Wittgenstein for attempting to defuse this question.[12] Yet it is surely the intended impact of the approach outlined by Reid to declare an amnesty on such scepticism: a form of epistemic "credulity" is justly *prior* (and not just logically prior, but chronologically prior in our initial coming to terms with the furniture of the world) to the raising of such anxieties about deception. What, then, if we were to extend the notion of "doxastic practices" well beyond those of ordinary sense perception (Alston's SP), and well beyond such neurotic checkings for initial sensory "reliability," to include such richly coded social undertakings as the bodily performances of liturgy (let us call these LP: "Liturgical Practices")? Could we claim that such performances, too, were justifyingly truth-conducive, and if so, in what ways?

A *detailed* account of how a liturgy could be thought of as a "doxastic practice" (or rather, several such practices) would, to be sure, require some considerable development of Alston's argument. It is true that Alston does sketch, briefly, some ways in which ramified "practices" involve a whole range of overlapping or "mutual involvement" of practices of different sorts: practices are "irreducibly plural," he admits.[13] The attempt to wrench them all into one underlying principle of justificatory efficacy is almost certainly doomed to failure: "Ultimate diversity is a fact of our epistemic life, however humbling this may be for our pride as theoreticians."[14] Liturgy too, it would seem, implicitly involves a full range of epistemological "practices" already sketched out by Alston: sense experience, introspection, memory, inference, evaluation, etc. But there is something else that needs to be caught here. It is the *primary* modelling of Alston's argument on the case of "ordinary" sense perception that implicitly restricts his approach and, when applied analogously to "perceiving God," leads to a strangely naïve failure to account for the *difference* between perceiving (say) a mango in a marketplace, and "perceiving" the source and cause of my very existence (God). Further, the specific, bodily ways in which Christians seek to "perceive" God through liturgy involve a range of ramified practices (including hymnody, or "walking in patterns," to revert to our opening cases) that are not merely straightforward analogues of "perception" in "immediate" response to God, but complex means of *training* the mind

12. Alston, *Perceiving God*, 154–55.

13. Ibid., 162.

14. Ibid., 163.

and senses, over time, in order to come into a right relation with God. As Nicholas Wolterstorff has recently argued, it is these developmental, and historically located, features of our epistemic negotiations that have been so strangely ignored in most analytic philosophy of religion to date. As Wolterstorff puts it, "We human beings are all hard-wired for belief; ... That's the beginning of the matter. ... [But it] cannot be the end of the matter. ... New dispositions emerge as the result of experiences of certain sorts ... [and m]uch of our programming is social, with the consequence that tradition becomes part of our belief-forming self."[15]

How, then, can such developmental, social, and tradition-based aspects of *liturgical* "cognition" be philosophically accounted for? And what, more fundamentally, is the ultimate matrix for such development in the first place? It is here that a brief, albeit surprising, excursus into feminist epistemology may greatly help our argument forward.

Feminist Epistemology and Knowledge by Relationship

The underlying problem seems to be that secular analytic epistemology has been inordinately invested in giving an account of the successful perception and re-identification of "medium-sized dry goods" over other forms of epistemic negotiation. The prioritizing of such a task then leads to a sidelining of other forms of "knowing," and a tendency to presume that "perceiving God" ought to have similar, or at least analogous, characteristics. But why should we take *this* form of knowing to be primary and basic? The important work of the Canadian feminist philosopher Lorraine Code may help here.[16] Code's sophisticated contribution to feminist epistemology questions the normative and paradigmatic status given in Anglo-American analytic epistemology to what she calls "perception at a distance" (that is, the conditions for the successful recognition of hard objects at a distance of five paces or so). Privileging *this* sort of knowledge, and the necessary and sufficient conditions for it, says Code, allows exponents to ignore both the "identity, circumstances, and conditionedness of the knower"[17] and the significance of the personal, familial, and communal interactions that enable and sustain such perception in the first place. Her point here is worthy of extended quotation:

15. Wolterstorff, "Historicizing," 127.

16. Code, "Subjectivity"; and, in more detail, in Code, *What Can She Know?*

17. Code, "Subjectivity," 15.

> If epistemologists require paradigms or other less formal exemplary knowledge claims, knowing other people in personal relationships is at least as worthy a contender as knowledge of everyday objects. Developmentally, learning what she or he can expect of other people is one of the first and most essential kinds of knowledge a child acquires. She or he learns to respond *cognitively* to the people who are a vital part of and provide access to her or his environment *long before* she or he can recognize the simplest physical objects. Other people are the point of origin of a child's entry into the material/physical environment both in providing or inhibiting access to that environment—in *making* it—and in fostering entry into the language with which children learn to name. Their initial induction into language generates a framework of presuppositions that prompts children, from the earliest stages, to construct their environments variously, according to the quality of their affective, intersubjective locations. . . . It is tempting to conclude that theorists of knowledge must either be childless or so disengaged from the rearing of children as to have minimal developmental awareness. Participators in childraising could not easily ignore the primacy of knowing and being known by other people in cognitive development, nor could they denigrate the role such knowledge plays throughout an epistemic history.[18]

Code's insistence that we take the identity of the embodied knower (S) "into account" when we consider the conditions of "S knowing P" is, we note, in general accordance with the line opened up by Alston's occasional admissions about the social situatedness of all religious knowing. It is certainly in line with Reid's interest in primary childhood "credulity"—though Alston does little to explore that strand in Reid's thought.[19] Code's further explication of the significance of personal relationships as a matrix for any "knowing that" is, I submit, of vast potential significance (though she, as a secular writer, does not know it) for philosophical reflection on knowing *God*. For it is in our first negotiations of sensual life (at the breast, in the arms of the primary caretaker), that we forge the potential for all cognitive developments that will occur later; without

18. Ibid., 32–33.

19. It is, of course, Wolterstorff who has been the most ardent promoter in recent years of Reid's alternative to a Lockean epistemological framework; see his *Thomas Reid*. It is not insignificant that Reid is the philosopher of modernity who gives most attention to the positive importance of childhood "trust" in human learning of how to negotiate the world.

primary relationships, without affective mobilization in the recognition of familiar faces, we will never even progress to the successful naming and negotiation of "medium-sized dry goods." All the more important, then, is the analogue here with "knowing God": whereas Alston often slips into talk about "perceiving God" in individualistic and merely *informational* terms, Code's insights about childhood psychology and epistemology suggest how the learned, sensual, and social responses of the liturgy might be the parallel, and indispensable, modes of coming to "know" the divine in some direct sense *different* from Alston's "perceiving" of God. For is not "knowing *God*"—"perceiving *God*"—more naturally analogous to encountering and loving and knowing a *person* (Christ, God incarnate) than it is to experiencing a moment devoid of hermeneutical content, or to stubbing one's toe on a hard object, or to noticing a novel item floating in the room? Yet from one's reading of the standard literature of analytic philosophy of religion on the veridical force of "religious experience" one would not always realize that.[20]

It is perhaps for that reason that Nicholas Wolterstorff has on occasion, though with the greatest affection and respect, characterized Alston's project as a "paraplegic" epistemology![21] Its overriding concern for the "justified true belief" tradition in epistemology, along with its desire for passively received "zappings" which would signal a nakedly "direct," but sporadic, perception of the divine, make it curiously blind to the possibility of a more fundamental, and ongoing, "knowledge" by acquaintance, founded in trust and sustained by repeated acts of adoration and worship.

But this now brings me to the third strand in my argument.

The "Spiritual Senses" Tradition of Epistemology

Let us suppose, then, that we have identified a possibly fruitful line of investigation for establishing how liturgy "is true" (i.e., it irreducibly conveys, announces, and even "justifies" certain theological truths *along with, and in the light of,* a primary relational access to intimacy with God-in-Christ). LP involves a subtle and complex set of "doxastic practices," is socially mediated, bodily enacted, sensually attuned, seeks ultimately to "know Christ," and commits no epistemic impropriety by *assuming*, until

20. I explore these points in more detail in relation to the standard analytic literature on "religious experience" in my "Dark Contemplation and Epistemic Transformation."

21. This in the context of a research seminar based at Calvin College on "Philosophy and Liturgy," 2006–2008, of which I was a co-member.

it is proven otherwise, that the social practices of the liturgy do give cognitive access to such personal knowledge.

But we have one more major and pressing question to answer to give this proposal philosophical "bite," and it is this: what *sort* of epistemological apparatus is involved in this process of liturgical response and growth in intimacy with Christ? Clearly the traditional mental faculties (intellect, will, memory) are actively involved in liturgical performance, and the intellect's significance in relation to propositional theological truth is self-evident. But what of the distinctly sensual dimensions of liturgy—do these not play some vital part in the growth in responsiveness to Christ's relational presence in intimacy, such as we have discussed? And do they not in some sense in turn inform our intellectual and affective responses? It is here that the so-called spiritual senses tradition in Christianity provides such an intriguing epistemological option, worthy now in my view of contemporary review and reconsideration.

It was Origen, in the third century, who was the first Christian author to argue that the epistemic and spiritual goal of the Christian life was to develop, over time, a sensual apparatus parallel to, but different from, the gross physical senses, and attuned finally to union with Christ. The development of these "spiritual senses," as he occasionally calls them, is for Origen a manifestation of the *mature* life "in the Spirit" (at the élite level of the contemplative, or *enoptic*), so that one can speak of an "inner" life of sense that is ultimately safely *disjoined* from the snares of physical and material sensuality. Indeed it has become subject to a unified and internal *noetic* focus that alone is destined to be embraced by the divine Logos in union. How, then, are the physical and spiritual senses *related* for Origen? This is an admittedly problematic exegetical question in Origen's case.[22] For there are some texts on the topic (mainly when Origen is addressing those of less spiritual maturity) when he enunciates what seems to be a deeply problematic "Platonic" disjunction between the two sorts of sense—between the material realm of the physical senses, on the one hand, and the spiritual realm where such "spiritual sensuality" can take place, on the other. (And this bespeaks an occasional parallel problem in Origen's

22. The best recent account of this exegetical problem is by McInroy, "Origen of Alexandria," which gives the lie to various previous, theologically massaged, accounts of the matter. Amongst those must be counted my own earlier assessment of Origen on this theme, "Resurrection and the 'Spiritual Senses,'" in which I overlooked Origen's various anticipations of Gregory of Nyssa's later transformational account of the physical/spiritual senses. See, more recently, "Gregory of Nyssa," nn. 25 and 26, 43, for my new account of the relation of Origen and Nyssen on this theme.

christological teaching about whether our material bodies are, after all, the locus of final redemption.) But there are also other texts and contexts, notably, in some portions of the *Commentary on the Song of Songs*, in which Origen begins to approach a position more robustly announced later by the fourth-century monk-bishop Gregory of Nyssa. Here the possibility of the training and purification of the physical senses is adumbrated, such that the gross physical body may itself be transformed, over time, into a "spiritual" entity. But it is hard to say that this is a consistently enunciated position in Origen's *oeuvre*.

In contrast, Gregory of Nyssa can, in his own *Commentary on the Song of Songs*, even talk, as Origen would never have done, of writing his commentary "*for* the fleshly minded"; for he sees the erotic metaphors of the *Song* as precisely those that will draw the attention of those seeking Christ and so lead them into the processes of sensual—and then also noetic—transformation.[23]

It has been pointed out recently, in fascinating complementary studies on spiritual sight and smell in the fourth and fifth centuries, that the period after the Constantinian settlement marked a rich set of developments in reflection on this "spiritual sense."[24] In part this arose from the new perception that the effects of incarnation now infiltrated the very fabric of Roman and Byzantine political and liturgical life. It was a time of many adult conversions, and excitement over being prepared for baptism at the Easter vigil. It was a time, then, when catechists such as Ambrose, Cyril of Jerusalem, and Theodore of Mopsuestia, were writing treatises for converts about what, sensually and spiritually, to expect as they moved through baptism into first communion and took Christ for the first time into their hands in the form of bread and wine. And it is important to understand, as Susan Harvey stresses, that even as extreme forms of asceticism arose within early monasticism—which was in part, of course, a reaction to the same imperial settlement with Christianity—bodily asceticism was increasingly compensated for by a lusher and more sensuous liturgy, especially in the Greek East.[25] Thus the ascetic work on the body could involve extreme deprivations at one level, but simultaneous heightened sensual retraining in the liturgical context.

As the priest's prayer before the Gospel, and some of the post-communion thanksgiving prayers in the Liturgy of Saint John Chrysostom, put

23. Coakley, "Resurrection," 136–40; Coakley, "Gregory," 42–43, 52–54.

24. Frank, "'Taste and See'"; Harvey, *Scenting*.

25. Harvey, *Scenting*, 5.

it explicitly (drawing on the tradition founded by Origen and Gregory): "Make the pure light of your divine knowledge shine in our hearts and open the eyes of our mind to understand the message of your Gospel." Or again, from Symeon the Translator, "Enlighten the fivefold simpleness of my senses." Or again, in a prayer addressed to the Most Holy Mother of God: "O you who gave birth to the true Light, enlighten the spiritual eyes of my heart, . . . give me compunction and contrition in my heart, humility in my ideas, and release from the imprisonment of my thoughts."[26]

Such strands in the liturgy are congruent with what I have argued, in my recent rereading of Gregory of Nyssa's doctrine of the spiritual senses, he himself took the doctrine to mean. For in his intriguing treatise "On the Soul and the Resurrection" Gregory actually makes explicit the possibility of *training* the gross physical senses so that they may come to anticipate something of the capacities of the resurrection body, and so not only sense Christ himself, but actually sense *as* he senses: "by the very operation of our senses," says Macrina, Gregory's sister and mentor in the dialogue, "we are led to conceive of that reality and intelligence which surpasses the senses."[27] It is this very claim of Nyssen's to which I want now to challenge analytic philosophy of religion to give its serious epistemological consideration. This, note, is no mere "seeing-as," as in the famous Wittgensteinian duck-rabbit example; instead it is the idea of a diachronic intensification and integration of the faculties and senses in order to respond appropriately and fittingly to the truth which is God. One might, in fact, see it an enriched and ramified account of epistemic "proper functioning": these are the conditions of transformed human response under which Christ makes us his own.

Let me now sum up: why is this tradition of "spiritual senses" of interest for one seeking an account of the truth claims of LP? Well, it seems to me to provide the perfect explication of the complex cognitive state of the knowing subject who engages, over time, in LP. That is, the cognitive functioning of such a knowing subject is not simply a "given"—a flat or universal mental *receptiveness* such as we find in Alston's MP. Nor is it a mere propositional consent with a nice aesthetic backdrop provided. Rather, what is distinctive to liturgical "knowing," I have argued, is the way that bodily movement, sensual acuity, affective longing, and noetic or intellectual response, are intricately entwined and mutually implicated in what is occurring, and indeed are being trained over time to intensify

26. *Divine Liturgy*, 15, 55, 56.

27. Gregory, *Soul*, 34. See Coakley, "Gregory," 45–52.

and deepen their capacity for response to the risen Christ. In an important sense, then, the epistemic apparatus of the liturgical subject is always *in via*; but there is a goal, and the goal is nothing less than divine truth itself.

What this line of approach suggests, then, is a liturgically conveyed form of the delivery of theological truth that involves, as a vital part of its practice (LP), a project of the refinement and purgation of "sensuality," and the integration of that evolving "spiritual" sensuality with an (enlarged) intellectual and affective response to the presence and power of Christ. Liturgy is, therefore, on this view *not* an "affective" *complement* to intellectual reflection, but rather the means of a full integration of all aspects of embodied selfhood into the life of Christ.

Clearly these are large and incautious claims to entertain afresh today. They are indeed to some extent "beyond [merely propositional] belief." They involve, amongst other endeavours, "singing hymns" and "walking in patterns," as we reflected on at the outset. And for analytic philosophy of religion to take on these suggestions again today, and give them a new cogency, would certainly involve philosophical boldness and innovation such as I have only hinted at preliminarily here.[28] But as John Chrysostom put it in the patristic era, it is all a matter of making "the unseen visible from the seen,"[29] a matter of training the bodily senses in attunement with Christ's presence. In the wonderful words of Cyril of Jerusalem on the physical reception of the eucharist, "Do not have your wrists extended or your fingers spread, but making your left hand a throne for the right, for it is about to receive a King, and cupping your palm, receive the body of Christ."[30] If analytic philosophy is to make sense of liturgy, to explicate its *ratio* as Nicholas Wolterstorff likes to put it, I suspect it must first acknowledge its own past rational limitations and past sins, and so cup its own empty palm to receive what only Christ can give.

Bibliography

Alston, William P. *Perceiving God*. Ithaca: Cornell University Press, 1991.

Asad, Talal. "Remarks on the Anthropology of the Body." In *Religion and the Body*, edited by Sarah Coakley, 42–52. Cambridge: Cambridge University Press, 1997.

Austin, J. L. *How to Do Things with Words*. Oxford: Clarendon, 1962.

28. Amongst other things it would involve giving new cogency to the very idea that God can in Godself *be* truth, as origin and cause of all propositional truths. For a new account of this neglected theme in Aquinas, see Wood, "Thomas Aquinas."

29. Frank, "'Taste and See,'" 635.

30. Ibid., 629.

Bell, Catherine. *Ritual Theory, Ritual Practice*. New York: Oxford University Press, 1992.

Bourdieu, Pierre. *Outline of a Theory of Practice*. New York: Cambridge University Press, 1977.

Coakley, Sarah. "Dark Contemplation and Epistemic Transformation: The Analytic Theologian Re-Meets Teresa of Avila." In *Analytic Theology: New Essays in the Philosophy of Theology*, edited by Oliver D. Crisp and Michael C. Rae, 280–312. Oxford: Oxford University Press, 2009.

———. "Gregory of Nyssa." In *The Spiritual Senses: Perceiving God in Western Christianity*, edited by Paul L. Gavrilyuk and Sarah Coakley, 36–55. Cambridge: Cambridge University Press, 2012.

———. "The Resurrection and the 'Spiritual Senses': On Wittgenstein, Epistemology, and the Risen Christ." In *Powers and Submissions: Spirituality, Philosophy, and Gender*, 130–52. Oxford: Blackwell, 2002.

Code, Lorraine. "Taking Subjectivity into Account." In *Feminist Epistemologies*, edited by Linda Alcoff and Elizabeth Potter, 15–48. New York: Routledge, 1993.

———. *What Can She Know? Feminist Theory and the Construction of Knowledge*. Ithaca: Cornell University Press, 1991.

The Divine Liturgy of Our Father among the Saints John Chrysostom. Oxford: Oxford University Press, 1995.

Ford, David F., and Daniel W. Hardy. *Living in Praise: Worshipping and Knowing God*. London: Darton, Longman & Todd, 2005.

Ford, David F., and C. C. Pecknold, editors. *The Promise of Scriptural Reasoning*. Oxford: Wiley-Blackwell, 2006.

Frank, Georgia. "'Taste and See': The Eucharist and the Eyes of Faith in the Fourth Century." *Church History* 70 (2001) 619–43.

Gregory of Nyssa. *The Soul and the Resurrection*. Translated by Catherine P. Roth. Crestwood, NY: St Vladimir's Seminary Press, 1992.

Harvey, Susan Ashbrook. *Scenting Salvation: Ancient Christianity and the Olfactory Imagination*. Berkeley: University of California Press, 2006.

Kerr, Fergus. *Theology After Wittgenstein*. Oxford: Blackwell, 1986.

Kretzmann, Norman. "Mystical Perception: St Teresa, William Alston, and the Broadminded Atheist." In *Reason and the Christian Religion: Essays in Honour of Richard Swinburne*, edited by Alan G. Padgett, 65–90. Oxford: Clarendon, 1994.

Martin, David. *Tracts Against the Times*. London: Lutterworth, 1973.

McInroy, Mark J. "Origen of Alexandria." In *The Spiritual Senses: Perceiving God in Western Christianity*, edited by Paul L. Gavrilyuk and Sarah Coakley, 20–35. Cambridge: Cambridge University Press, 2012.

Swinburne, Richard. *Epistemic Justification*. Oxford: Oxford University Press, 2001.

Wolterstorff, Nicholas. "Historicizing the Belief-Forming Self." In *Knowledge and Reality: Essays in Honor of Alvin Plantinga*, edited by Thomas M. Crisp, Matthew Davidson, and David Vander Laan, 111–35. Dordrecht: Springer, 2006.

———. *Thomas Reid and the Story of Epistemology*. Cambridge: Cambridge University Press, 2001.

Wood, William. "Thomas Aquinas on the Claim that God is Truth." *Journal of the History of Philosophy*, forthcoming.

Wynn, Mark. *Emotional Experience and Religious Understanding: Integrating Perception, Conception and Feeling*. Cambridge: Cambridge University Press, 2005.

11

Wonder-Voyaging

The Pneumatological Character of David Ford's Theology

Ben Quash

King's College London

Introduction: An Island Pneumatology

In this chapter I want to propose that David Ford's theology is at heart pneumatological. In addition, I suggest that this pneumatology has taken on particular features that are appropriate to the context in which it has developed: it is an "island pneumatology," and this gives it illuminating continuities with the artistic traditions that have been formed in that same environment.

The poet and artist David Jones wrote an introduction to Coleridge's *The Rime of the Ancient Mariner* in the early 1960s—a work that he had illustrated more than thirty years earlier. It is a long essay, and a wide-ranging one, that moves associatively and suggestively from analysis of the poem, to reflections upon the techniques of copper engraving that Jones used to illustrate it, to aspects of marine geography and European history, and to theological reflections on the nature of Christ and of grace and of the Mass. Some of the most intriguing sections of the essay, however, are about the place that the *Rime* has in a long tradition of Anglo-Celtic art (mainly, but not at all exclusively, literary art): art about the sea. The "deep things" in this complexly layered poem resonate with other "deep things" (in other great works, and in us who read or hear it) precisely, as Jones points out, through *the sound of cataracts.*[1] "[T]he voice of the water-floods and the cataracted foam" that resounds in Coleridge's poem is in continuity with voices that are audible "throughout so much of our heritage store," writes Jones.[2] For this reason, the poem has "a connatural appeal to the people of an island," who are never far from the noise of "the limitless ocean's ceaseless surf-break."

For "island" we might substitute "islands" and in doing so better acknowledge that the maritime fringe of Europe, west of the English Channel, is dotted with many big and small islands, and that its complex heritage includes Irish alongside British people, traditions, and languages. It is an "Anglo-Celtic" tradition that some historians designate with the name "insular" (by which no negative judgement is intended), and it still finds itself assimilating new influences and additions to its already variegated identity.

But in all the variations of these islands' history and their people's imaginations, the sea is a constant feature. So, as Jones reminds us, a tenth-century entry in the *English Chronicle* sings of "the gannet's bath," "the teeming waters," "the whale's domain." And there is an early and little-known Welsh narrative of King Arthur's making an expedition with his men in a ship called Prydwen, in order to raid northwards. Then, more famously, there are "copious Irish accounts of . . . Celtic wonder-voyagings,"[3] including St Brendan's voyage to the islands of the Blessed, as well as the journey of Bran son of Febal, and the adventure of Maeldúin, "with its innumerable fantasies and strange varieties of experience as involved and intricate as the interlacings on a page from Kells."[4]

The first thing I want to celebrate in this essay in honour of David Ford's island pneumatology is his sense of life as a sort of "wonder-voyage," and his capacity to communicate that sense in a way that has much in common with Coleridge, with David Jones, and with a select tradition of others who are simultaneously theologians and artists. Like Coleridge

1. The reference here is Jones's, and is, of course, to Psalm 42:7: "deep calls to deep in the thunder of your cataracts."

2. Jones, *Dying Gaul*, 189.

3. Ibid., 192.

4. Ibid., 191.

and Jones, his work is interested in *everything* (Ford once described his ambition to initiate something called the "*Passim* Project," in which all domains of human life, knowledge, and experience would be explored in as rich a way as possible in dialogue with theology). Like their work, his suggests layer upon layer of significance and possibility, but in a way that is never artificially tidied up or forced prematurely into some sort of theoretical framework. Because it is "voyaging" theology, it is marked by qualities of open-endedness, principled (and often highly generative) irresolution, and conversational interaction. It, too, can be involved and intricate like the Book of Kells, but what is said by David Jones about Coleridge's *Rime* can, I think, be said of David Ford's theology too: "Its achievement is all the more astonishing in that while it evokes these deeps of meaning to which I have referred, it manages to do so with ease and grace and lightness of touch, without a suspicion of ponderousness or of the heavy burden with which it is cargoed-up."[5]

As a voyaging theology, Ford's theology does not resist the fluidity and instability and changeability of its medium, wishing always for less watery and shifting foundations. On the contrary, it is well adapted to these qualities in its environment: it both celebrates and harnesses them. We experience many aspects of our world as ocean-like; theology should rejoice in this fact (note how Ford's theological language is often water-related, and talks enthusiastically of overwhelmings and immersions). Moreover, to travel by sea means to appreciate more sensitively and fully not only the endless variegation of these great waters themselves, but the oddities, complexities, uniquenesses of the *land* as well, wherever the land's edges are raggedly interlaced with the deeps. It is a good place from which to appreciate "a world infinitely differentiated,"[6] in which, as T. S. Eliot put it, "nothing . . . is a substitute for anything else."[7] To travel by land is often to travel on a road or a railway, which imposes a humanly contrived order on a complex and folded landscape—mitigating its bends and contours. Some theology does that too: disciplining and formalizing its material and its experiences of the world. But it is possible to move across the surface of water in a floating vessel (especially a small one) in a way that permits each twist and turn of a coastline to be followed with no artificial reduction of its shape. David Ford's theology journeys in

5. Ibid., 193.

6. Pechey, "Pointed Remarks," 25. I am most grateful to Graham Pechey for his insights on this theme, both in print and in conversation.

7. Eliot, *Use of Poetry*, 113.

that way. It has a special responsiveness to the particular and the new or unprecedented—"all things counter, original, spare, strange,"[8] as Hopkins (self-consciously an Anglo-Celt) puts it. The sea embraces the land and hugs its every intricacy, enabling those who travel on it to do the same.

Another description of such theology might be that it is concerned with the "ambient": not the analysis of particular and artificially isolated objects, but with the whole environment in which we live and move and have our being, and here the central and generative role that pneumatology plays in Ford's work displays itself. In a recent paper given in the Research Institute of Systematic Theology at King's College London, Ford focused especially on questions of pneumatology, and named one of the key features of the Holy Spirit in Christian understanding as its "circumambience."[9] The Spirit is not best understood as an object of study in the way that (for example) the life of Christ has been for historical critical scholars. Giving a theological account of the Holy Spirit is not best achieved by the analysis of specific "acts" of the Spirit, in the past or in the present. A doctrine of the Holy Spirit will be concerned with describing an embracing environment in which many *other things* come to definition. To put it in island terms which owe something to Eugene Rogers[10]: the land's edges appear in all their unstandardizable intricacy because of the surrounding sea which dilates to give them space (while also beating shapingly upon them); the wind is appreciated as that which causes other things to move. We realize the meaning of the *Spirit* as we are drawn more and more fully into an appreciation of the things we find in the *world* as (sacramental) signs of God. This is not a closing down of that which in our environment has significance for us; it is a multiplication of it (we get to visit this coastline in detail, as we would in a boat, not as we would on a motorway). Viewed in the light of a circumambient pneumatology, the world opens up not as a road map, but in its magnificent and multiple particularity. As God becomes freely present as an all-encompassing environment—both public and intimate (like wind, air and water)—the world becomes more present to us too. The ambient Spirit, like water around an island, brings us into closer relationship with the world that this same God made and is transforming for perfection.

8. Hopkins, "Pied Beauty," 68.

9. Following David Kelsey, who deploys this concept in his recent book *Eccentric Existence*.

10. Rogers develops the idea of "dilation" as a way of understanding the operation of the Holy Spirit in Rogers, *After the Spirit*, 104–11.

I want to return to the notion of the ambient in closing, but in the central section of this essay that follows I want to develop my initial suggestion that a pneumatological approach of the kind that David Ford embodies in his *theology* has instructive parallels with a particular character discernible in the *arts* (especially, but not exclusively, the literary arts) of an Anglo-Celtic tradition. My guiding assumption will be that such a tradition has features to it that are typically Anglican—though they are no doubt shared by many other ecclesial traditions too—and mark a church that has a "voyaging" character, attentive to the uniqueness of local places and novel circumstances. Above all, a "Fordian" theology shares with the native arts of these islands a *responsive* mode that, like the sea, is always ready to embrace the particular shapes it meets, and, like a nimble sea vessel, can come into close and observant proximity to them. To put it another way, what follows is the description of an artistic heritage in the belief that it offers resources for understanding and appreciating a valuable theological method.

An Island Beauty

In describing David Ford's theology by correlating it with what might be called an Anglo-Celtic (or "insular") *aesthetic*, I am conscious that I am describing the theology of some of his friends and closest dialogue partners too—and above all, his father-in-law, the late Daniel Hardy.

Peter Ochs has ventured a description of the strain of Anglican postliberalism (as he calls it) that he observes in Ford, Hardy, and a number of others.[11] For such Anglican theology, he says, reason does not begin with itself but with the "found objects of the world" or with what Dan Hardy called "whatever we find before us." This attitude leaves room for an appreciation of the infinite modulation of things (like the sea's surface) and their detailed particularity (like the interlace of the landscape or the ragged edges of a coast), by contrast with a desire to make them conform to some pre-existing type or ideal. Human beings, in their theological activity as well as in other ways, do, of course, have much to contribute to the sorting, interpretation, and articulation of their experiences (finding is never simply passive), but they ought not ever to abandon what is fundamentally a responsive mode of engagement. They ought not, in other

11. See Ochs, *Another Reformation*, and especially his brilliant analysis in chapters 6 and 7, 167–221.

words, to expect the world to comport itself all the time in accordance with their "given" presumptions.

Ochs recalls Dan Hardy delivering a lecture at the University of Virginia in 2004. He had stood, while there, at Thomas Jefferson's "Rotunda," which (as Peter Ochs points out) is the symbol of UVA and "the defining mark of Jefferson's architecture for the school."[12] If you stand there, at the northern head of the main campus, and look south over what is called "The Lawn," you see elegant brick buildings to left and right. What you see straight ahead of you, once these apartment buildings stop, has undergone change since the campus was first designed and built. Originally, according to Jefferson's vision, you would have seen an "unenclosed wilderness beyond." Now, the pressure for more facilities has caused the southern view to be closed off, so that instead of what Ochs calls the "open forests" you now see an auditorium and a large classroom building.

For Hardy there was something significant to be discerned about an American rationalism *both* in the original vision *and* in this later cut-off. It symbolized for him an important aspect of an American understanding of the human being's place in God's creation.

> For the American Jefferson, he said, reason is a human construct, informed by a priori principles inherent in our being or "nature." This means that the other "nature" we find out there is ultimately unknown and threatening: in Jefferson's time, the place of potentially unfriendly indigenes of the Americas and untamed wildlife and climates. Nature is beautiful, to be sure, but also sublime and dangerous; it can be cognized only to the degree that it is domesticated, and it is domesticated only by human rationality.[13]

Hardy went on to suggest that this initial way of thinking about nature as "other" already contained within itself the seeds of the next stage of architectural activity: the closing off of the south side so as to *en*close "The Lawn." Whatever the practical reasons may have been for doing it, this too (he felt) symbolized an ongoing failure of vision. Jefferson's American enlightenment "standard of rationality"[14] could be read as reflecting a distrust of the unknowable in nature: "[N]ature is acceptable only when it accommodates our rational constructs. When nature displays its fury,

12. Ibid., 169.
13. Ibid., 170.
14. Ibid.

we would judge it irrational and close it off, limiting reason's gaze to what lies within our precincts."[15]

So much for newly independent America.[16] But does one really find a different vision on the other, north-*eastern*, side of the Atlantic?[17] And, if so, does it have any theological interest: might it issue in a theology of natural beauty, for example, with affinities to other theological loci (including a doctrine of the Holy Spirit)?

John Ruskin is one of the most robust thinkers to have suggested just this, and what he celebrates in the art of these north-eastern islands is such art's attention to the particular, the peculiar, and the infinitely varied concreteness of things. Here too, in a way that rather precisely recalls Peter Ochs description of Anglican postliberalism, the emphasis is on the "foundness" that is honoured in that art, rather than an ideal of what things *ought* to be. In *Modern Painters*, for instance, Ruskin writes as follows:

> I assert with sorrow, that all hitherto done in landscape, by those commonly conceived its masters, has never prompted one holy thought in the minds of nations. It has begun and ended in exhibiting the dexterities of individuals, and conventionalities of systems. . . . The sense of artificialness, the absence of all appearance of reality, the clumsiness of combination by which the meddling of man is made evident, and the feebleness of his hand branded on the inorganization of his monstrous creature, are advanced as a proof of inventive power, as an evidence of abstracted conception; nay, the violation of specific form, the utter abandonment of all organic and individual character of object . . . is constantly held up by the unthinking critic as the

15. Ibid.

16. For reasons of space, I bracket here a later neo-Romantic American tradition in the works of Whitman, Thoreau, and others that rejoices in untamed nature.

17. It was a widespread assumption in the nineteenth century, though considerably harder to identify now, that there can be a national character, a distinctive national genius even, in the production of art. We are nervous of such claims because of the ease with which they shade into the concept that there are racial strengths and weaknesses, racial types, and even (by way of another short step) a hierarchy of such types. But in rightly rejecting an essentialism about racial characteristics on account of all the ideological perils that attend it, there is a risk that we cease to ask the question whether certain kinds of historical inheritance, familiarity with certain kinds of landscape, a certain tradition of language use, certain cherished and transmitted habits of mind and types of judgment, certain shaping stories, may together have a formative influence on the art that is produced in a particular place—literary, visual, and musical.

> foundation of the grand or historical style, and the first step to the attainment of a pure ideal.[18]

But (he insists):

> It is just as impossible to generalize granite and slate, as it is to generalize a man and a cow. An animal must be either one animal or another animal: it cannot be a general animal, or it is no animal; and so a rock must either one rock or another rock; it cannot be a general rock, or it is no rock. If there were a creature in the foreground of a picture of which he could not decide whether it were a pony or a pig, the *Athenæum* critic would perhaps affirm it to be a generalization of pony and pig, and consequently a high example of "harmonious union and simple effect." But *I* should call it simple bad drawing . . .[19]

George Eliot, when writing about her literary creations, emphasizes her belief in something very similar to what Ruskin calls for in painting. It is precisely as a novelist that she feels her greatest discomfort at the ideas of the Comtean positivists to whom she was in so many other respects sympathetic. As E. S. Shaffer observes, she was "altogether less fond of systems than Comte. . . . [T]he qualities of humility, tolerance, sympathy and humour [so evident in her novels] are noticeably absent from Comte's writing. His Religion of Humanity, it might be said, gained in her work the quality of humanity."[20] The positivist Frederic Harrison was pressing her in the late 1860s to produce a novel to illustrate the "normal relations" within a positivist society, in particular the influence of the local physician. But Eliot responded:

> That is a tremendously difficult problem which you have laid before me, and I think you see its difficulties, though they can hardly press upon you as they do on me, who have gone through again and again the severe effort of trying to make certain ideas thoroughly incarnate, as if they had revealed themselves to me first in the flesh. . . . I think aesthetic teaching is the highest of all teaching because it deals with life in its highest complexity. But if it ceases to be purely aesthetic—if it lapses anywhere from the picture to the diagram—it becomes the most offensive of all teaching. Avowed Utopias are not offensive, because they are understood to have a scientific and expository character: they

18. Ruskin, *Modern Painters*, 135–37.

19. Ibid., 142.

20. Wright, *Religion of Humanity*, 201.

> do not pretend to work on the emotions, or couldn't do if they did pretend. I am sure, from your own statement, that you see this quite clearly. Well, then, consider the sort of agonizing labour to an English-fed imagination to make art a sufficiently real background for the desired picture, to get breathing, individual forms, and group them in the needful relations, that the presentation will lay hold on the emotions as human experience—will, as you say, "flash" conviction on the world by means of an aroused sympathy.[21]

Incarnation, or embodiment, is a massive concern of the book *Middlemarch*, for instance. The novel repeatedly indicates that ideas are of doubtful value unless they can be put into action. Dorothea's high ideals have to be chastened and tempered into something that can actually be made effective. The more political and less "angelic" life she eventually takes on as Will Ladislaw's wife is not to be seen as a failure or a grubby compromise; it is a vital "realization" (in more than one sense). Bulstrode the banker does not incarnate his ideals; his religious convictions are allowed to float horrifyingly free of any material or ethical expression (and become the occasion for a devastating critique of the doctrine of double predestination). In effect, Bulstrode's ostentatious piety barely conceals the fact that he is one of the most materialistic characters in the book. By contrast, Caleb Garth—one of the characters who is most involved in working materially with things—shows their almost religious value:

> "[B]ut it's a fine thing to come to a man when he's seen into the nature of business; to have the chance of getting a bit of the country into good fettle, as they say, and putting men into the right way with their farming, and getting a bit of good contriving and solid building done—that those who are living and those who come after will be the better for. I'd sooner have it than a fortune. I hold it the most honourable work that is." Here Caleb laid down his letters, thrust his fingers between the buttons of his waistcoat, and sat upright, but presently proceeded with some awe in his voice and moving his head slowly aside—"It's a great gift of God, Susan."[22]

We might say that Eliot the novelist shows the passion of a Dorothea alongside Caleb's delight in the modest, and his promotion of the mundane, the proximate, the locally responsible. Her own work as a novelist

21. Quoted in Shaffer, "*Kubla Khan*," 228–29.

22. Eliot, *Middlemarch*, 387.

could be described as a lifting up of the mundane by passion, and a tempering of passion by the mundane, to the good of each.

A third example of the "island aesthetic" we are pursuing might be Gerard Manley Hopkins, to whom we have already referred. Hopkins, of course, was himself deeply influenced by Ruskin. He also shared George Eliot's distrust of intellectual abstraction. His suspicion of "the value of universal concepts" is well observed by Hans Urs von Balthasar in volume three of *The Glory of the Lord*, as part of what Balthasar calls "Studies in Theological Style."[23] He also recognizes Hopkins' joy in the *found wildness* of the natural world (*contra* Thomas Jefferson, we may speculate), and his sensitivity to the way humanity has mutilated nature's purer forms. The word "wild," Balthasar points out, is everywhere in Hopkins, and signals the importance of what is for him an "almost primeval experience."

For Balthasar, the marks of a common concern that he notes in different representatives of an island art are not the consequence of chance convergences of taste; they genuinely represent a native Anglo-Celtic tradition.[24] Balthasar identifies in this insular aesthetic a particular celebration of "the irreducibility of the individual, be it material or personal,"[25] which has its summit in Shakespeare, "the greatest creator of unique, incomparable characters."[26] There is no place in this perspective for spurious ideas of "perfection in general." There is instead "the absolute, hard reality in which alone the true glory of being shines forth."[27] There is a celebration of the "uniqueness . . . of each image met with every day in nature or the world of men."[28]

His discussion of Hopkins leads him to make some more general remarks about the correlation between this "island" *aesthetic* and a correlative *theological* outlook; this is already hinted in his remark about "the true glory of being." Hopkins's poetic concern to pay due attention to the God-given, glorious "reality" that is before one in nature—not meddling with it, or allowing one's own shadow to fall distractingly upon it, and never abstracting—is, according to Balthasar, the product of a correspondence with the Scotist notion of *haeccitas*, "individual form," as "the basis

23. Balthasar, *Glory*, 3:354–55.

24. One over which, he contends, Duns Scotus is a sort of presiding genius.

25. Balthasar, *Glory*, 3:355.

26. Ibid., 356.

27. Ibid., 357.

28. Ibid., 356–57.

for any consideration of universal constructions."[29] When Hopkins first read Scotus in the summer of 1872, he enthusiastically embraced him as a fellow spirit, for Scotus was (Balthasar says) "the first to maintain philosophically the uniqueness of things, withstanding the temptation to dissolve them into general ideas, forms, or laws."[30] This is music to the ears of the Hopkins who wants to depict in his art the "arch-especial spirit" of things;[31] who wants to emphasize their distinctiveness, and not allow "unifying laws" to drown such distinctiveness.

To the extent that an "island" *theology* has shared this focus on the concrete form—"the unique, the irreducible"[32]—then Balthasar rejoices to celebrate its advantages over his own continental tradition, for "reared in an hereditary empiricism" it has "preserved the native rights of imagery in religious thought . . . right up to the present day."[33] And for this reason, it makes perhaps a better sense to an English or a Celtic mind to say that the theologian should talk to the poet.

So, then, Hopkins and Scotus stand here alongside Ruskin and George Eliot in the support of the case for an insular theology of beauty,[34] and (beyond that) *a particularist theological method* more generally, to which attention to beauty is an apprenticeship. Although the theology in his work is often implicit, we might turn back to David Jones at this point too, and to the fascinating essay fragment published after his death and titled "An Aspect of the Art of England."[35] It is speculative—almost whimsical—but also rings true in its identification of a "distinguishing quality" of the art of what "the Greek geographers," Strabo and Diodorus of Siciliy called "the Pretanic Isles": "[T]he Romans got their 'Picti' from the same source—the Old Welsh *Priten*, the Old Irish *Cruithin*, the speckled, mottled, variegated, painted men."[36] The distinguishing quality in question is a love of the

29. Ibid., 357.

30. Ibid., 374.

31. Hopkins, "Henry Purcell," 78.

32. Balthasar, *Glory*, 3:357.

33. Ibid., 354.

34. Are there signs of this tradition alive and well in contemporary poetry? We might point to Geoffrey Hill's highly charged attention to the layered depths of Western history which make his poems like literary cross sections through countless geological strata (which are in fact *human* strata—with all their knots and twists, profane and religious, vicious and exalted) in order to lay open the fragile possibilities we have for responsible life *now*.

35. Jones, *Dying Gaul*, 59–62.

36. Ibid., 59.

"fretted, meandering, countered image," and it is paradigmatically found in "*the* one art which has taken its name from us," namely, "that kind of needlework called 'Opus Anglicanum.'" Eclectic as ever, Jones traces this "flexible, delicate and chequered art"[37] through the English Gothic tradition in architecture, and the poetry and watercolours of William Blake, and ends up in a garden: "It is said that the 'cottage garden' is peculiar to this island, and that is not without interest—for the dappled complexity that makes the unity of those small gardens . . .—especially after sunset, when each colour and each form is distinct and like an embroidery and as complex as an embroidery—is very much akin to the quality I mean . . ." Which neatly returns us to Ochs's discussion of the Anglican postliberalism of David Ford and Dan Hardy, for—he suggests—their alternative to the nature-excluding rationalism of the Virginia campus would find better expression in a garden. Not the highly regimented, geometrical gardens of continental Europe and its imitators, but the tumbling, intertwining, organic shapes of, say, Sissinghurst in Kent, which represent not an imposition on wild nature, nor an attempt to suppress it, but rather a sort of "settlement with" it. Such a sampling of wild nature cannot regard it as simply "other" or even "irrational." On the contrary, it expresses the view that we can be at home with the non-human creation, and that our loves—the things that give us pleasure—are qualities that reside in nature already, and that can be elicited further by our human interaction with them.

Ford, Hardy, and others would not find it difficult to provide a theological rationale for such joy in the found. Their theology seeks what Balthasar, in his discussion of Hopkins, calls "an exact experiencing of the forms of the world . . . not concepts (of 'universal,' abstract truth), but images (of the unique, personal, divine-human truth)."[38] This is a characteristically Anglican theological sensibility, affirming what we find "out there" in the world; seeing "not some independent 'nature,' but God's creation and creatures."[39] We belong among non-human creatures, neither identical to them nor wholly separate, but *in relation to them as well as to their creator*. "Wisdom" is the deepening of our relationship to creation and its ongoing history, and is not something accomplished by an *a priori* "reason" located strictly in *us*. Reason is "nothing less than the Logos, God's Word as it continually creates the world and as it is revealed to us in

37. Ibid., 60.

38. Balthasar, *Glory*, 3:391.

39. Ochs, *Another Reformation*, 170.

Scripture and in the body of Jesus Christ."[40] And the primary *place* where wisdom is fostered through the relational and communicative exercise of such reason is *the church*, the Spirit-gathered body of Christ in whom God's Word speaks, and through whose members creation also speaks. In its chief sacrament, the Eucharist, this Anglican ecclesial tradition identifies a real presence of the divinity, realized pneumatologically by the work of the Spirit, but it also affirms this presence as manifesting itself in a non-centralized, variegated, and distributed form: always *local*, and affected by its locality.

A pneumatology based upon this understanding of foundness, and the affinity of human reason with the grain of the world, stands in the tradition of Hooker, Traherne, Herbert, Coleridge, and many others and offers not just a set of theological resources for identifying (or *finding*) the church, but a warrant for something else too: a warrant for celebrating certain habits in an island art. Ones that Ruskin would surely have wanted to endorse as he searched tirelessly and passionately for "specific form" for the "organic and individual character" of objects, in the face of all the "sense of artificialness . . . [and] abstracted conception" he longed to overcome.

Ambience

Finally, in a closing section, I want to return to the idea of ambience, and offer some reflections on the faculty of hearing.[41] This faculty, I suggest, has a particular importance for David Ford, and also plays a crucial role in the life of a church characterized in terms of community, historical openness, and receptivity in the Spirit. It is central to the worshipping and conversational practices that are, for Ford, the church's life.

What has hearing got to do with all we have been discussing so far? Of the five senses (with the near parallel of smell), it is the most attuned to an embracing, enwrapping, ambient environment. Touch and taste require physical contact at a specific spatial location. Sight must be directed somewhere. Hearing relates us in every direction at once to what is around us. This distinctiveness of hearing may seem all the more acute to us moderns—especially in its contrast with sight—since the way that

40. Ibid., 170.

41. I am indebted to my research student Corinne Williamson for conversations about the importance of audition in the church, and I draw on those conversations in what follows.

powerfully influential metaphors of sight came to dominate the rhetoric of Enlightenment philosophy. Descartes, for example, describes the act of seeing an object as like poking it with a stick (the "stick" being the light that mediates between our eye and the object we view).[42] It is an image riddled with implications of detachment, overview, dominance, and limited directionality: it is hard to think of anything *less* like relationship with an ambient environment. It expresses what Merleau-Ponty called *survol*—a looking down from above[43]—and in terms which both David Ford and I have had occasion to use before, it is characteristic of what might be called an "epic" relation to the world.[44] (It is interesting that hearing, by contrast, seems to be the faculty to which Descartes made the least reference in his philosophy.[45])

Whether or not sight *must* be construed in this Cartesian way—or whether there are neglected possibilities for thinking of it much more as a communal medium—is something that has been interestingly explored by Catherine Pickstock and others, through an appeal to Augustine's treatment of the senses in Book Two of *De Libero Arbitrio*.[46] Augustine celebrates the fact that sight, like hearing, is not a possessive faculty. Many people can see (as they can hear) the same things at one and the same time—and this is therefore unlike the appropriative action of breathing or ingesting something, by which that thing becomes unavailable to others (in this respect, to recall again the typology of genres, smell and taste embody a "lyric" relation to the world—i.e., private and intimate—and touch has some of these qualities too). Augustine seems to imply a certain hierarchy to the physical senses, in which sight and hearing have particular dignity because they are more communal than the others: "Therefore, the things that we touch or taste or smell are less similar to [the] truth than are the things that we hear and see. For every word that is heard is heard simultaneously and in its entirety by everyone who hears it, and any form that is seen by the eyes is seen equally by every eye that sees it."[47] There is a profoundly ethical concern at work in this implicit hierarchy, which

42. Descartes, *Optics*, 67.

43. See, for example, Merleau-Ponty, *Visible and Invisible*, 13.

44. See Quash, *Drama of History*; Ford, *Future of Christian Theology*.

45. Jennifer Spencer of the University of Cambridge made this observation in an unpublished paper in 2007 titled "A Theology of Vision."

46. Augustine, *On Free Choice*; see Pickstock, "What Shines Between."

47. Augustine, *On Free Choice*, 57.

mirrors the Christian value of a life in which shared goods replace private ones.

But whatever injustices may have been done to sight's good reputation by Descartes and others, the auditory retains this one remarkable "excess" over the visual, namely, that it is genuinely immersive; it *receives ambiently*. It is more receptive, because you cannot stop hearing as easily as you can stop looking. There is a more radical openness to this faculty—and perhaps, therefore, an even more radical communality—than there is to the faculty of sight. If sight tends to the "epic," and smell, taste, and even touch tend to the "lyric," then hearing may correspond best to the relation to the world which I, like David Ford, have called "dramatic." We are most open to each other—and (*together*) most open to the world around us—through audition. We do not master or comprehend or possess when we hear; we participate. It is one of the fascinations and successes of Ford's theology that it has a special relationship with the auditory. For example, in his paper on the Holy Spirit given at the Research Institute of Systematic Theology at King's College London, to which I referred earlier, Ford concluded by proposing four particular "signs" of the Spirit. They were not in any way intended to be comprehensive, but it was interesting that three of the four involved sound: the "cathedral of sound" (the "pure cry") of *glossolalia*; the singing (and dancing) of genocide survivors in Rwanda, demonstrating that there can be a simultaneity of praise with grief; and the abundance, innovation, and freedom-in-community of jazz.[48] In these examples, he presented a *dramatic* church as preeminently a "church of hearing."

I do not think that this needs to lead to a dismissal of vision, but rather an appreciation of different ways we might see *by analogy with* hearing: more radically participatory; more alert to the unfinished or to that which cannot be appropriated. Certain traditions of visual art are, in fact, "dramatic," because open-ended, social, time-full. They do not "see all clear";[49] they invite response. But they are dramatic exactly because of what they share with the auditory; they tend to be a bit like listening. Ford's own meditations in *Self and Salvation* on the face of Jesus Christ—and on our own faces—are of a piece with his discussions of what it is to

48. The fourth one was the occasion for love opened up by dealing with the pee and poo (the "pipi et kaka") of the severely disabled in L'Arche communities, as described by Jean Vanier.

49. I am echoing Henry Vaughan; Vaughan, "The Night," 289.

be a "singing self";[50] to relate to the world mutually, dialogically, and in a way that involves a certain surrender. And the ambient environment of a cottage garden, or of an ocean, requires a special sort of seeing that is immediately dispossessed of its ability to "poke" or dominate the objects of sight, and will thus always be a more dramatic (or quasi-auditory) sort of seeing than that exemplified in the carefully framed vista of Jefferson's rationalist Virginia campus. The receptivity of such sensing will be a correlate of the genuine freedom from us and from our designs that found objects have. And, as Augustine would affirm, it will ultimately be a mode of *wisdom*, for wisdom is supremely ambient, supremely communal: "We can all enjoy it equally and in common; there is ample room, and it lacks for nothing. . . . No part of it ever becomes the private property of any one person; it is always wholly present to everyone."[51] There are words here that may act as a fitting tribute to David Ford's theological vision, and to the ambient pneumatology at its heart. It is a theology that has "ample room," an emphasis on the God-given importance of "enjoyment," a belief that there is around us an abundance of things *to* enjoy, and a desire to make these good things as "wholly present" to everyone as it possibly can.

Bibliography

Augustine. *On Free Choice of the Will*. Translated by Thomas Williams. Indianapolis: Hackett, 1993.

Balthasar, Hans Urs von. *The Glory of the Lord*. Vol. 3. Edinburgh: T. & T. Clark, 1986.

Descartes, René. *Optics*. In *Discourse on Method, Optics, Geometry, and Meteorology*, translated by Paul J. Olscamp, 65–175. Indianapolis: Hackett, 2001.

Eliot, George. *Middlemarch*. Harmondsworth, UK: Penguin, 1994.

Eliot, T. S. *The Use of Poetry and the Use of Criticism*. London: Faber & Faber, 1933.

Ford, David F. *The Future of Christian Theology*. Oxford: Wiley-Blackwell, 2011.

———. *Self and Salvation: Being Transformed*. Cambridge: Cambridge University Press, 1999.

Hopkins, Gerard Manley. "Henry Purcell." In *The Major Poems*, edited by Walford Davies, 68. London: Dent, 1979.

———. "Pied Beauty." In *The Major Poems*, edited by Walford Davies, 68. London: Dent, 1979.

Jones, David. "An Aspect of the Art of England." In *The Dying Gaul, and Other Writings*, 59–62. London: Faber & Faber, 1978.

———. "An Introduction to *The Rime of the Ancient Mariner*." In *The Dying Gaul, and Other Writings*, 186–225. London: Faber & Faber, 1978.

50. Ford, *Self and Salvation*, 107–36.

51. Augustine, *On Free Choice*, 57.

Kelsey, David. *Eccentric Existence: A Theological Anthropology*. Louisville: Westminster John Knox, 2009.

Merleau-Ponty, Maurice. *The Visible and the Invisible*. Translated by Alphonso Lingis. Evanston: Northwestern University Press, 1968.

Ochs, Peter. *Another Reformation: Postliberal Christianity and the Jews*. Grand Rapids: Baker Academic, 2011.

Pechey, Graham. "Pointed Remarks: Scholasticism and the Gothic in the English Counter-Enlightenment." In *Christianity and Literature* 57.1 (2007) 3–33.

Pickstock, Catherine J. C. "What Shines Between: The *Metaxu* of Light." In *Between System and Poetics: William Desmond and Philosophy after Dialectic*, edited by Thomas A. F. Kelly, 107–22. Aldershot, UK: Ashgate, 2007.

Quash, Ben. *Theology and the Drama of History*. Cambridge: Cambridge University Press, 2005.

Rogers, Eugene F., Jr. *After the Spirit: A Constructive Pneumatology from Resources Outside the Modern West*. London: SCM, 2006.

Ruskin, John. *Ruskin's Modern Painters*. Abridged and edited by A. J. Finberg. London: Bell, 1927.

Shaffer, E. S. *"Kubla Khan" and* The Fall of Jerusalem: *The Mythological School in Biblical Criticism and Secular Literature*, 1770–1880. Cambridge: Cambridge University Press, 1975.

Vaughan, Henry. "The Night." In *The Complete Poems*, edited by Alan Rudrum, 289–90. Harmondsworth, UK: Penguin, 1983.

Wright, T. R. *The Religion of Humanity: The Impact of Comtean Positivism on Victorian Britain*. Cambridge: Cambridge University Press, 1986.

12

"A Secular and Religious World"

David Ford's Contribution to the Secularization Debate

Timothy Jenkins

University of Cambridge

I want to look from a sociological perspective at David Ford's contribution to the secularization debate, a contribution that forms part of his developed approach to theological and institutional questions. I shall do so by drawing him into conversation with the recent work of two historians, Thomas Howard and Callum Brown.

Two Theories of Secularization

Let me begin with a synopsis that derives from Howard's *God and the Atlantic*. If you take a European perspective, two issues dominate all questions concerning the place of religion: the relation of the state to the church and the significance of the French Revolution. For intellectuals, the Revolution is conceived as an absolute beginning, a break with the past in which new relationships were forged and in which, in particular, the relation between church and state became central. Historically, the first responses to the Revolution were right-wing and sought to "restore" the place of religion as part of returning to the values of the Ancien Regime, modelled on an organic conception of society characterized by the separation of social ranks and a hierarchical relation between them, moderated by an awareness of their interdependence, an order in which religion played its part. Subsequently, left-wing responses developed, also taking a holistic or universalist conception of society, but emphasizing individualism, equality, and self-making, and looking to the state as the agency that created free citizens and guaranteed their rights. In this latter account, religion could either be incorporated, as the servant of the state involved in the education of individuals and inculcating the appropriate egalitarian moral order, or rejected as an enemy of and competitor to the state, incapable of adopting modern values and therefore to be excluded from the public sphere. The view that came to predominate however saw religion by definition as part of the old order, due to disappear in the advanced, enlightened political settlement we now enjoy, but present as a matter of individual freedom and choice to those who cling to the older forms for some secondary reason—the nostalgia of a defeated class fraction, an individual need for (illusory) comfort or, more sinisterly, in order to promote reactionary political values under the cover of a democratic ideology or licence. None of the positions in this spectrum escapes from the view that religion is harnessed to the state in one form or another, and that this potential for collaboration or competition is the exclusive and only option under our modern (post-Revolutionary) condition.

Such an optic is, of course, an intellectual perspective or "world view." It has its own concerns—notably, how intellectuals relate to other clerks, to priests and civil servants—and its unconscious models—drawn for the most part from post-Tridentine Catholic thought, deriving systematic and totalizing accounts of society from initial abstract principles of explanation. It is not particularly concerned with the complexities of life on the ground, with the life of congregations, for example, or with the everyday beliefs and practices of populations, or with the practical challenges of government. These are effectively invisible or, when considered, examined within categories that draw from the perspective of secularization, which is taken simultaneously to be a theory and a description of ineluctable processes taking place in the world.

The problems of misreading are particularly acute when the European perspective pays attention to the example of the United States, which has been an object of consideration at least since the War of Independence. From the European perspective, the American Revolution may be considered a precursor and anticipation of the French, and the society that resulted as representing European values freed from the legacy of the institutions of the Ancien Regime, for the values of individualism, equality, and self-making are there written large and the citizens of the United States are notable both for their freedom and their industry. Yet the consequences of this anticipated prototype of European liberation were curiously mixed and, as Howard notes, reactions focused particularly on American religion which, instead of withering as it should have, according to European prognostications, flourished and multiplied, serving instead then as a metaphor for the perceived naivety, lack of political and other culture, insincerity, self-interested greed and so forth that Europeans attributed to Americans as rivalries between the two continents emerged in the later nineteenth century. Howard claims that a reading of American religion through European categories gives form to many of the familiar tropes of anti-American rhetoric.

From an American perspective, things look somewhat different. In Tocqueville's terms, the spirit of religion and the spirit of freedom are intimately united in America, not, as in Europe, moving in contrary directions. Howard's thesis may be put simply: while in post-Revolutionary Europe religion—whether conceived positively or negatively—is always thought of primarily in relation to the state, in America the separation of church and state is considered to be a precondition for the flourishing of religion. In the European frame, religion is always a function of political power, either forming or oppressing citizens according to the optic taken; while in the American mind, citizens form themselves under the minimum tutelage of the state, and are free to seek appropriate kinds of religious expression to help them do so. In the one, liberty is considered abstractly, as a function of the right kind of government, and religion is an instrument to aid or obstruct its development; in the other, liberty belongs to individual men and women who make their own lives, in which religion may play a part.

Two quite different accounts of secularization emerge out of these different perspectives, each—as is the tendency of social theory—anticipating a different future. On the one hand, there is the European "zero-sum" game in which either the state will come to dominate the public sphere entirely and eliminate religion as a voice or, hypothetically, religion will "return" and make itself felt again in the public sphere, re-establishing traditional practices and beliefs. But this "return" will be on the basis of the sum of individual choices. On the other hand, there is an "American" account where religion and political institutions live together in some form of coexistence. These accounts are intellectual visions rather than accurate descriptions of what is happening on the ground, although they each show affinities with their place of origin. It is perfectly possible, however, for American intellectuals to adopt European categories, and it is conceivable too that the "coexistence" model may provide more insight into the place of religion in everyday life in Western Europe than does the narrative of inevitable secularization. For while the European model generates the categories of the sociology of religion, there is also a good deal of work from contemporary American ethnographers and social historians which is more comprehending of the beliefs and practices of what appear to European eyes to be eccentric sects. Instead of recording a battle between the state and religion, these latter accounts offer the possibility simultaneously of getting in touch with the ordinary concerns of citizens and their rulers and of repairing sociological categories, including the narrative of secularization.

A "Religious and Secular World"

David Ford is a theologian who to an unusual extent has developed a conversation between North American and European concerns; this commitment has its roots in his education (and his marriage), and provides the ground for his subsequent engagement with other faiths. I want to draw attention to a single feature of his thinking; his recent development of the idea of a "religious and secular world," in an attempt to do justice to the complexity of the world we find ourselves in.

Being a theologian placed between two continents, Ford employs elements of both the models we have been discussing. He introduces the need to face up to "the religious and secular reality of our world"[1] in the context of what might be termed the "failure of secularism," a failure to be thought of both in terms of the loss of plausibility of a neutral, utilitarian framework for appraising human activity and in terms of recognizing the subscription on vast parts of the world's population to one or other of the world faiths. This account then combines both an element of critique of the all-or-nothing category of secularization theory together with a suggestion of what has been called the "return of religion." This pairing also appears in a lecture in 2005 on the place of faith in the modern university, in which Ford sets the intellectual context as the seeming failure of the

1. Ford, *Shaping Theology*, 51.

categories of liberalism to offer ways of orienting ourselves in the modern world, drawing particularly on Asad (*Formations of the Secular*) and Stout (*Democracy and Tradition*), at the same time pointing to the empirical fact of the (global) persistence of belief.[2]

These discussions set a frame for a "secular and religious" account, but the idea is developed further in the recent "manifesto," *The Future of Christian Theology*, where Ford presents a reading of modern social order through an analysis of "dramatic codes." This work draws on Quash's account of Von Balthasar's Hegelian categories.[3] Ford identifies the two tendencies with which we have been concerned as follows. The modern, secular account may be characterized as "epic," as a third person perspective that focuses on "clarity, completeness, and objectivity, systems, overviews, and comprehensive structures."[4] Opposed to this is the "lyric" nature of personal religious discourse, to do with "inwardness, self-expression, and the present moment," in which overall coherence may give place to subjectivity and the event. This is a considerable advance over the characterization introduced in the earlier pieces, for it brings out both the strength and the limitations of each position; the objectivity of the account of secularization which, nevertheless, seems to miss so much, and the fashion in which any turn to subjectivity seems, while comprehending so much more, incapable of giving any overall principle of intelligibility. But, of course, to characterize American religion as lyric would be to repeat what has been outlined above as a European misreading. Beyond this development, and most important of all, then, Ford presents a third moment of synthesis, "drama," which is able "to embrace the objective and the subjective, to maintain a sense of plot and purpose without suppressing individuality, diversity, and the complexity of levels, perspectives, motivations, and ideas."[5] The moment of drama clearly could correspond to a renewed "secular and religious" account of society, avoiding both the limitations of contemporary (epic) social theory and the traps of an over-individualized (lyric) personal religion.

This possibility is explored by Ford in his third chapter.[6] He identifies the narrative of secularization as "an epic of modernity in which a

2. Ibid., 115.
3. Quash, *Theology and the Drama of History.*
4. Ford, *Future of Christian Theology*, 25.
5. Ibid., 26.
6. Ibid., 45–50.

religious society turns into a secular society"[7] over a period of five hundred years. This epic has however lost plausibility, to the extent that Europe has begun to be seen as the exception globally rather than the rule (he cites Davie),[8] and other, alternative epics—such as Habermas's "post-secular age"—developed. Ford suggests, however, that rather than impose a single, externally defined, objective overview it might be better to recount the interaction of forces in a dramatic narrative form. In catching up the options both of epic and lyric in the dramatic synthesis, he is moving from a logic of "either/or" to one of "both-and."

Such a complex narrative has a place for the secular, Ford claims; in particular identifying the importance of the state in enabling a "minimum secular settlement," developed in the light of religious wars and symbolized by the Peace of Westphalia (1648).[9] This settlement enabled both states to avoid war and citizens within a single state to live together in peace.[10] Such an arrangement, he seems to suggest, also underwrites the unique American settlement. "The . . . beneficial thrust of minimal secularism . . . was toward peaceful accommodation of religious differences . . . minimal rules and values that might be called 'secular' allowed a conception of the public good that was not constantly threatened by religious conflict."[11] In this account, epic conceptions of religion were brought, through the bitter experience of conflict, to share in a drama that allowed the possibility of common aims and values to emerge. Ford links this process of education to the creation of the national institutions of democracy, including the development of independent corporations, and suggests that the same issues will underlie the history of the European Union.

At the same time, these "dramatic" developments are threatened, or at least accompanied by possible threats, from two sides. The one is to replace the religious epic "by secularism in a comparably epic mode,"[12] whether in imperial, nationalist, or revolutionary form, or in the subtler form of state-welfare ideologies that seek to exclude all traces of civil society—all intermediate groups including religious ones—from the public sphere. The other is the lyric reaction to such grand narratives, the

7. Ibid., 45.

8. Davie, *Europe.*

9. Cf. Nexon, *The Struggle.*

10. Cf. the discussion of a minimum secular settlement in Jenkins and Quash, *Cambridge Inter-faith Programme.*

11. Ford, *Future of Christian Theology*, 46–47.

12. Ibid., 48.

fragmented, feeling response to the threat of the epic, whether expressed in the "revival" of conservative religion or the chiliastic despair of postmodernisms. Ford characteristically spends little time exploring the negative; instead, his positive vision (drawing in particular on Stout, *Democracy and Tradition*) concerns a pluralism of contributions building on a minimal secular settlement and working towards a sustained common good: in short, demanding that the various players see themselves in dramatic terms, integrating both epic and lyric tendencies. This vision is then, we might say, a European proposal for an Americanized secular settlement, weaving together elements of formation, worship, culture, and politics—a synthesis that both pays attention to the details of the past and maintains an attitude of openness towards the present and future.

It is interesting to contrast this approach to that of Charles Taylor in *A Secular Age*, on which Ford offers an interesting commentary. He retells Taylor's analysis of secularity in terms of a shift from epic/lyric (narrative/experience) in the premodern period to drama (integration) in the modern. Taylor, as he notes, tends to reproduce a version of the Catholic critique, attributing the breakdown of the epic, lived world and the rise of the lyric (subjectivity) to the "Reform Master Narrative," identifying tendencies in the new subjectivity to adopt new master narratives, but seeing its culmination in the post-war "cultural revolution in the North Atlantic world, with its 'expressive individualism' on a mass scale, a new consumer culture, an ethos of authenticity and personal fulfilment, gender equality and sexual pleasure, emphases on creativity, feeling, imagination, choice, individual responsibility, and accompanying spiritualities beyond religious institutions."[13] The end point is the "buffered," "disembedded" individual. This is the European narrative of secularization without remainder, though written by a North American. Ford further points out that Taylor relies on a Hegelian model of this present period being a necessary stage in the education of humankind within a providentialist perspective. Ford does not labour the point, but the contrast with his own approach is striking: Taylor's tends towards a closed narrative, capable of redemption by divine intervention, while Ford's is humanist, under-determined, and open.

Both Taylor and Ford come together, however, in the importance they attribute to practices of formation. For if one is dealing in the power of ideas and ways of thinking about the world, the heart of the issue concerns where ideas come from, and how they are effective. Ideas

13. Ibid., 53, referencing Taylor, *A Secular Age*, 473ff.

emerge from people brought up in and shaped by some quite small-scale practices, and they in turn repair and reshape these practices. There is then a further claim made, that these practices and their repairs can have widespread implications for broader social practices that shape and condition the possibilities of the various members of a given social order.[14] In this way, ideas, social processes and the details of ordinary lives are all interconnected, and one can begin to identify various points at which turnings were made whereby—to characterize the way we live now—the state has become the trusted arbiter of truth, civil society is seen largely as an irrelevance, and each sex dies alone. In this perspective, it is clear that social science and social history may be able to offer detailed accounts to supplement, fill out, and refine the broad picture sketched in Ford's short book and Taylor's long one.

A Sociological Description of a Religious and Secular World?

The question that remains, then, is whether there is any sociology that begins to carry out research along the lines Ford has indicated. The answer is both yes and no. We could look to Grace Davie's identification of "European exceptionalism,"[15] which limits the processes of secularization to a European history and sees the emergence of modern individualism as part of a separate, North American history. But this approach does not distinguish clearly enough, for our purposes, the complex history of the formation and dissemination of the sociological concepts in contrast to the social processes they purport to describe. Instead, I want to draw attention to a recent transformation of British historiographical perspectives on secularization by Callum Brown which has contributed both detail and substance to the questions raised by Taylor and Ford.

Brown, for our purposes, makes two significant moves. First, he offers a genealogy of the idea of secularization in a British context. And second, he identifies some broad categories of thought and behaviour—a "social imaginary"—which he terms "discursive Christianity," and for which he claims both widespread application and pretty precise dating: these categories constitute an unquestioned set of presuppositions between approximately 1800 and 1950. Through this second topic, Brown moves away from the institutional focus, which reproduces the zero-sum

14. Cf. Taylor's recent work on "modern social imaginaries": Taylor, *Modern Social Imaginaries*; Taylor, *A Secular Age*.

15. Davie, *Europe*; cf. Berger, *Desecularization*.

game between church and state, and looks instead to the forms of social life which are expressed in the everyday.

Let us look first at the concept of secularization. In a nutshell, Brown suggests that rather than being a description of a state of the world or of a process with stages that can be identified and monitored, secularization is better considered as a way of speaking about the world. This is a shift that we might characterize as being from function to meaning: religion is no longer taken to be a set of objective institutions and beliefs that can be measured and which diminishes in importance as its purpose or function is taken on by other institutions and beliefs. Instead, we look to ways of classifying human behaviour that emphasize flourishing and failure, which are matters of evaluation rather than objective concepts. Brown, therefore, replaces a naturalistic account of religion, which assumes that facts are open to observation, with an account that sees religion as something spoken about, as an expression of human attempts to make sense in and of the world. Once this shift in approach is made, the crucial question becomes: who is speaking when the idea of religion is evoked, and with what intention?

Brown offers us an etymology of the idea of secularization by suggesting that "religious decline" was a concept that emerged within evangelical circles round about the end of the eighteenth century. The idea of decline was conceived around the opposition of town to countryside, expressed in what Brown terms "the myth of the unholy city." "The clergy of Britain," he suggests, "were the first [of the professions] to engage with the theoretical and practical problems of urbanity and the human condition,"[16] and they did so on the basis of categories that took for granted the idea of a Christian countryside and the contrasting irreligion of the industrial town. This opposition covered another, relating to social class: the religious middle classes were conceived in contrast to the irreligious working classes, and with the vocation to endeavour to improve their ways and influence their fate. The model conceived on this basis organized extensive Christian efforts in the form of "home mission."

Brown identifies the importance of Thomas Chalmers in the formulation of the model. Chalmers, who worked in Glasgow in the early years of the nineteenth century, created a variety of organizations to serve the locality and, at the same time, formulated a strategy for combating irreligion on the basis of "statistics of religiosity," these indicating both the size of the task and monitoring the means undertaken to remedy the situation.

16. Brown, *Death of Christian Britain*, 20.

Home evangelism was thus planned in a rational fashion, focused on a locality and taking the initiative in what was called the "aggressive system." This approach was to be extremely influential in terms of how the issues were understood. "After Chalmers," Brown writes, "the language of class placed religiosity and its absence at the centre of the conception of society, its ordering and its problems."[17] But it was equally important in terms of providing the methods for tackling the problems so conceived: these problems were objectified in the form of statistics, in the "moral statistics" of crime, prostitution, drink, and gambling, and resolved in forms of rational management advanced to tackle the issues, also monitored through statistics of visits, attendance, conversions, membership, and so forth. In this fashion, the model not only served the clergy working in the cities, but also created the basis for the "social scientific study of urban religion and morality."[18]

Brown makes two points concerning this myth of the unholy city, which was created in the context of mobilizing energies for Christian work and was expressed in a strategy of reversing the urban decline or absence of religion. The first concerns the state of affairs at the end of the eighteenth century in which it arose. The original anxiety that was translated into the myth of the decline of religion was, Brown suggests, Anglican disquiet at the rise of Dissent and, therefore, at a loss of hegemony, in particular at the local as opposed to the national level. Rather than not being Christian, people were the wrong kind of Christian; the appearance of Christian pluralism was projected (not for the first time) as a myth of irreligion. The rise of Nonconformity can, of course, be linked to other social changes, which Brown summarizes as a breakdown in paternalism: in sum, "the *idea* of religious decline was born in Britain within the breaking of social bonds, the decline of what E. P. Thompson called the 'paternalism-deference equilibrium.'"[19] One settlement was coming to an end, and another, with very different dimensions, coming into being—a settlement in which the values of Nonconformity are prominent.

The second point, already hinted at, concerns the emergence of secularization theory as an academic discipline properly speaking; this, Brown claims, only occurs with E. R. Wickham's study of urban religion in Sheffield, published in 1957. The substantive point is that Wickham takes Chalmers both as authority and as evidence: he adopts Chalmers'

17. Ibid., 25.

18. Ibid., 23.

19. Ibid., 18.

categories and methods while at the same time "relying on Chalmers and his clerical ilk as the 'sources' to 'prove' the theory."[20] The social science theory of secularization is simply a later retelling of an evangelical account designed to mobilize resources, and it perpetuates the myth through subsequent revisions as more refined data and statistical methods are applied. In brief, "the story told by academics in the second half of the twentieth century has been the same story as that told by clergymen in the 1810s and 1820s."[21]

The narrative of secularization is then a version of the myth of the unholy city—the decline of religion taken as literally true—and it pays very little attention to what might be happening on the ground. There is what I would call a lack of ethnography; no heed is paid to local categories and practices, nor to indigenous ways of making sense and how "religious" thought and institutions are deployed by local populations in constructing their lives. Brown acknowledges this need, pointing to works that look at issues of "religious identity," "informal religion," and "popular religiosity." Sarah Williams' work in particular is important in Brown's thinking and his project of describing how Christian thinking appears and persists in popular categories and their expression, which is his second topic.[22]

Here, however, we do not find the ethnography we might have hoped for, but instead, in order to offer a positive account of what is going on in fact on the ground, he turns to discourse analysis, to a concept of "discursive Christianity," a set of codes which create the ground rules for much of ordinary life among the British population between 1800 and 1950. He offers four substantial observations or claims.

His first observation is that discussions and debates essentially within the churches' sphere have effects beyond their boundaries.[23] Quite small-scale Christian social debates and practices are received and put to work, or at least make a contribution, shaping wider debates and reforms. A price has to be paid for this influence; Brown suggests that the Christian narrative of secularization succeeds in becoming generalized because it joins in with a wider project and myth of progress, becoming the mark of a modern person.

On this basis, Brown claims that the evangelical understanding of the self, formed through individual self-examination, the moment of

20. Ibid., 27.

21. Ibid., 30.

22. Williams, *Religious Belief.*

23. Cf. Harding, *The Book of Jerry Falwell*, which makes the same point.

conversion, and subsequent self-accounting, became universalized, and was expressed and refined through congregations of believers and the voluntary associations that emerged in the period. Just as the individual has to separate him or herself from the troubled world and set out to create a new self, so the congregation of believers has a similar task, both of separation from and the redemption of those who surround them, through a labour of love. This new account of transformation of self and society was disseminated through hymns, biographies, and magazine stories, and set the narrative forms that characterized popular literature, so that every life was touched and shaped by these forms of piety.

His third claim is that gender relations, as opposed to social class, were primary in organizing this discursive Christianity. By this he means that men and women are placed differently in the narratives of piety, so that women become central to the construction of social order, through self-sacrifice, while men are allowed a more troubled relationship to the world, with greater freedom of action but, by the same token, a more peripheral role. He calls this the feminization of piety.

This last claim, of the centrality of gender relations and of women's piety to discursive Christianity, prepares the way for Brown's last and most controversial move, which is to suggest that the entire discursive apparatus breaks down in the second half of the twentieth century because of the redefinition of the settlement between the sexes under the impulse of feminism. This thesis, although challenged, has been influential;[24] it allows him to rejoin the conventional narrative of secularization—"the death of Christian Britain"—while offering a radical revision of the timeline.

This sudden capitulation to the narrative which he had so successfully identified and described is striking, the more so because this persuasive account is similar in kind to the "urban unbelief" myth of the early nineteenth century. It is based in the personal experience of a generation of intellectuals: Brown grew up in the sixties, was involved in both youth culture and church life, and subsequently gained experience of aspects of the feminist movement. He gives this widespread experience of personal growth and social change a universal interpretation, drawing on certain salient features to describe a radical break in the order of civilization, just as evangelical clergy transformed the experience of Dissent and urban ministry into a picture that allowed them to make sense of their contemporary world.

24. For more nuanced treatments, see McLeod, *The Religious Crisis*; Green, *The Passing of Protestant England*.

This ambiguity explains my earlier "yes and no" to the question of whether we have any sociological developments that might fill out Ford's "religious and secular" idea. Brown does precisely what Taylor and Ford demand in situating the production of the secularization narrative and identifying the milieu both of its creation and transmission. Yet by opting for the analysis of a discursive formation, however rich, Brown still pays insufficient attention to the improvisatory powers of those who constitute the field of social activity.[25] He neglects both alternative institutional and clerical strategies and other theologies, and the self-orderings of ordinary lives in specific places over time. Sarah Williams' detailed local history constitutes a unique reference for Brown, but he has not fully drawn the lesson from it that if attention is turned towards popular categories, an ethnographic dimension is necessary. Discourse analysis gives an unexamined authority to the written word: it is as if our reading (or use of other media, such as films) gave us the uncritically absorbed means by which we live our lives—our possibilities and our limits, the thinkable and what never occurs to us. This is too great an assumption; the role of popular literature in common lives is a crucial topic, but it demands more nuanced theorizing, investigation, and description. Last, he neglects to give any account of the place of the state as a social actor seeking to establish and expand the bounds of a minimum secular settlement, and yet this may be the key to any account of church-state relations in the sixties and later.[26]

In order, then, to fulfil the promise of Ford's idea, we need to carry out the programme Brown has set out. By portraying secularization theory as a way of talking and not concerned with the objective description of natural facts, Brown brings academic talk into the field of social facts. In the early analysis of Chalmers et al., he also identifies the active, improvisatory intelligence of leaders and small groups that together create new categories and possibilities for the ordinary lives and practices with which they come into contact. This is a crucial feature; for this kind of reason, the present is, to a great degree, indiscernible, and the future open. And Brown is surely right, too, to focus on gender relations as an area of extraordinary contemporary interest; we might look to the improvisations of Charismatic churches in the area of the family and the settlement between

25. See Morris, "The Strange Death of Christian Britain"; Morris, "Secularization in Modern Britain."

26. See, for example, Prochaska, *Christianity and Social Science*; Green and Whiting, *The Boundaries of the State.*

the sexes as a topic to watch in the unpredictable future of Britain, neither precisely Christian nor secular.

Conclusion

It is possible following Howard to distinguish European and American styles of approach to secularization. The first regards church-state relations as a zero-sum game, on the one hand, and instances of continuing faith as entirely individually motivated, on the other. The second conceives the vocation of citizens to make their own lives as a process carried on under minimum conditions set by the state, a process in which religion may play its part. Ford identifies these three possibilities dialectically as epic, lyric, and dramatic forms. The question then arises of whether there is any sociological account that corresponds to the dramatic form. Brown's work gives a "dramatic" account of the formation of the European categories, but falls short to a degree in failing to study both the practices of believers and, to a greater extent, the practices of the state that negotiate a minimum secular settlement amongst its citizens.

Ford's work then sets the agenda for the repair of the sociology of secularization. What general lessons can be drawn for the work of theologians? In the first place, theologians tend to pay insufficient attention to the various histories that lie behind the production of certain social categories, especially categories that arise in other disciplines but which they wish to use. In the second place, sociologists (with certain exceptions) tend to make a version of the same mistake, so that theologians' borrowings import the sociological neglect of attention to local particularity. The result is that, although theologians are right in their wish to include the social aspects of religious life in the phenomena they discuss, these discussions are frequently flawed or even rendered meaningless. Rethinking the category of "the secular" is then an urgent theological task and, if we follow the indications of this conversation I have traced, it will be best pursued through attention to specific histories and localities.

Bibliography

Asad, Talal. *Formations of the Secular: Christianity, Islam, Modernity*. Stanford: Stanford University Press, 2003.

Berger, Peter L., editor. *The Desecularization of the World: Resurgent Religion and World Politics*. Grand Rapids: Eerdmans, 1999.

Brown, Callum G. *The Death of Christian Britain: Understanding Secularization*, 1800–2000. London: Routledge, 2009.

Davie, Grace. *Europe: The Exceptional Case: Parameters of Faith in the Modern World*. London: Darton, Longman & Todd, 2002.

Ford, David F. *The Future of Christian Theology*. Oxford: Wiley-Blackwell, 2011.

———. *Shaping Theology: Engagements in a Religious and Secular World*. Oxford: Blackwell, 2007.

Green, S. J. D. *The Passing of Protestant England: Secularization and Social Change, c. 1920–1960*. Cambridge: Cambridge University Press, 2011.

Green, S. J. D., and R. C. Whiting, editors. *The Boundaries of the State in Modern Britain*. Cambridge: Cambridge University Press, 1996.

Harding, Susan Friend. *The Book of Jerry Falwell: Fundamentalist Language and Politics*. Princeton: Princeton University Press, 2000.

Howard, Thomas Albert. *God and the Atlantic: America, Europe, and the Religious Divide*. Oxford: Oxford University Press, 2011.

Jenkins, Timothy, and Ben Quash. *Cambridge Inter-Faith Programme Academic Profile*. 2006. Online: http://www.interfaith.cam.ac.uk/en/resources/papers/cip-academic-profile.

McLeod, Hugh. *The Religious Crisis of the 1960s*. Oxford: Oxford University Press, 2007.

Morris, Jeremy. "Secularization in Modern Britain since 1800." *The Historical Journal*, forthcoming.

———. "The Strange Death of Christian Britain: Another Look at the Secularization Debate." *The Historical Journal* 46 (2003) 963–76.

Nexon, Daniel H. *The Struggle for Power in Early Modern Europe: Religious Conflict, Dynastic Empires and International Change*. Princeton: Princeton University Press, 2009.

Prochaska, Frank. *Christianity and Social Service in Modern Britain: The Disinherited Spirit*. Oxford: Oxford University Press, 2006.

Quash, Ben. *Theology and the Drama of History*. Cambridge: Cambridge University Press, 2005.

Stout, Jeffrey. *Democracy and Tradition*. Princeton: Princeton University Press, 2004.

Taylor, Charles. *Modern Social Imaginaries*. Durham: Duke University Press, 2004.

———. *A Secular Age*. Cambridge, MA: Belknap, 2007.

Williams, Sarah. *Religious Belief and Popular Culture in Southwark, c. 1880–1939*. Oxford: Oxford University Press, 1999.

13

Theology among the Humanities

Rowan Williams

Magdalene College, University of Cambridge

The exact sciences constitute a monologic form of knowledge: the intellect contemplates a **thing** *and expounds upon it. There is only one subject here—cognizing (contemplating) and speaking (expounding). In opposition to the subject there is only a voiceless thing.*[1]

This is how the great Russian critic Mikhail Bakhtin defines the sort of academic labour that does *not* belong in the humanities: science is the study of what does not answer back, whereas the typical mode of the humanities is "dialogical." In fact, of course, such a definition is a travesty of what actual science does. The sciences (the "exact" sciences) do not constitute the monologic practice that Bakhtin sketches, a single subject mapping a passive object; for one thing, the subject in scientific research is someone who has learned a practice along with others and whose observations and utterances are offered for scrutiny to a very demanding community of practice. But it is also true that what the scientist studies is the *product* of conversation and community: the researcher does not—as Bakhtin's language might suggest—approach a raw phenomenon, if such a thing is even thinkable, but an object whose boundaries and properties have been settled in a long process of negotiation. The object is, we

1. Bakhtin, *Speech Genres*, 161.

might say, *proposed* to the researcher; it is already a "text." And once the researcher has done his or her work, the text continues to be elaborated; there are new "proposals" to be engaged. Unless we are searching for a single reductive register in which to discuss and explain all possible phenomena—a fantasy more popular with non-scientists than with working researchers, it must be said—the dialogic elements in science have to be acknowledged. All sciences are human sciences, it has been said; and the work of philosophers of science like Joseph Margolis or—from a rather different point of view—Roy Bhaskar has stressed the ways in which both reductive methods (there is only one adequate mode of explanation) and non-realist theories (scientific discourse is simply one form of learned behaviour with no claim to truth) miss the essence of what scientists do.[2] They cannot but work on "texts; but the context of the textually based labour is not a groundless abyss."[3] "A history," says Margolis, "is the intentionally unified or coherent diachronic career of (or assignable to) a text"; and "texts exist, are found, are recognized, and are understood only in the world or space of human culture—(*only*) by persons, being naturally groomed within their respective societies to be apt for producing and understanding themselves and their texts."[4]

As Alan Jacobs notes in a very helpful discussion of the Bakhtinian judgement,[5] the Russian scholar is deliberately addressing an ethical rather than a methodological issue: the question that concerns him is what happens when someone lays claim to a form of knowing in which what ought to have a voice is made voiceless. It is part of a polemic against the misconstruction of what the "human sciences" might come to mean. As such, its usefulness is as a heuristic tool for thinking about thinking rather than a way of distinguishing between "arts and sciences." Together with Margolis' suggestive phrasing of the intrinsic connection between text and history, it holds our attention upon the temporal character of human thinking. Our temptation is constantly, it seems, to spatialize our thought, in the sense of imagining the activity of thinking in terms of two spatial standpoints, observer and observed, which allow us to give a definitive account of what can be observed. But the truth is that complex space, three-dimensional space, is mentally constructed through time,

2. See, for example, Margolis, *Science Without Unity*, chapter 11.

3. Ibid., 391.

4. Ibid., 377–78.

5. Jacobs, *Theology of Reading*, 51.

through the bringing together of various imagined standpoints,[6] so that the crude binary confrontation of observer and observed in an ideal and isolated moment will deliver very little in understanding what it is to react intelligently to our environment. Where we are talking about our relation with other literal speakers, it is obvious that the active-passive polarity is only a very small part of the picture—hence the moral concern about what renders another "voiceless." But Bakhtin could be read as warning us against a *general* privileging of monologic, even where it is not obvious that our objects have a "voice." If we are always engaging with texts, we are always contributing to a dialogue of sorts; and the fact that complex space requires us to think about the dimension of time reminds us that the construction even of a supposedly passive object involves allowing it to make different successive impacts upon us: it is not simply *possessed* in one act of perception or comprehension. And this is at least analogous to allowing the object a voice, in the sense that it allows the object to be at any given moment more than it then appears, more than we can consciously take in.

Against this background, it is possible to see that serious intellectual labour, whether we call it science or humanities, is an activity that can never be done for the last time; the point is not that we do it so as to "have done" (with) it, but that the encounter of thought or contemplation, in Bakhtin's wording, continues to press us to begin again or at least to recognize that the encounter of thought has changed the world it thinks. An intellectual culture that privileges the hope of closure is a dangerous and sterile one. As I shall be arguing later in this chapter, one of the chief functions of the humanities when such a culture threatens to distort the intellectual enterprise is to protest, along with genuine science, against the reduction of thinking to closure-oriented problem solving; not, as they say, an entirely academic issue just at the moment. When David Lodge, in his splendid university comedy of 1975, *Changing Places*, created the American literary critic Professor Morris Zapp, whose great aim in life is to provide totally exhaustive commentaries on all the novels of Jane Austen "so that when each commentary was written there would be simply *nothing further to say* about the novel in question,"[7] he was no doubt painting with what seemed a very broad brush at the time; the barbarically obsessive quantifying of scholarly output still lay well in the future. But the sting is in the idea that the point of scholarly interpretation is ultimately

6. One of the most suggestive discussions in twentieth-century philosophy remains Merleau-Ponty, *Phenomenology of Perception*, especially Part 2.

7. Lodge, *Changing Places*, 44.

to silence any further conversation ("periodicals would fall silent, famous English Departments be left deserted like ghost towns . . ."); [8] to provide the last reading of texts, to have done with them. It is a vision of leaving the object terminally voiceless and silencing whatever possibilities of common discourse are connected with its continuing life.

Because the "exact sciences" are capable of establishing comparatively lasting consensus, they will always carry with them, in the eyes of a not too well instructed observer, the seductive possibility of coming to an end of learning. Which is why the presence of the humanities in the intellectual community is so crucial for the health of the whole enterprise: with due respect to Morris Zapp, it is simply not possible to imagine the humanities in such terms. At the very least, if there are any signs of hubris or fantasy among scientific neighbours, the humanities can remind the sciences that they have a history.

All of which so far is a relatively commonplace set of observations on the vagaries of intellectual method; but the point of this chapter is to push a bit further. The place of theology in the academy is clearly not among the "exact sciences"; but what precisely does it mean to count it among the humanities in the light of the brief foregoing discussion? I propose to argue that what the humanities in general can do for the academic community, theology itself can do for the humanities by offering a possible ground or context for sustaining the vision of dialogical encounter. It is not that theology is uniquely a discipline devoted to the dialogical; some would say that it should forfeit its place in the academy precisely because it is not and cannot be truly dialogical since it always assumes truths that cannot be established in rational public argument. But—given that there is a point there that will need addressing—there are ways of configuring the theological task that underline very strongly the model of theology as an *exemplary* case of the humanities—or, more properly, of the kind of discipline that resists the binary "active mind/passive object" disjunction that we have been warned about.

To begin with, then, we need to think for a moment about theology as a discipline of reading. It is very clear, certainly where the "Abrahamic" religious traditions are concerned, that religious practice and reflection are textually based: Judaism, Christianity, and Islam all work with a sacred text believed to be given by God—though the exact nature of that givenness is a matter of debate within and between the traditions. This means that all reflection within the community of faith has the character of response, of

8. Ibid., 45.

attempting to reply appropriately to what has come from another *subject*. It could be said that one of the central issues for theology has always been the question of how to avoid this prior subjectivity being absorbed into the *self*-reflection of the community of belief; and in Reformation and modern Christian theology, this has been a specially sharply contested area. Both in the Reformation insistence that *hearing* what is revealed is prior to *seeing*, because we are more obviously "passive" when we hear than when we see, and in the twentieth century, with Karl Barth's revolt against a theology in which God was, as it were, passively available for inspection or discovery, there is a manifest concern that theology should not become a monological activity—and a monological activity of a particularly malign sort, in that it can so readily degenerate into a self-indulgent focus on our feelings about an object that is not available in history or language. The materiality of the text serves theology as a reminder of its responsive character; and the nature of the text itself as something presented and received as an *address*, thus as an event of hearing, reinforces this. In the late T. F. Torrance's forceful discussion of these questions in the opening chapter of his underrated 1969 work, *Theological Science*, something of a *locus classicus* on the issue of the priority of hearing, he sums this up by saying that for theology, "[t]he given fact is *not a mute fact*—that is the kind of fact we have in the natural world, a fact that is only made to 'talk' as it comes to cognition and expression in our rational experience."[9] While, as we shall see, this formulation needs a good deal of qualification, it is a powerful crystallizing of Christian theology's historic starting point; revelation is not the provision of propositionally exhaustive information, but it is the provision of a datum from elsewhere that demands an appropriate reply. The text of revelation is the stimulus to a dialogue, a dialogue that is in principle unlimited, since the initial speaker is conceived as wholly and eternally free and thus not to be absorbed into the discourse of response.

Both the patristic and Orthodox tradition of "negative theology" and the Barthian emphasis on divine freedom to speak imply a provisionality in theology; not a provisionality of polite hesitation to affirm or a reluctance to make clear statements about the divine, but a fundamental disposition of intellect and spirit to question how honestly, vulnerably, or repentantly the divine communication is being received.[10] Barth's genius was to show at magisterial length how the affirmations of creedal orthodoxy about the incarnation and the Trinity, so far from being "speculative," are essentially

9. Torrance, *Theological Science*, 29.

10. E.g., Lossky, *Mystical Theology*, 42; cf. Williams, *Wrestling With Angels*, chapter 1.

the basic things that have to be said in order to establish precisely God's freedom to speak—and thus also to establish the universal imperative need for us to seek to open ourselves more fully to the truth God is communicating. The fundamentals of doctrine, in this context, represent an agenda for the Spirit—of self-examination and the "de-centring" of the ego's agenda. The mature doctrinal formulations of the early church are not supposed to be comprehensive maps of the divine life; they affirm simply what must be affirmed of God if the practice of Christian prayer, listening, and self-questioning is to be valid and to make sense.

Theology is a discipline of reading and thus a discipline of holding together active and passive engagement; it belongs with the humanities because of its exemplary inability to reduce its "object" to silence. And it is this "exemplary incapacity" that makes it, we could say, the most extreme case of the humanities: what it studies is always expected to make a contemporary and transforming difference that overcomes the individual resistance we put up, the assumptions that would absorb object into subject. As John Webster has recently argued,[11] theology offers an account of the life of intellect as such, which is essential to each and every specific discipline (so that it is never quite enough *for the theologian* to think about it as simply one among others). "A theology of the humanities derives from a more general theology of the intellectual arts—that is, from a theological portrayal of what happens when the reconciled creaturely intellect is at work."[12] Such a theology presupposes that the "reading" activity of the mind is—in every aspect of its interpretative engagement with the world—picking up the traces of the world's origin in an act of intelligible, structured love: the creation of finite being, and the bestowal upon it of an interconnectedness, which guarantees that from every point in finitude it is possible to arrive at a vision of this originating act.[13] I would add only that it is theology that decisively illustrates the importance in this of the perennial centrality of humility, the readiness to *be* questioned rather than to do all the questioning. And this is, incidentally, a model of intellect that encompasses the exact sciences as much as the humanities: the interconnectedness charted by the sciences is in this context no more voiceless than the textual interlocutor in the humanities. The monological subject examining a silent and passive bit of raw material is blocking off

11. Webster, "*Regina Artium.*"

12. Ibid., 57–58.

13. Ibid., 51; cf. Fishbane, *Sacred Attunement*, 37–43, for a strikingly comparable Jewish approach.

the journey into the originating act of being; and to the extent that the sciences refuse such a model of looking at an object that can in principle be seen through and round and once and for all, they align themselves with what Webster and others want to say about intellect theologically understood. Where intellect refuses to treat the object as a system whose comprehension can be definitively closed off, it retains its theological significance. *Pace* Torrance, it is not then quite true to say that the objects of scientific enquiry "talk" only when licensed to by the enquirer. Something like a "summons" to understanding is part of what is presupposed by the openness of intellect. And the disagreement between religious and secular accounts of scientific knowing will be about how much more than useful metaphor is this language of invitation and its implications of address.[14]

But there is another dimension to this discussion of theology as an "exemplary incapacity" to close off the intellectual process, one that is recognized in every exercise in theological exegesis, yet not all that often thought through in detail. What theology in the Abrahamic traditions read is a text always already *reread.* Orthodox Jewish reflection begins with the monumental accumulation of readings and rereadings that constitutes the Talmud. Hebrew Scripture in its broader definition, the Tanakh as a whole, includes major acts of rereading and reconceiving narrative, from the doubled narrative in Genesis of the creation of the human, to the Chronicler's reworking of Samuel and Kings and, less obvious but hard to deny, the author of Ruth's rereading of a history widely assumed to be one of essential ethnic purity.[15] For the Christian, the Four Gospels themselves represent a sequence of new readings and new configurings of received material, a sequence whose details are notoriously resistant to decisive mapping. And the entire corpus of Christian Scripture, of course, is as a whole an exercise in rereading Jewish Scripture—with all the spiritual and moral ambivalence that this now presents to us, it has also to be said. The devout Muslim will hear the Qur'an as a setting-right of the distortions of primordial Scripture represented by the Christian's text, a therapeutic and corrective rereading. And as if emboldened by this scriptural practice of rereading, the theologians of Christian history have consistently reread their own theological texts: there are the various reappropriations of Augustine in the Middle Ages, not to mention the rich history of rereading

14. Cunningham, *Darwin's Pious Idea*, is a profoundly suggestive contribution to discussion on these themes; see especially 303–45.

15. For a fuller discussion, see Williams, "The Discipline of Scripture," in *On Christian Theology.*

and indeed creatively *mis*reading Pseudo-Dionysius;[16] the immense revisionist project of the Reformation, especially in the hands of someone like Calvin;[17] and the twentieth- and twenty-first-century recoveries of earlier theologians, from the *nouvelle theologie* of postwar France and the neopatristic theologies of Russian Orthodox writers like Lossky and Florovsky to the various bids for the "essential" Luther made by scholars as diverse as Holl, von Lowenich, Ebeling, and the more recent Finnish school.[18] Theology's attention to its own past is often critical, unmistakeably dialogical. The theologian is summoned not to repeat but to engage with a set of texts already internally "engaged," already in conversation.

Like other humanities, theology, in watching how texts "behave" is watching thought at work. Confessional theology is different only in the fact that the theologian's behaviour is bound up with the behaviour of the texts and traditions under consideration; this is his or her conversation, his or her native language. The formidable Canadian poet and critic, Robert Bringhurst, has written about how, even with the supposedly anonymous creators and performers of oral art, what we are seeing is a speaker taking risks with what has been inherited, risking themselves and their tradition.[19] In what may seem a paradoxical way, the individual performer has to have immense confidence in him or herself as well as in the tradition to be able to take such risks: they have to believe that the tradition is capable of surviving tough probing and reworking—which is very much the assumption of Talmudic discussion. The individual theologian practising theology as an exploratory matter, not only as description, is entering a world in which dialogue is possible with an unbounded freedom: that freedom is shown in the constant rediscovery of the inadequacy of the concepts you began with and the constant discovery of the (already conversational and self-questioning) text's "excess," its capacity to generate

16. On this, see the special issue of *Modern Theology* edited by Coakley and Stang in 2008—a collection of outstandingly interesting essays covering the reception of Dionysius from the early Middle Ages to the present. Now available as a book, *Re-Thinking Dionysius the Areopagite.*

17. MacCulloch, *History of Christianity*, 632–36, gives a fine brief digest of the rationale for seeing Calvin as consciously seeking to repristinate the patristic heritage; for an impressive longer account, see Canlis, *Calvin's Ladder.*

18. On this last, Braaten and Jenson, *Union With Christ*, provides an excellent introduction. On the *nouvelle theologie*, Milbank, *The Suspended Middle*, is a typically original and insightful discussion. Gallaher, "Waiting for the Barbarians" is a groundbreaking study of the historical ambiguities traceable in the neo-patristic movement in Eastern Orthodoxy.

19. Bringhurst, *Everywhere*, 84.

new meanings. In relation to the other humanities, it claims that the indeterminacy and revisability of a discipline that refuses to silence the voice of the other is grounded in a fundamental inexhaustibility of "being"—but also that this inexhaustibility is not simply a limitless, trackless infinity of possible meanings. Theology—and again I have in mind the self-reflection of the Abrahamic traditions—points to a narrative in which the excess or indeterminacy of being is presented as the excess of a giver over the gift; it asserts in and through its basic narratives that what prevents a collapse into universal indeterminacy is the grounding of being in love. And it is this grounding in love that gives boldness to the theologian to live in the critical awareness of the negative—not this, not yet, but also not other than this, nowhere else but here. The dispossession of theology, its "exemplary incapacity" to present a fixed and final conceptual scheme, is always contained within the affirmation of an originating gift, an originating act that bestows life, intelligence and the capacity for love. This ontological affirmation allows all excess and all indeterminacy, the constant reimagining work of the humanities, to remain—in the proper sense of the word—"humanistic," oriented to a mystery in human affairs that attracts and demands reverence.

For Christian theology there is, of course, the further point that the originating act of gift is itself grounded in the grammar of God as such: God's identity is always an identity that cannot be rendered as a simple *self*-identity. God is always God in relation to a *divine* otherness (not just the difference of finite reality): at each point at which we "stop" to think of God—Fatherhood, Sonship, the Spirit—there is a divine excess, a something not-yet-said, a relatedness such that we cannot speak truthfully if we ignore it. To speak of the divine embodiment in Jesus of Nazareth is unintelligible without referencing the divine otherness to which he prays. To speak of an indwelling divine Spirit is unintelligible unless it is connected to the specific shape in Jesus of this embodied life of prayer, suffering and transforming compassion. To speak of the source of divine life is unintelligible if we do not specify that what eternally comes from this source is "filial" relation and the energy that opens up this mode of relation without limit, opens it to what is created. There is no point to stop and "freeze" an identity. The most basic ontology of all is one of irreducible difference and irreducible mutual dependence.

Robert Bringhurst intimates in a brilliant discussion of Native American models of mind that the ultimate skill of language is to make sure that we are not always of one mind, so that we continue actually to *live* in a constantly shifting balance of forces.[20] Bringhurst describes a feature of the "phenomenology of spirit," found in the literature of the Wakashan group of languages, that has some relevance to the wider issue here. In addition to the tenfold division of mind, there is an eleventh element whose name is best translated as "Continuing to Live": this is, says Bringhurst, "a kind of blind ecological conscience: the thought that mind embodies, which is always inaccessible to mind."[21] It is a teasing and pregnant phrase. Mind cannot capture itself: despite any amount of analysis of mental process and its neurological mapping, the fact remains that it is an attempt to fix as an object what is simultaneously and absolutely necessarily known from within as a subject. Insofar as we can say anything intelligible about this, it is—Bringhurst implies—by thinking of thinking as an ecological instinct, a constant adjustment to an environment that cannot be controlled but can be negotiated. In such a context, speaking truthfully is speaking in a way that continues to make life possible, that allows the ecology of human thought-in-relation-to-what-provokes-it to keep a viable balance. David Ford's image of an "embracing mood" catches something important here.[22] From nuclear physics to poetry and back again, truthfulness is what generates the capacity for shared life and speech within the given constraints of a finite world—a matter certainly of truth *claims*, as this is not a recipe for relativism or constructivism (we cannot just "say what we like" if it is a question of preserving a life-sustaining balance), but also a matter of constant readjustment, like the adjustment of the swimmer to the sea.

And if we then ask what truthfulness and intellectual accountability might look like in theology, the answer would have to be in terms of what sustained the capacity to go on living in the "shape" of God's self-bestowing in love. If the trinitarian love of God is the ultimate context for everything that is, any comprehensive "ecology" for human life will finally find itself adjusting and readjusting to this if it is to continue to live. Truthful Christian theology (and I leave it to others to spell out what this would mean in other theologies) is Christian reflection and confession (acknowledgement) negotiating with the given pattern of parental self-gift and filial love in God, as this pattern is embodied in biblical narrative, in the various historical readings of that narrative, and specially in those "readings" that are actual performances in worship and in holy life. And if the objection is made that this is not robust enough as an account of

20. Ibid., 282–83.

21. Ibid., 283.

22. Ford, *Christian Wisdom*, 50.

Christian truth-claims, the reply must be that the continuing labour of adjustment to what is believed to be the context in which life continues *shows* its obedience to and seriousness about an abiding and mind-independent reality in its willingness to go on testing what is said—intellectually, spiritually, and in terms of practice in general—with confidence and courage. It is a courage that includes the willingness to say of this or that formulation, "This is our best verbal 'strategy' for responding to the current of God's action, and we may not be able to imagine any better; but we are not claiming that what is on offer is a simple descriptive summary." Or, in slightly different terminology, exactly *how* such theological formulation refers is not something we can scrutinize; but the way in which the language operates, its points of strain or self-criticism, tells us that we cannot set aside the intention to refer, to tell a truth not reducible to an account of our own feeling or to speculative play.

To sum up: Christian theology as a discipline displays "exemplary incapacity," a systemic resistance to the monological temptation, the silencing of the object of study. As such, it is "exemplary" for intellectual life itself, science as well as humanities; but it has a particular significance for humanities liable to be seduced by a monological view of science that is a fair distance from what serious scientists actually do. Theology's incapacity is anchored in the recognition that its "object" can only be imagined as an inexhaustible act of gift, bestowal: this is what divine action is constructed as in the narratives of believing communities, in Scripture, and in the history of the reading of Scripture. Through this recognition, the theologian implicitly locates all intellectual enterprise within the same horizon of engaging with an excess of meaning that witnesses to the "given" nature of finite reality. Theology's claim to be not only a legitimate partner in the work of the humanities but in some sense the bearer of a crucial critical insight about their character can be sustained only by the theologian's willingness to work responsibly at the specific ways in which and the points at which the language of doctrine compels a radical self-recognition not only as finite but as constantly capable of self-justificatory fabrication, constantly tempted (in Simone Weil's terms) to "fill the void" in speech or (in more positive idiom) to deny the uncapturable excess. And, in a hopelessly paradoxical fashion, this refusal to deny excess and fill up silence is inseparable from a particular ontology of difference grounded in a particular (trinitarian) apprehension of God. The practice of theology seeks to sustain life: to represent in its verbal exercise the ecology of mind itself in its receptive and creative interaction with what it is not, the probing and yielding in encounter with what is ultimately an act of absolute gift that can be received only in the "embrace" that David Ford's phrase points us to.

It is an ambitious self-description for any intellectual discipline, and we should not be shy of acknowledging that it is not like other disciplines. Nor should we be shy of underlining the fact that, as characterized here, it is inescapably a practice belonging with a range of other spiritual practices, not simply a detached and speculative matter. That it can be responsibly, even creatively, studied by those who do not see it as *their* practice—studied as a subject among others in the academy—is by no means impossible, however, so long as it is seen not as what Nietzsche classically identified as a science of unreal objects but precisely as a practice of self-aware commitment, of *wisdom*, to use David Ford's favourite category. But as a practice simultaneously of humility and ambitious truth telling it is always likely to unsettle even the uncommitted student. If the registers of both proper fear and love cannot be excluded from theological speech, it is bound to put some questions to what we assume we know about knowing. But to raise the question of how we may come to *know* something about "how to be human before God"[23] is surely not an ignoble goal for theology in its engagements with the human sciences.

Bibliography

Bakhtin, Mikhail. *Speech Genres and Other Late Essays*. Translated by Vern W. McGee. Edited by Caryl Emerson and Michael Holquist. Austin: University of Texas Press, 1986.

Braaten, Carl E., and Robert W. Jenson. *Union With Christ: The New Finnish Interpretation of Luther*. Grand Rapids: Eerdmans, 1998.

Bringhurst, Robert. *Everywhere Being is Dancing: Twenty Pieces of Thinking*. Kentville, Nova Scotia: Gaspereau, 2007.

Canlis, Julie. *Calvin's Ladder: A Spiritual Theology of Ascent and Ascension*. Grand Rapids: Eerdmans, 2010.

Coakley, Sarah, and Charles M. Stang, editors. *Re-Thinking Dionysius the Areopagite*. Directions in Modern Theology. Oxford: Wiley-Blackwell, 2009.

Cunningham, Conor. *Darwin's Pious Idea: Why the Ultra-Darwinists and Creationists Both Get It Wrong*. Grand Rapids: Eerdmans, 2010.

Fishbane, Michael. *Sacred Attunement: A Jewish Theology*. Chicago: University of Chicago Press, 2008.

Ford, David F. *Christian Wisdom: Desiring God and Learning in Love*. Cambridge: Cambridge University Press, 2007.

23. Ibid., 369.

Gallaher, Brandon, "'Waiting for the Barbarians': Identity and Polemicism in the Neo-Patristic Synthesis of Georges Florovsky." *Modern Theology* 27 (2011) 659–91.

Jacobs, Alan. *A Theology of Reading: The Hermeneutics of Love*. Boulder, CO: Westview, 2001.

Lodge, David. *Changing Places*. London: Secker & Warburg, 1975.

Lossky, Vladimir. *The Mystical Theology of the Eastern Church*. London: Clarke, 1957.

MacCulloch, Diarmaid. *A History of Christianity: The First Three Thousand Years*. London: Allen Lane, 2009.

Margolis, Joseph. *Science Without Unity: Reconciling the Human and Natural Sciences*. Oxford: Blackwell, 1987.

Merleau-Ponty, Maurice. *Phenomenology of Perception*. Translated by Colin Smith. London: Routledge & Kegan Paul, 1962.

Milbank, John. *The Suspended Middle: Henri de Lubac and the Debate concerning the Supernatural*. Grand Rapids: Eerdmans 2005.

Torrance, Thomas F. *Theological Science*. London: Oxford University Press, 1969.

Webster, John, "*Regina Artium*: Theology and the Humanities." In *Theology, University, Humanities: Initium Sapientiae Timor Domini*, edited by Christopher Craig Brittain and Francesca Aran Murphy, 39–63. Eugene, OR: Cascade Books, 2011.

Williams, Rowan. *On Christian Theology*. Oxford: Blackwell, 2000.

———. *Wrestling With Angels: Conversations in Modern Theology*. London: SCM, 2007.

PART FOUR

Reasoning between Faiths

14

What Kinds of Thinking Complement What Kinds of Societal Action?

Peter Ochs

University of Virginia

David Ford has been my theological and theo-social dialogue partner for twenty years. Over a lifetime, I have enjoyed just a very few such partnerships, and in each I have experienced what Aristotle says of friendship—that we seek in the other what raises us up in ourselves. By way of illustration, each time I have written about David Ford's work, I appear to have focused on an aspect of it that best raised me to what I was then seeking. In one essay on Ford's work, this was dialogue; in another, it was poiesis; in another, salvation.[1]

On this occasion, I seek to gain traction on an issue which those engaged in the interfaith activity of Scriptural Reasoning have not yet treated systematically: whether specific modes of theological and scriptural thinking correspond to specific patterns of societal and political work

1. For example: (a) on Ford on the reparative spirit and poiesis, Ochs, "Wisdom's Cry," in Ochs, *Another Reformation*; (b) on Ford on a God-centred soteriology of cry-and-repair, Ochs, "On *Christian Wisdom*"; (c) on wisdom in the world and on Ford in SR, Ochs, "Coda"; (d) on pneumatology and Anglican postliberalism in Ford and Hardy, Ochs, "Judaism and Christian Theology," 655–56.

and, if they do, how. David Ford's career should offer us a prime test case, since he invests his theological work equally in academic writing and in the performance of institution-, community-, and relationship-building and repair. To honour David in this essay, I shall not burden him with yet another examination of his work but shall instead treat him to some storytelling about an early modern Jewish theologian who integrated scholarly and performative work in a way that I believe Ford would appreciate. It is only by dint of historical contingencies that Don Isaac Abravanel's public work was more swashbuckling than Ford's, and we can only pray that this particular difference continues. After the storytelling, I shall speculate about the kinds of correlation we might, through more disciplined scholarship, observe between theological thinking and public performance in the history of Jewish thought. I offer these speculations in the hope that more qualified scholars (most especially those engaged in the practice of Scriptural Reasoning and text-historical scholars in particular) may soon pursue such work for real: searching out within the work of thinkers from Philo to Ford what we might call the virtues and measures of performative thinking as a theological vocation.[2] Those of us who have been engaged in interfaith work of Scriptural Reasoning have become fairly accomplished in understanding the patterns and practices of inter-Abrahamic scriptural study. We engage in this work all for the sake of repairing the academy, the seminaries, the social relations, and institutions that are influenced by them. But what are the patterns of repair that will, to some degree of probability, lead from study to societal performance? Thinking about Ford's work at this time "raises me up" to this question, and I ask it to set an agenda for the vocation of theology today.

The Case of Don Isaac Abravanel

To examine this question, I choose the case of Don Isaac Abravanel. I do so because he is such a colourful and even extreme case of a thinker whose life was as much in the world as it was in the ivory tower. This is only a first step, however. A second step would be to show which particular kinds of ivory tower study might complement which particular kinds of societal repair. I hope others will soon undertake that study as their vocation in earnest.

2. I am no historian, nor even a qualified scholar of medieval and early modern Judaism. I venture into the subject of this essay strictly in the hope that some qualified text historians may rush to do it the right way.

Abravanel was a remarkable figure in the history of Judaism in the fifteenth century. His life story reads like an adventure movie and, at times, a disaster movie. He lived in Portugal and Spain in the years when the once proud and secure Jewish civilization in Spain was, step by step, headed to destruction and dissolution. During many of those years he was the effective leader and spokesperson for the Jewish community-in-exile in Portugal, then Spain, then various principalities in Italy. Often, his movement from one settlement to the next was alongside the Jewish community's flights from persecution; at times, it was to avoid this or that prince's personal vendetta against him. Remarkably, he achieved political roles somewhat like that of the biblical Joseph with the princes or kings of each of the states he lived in or fled to. He often served as the royalty's economic or also politico-economic advisor. As one might therefore expect, he was a man of great inherited wealth and also earned wealth, a man of great prudential and practical judgment, courage, audacity, verve. He was profoundly dedicated to the Jewish people, and he was cautiously and effectively self-protective and self-promoting as well. Alongside all this, he was also a deeply learned scholar of biblical, rabbinic, and medieval Judaism, of scriptural interpretation, of law, and of Kabbalah, and he was a prolific writer. Somehow, he wrote books of Jewish law and scholarship that accompanied each of his periods of political calamity and exile as well as each intervening periods of relative peace. These works are all the more of interest to us because the interpretive focus of each study appears to reflect his thinking about the place of Judaism and of the human being in each of the political turmoils he faced. While my report is merely introductory, drawn from secondary and tertiary sources, I trust it may demonstrate why the life and work of thinkers like Abravanel merit attention from scholars qualified to search out instructive patterns of what I shall call *performative thinking*—or thinking that moves successfully between study and societal repair.[3]

3. Among sources consulted are Feldman, *Philosophy in a Time of Crisis*; Ben-Sasson, *History*; Abravanel, *Letters*; Netanyahu, *Don Isaac Abravanel*; Borodowski, *Isaac Abravanel*; Ogren, *Renaissance*; Abravanel, *Principles of Faith*; Abravanel, *Perush Abravanel'al ha-Torah*; Abravanel, *Perush Abravanel al sefer Moreh Nevukhim*; Abravanel, *Ateret zekenim*.

Stages in Abravanel's Life Story

Abravanel was born in Lisbon in 1437. For generations, his was *the* family of great wealth and political influence, highly respected within the Jewish communities of Portugal and Spain. It was also a family of deep Jewish and classical learning. His father and grandfather were financial advisors to the Portuguese royalty and their households were places of learning. As a youth, Abravanel was trained in the Latin-scholastic classics and in the sciences of his day, as well as in rabbinic learning. From early in his adult years, he was also a student and active contributor to the literatures of Jewish mysticism and apocalypticism.

A Family of Spanish Exiles in Portugal

While Abravanel's family's occupied prestigious positions in the Court, the young Abravanel must also have been exposed to Portugal's significant anti-Semitism, including anti-Jewish riots in Lisbon. In his young adulthood, during the more benign rule of King Alfonso, Abravanel composed his first philosophic monograph, *Forms of the Elements*; a study of the Aristotelian elements written within the frame of Maimonides' philosophic work. About ten years later, in his late thirties, he composed *Crown of the Elders*, in which his respect for Maimonides was tempered by a growing interest in mysticism and, later, apocalypticism.[4] This study of the wisdom of the prophets marks a "radical shift in his thinking,"[5] and anticipates many of his lifelong theses. Without abandoning the discipline of systematic reasoning, he criticizes the kind of rationalizing Aristotelian philosophy that will become the hallmark of Gersonides' work, favouring instead a reasoned reading of prophetic visions of the future and of mystical engagement with the divine presence.[6] In the latter years of his days in Portugal, Abravanel wrote *Vision of God*—another study of prophecy, respecting but also challenging Maimonides' account of how prophecy works.[7]

4. Abravanel, *Ateret zekenim*.

5. Feldman, *Philosophy in a Time of Crisis*, 7. See also Feldman, "Prophecy and Perception."

6. Students of Scriptural Reasoning may appreciate some analogies between his turn away from Aristotelian philosophy and that of Al-Ghazali, whose work he sometimes cited.

7. Abravanel completed *Vision of God* (*Mahazeh Shadai*) in Spain.

By this time, Abravanel also began to enter into what would become his lifetime occupations in the world of political action. With the aging, then passing of his father, he began to assume political and communal responsibilities in both the Portuguese Jewish community and the Portuguese Court. In the fashion of what historians of European Judaism call "Höf Juden" (Court Jews), part of Abravanel's role was to represent Jewish society to the court, protecting its economic and social interests and often its bare survival.[8] Under King Alfonso V, whose rule was more benign towards the Jews then his predecessors, Abravanel became national treasurer, at times drawing on his own funds to assist the crown. At the same time, in addition to various intra-communal affairs, he contributed to dramatic efforts to protect Jews. When, for example, the King conquered a city in Morocco and held 250 of its Jews for ransom, Abravanel raised funds to redeem them, and—using his own resources—to support them for two years until they were prepared to speak Portuguese and earn a living.

One of the most revealing archival sources on Abravanel in this period is the set of his correspondences with a fellow Jewish courtier, Yehiel, whose assistance Abravanel sought concerning several matters of political intrigue. Abravanel explains to his friend, for example, how he sought the favour of two Portuguese ambassadors to the Pope to deliver a successful entreaty on behalf of the Portuguese Jewish community. He then sought Yehiel's assistance to pay the ambassadors for this service. In explanatory commentary from the editor of the archive of these letters, the editor notes how Abravanel draws on extensive scriptural and rabbinic textual knowledge to provide tropes that serve his entreaty; how his language is fashioned in the manner of Portuguese letters; and how he describes, in passing, his own Jewish scholarship, and the way his house serves as a place of Jewish learning.[9]

Escape from Portugal

After Alfonso V died and Joao II became king (or, in Abravanel's terms, "tyrant"), the court was more accepting of popular Portuguese sentiment against the Jews. Seeking to limit the power of the feudal lords, Joao appealed for power directly to the people and against those, like the economic counsellor Abravanel, who were favoured by the feudal princes.

8. On "Court Jews," see Ben-Sasson, *History*, 76, 396ff.

9. Abravanel, *Letters*.

Joao encouraged public enmity against Judaism, the prejudice always available among the populace but previously subdued by the king and the nobles. Just before the Jewish population itself fled persecution, Abravanel escaped over the border to Spain, learning soon after that Joao's agents had engineered a plot against him in Portugal. During this period in Spain, Abravanel took time to develop lectures on the Former Prophets, composing within one year commentaries on Joshua, Judges, and Samuel. In these, he addressed specific questions of biblical exegesis and more generalizable questions about the life and fate of kings and other government leaders.

Entry into the Favour of Spain's Catholic Kings

Soon after his move to Spain, Abravanel sought the attention of the Spanish court. Indeed, in 1484, Ferdinand and Isabella invited him for an audience and soon thereafter he became financial counsellor to the crown. All this occurred less than a decade before the expulsion of all Jews from Spain. In Spain as in Portugal, Jewish influence tended to lie with the nobles, to whose economic goals Jewish financiers could offer counsel. As in Portugal, the interests of the Spanish crown gradually turned away from the nobles and, in the name of the populace and of the clerics' Inquisition, the crown became an enemy of the Jews and sought their exile. The goal was undoubtedly not so much conversion, which would have failed to provide any economic benefit for the crown, but literal removal, and—with it—the possibility of retaining much of the former wealth of the fleeing Jewish populations. Throughout this trying period, Abravanel maintained his two public occupations of caring for the Jewish community and serving as counsellor to the crown. As conditions worsened, his two activities became increasingly interconnected as he sought, often with his own wealth, to influence the court away from its anti-Jewish machinations. In the end, his efforts were futile and he may, perhaps, have misread the situation, overworking to repair the Jews' plight rather than planning earlier for mass exile. He apparently did not complete any recognized works in this period, which ended with his fleeing Spain for Naples in 1492.

Troubled Life in Italy

Thousands of Jews perished during the period of expulsion from Spain, many under the terrible conditions of sea or land passage. If some sought exile in Italy, it was not for an easy life. At this time, the ten northern states of Italy had rather bad records concerning the treatment of the Jews and, for that matter, one another. In many of these states, the merchant class opposed the Jews, whom they considered financial rivals, while the Papal States opposed the Jews for religious reasons. Abravanel settled first in Naples, where kings remained stronger than the merchants and clerics, and where financial advisors like Abravanel could gain favour. King Ferrante, in fact, allowed ships of the miserable Jewish exiles to land in Naples, despite popular sentiment against them. The family Abravanel found their way there as well. Soon, Abravanel was able to contribute his talents to Ferrante's court as an economic and political advisor.

During his first year in Naples, Abravanel completed a commentary on the books of Kings, once again offering textual commentary on the vagaries of kingship alongside his biblical exegesis. Next, he wrote a theological piece called *Eternal Justice* (*Tsedek Olamim,* now lost), addressing questions of theodicy. He then began a work to be entitled *The Days of the World.* His goal was to examine the phenomena of Jewish survival throughout the terrible events of world history. One may assume that Abravanel had significant contact during these years with Naples' Jewish as well as Christian intelligentsia (such as Giovanni Potano, the noted humanist, and the Jewish intellectuals Judah Messer León and Elijah del Medigo). Abravanel's son Judah was deeply influenced by the Neoplatonism of the time, and Abravanel took up some of these influences as well, evident in his philosophic work *The Deeds of God.*

Out of Naples to Sicily

It was a time of war and conflict in Naples, and Abravanel fled once again in front of the French invasion by Charles VIII. Abravanel followed Naples' King Alfonso into Sicily. Behind him, French troops and local Neapolitans conspired in a pogrom against the Jewish community, killing some, enslaving and converting others, and in the process plundering a good part of Abravanel's wealth.

Corfu

In between warring parties of French, Spanish, Neapolitan, and other invaders and defenders, Abravanel fled to Corfu, Turkey, where he joined other exiled Jewish leaders and scholars. Just after arriving in Corfu, in his mid-sixties, Abravanel began a commentary on Isaiah and then interrupted that work to compose *Principles of Faith*, an examination of the fundamental tenets of Jewish faith. Arguing on behalf of Maimonides' thirteen articles of faith, he also argued, beyond Maimonides' rationalism, that "each sentence, word and letter of the Law is a principal and a root in itself."[10] During his two years in Corfu, Abravanel also completed the commentary on Deuteronomy he had begun in the mid-1470s.

Some Quiet in Monopoli

Choosing not to stay for an extended period in Turkey, Abravanel moved in 1495–96 to Monopoli, a seaport on the Adriadic coast controlled by Naples. Here, for a time, he was out of danger and unburdened by responsibilities towards any royals or towards the Jewish community. He evidently resumed *Days of the World*, but then interrupted it for a time to compose *Passover Sacrifice* (a study of the redemption of the Jews), after which he began *Inheritance of the Fathers* (a commentary on *Ethics of the Fathers* (*Pirke Avot*)). In the latter, he deplored the moral state and materialism of the surviving Jewish people and argued for the need to recover the truth and life-sustaining values of the rabbinic sages. Then, he wrote *Wells of Salvation*, the first of his messianic trilogy, offering prophecies of the political future of the world, predicting major conflicts between Christianity and Islam, Christendom and Turkey, and predicting that the final redemption would come soon, in 1503. He then added two more volumes on messianism.[11] The trilogy offered an extended, prophetic reading of the Bible along with an extensive account of post-biblical mysticism, all focused on messianic prediction. He then wrote *New Heavens*, a study of the account of creation in relation to contemporary views of the heavens—at once a Maimonidean and post-Maimonidean argument. Then, in 1498, he completed his commentary on Isaiah, which combined biblical exegesis with continued prophecies of the world's future. His seven-year stay in Monopoli ended with the Spanish conquest of Naples and subsequent war between Spain and France.

10. Abravanel, *Rosh Amanah*. See Kellner, *Principles of Faith*.

11. *Ma'aynei ha-Yeshuah* (*Wells of Salvation*), *Mashmi'a' Yeshuah* (*Announcer of Salvation*), and *Yeshu'ot Meshicho* (*Salvations of His Anointed*).

A Final Refuge in Venice

When Abravanel settled in Venice in 1503, it was a place of political stability, wealth, and relative quiet. As in most of his previous settlements, he sought in Venice a place of both political influence and refuge for study and writing. Soon after his arrival, he offered himself to the Venetian Council, and was soon summoned to the task of mediating a resolution to the economic conflict between Venice and Portugal. At the same time he turned to complete many of his literary projects. He completed his commentaries on the Latter Prophets and wrote commentaries on the first four books of the Pentateuch. He completed his *Commentary on the Guide for the Perplexed*, a project he had begun early in his career and continued off and on until these final years. He wrote, then at age seventy, *Answers to Saul*, a response to philosophic questions posed to him by Saul ha-Kohen Ashkenazi, a disciple of the Aristotelian del Medigo. While in some ways a Maimonidean, Abravanel displayed once again his critique of strict Aristotelianism, and his respect for the limits of reason and the power of mystical knowledge. Abravanel's biblical commentaries continued to display his signature combination of biblical exegesis and political commentary. In his study of Genesis, for example, he read prophetic qualities into the story of Jacob, differing here from Maimonides and complementing his own messianic studies.

The Topics of Prophecy and Miracles in Abravanel's Writing

Abravanel's signature topics are prophecy and divine creativity.[12] Prophecy is the subject of many of his biblical commentaries, his commentary on Maimonides' guide, and several of his thematic writings. These studies are noteworthy, for one, because of his interpretive method. Abravanel distinguished himself from most of his predecessors by paying careful attention to historical context, attending in particular to political accounts in the Bible, from which he also drew lessons for contemporary politics. Abravanel's studies are noteworthy, secondly, for the distinctive way that he characterizes prophecy. Identifying four different species of prophecy (by way of the intellect, of the imagination, of the senses, and of any

12. See Feldman, *Philosophy in a Time of Crisis*, 41–43, 61–69, 91–95. See also Feldman, "Prophecy and Perception," 223–30; Borodowski, *Isaac Abravanel on Miracles*, 77–91.

combination of these), he offered his signature claims about the senses, or what he named "perceptual prophecy":

> In his midrash on the Sinaitic revelation Abravanel recognized a kind of prophetic cognition that requires no intellectual or imaginative operations at all. Since Maimonides defined prophecy in terms of influence upon these faculties, their perfection had to be made essential to the reception of the prophetic emanation. Thus he was blind or uninterested in another sort of prophetic illumination, one that can be received by ordinary people who have not reached the level of intellectual and imaginative perfection that Maimonides had stipulated. This is *perceptual prophecy.* The possibility of this kind of prophecy allows Abravanel to develop a different typology of prophetic illumination [including intellectual, imaginative, perceptual, and mixed forms].[13]

In perceptual prophecy, "only the senses are operative. Everyone with normal sense-perception is therefore eligible to receive this kind of prophecy if God so wills."[14] It comes by way of "a perceptual experience that resembles ordinary perceptual experiences in all respects but one: it is produced by God."[15] For Abravanel, the paradigmatic case of perceptual prophecy is that of Abraham at Mamre. Abravanel criticizes Maimonides' account of Abraham for misidentifying the case as one of imagination rather than perception. He criticizes Ibn Ezra and Gersonides for naturalizing the case as if Abraham saw three actual men who were prophets. He criticized Nachmanides and some kabbalists for offering too mysterious a notion that the three visitors were three angels who became incarnate for this purpose. According to Abravanel,

> Abraham had an experience of perceptual prophecy whose author was God alone: had Ishmael been seated there, he would not have received the vision. . . . For this emanation to be called "perfect prophetic emanation': it is necessary that it affect first the intellect of the prophet and then spread from it to the imagination. From there it passes over to the external senses, and that prophet alone experienced that very perceptual apprehension not because of the overpowering of his imagination or the

13. Feldman, *Philosophy in a Time of Crisis*, 93.

14. Ibid., 94.

15. Ibid.

> weakness of his intellect . . . but because of the perfect employment of his senses.[16]

For Abravanel, as opposed to Maimonides and his followers, "the decisive criterion . . . [is not the intellect, but] the nature of the link, or 'conjunction' (*dibbuq*), between the prophet and God."[17]

Abravanel's approach to prophecy complements his approach to miracles, the occurrence of which he regarded as within the scope of logical possibility. His approach to miracles is:

> strengthened by an argument that he explicitly borrows from the Muslim theologian Al-Ghazali. Al-Ghazali had argued against the Muslim followers of Aristotle . . . [t]hat if two events are genuinely distinct, then there is no inherent necessity that binds them together . . . or, as the 18th century philosopher David Hume put it, causal connections are not necessary. For both Ghazali and Abravanel the laws of nature are "weak": they are just logically contingent propositions, whose truth has been confirmed empirically, but which have no inherent necessity. Once we appreciate this logical point, it is easy to see how miracles are possible.[18]

Abravanel's approaches to prophecy and miracles, finally, complement his great attention to divine creativity. For Abravanel, "Miracles constitute an actual testimony to the possibility of the greatest unnatural act: creation," and *Mifa'lot Elohim* (*The Works of God*) is devoted to a definitive proof of creation *ex nihilo*.[19] Unlike the followers of Maimonides and Gersonides, Abravanel conceived of God's creativity under the attribute of omnipotence rather than of wisdom. Explaining his doctrine of perceptual prophecy, Abravanel noted that God may bring one to perceive that which our wisdom would regard as nonexistent; just as in creation, God brings into being that which had been nonexistent. At the same time, Abravanel considers divine creativity to operate within the bounds of logi-

16. Feldman, "Prophecy and Perception," 230.

17. Feldman, *Philosophy in a Time of Crisis*, 97. Feldman continues, "Maimonides and his followers . . . focused on the presence or absence of specific mental faculties in the prophetic experience. If the imagination was present, this fact alone rendered the prophetic emanation inferior to the emanation which affects only the intellect. Although Abravanel did distinguish types of prophecy according to the roles of the various mental faculties, he does not use these distinctions to rank prophets, at least not in the way Maimonides did" (ibid.).

18. Ibid., 68.

19. Borodowski, *Isaac Abravanel on Miracles*, 79.

cal possibility, adding that this possibility is much much larger than we may have imagined.

Correlating Study and Societal Repair

A clever, interpretive Jewish historiographer—what I label a "depth historiographer"—might seek out the patterns of Abravanel's performative inquiry by constructing sets of correlations (measured to some degree of probability) between patterns of scholarly reasoning displayed in his religious writings and patterns of economic, social, and prudential reasoning displayed in his work with the Jewish community and with various kings. This would, of course, be a speculative endeavour, shaped by the questions such a historiographer would ask on the basis of contemporary concerns. It would be anachronistic to read such concerns into the historical materials. But it would be fully appropriate to offer illustrations and analogies from Jewish intellectual and social history as resources for gaining insights—per hypothesis—into contemporary problems.

David Ford's writings on the university and on Scriptural Reasoning bring attention to the problem that stimulates this essay: how to educate future academics to contribute some of their skills and energies to the work of societal repair without sacrificing the quality of their intellectual endeavours. This essay's working hypothesis is that one significant source of educational models is the history of medieval and early modern religious thinkers: those who, in the generations before the rise of the professionalized university, worked as public servants while writing books of religious commentary and thought.[20] The concluding work of this essay is, by way of illustration, to suggest how the life and work of Isaac Abravanel might be scoured for evidences of the virtues that might inform a life of intellectual and public service. If this exercise bears any fruit, then there may be good reason for qualified scholars to scour the lives and work of a broad set of Muslim, Christian, and Jewish religious and public thinkers, from the early medieval period to today, in search of promising correlations between a thinker's patterns of religious thinking and of public action. The measure of "promise" would depend on what the contemporary scholars are seeking. Peers and students of David Ford may, for example,

20. David Ford's study of the University of Berlin is motivated in part by a concern to identify how and when Western intellectuals began to divorce their intellectual endeavours from work in or related to public service. See Ford, "Shaping Universities"; Ford, "The Responsibilities of Universities"; Ford, "Faith, Scriptures and Universities."

seek models for nurturing virtues that integrate patterns of theological enquiry and patterns of educational reform, public inter-religious dialogue, and institution building.

In these terms, what correlations might one perceive between Abravanel's modes of study and of societal action?

1. Possibly Generalizable Features of Abravanel's Life Story

All the following features appear to complement all the primary areas of Abravanel's public work. We need to ponder the fact that many of these features, even of privilege, may be evident in the life stories of other noted performative thinkers as well.

a. Living at a time of disaster or major cultural transition
b. Being brilliant nearly from birth
c. Having unusual energy and drive
d. Inheriting wealth
e. Inheriting education, learning, prestige
f. Ambition in the sociopolitical world: Seeking access to worldly political authority and/or taking responsibility for the Jewish community, seeking or receiving position of leadership in the Jewish world
g. Ambition and desire in the world of letters or thought
h. Seeking moral, spiritual, intellectual, religious, and political virtues and excellences

2. Possibly Generalizable Patterns of Abravanel's Jewish Study and Inquiry

Note that all these kinds of thinking are applied, in varying degrees, to the study of biblical, rabbinic, and post-Talmudic Jewish sources and, where appropriate, to the arts, letters, and sciences.

a. Messianic thinking
b. Scientific thinking
c. Pragmatic and reparative thinking
d. Rabbinic-halakic thinking

e. Rabbinic-midrashic thinking

f. Historicist thinking

g. Historical-hermeneutical thinking

3. Possibly Generalizable Patterns of Abravanel's Societal and Political Action

Where possible, I name these after biblical prototypes.

a. Joseph-like (economic-political advisor to king or authority)

b. Messianic-monarchical (supporting worldly powers for the sake of a messianic vision of the Jewish community's future)

c. Pragmatic-prudential (working for the sake of the Jewish community)

d. Moses or Ezekiel or Akiba-like (working to increase Torah learning and practice)

e. Self-serving (for family or self)

f. Monarchical-realpolitik (supporting worldly powers for utilitarian purposes, for the sake of the Jewish community)

Possible Correlations among 1, 2, 3 in Abravanel's Life and Work

The purpose of this concluding section is, for the sake of illustration, to speculate about which patterns of Abravanel's thinking (2 above) appear most often to complement the major areas of his public work (3 above). Note that certain areas of thinking seem to combine more often with certain others.[21]

- *Messianic-prophetic thinking* is evident in much of Abravanel's work, primarily complementing his Joseph-like and messianic-monarchical work. There also appears to be a negative complement—that his messianic thinking might interfere with his prudential and reparative

21. The way these modes of thought combine seems analogous to Max Kadushin's notion that rabbinic "value concepts" (virtues) tend to "interweave." See Kadushin, *Rabbinic Mind*, 22–23.

judgments and vice versa. One wonders, for example, if his messianism led him to misjudge the strength of Spanish anti-Judaism.[22]

- *Scientific thinking* is another major area of Abravanel's work, displayed most typically in his economic and political judgments, and, therefore, in his monarchical real politick, his prudential-reparative work, and also supporting his monarchical-messianic work.
- *Pragmatic and reparative thinking* combines, in contradictory ways, with Abravanel's messianic thinking, on the one hand, and with his scientific thinking, on the other. The pragmatic-scientific complex complements his pragmatic-prudential work and his non-messianic monarchical work, while the pragmatic-messianic complex complements his Joseph-like work in its messianic uses and, therefore, his messianic monarchical work.
- *Rabbinic-halakic thinking* can combine with his scientific thinking, in which case it complements his pragmatic-prudential work and his Akiba-like work. It can also combine with his messianic thinking, complement his Joseph-like and messianic-monarchical work.
- *Rabbinic-midrashic thinking*, when non-halakic, combines with his messianic thinking to complement his messianic-monarchical work.
- *Historicist thinking* usually combines with his scientific thinking to complement his pragmatic-prudential work and his monarchical work (perhaps when non-messianic).
- *Historical-hermeneutical thinking* can complement his Joseph-like and messianic-monarchical work.

In Sum: Abravanel's Primary Performative Tendencies

My concluding speculation, offered strictly for the sake of illustration, is that Abravanel's oeuvre displays contradictory tendencies:

a. *Messianic-prophetic thinking*, which combines with rabbinic-midrashic and historical-hermeneutical thinking to complement his monarchical-messianic political work and often his Joseph-like work.
b. *Scientific thinking*, which combines with rabbinic-halakic and historicist thinking to complement his pragmatic-reparative work on

22. A speculation offered by Netanyahu, *Don Isaac Abravanel*, 88–91, 255–57.

behalf of the Jewish community and, instrumentally, as a means of serving various kings as economic-political advisor.

Note that Abravanel's messianism appears to contradict his scientific values when messianism engenders political apocalypticism. In this case, his messianism runs contrary to his pragmatic-prudential work. Since his public influence drew heavily on his economic science, and since his religious thinking grew increasingly apocalyptic, it is difficult to imagine his life freed from the inner contradictions between science and apocalypticism.

Are there no integrative tendencies in his life's work? If we cannot imagine separating the man from the contradictions that animated his life, we can nonetheless ask what lessons his future students might learn for themselves. If the students were attracted to practices in the form of Scriptural Reasoning (or something comparable), I would imagine they would, on the one hand, choose science over apocalypticism while, on the other hand, choosing Abravanel's trust in prophecy, miracles, and creationism over rationalism or a rationalist empiricism. A scripturally grounded pragmatism would provide one model for integrating trust in both science and miracles; such a pragmatism would, of course, complement most practices of Scriptural Reasoning, and the likes. I see no a priori reason why a pragmatic student of Abravanel's would necessarily refrain, in certain circumstances, from his Joseph-like, Akiba-like, at times self-serving, or, of course, pragmatic-prudential work.

What virtues would conceivably nurture such a student? Apparently, these virtues are certain rabbinic virtues when enacted by a pragmatic, prudent and scientific public servant—at once generous, pious, and self-serving in the normal human way—who inhabited a monarchical society marked by unpredictable tensions among the Abrahamic communities and among the various monarchies.

There are, of course, many kinds of Jewish performative thinkers in history whose life's work would display evidence of many different kinds of performative virtues, including many kinds of scripturally grounded pragmatic ones: from Saadya Gaon to Maimonides to the Vilna Gaon and so on. We have much to learn from examining their performative virtues—and from examining the performative virtues of Abrahamic thinkers more broadly, from Augustine and Al-Ghazali to present practitioners of these performative virtues. So, who will be the first to examine David Ford's work from this perspective? And then?

Bibliography

Abravanel, Isaac. *Ateret zekenim*. Lemberg: Shrentsel, 1859.

———. *The Deeds of God*. Lemberg: Back, 1863.

———. *Letters*. Translated and edited by Cedric Cohen Skalli. Berlin: De Gruyter, 2007.

———. *Perush Abravanel al ha-Torah*. Jerusalem: Horev, 2007.

———. *Perush Abravanel al sefer Moreh Nevukhim le-Rabenu Mosheh ben Maimon*. Prague: Landa, 1831–32.

———. *Principles of Faith (Rosh Amanah)*. Translated by Menachem Kellner. Oxford: Littman Library, 1982.

———. *Rosh Amanah*. Königsberg: Grüber, 1861.

Ben-Sasson, H., editor. *A History of the Jewish People*. Cambridge: Harvard University Press, 1985.

Borodowski, Alfredo Fabio. *Isaac Abravanel on Miracles, Creation, Prophecy and Evil: The Tension between Medieval Jewish Philosophy and Biblical Commentary*. New York: Lang, 2003.

Feldman, Seymour. *Philosophy in a Time of Crisis: Don Isaac Abravanel, Defender of the Faith*. New York: Routledge Curson, 2003.

———. "Prophecy and Perception in Isaac Abravanel." In *Perspectives on Jewish Thought and Mysticism*, edited by Alexander Altmann et al., 223–36. Amsterdam: Harwood, 1998.

Ford, David F. "Faith, Scriptures and Universities in an Inter-Faith and Secular Society." Public lecture given at the University of Sheffield, February 2007.

———. "The Responsibilities of Universities in a Religious and Secular World." *Studies in Christian Ethics* 17 (2004) 22–37.

———. "Shaping Universities in a Religious and Secular Europe." Keynote address at the International Forum Bosnia, August 2010.

Kadushin, Max. *The Rabbinic Mind*. Binghamton, NY: Global, 2001.

Kellner, Menachem Marc, translator. *Principles of Faith (Rosh Amanah)*. Rutherford: Fairleigh Dickinson University Press, 1982.

Lindbeck, Kris. "Scriptural Reasoning and Depth Historiography." *The Journal of Scriptural Reasoning* 2.1 (2002). Online: http://etext.lib.virginia.edu/journals/ssr/issues/volume2/number1/ssr02-01-gr04.html.

Netanyahu, Benzion. *Don Isaac Abravanel: Statesman and Philosopher*. Ithaca: Cornell University Press, 1999.

Ochs, Peter. *Another Reformation: Postliberal Christianity and the Jews*. Grand Rapids: Brazos, 2011.

———. "Coda." In *Spreading Rumours of Wisdom: Essays in Honour of David Ford*, special issue of *The Journal of Scriptural Reasoning* 7.1 (2008). Online: http://etext.lib.virginia.edu/journals/ssr/issues/volume7/number1/ssr07_01_e09.html.

———. "Editor's Introduction." In David Weiss Halivni, *Breaking the Tablets: Jewish Theology after the Shoah*, edited by Peter Ochs. Lanham, MD: Rowman & Littlefield, 2007.

———. "Judaism and Christian Theology." In *The Modern Theologians*, edited by David Ford with Rachel Muers, 645–62. 3rd ed. Oxford: Blackwell, 2005.

———. "On *Christian Wisdom*—by David Ford" *Conversations in Religion & Theology* 7 (2009) 134–46.

———. "Reparative Reasoning: From Peirce's Pragmatism to Augustine's Scriptural Semiotics." *Modern Theology* 25 (2009) 187–215.

Ogren, Brian. *Renaissance and Rebirth: Reincarnation in Early Modern Italian Kabbalah.* Leiden: Brill, 2009.

Rüegg, Walter. "Themes." In *Universities in the Middle Ages.* A History of the University in Europe, vol. 1. Edited by H. De Ridder-Symoens. General Editor Walter Rüegg. Cambridge: Cambridge University Press, 2003.

15

Theology as a Vocation

A Weberian Perspective

Basit Bilal Koshul

Lahore University of Management Sciences

I took up my first teaching position in September 2002 in the Religion Department at Concordia College in Minnesota, USA. I had to attend a day-long orientation for all new faculty and staff before classes began. One of the sessions at the orientation was led by the college pastor, Phil Holton. I do not remember much from the many sessions at the orientation or from Pastor Holton's session itself—but the opening sentences of his presentation have been with me ever since I heard them for the first time that day: "The Scriptures say: 'Renewal comes through the stranger.'" The feeling I experienced upon hearing these words was nothing short of sublime. In retrospect I can say that this is primarily because these words helped me to become conscious of something I already knew in a very real and deep sense but was conscious of only superficially. In the three to four years before I heard these words I had come to know a group of "strangers" and many new "strange" ideas. David Ford was among this group of "strangers," along with Peter Ochs and Daniel Hardy (of blessed memory). Given the fact of my Pakistani/South Asian cultural background in which medicine, engineering, and computer sciences are considered to be the only worthwhile areas of study for males, sociology of religion, religious studies, and theology were very "strange" ideas. And while I was familiar with interfaith dialogue at that time, the idea of Scriptural Reasoning was also "strange." Furthermore, while I was familiar with Christianity and Judaism to some degree, these traditions were also "strange" in a very real sense because my relationship with a living Christian or Jew did not go beyond institutional formality or collegiality.

As my familiarity with certain human beings (Ford, Hardy, and Ochs) grew, the strangeness of certain ideas and traditions (theology, religious studies, Christianity, and Judaism) was also transformed into familiarity. Looking back, I can delineate a causal chain. First a group of strangers became mentors and teachers and shortly thereafter friends. As a direct result of their mentoring and friendship the strangeness of theology, religious studies, Scriptural Reasoning, Christianity, and Judaism gradually dissipated to be replaced with familiarity, understanding, and appreciation. This newfound understanding and appreciation of that which was once strange with the help of those who were once strangers, in turn, had a transformative effect on me as a person. The reason the words "renewal comes through the stranger" struck such a sensitive chord inside me in when I first heard them and have remained with me every since is that I was in the midst of being renewed by the "strangers" and "strange" ideas at that time. I am very confident (and I pray that I am right) that my understanding and appreciation of that which had been relatively familiar (Islam) has been affected for the better as a result of my interaction with the strangers and the strange named above.

As a (small) token of my gratitude towards and friendship with David Ford, I will use the gracious invitation extended to me to contribute to this Festschrift to offer some reflections on the relationship between strangers, renewal, and what Max Weber has called the "fate of our times." In the following pages I will put forth the hypothesis that a careful reading of David Ford's "Muscat Manifesto" represents a cry of wisdom in our disenchanted, global culture to take the words "renewal comes through the stranger" seriously. Before teasing out the relationship between the Muscat Manifesto and the words "renewal comes through the stranger," I will detail Weber's description of the "fate of our times" and the significance of theology as a vocation in the face of this fate. This analysis will show that the strange, strangers, and strangeness are so much a part of the contemporary cultural condition that for any theology to be relevant at this juncture in history it must face and address the reality of strangeness condition directly. I will argue that the theology on which the Muscat Manifesto is based does this marvellously well. The most compelling evidence in favour of this claim is the fact that not only have many Christians been renewed and strengthened as a result of their friendship and collegiality with the Christian theologian advocating this theology (David Ford), but also many "strangers" (Jews and Muslims) have been renewed and strengthened as well.

Theology in an Age of Disenchantment

Max Weber begins the concluding section of his last public lecture (titled "Science as a Vocation") with these words: "The fate of our times is characterized by rationalization and intellectualization and, above all, by the 'disenchantment of the world.'"[1] After noting that there is no doubt that rationalization and intellectualization have developed far more in modern culture than in any premodern culture, Weber goes on to note that this does not mean that the modern knows more or knows better than the premodern. After detailing what rationalization, intellectualization, and disenchantment do not mean, he goes on to describe what they do mean: "The increasing intellectualization and rationalization do *not* . . . indicate an increased and general knowledge of the conditions under which one lives. It means something else, namely, the knowledge or belief that if one but wished one *could* learn it any time. Hence, it means that principally there are no mysterious incalculable forces that come into play, but rather that one can, in principle, master all things by calculation. This means that the world is disenchanted."[2]

While there are innumerable factors that have contributed to the process of disenchantment, there is one factor that has played an especially prominent role: "Scientific progress is a fraction, the most important fraction, of the process of intellectualization which we have been undergoing for thousands of years."[3] The progress of mathematics, physics, biology, chemistry, and the social sciences over the centuries is both the manifestation of and the catalytic element in the process of disenchantment.

After talking at length about the definition of science, its impact on occidental history and culture, its place in the university, its constituent elements, and the possibility of pursuing science as a vocation in the face

1. Weber, "Science as Vocation," 155.

2. Ibid.

3. Ibid., 138.

of disenchantment, Weber tackles a very tricky issue: "Which stand does one take towards the factual existence of 'theology' and its claims to be a 'science'? Let us not flinch and evade the answer."[4] Science is the intellectual rationalization of some particular subject matter—biology is the intellectual rationalization of "life," physics of "matter," economics of "money/wealth," etc. Given an objective and value neutral definition of science, Weber argues that theology must be labelled as a science because it "represents an *intellectual* rationalization of the possession of sacred value."[5] There is no difference between theology and the other sciences insofar as it represents the intellectual rationalization of a particular subject matter. What sets it apart from the other sciences is the particular subject matter that it rationalizes, i.e., "the possession of a sacred value." The fact that it rationalizes a unique subject matter that is different from the other sciences is no reason to disqualify it as a science because every science, no more and no less than theology, intellectually rationalizes a unique subject matter. For Weber this makes theology as much of a rational, intellectual enterprise as any other science.

Being a science, theology has one more characteristic in common with the other sciences: it is based on presuppositions that it itself cannot prove. Weber cites the philosophical authority of Kant to support his claim that all of science rests on a presupposition that science cannot prove. Commenting on Kant's epistemology Weber notes: "He took for his point of departure the presupposition: 'Scientific truth exists and it is valid,' and then asked: 'Under which presuppositions of thought is truth possible and meaningful?'"[6] Weber goes on to note that the presupposition on which all scientific inquiry is based is "essentially religious and philosophical."[7] Furthermore, the affirmation of this presupposition is as much a matter of faith as the affirmation of any religious teaching/dogma. Weber notes: "No science is absolutely free of presuppositions, and no science can prove its fundamental value to the man who rejects these presuppositions."[8] If science cannot prove its value to the individual who rejects the presuppositions on which science is based, we are faced with the following question: On what basis does the practising scientist accept the presuppositions on which science is based and thereby affirm the validity of the value of

4. Ibid., 153.

5. Ibid.

6. Ibid., 154.

7. Ibid.

8. Ibid., 153.

science? Weber answers this question directly: "Only on the assumption of belief in the validity of values is the attempt to espouse value-judgement meaningful. However, to *judge* the *validity* of such values is a matter of *faith*."[9] In sum, the praxis of science becomes possible only in the aftermath of a faithful affirmation of an "essentially religious and philosophic" presupposition. In light of what Weber has said elsewhere, we may add that wherever we can observe the praxis of scientific inquiry we can rest assured that such an affirmation has taken place. Earlier we saw that for Weber rationality is as much a part of theological inquiry as any scientific inquiry. Now Weber shows us that faith is as much a part of the foundations of science as of theology.[10] Putting these two points together, we can say that Weber's analysis shows us that theology and science are connected at the heart as well as the head.

The foregoing discussion suggests that the more a culture is shaped by scientific rationality the more conducive it would be to the pursuit of theology as a vocation. From this we may be tempted to conclude that theology (and the theologian) would be more at home in the contemporary cultural setting than at any time in history because it is the most scientific of all cultures. But Weber forces us to face the reality that the case is much more complex and difficult due to two different but intimately related reasons. The first is the fact that the fundamental presupposition with which theological inquiry begins (i.e., that there is meaning [*Sinn*] in the universe) is categorically rejected by the final conclusion that scientific enquiry reaches. The second is that the worldly spheres in modern culture challenge the central religious ideal (i.e., universal brotherhood) more directly and pointedly than ever before. Both of these factors have created a cultural situation in which religion, theology, and the theologian

9. Weber, "Objectivity," 55.

10. Here Weber is echoing the observation that Nietzsche had made a few decades earlier: "But you will have gathered what I am driving at, namely, that it is still a *metaphysical faith* upon which our faith in science rests—that even we seekers after knowledge today, we godless anti-metaphysicians still take our fire, too, from the flame lit by a faith that is thousands of years old, that Christian faith which was also the faith of Plato, that God is the truth, that truth is divine" (Nietzsche, *Gay Science*, 283).

It is worth noting that the fact that science is made possible by certain presuppositions that it itself cannot prove is not a discovery of the modern social sciences or modern philosophy. Even Euclid knew that his geometry was based on certain postulates and axioms that geometry could not prove. Peirce notes that Euclid "does not reckon them [i.e., axioms and postulates] among his *koinai ennoiai*, or things everybody knows, but among the *aitèmata*, postulates or things the author must beg you to admit, because he is unable to prove them" (Peirce, *Collected Papers*, 1.130).

have become strangers in a way that has not happened in any premodern culture. We will look at both reasons in some detail.

As with all other intellectual endeavours, theology is based on a particular presupposition: "At all times and in all places, the need for salvation—consciously cultivated as the substance of religiosity—has resulted from the endeavour of a systematic and practical rationalization of life's realities. . . . [O]n this level, all religions have demanded as a specific presupposition that the course of the world be somehow *meaningful*, at least in so far as it touches upon the interests of men."[11]

Science first leads us to question the claim that the universe is "somehow *meaningful*"—the empirical facts that are most difficult to reconcile with this presupposition are the facts of unjust suffering and undeserved reward. Then with the progressive accumulation of scientific knowledge the thesis of natural causality emerges to replace the religious claim of ethical causality in the universe. The final result is that the presupposition of religion has to be abandoned in the face of advancing scientific knowledge:

> The tension between religion and intellectual knowledge definitely comes to the fore wherever rational, empirical knowledge has consistently worked to the disenchantment of the world and its transformation into a causal mechanism. For then science encounters the claims of the ethical postulate that the world is a God-ordained, and hence somehow meaningfully and ethically oriented cosmos. In principle, the empirical as well as the mathematically oriented view of the world develops refutations of every intellectual approach which in any way asks for a "meaning" of inner-worldly occurrences.[12]

A relationship between the presupposition of theology and the conclusion of science could be maintained while science was still in the initial phases of its development. But once science has matured it becomes virtually impossible to maintain this link:

> Who—aside from certain big children who are indeed found in the natural sciences—still believe that the findings of astronomy, biology, physics, or chemistry could teach us anything about the meaning of the world? If there is any such "meaning," along what road could one come upon its track? If these natural sciences lead to anything in this way, they are apt to make the belief

11. Weber, "Religious Rejections," 353.

12. Ibid., 350–51.

> that there is any such a thing as the "meaning" of the universe die out at its very roots.[13]

In addition to making it impossible to affirm the presupposition that there is such a thing as meaning in the universe, a culture shaped by the scientific ethos has first challenged and eventually rejected the supreme worldly ideal for religion. This ideal is encapsulated in the Golden Rule (universal brotherhood). Just as the idea of "meaning" should come to believer's mind when looking at any natural phenomenon in the universe, the idea "brother" (or "sister") should come to the believer's mind when looking at any fellow human being. We have already seen that the progressive rationalization of science causes it eventually to reject the presupposition of theology. Now Weber makes us face the fact that progressive rationalization of the worldly spheres (politics, economics, aesthetics, and the erotic sphere) first makes the worldly spheres challenge and then eventually reject the religious ideal of universal brotherhood .

From the perspective of a salvation religion, there is a direct link between living one's life in line with the ideal of universal brotherhood in this world, and attaining salvation in the hereafter: "The more imperatives that issued from the ethic of reciprocity among neighbors were raised, the more rational the conception of salvation became, and the more it was sublimated into an ethic of absolute ends. Externally, such commands rose to a communism of loving brethren; internally they rose to the attitude of *caritas*, love for the sufferer *per se*, for one's neighbor, for man, and finally for the enemy."[14]

The ideal of love of neighbour or universal brotherhood is directly at odds with the inner logic and highest value of the different worldly spheres: "The religion of brotherliness has always clashed with the orders and values of this world, and the more consistently its demands have been carried through, the sharper the clash has been. The split has usually become wider the more values of the world have been rationalized and sublimated in terms of their own laws."[15] The clash between the religious ideal of brotherhood and the worldly spheres is especially acute when the religion in question is a monotheistic, universalist religion: "The problem only arose when these barriers of locality, tribe, and polity were shattered by universalist religions, by a religion with a unified God of the entire

13. Weber, "Science as Vocation," 142.

14. Weber, "Religious Rejections," 330.

15. Ibid.

world. And the problem arose in full strength only when this God was a god of 'love.'"[16]

Each of the different worldly spheres seeks to replace the ideal of love of neighbour with its own supreme value. In addition to replacing the religious ideal with a variety of worldly ideals, each of the worldly spheres has come up with specific means and institutions that facilitate the pursuit of the new value. This part of Weber's reflections on the sociology of culture can be summarized in the following way:

	Highest Value, Ultimate End, or "God"	Primary Means of Pursuing End or "Serving God"	Institutional Manifestation or "Temple in Service of God"
Political Sphere	Power	Violence	Bureaucracy of nation-state, w/ monopoly on legitimate use of violence
Economic Sphere	Profit	Money and quantification of value	Impersonal exchange in marketplace
Esthetic Sphere	Beauty	Free play of imagination, free of any ethical norms	Discovery of new forms in which beauty can be expressed
Erotic Sphere	Pleasure	Sexual union	Lifelong commitment to one partner excluding any third
Intellectual Sphere	Knowledge	Science—i.e., abstract concept + controlled experiment	The University

The reader may be puzzled why the term "God" has appeared in relationship to the different aspects of the worldly spheres. Weber turns to explicitly religious imagery when detailing the fact that science cannot and should not pass judgment on the validity of any value. He uses the terms

16. Ibid., 333.

"god" and "devil" to refer to the supreme value and the most abhorrent value, respectively, of any sphere of culture:

> What man will take upon himself the attempt to "refute scientifically" the ethic of the Sermon on the Mount? For instance, the sentence, "resist no evil," or the image of turning the cheek? And yet it is clear, in mundane perspective, that this is an ethic of undignified conduct; one has to choose between the religious dignity which this ethic confers and the dignity of manly conduct which preaches something quite different; "resist evil—lest you be co-responsible for overpowering evil." According to our ultimate standpoint, the one is the devil and the other God, and the individual has to decide which is God for him and which is the devil. And so it goes throughout all the orders of life.[17]

Not only has the progressive rationalization of the worldly spheres caused them to directly challenge and reject the Golden Rule of religion, it has also caused open conflict to emerge among the worldly spheres themselves. In the premodern cultural setting, the religious ethic had the effect of partially suppressing the tensions and struggles between the different worldly spheres by striving to focus attention on the "one thing that is needful"—other-worldly salvation.[18] But in the modern disenchanted cultural condition, the suppressed struggles among the worldly spheres break out into the open in much more stark terms: "Our civilization destines us to realize more clearly these struggles again, after our eyes have been blinded for a thousand years—blinded by the allegedly or presumable exclusive orientation towards the grandiose moral fervor of Christian ethics."[19]

The demise of the unifying impetus of the teaching of "love thy neighbour" has led to the resurgence of a very particular type of polytheism in modern culture: "We live as did the ancients when their world was not yet disenchanted of its gods and demons, only we live in a different sense. As Hellenic man at times sacrificed to Aphrodite and at other times to Apollo, and above all, as everybody sacrificed to the gods of his city, so do we still nowadays, only the bearing of man has been disenchanted and denuded of its mystical but inwardly genuine plasticity."[20] When looked at from the perspective of the relationship between the different worldly

17. Weber, "Science as Vocation," 148.

18. Ibid., 149.

19. Ibid.

20. Ibid., 148.

spheres, the modern cultural condition resembles the proverbial "war of each against all:" "Many old gods ascend from their graves; they are disenchanted and hence take the form of impersonal forces. They strive to gain power over our lives and again they resume their eternal struggle with each other."[21]

In light of what Weber has said about science, theology, the supreme ethical value of religion and the supreme values of the different worldly spheres, we can draw the following conclusions: 1. Even though they are joined at the head and the heart, science and theology have become completely estranged from each other. 2. Because of the death of meaning (Sinn) in the universe, the human being has become a complete stranger in the universe. 3. With the unifying ethical impetus of religion consigned to the domain of the irrational, modern culture becomes an arena where mutually estranged worldly spheres battle each other for survival and supremacy.

In sum, the strange, strangers, and strangeness have become our most intimate companions in modern culture. It does not take a genius to figure out that this is an intolerable situation in which to live. At this point in the discussion Weber's description of the attempts of two groups of people to redress this situation is of interest to us: a) the response of the theologians; and b) the response of the university professors. Among the first group there is a subgroup whose response to the "fate of our times" is to try to bring religion and science into relationship with each other, thereby challenging disenchantment at its very roots. Weber calls these theologians "liberal theologians." In contrast a significant subgroup among the secular intellectuals attempts to build a naturalistic metaphysics on the findings of science and then use this artificial concoction to replace religion. Weber uses the phrase "academic prophecy" to describe this latter approach—and he has nothing but contempt for such shenanigans: "If one tries intellectually to construe new religions without a new and genuine prophecy, then, in an inner sense, something similar will result, but with still worse effects. And academic prophecy will, finally, create only fanatical sects but never a genuine community."[22] This academic prophecy is probably a greater threat to the integrity of science than to religion. This is due to the fact that "in the lecture-rooms of the university no other virtue holds but plain intellectual integrity."[23] Academic

21. Ibid., 149.

22. Ibid., 155.

23. Ibid.

prophecy is an obvious violation of intellectual integrity "which sets in if one lacks the courage to clarify one's own ultimate standpoint and rather facilitates this duty by feeble relative judgments."[24]

In contrast, after Weber looked at the work of some theologians in Rome he says that he "became convinced how hopeless it is to think that there are any scientific results that the church cannot digest."[25] In a personal letter to his friend Ferdinand Tönnies, he goes on to offer some self-reflective comments on his personal fate in a disenchanted world:

> It is true I am absolutely unmusical in matters religious and I have neither the need nor the ability to erect any religious edifices within me—that is simply impossible for me, and I reject it. But after examining myself carefully I must say that I am neither anti-religious nor irreligious. In this regard too I consider myself a cripple, a stunted man whose fate it is to admit honestly that he must put up with this state of affairs (so as not to fall for some romantic swindle). I am like a tree stump from which new shoots can sometimes grow, but I must not pretend to be a grown tree.[26]

Towards the end of the letter he draws the following contrast between the liberal theologian and the academic prophet: "From this follows quite a bit: For you a theologian of liberal persuasion (whether Catholic or Protestant) is necessarily most abhorrent as the typical representative of a halfway position; for me he is in human terms infinitely more valuable and interesting . . . than the intellectual (and basically cheap) pharisaism of naturalism which is intolerably fashionable and in which there much less life than in the religious position."[27] For Weber, the theologian attempting to transform the estrangement of religion from science into familiarity and relationship is an "infinitely more valuable and interesting" human being than the university professor who would replace religion with scientistic metaphysics. And he finds much more promise and life in the position of the theologian than the university professor.

Given Weber's analysis we can offer the following observations on theology as a vocation in the age of disenchantment. On the one hand, theology is the most difficult of vocations to pursue in modern culture. The advancement of scientific knowledge strikes at the very foundational

24. Ibid.

25. Schluchter, "Paradox of Rationalization," 82 n. 44.

26. Ibid.

27. Ibid.

presupposition of religion (there is meaning in the universe). The development of the different worldly spheres is possible only to the degree the foundational religious ethic (universal brotherhood) is rejected. On the other hand, the theological position seeking to find meaning (*Sinn*) in the face of scientific advancement and to affirm brotherhood in the face of advancing secular culture shows more promise for life than any "scientific" secular alternative. Weber seems to be saying that while the theologian should be prepared to live the life of an alien in modern disenchanted culture, the theologian's "cry of wisdom" appears to hold the most promise of life if modern culture is to repair its rupture. The wisdom of Scripture captured in the words "renewal comes through the stranger" is so compelling that even an individual who is "absolutely unmusical in matters religious" acknowledges that this wisdom is far more likely to yield life than the attempt to conquer, marginalize, and destroy the stranger. Much more so in our day than in Weber's day, this particular cry of wisdom is the need of the hour—and even a cursory look at the Muscat Manifesto shows that it is a cry of this wisdom in the wilderness that is our disenchanted cultural condition.

The Muscat Manifesto as a Cry of Wisdom

David Ford is the author of the Muscat Manifesto. It would be worthwhile to pause and look at the elements that went into constructing the manifesto. To begin with we have a theologian who is first and foremost a human being living at a particular time in history and is part of a community that stands in very close proximity to other communities. When he looks around him, he describes what he sees to an audience of Jews, Christians, and Muslims: "This is a moment of great danger in the history of our three faiths and of our world. There are tensions, crises and conflicts, and widespread misunderstandings and suspicions. But there are signs of hope too, and we must believe that God wants us to create many more such signs."[28]

This particular human being is a part of the Christian community and when looking for ways to better understand the dangers in the environment and recognize the signs of hope, one of the places he turns to is the Christian Scriptures. In the Scriptures the following passage catches his attention:

28. Ford, *Muscat Manifesto*, 8.

> Wisdom cries out in the street;
> in the squares she raises her voice . . .
> Beside the gates in front of the town,
> at the entrance of the portals she cries out:
> "To you, O people, I call,
> and my cry is to all that live . . .
> Take my instruction instead of silver,
> and knowledge rather than choice gold;
> for wisdom is better than jewels,
> and all that you may desire cannot compare with her . . ."
> (Prov 1:20; 8:3, 4, 10, 11)

Meditating on these words of Scripture in the midst of the dangers and opportunities that he is surrounded by, he imagines "What might wisdom urge us to do today?"[29] The Muscat Manifesto is the scripturally reasoned answer to this question. Because of my personal relationship with the author of the manifesto, the thing that struck me when I first read the text was that it embodies a particular aspect of the innumerable dimensions of wisdom—the aspect that is best captured by the words "renewal comes through the stranger."

The first point in the manifesto is a call to love the stranger, whether the stranger is divine, a human neighbour, or the non-human natural world. As Rudolf Otto has noted, whether we encounter God as *mysterium fascinans* or *mysterium tremendum*, the initial encounter with God always has an element of mystery attached to it. As difficult as it is to keep one's bearing in the face of this divine strangeness one must work hard to become familiar with the mystery that one has experienced because one's renewal depends upon it. Similarly God's creation may look to be a strange non-human alien—at best, something to be used for utilitarian purposes. But one must love it as one must love God. The second point leaves no doubt that the "neighbour" referred to in the first point is not just the neighbour who belongs to one's own faith community but also the neighbour who belongs to a different faith community. In other words, it does not matter whether the neighbour is a brother or sister in faith or a stranger, the neighbour must be loved. It is important to note from the second point of the manifesto that this is not a call for some type of religious syncretism or a search for the lowest common denominator among faiths. This is clear from the fact that one is first called to go deeper into one's own faith and to engage with the other from this particular

29. Ibid.

vantage point. This is the simultaneous affirmation of the uniqueness of one's self, a recognition of the irreducible worth of the other and a call to establish a relationship between the self and the other to work towards a common good. While the second point aspires for renewal by embracing the strange other in the form of different faith traditions, the third point of the manifesto moves towards the same goal by embracing the strange in the form of different intellectual traditions. In the third point, we have a theologian explicitly stating that wisdom is not something that is confined to the area of theology, it is to be found in "strange" secular disciplines. Science, history, the arts, philosophy, and others are not strange aliens that are to be shunned in the search for wisdom. These non-theological disciplines are to be considered fellow-travellers that are walking/creating the path towards wisdom. The fourth point, "Engaging with the Modern World," teaches us that even though elements of secular modernity are, indeed, harmful to the human well-being, we should not view them as tumours that have to be excised. On the contrary, when seeking to treat the diseases caused by secular modernity we need to develop the antibody serum from elements of secular modernity itself. The fifth and sixth points of the manifesto bring to our attention the fact that just as the source of wisdom is not limited to the religious sphere, the task of spreading wisdom is a responsibility that has to be shared with groups and institutions outside of the religious sphere. The editorial pages, art canvases, university classrooms, theatre stages, etc. are as valuable as pulpits in spreading the teachings of wisdom. The seventh point forces us to recognize the fact that we are indebted to God and those who came before us for the fact that we have inherited a habitable world. The only way to repay this debt is that we leave a habitable world behind us for future generations. The eighth point of the manifesto can be restated as follows: "Continue to utter words of wisdom and do wise deeds and respond to the call of wisdom—especially the call that is uttered by a stranger." The final point reminds us that irrespective of particular scientific and philosophical stances, we affirm that there is purpose and meaning in the universe. It is our hope that the purposes and meanings that we have chosen for ourselves are ones that are pleasing to God.

A plain sense reading of the Muscat Manifesto suggests that its significance is limited to healing the rupture in interfaith relations. In my opinion this is a shallow reading of the manifesto. When read carefully, we find that the manifesto goes beyond repairing the relationships among different religious communities; it challenges disenchantment as the fate of our times and points the way towards repaired relationships in contemporary culture at large. The first point in the manifesto asks us to affirm the ethic of universal brotherhood and the last point affirms the reality of meaning and significance in the universe. Between the first and the last points we find a confident and gracious embrace of non-religious knowledge (especially knowledge from the secular sciences—natural, physical, and humanistic). We find repeated calls to open ourselves up to the cry and face of the stranger (especially the religious other). As we gain the courage and wisdom to do this, the loneliness brought about by disenchantment gradually dissipates and is replaced with mutually affirming relationships. Finally, this "religious" undertaking becomes the starting point for ameliorating the conflicts among the different non-religious spheres. While it is not explicitly stated anywhere in the manifesto, it is difficult to escape the conclusion that the litmus test which will determine if this "religious" undertaking is of any value is the degree to which it contributes to the worldly well-being of all of God's creation in the present as well as the future. The vision of the Muscat Manifesto is a cry of wisdom in an age of disenchantment that calls upon us to challenge the "fate of our times"; imagine new possibilities; and work with others to actualize these possibilities. In light of what has been said in the previous section about strange, the stranger, and strangeness being the outcome of disenchantment, we can offer the following observations about the Muscat Manifesto: 1. Since theology and secular knowledge (especially science) are joined at the head as well as the heart, theologians must work to bring the two into deep conversation and intimate relationship. 2. Because God created the universe for good purposes, human beings must discover meaning and significance in each and every nook of the universe (especially in the face of the strange other). 3. Because God's love is boundless it expresses itself in bewildering variety. Politicians, businessmen, artists, and intellectuals (no less than theologians) have a responsibility to translate/manifest God's love in the world by making their unique contribution to cultivating and sustaining the common good.

A Final Word

Weber notes that the "two highest conceptions of sublimated religious doctrines of salvation are 'rebirth' and 'redemption.'"[30] In the past, religious revivals have resulted from the efforts of religious intellectuals

30. Weber, "Social Psychology," 279.

working to "sublimate the possession of sacred values into a belief in 'redemption.'"[31] He goes on to posit that, while in very general terms "redemption" has meant liberation from all sorts of suffering in the world, it "attained a specific significance only where it expressed a systematic and rationalized 'image of the world' and represented a stand in the face of the world. For meaning as well as the intended and actual psychological quality of redemption has depended upon such a world image and such a stand."[32] For Weber, beyond the commonly understood meaning of "redemption," it means "a stand in the face of the world": a claim that the world and the human condition in the world do not have to be as they presently are; they could be otherwise. This stand is a protest against the present "is" and a call / hope for a better "ought." Weber also emphasizes that the kind of practical stand that one can take (what one can protest against or hope for) depends on the image of the world that one has: "'From what' and 'for what' one wished to be redeemed and, let us not forget, could be redeemed, depended upon one's image of the world."[33] From this perspective, an intellectual who formulates an image of the world that offers novel possibilities of being human in the world is fulfilling the most basic prerequisite for the beginning of a "religious revival."

There can be little argument that at the beginning of the new millennium disenchantment has given birth to a cultural condition from which redemption is necessary. From this perspective it is obvious that theology becomes the most crucial of sciences in an age of disenchantment—without ever losing sight of the fact that it is the most difficult of sciences to practise in the material conditions created by the different disenchanted worldly spheres. The vocation of the theologian is to formulate an image of the world that makes it possible to take "a stand in the face of the world"—a claim/hope that something better is possible. As unlikely as it appears at first glance, there is compelling evidence that a stranger who is "absolutely unmusical in matters religious" is a uniquely valuable resource for theologians of the twenty-first century. For the most part this chapter has used Weber's insights to facilitate an analysis of "theology as a vocation" in an age of disenchantment. But there is much more to Weber. This essay could only hint at the insights that Weber's corpus contains for those who want to construct a world image that makes it possible for a clear and sober "stand in the face of the world." But to discover these insights one

31. Ibid., 280.

32. Ibid.

33. Ibid.

has to open oneself up to the risks and surprises that are contained in the words "renewal comes through the stranger." May God give us the faith, courage, and wisdom to be worthy of His Grace that comes in the form of such openings.

Bibliography

Ford, David F. *A Muscat Manifesto: Seeking Inter-Faith Wisdom*. Cambridge: Cambridge Inter-Faith Program and Dubai: Kalam Research & Media, 2009.

Nietzsche, Friedrich. *The Gay Science: With a Prelude in Rhymes and an Appendix in Songs*. Translated by Walter Kaufmann. New York: Vintage, 1974.

Otto, Rudolf. *The Idea of the Holy: An Inquiry into the Non-Rational Factor in the Idea of the Divine and Its Relation to the Rational*. Oxford: Oxford University Press. 1970.

Peirce, Charles. *Collected Papers of Charles Sanders Peirce*. Edited by Charles Hartshorne, Paul Weiss (vols. 1–6) and A. Burks (vols. 7–8). Cambridge: Harvard University Press, 1931–1958.

Schluchter, Wolfgang. "The Paradox of Rationalization: On the Relation of Ethics and World." In *Max Weber's Vision of History: Ethics and Methods*, edited by Guenther Roth and Wolfgang Schluchter, 11–64. Berkeley: University of California Press, 1979.

———. "Value Neutrality and the Ethics of Responsibility." In *Max Weber's Vision of History: Ethics and Methods*, edited by Guenther Roth and Wolfgang Schluchter, 65–116. Berkeley: University of California Press, 1979.

Weber, Max. "'Objectivity' in Social Science and Social Policy." In *Max Weber on the Methodology of the Social Sciences*, translated and edited by Edward A. Shils and Henry A. Finch, 49–112. Glencoe, IL: Free Press, 1949.

———. "Religious Rejections of the World and Their Directions." In *From Max Weber*, edited by H. H. Gerth and C. Wright Mills, 323–59. New York: Oxford University Press, 1946.

———. "Science as a Vocation." In *From Max Weber*, edited by H. H. Gerth and C. Wright Mills, 129–56. New York: Oxford University Press, 1946.

———. "Social Psychology of World Religions." In *From Max Weber*, edited by H. H. Gerth and C. Wright Mills, 267–322. New York: Oxford University Press, 1946.

16

Dialogue in the Dust

On the Wisdom of Inter-Religious Encounter

Michael Barnes SJ

Heythrop College, University of London

My introduction to David Ford came through a conference for interfaith practitioners. David had just been appointed Regius Professor of Divinity at the University of Cambridge. He began his keynote address by responding graciously to the congratulatory introduction and spoke warmly about his experience as a theologian living and working in multifaith Birmingham. He then paused, rubbed his hands, and announced gleefully: "Now let me just perform a few arabesques on my paper." What followed, of course, was less a dance around the subject than variations on a theme—and what intrigued me was less the content of the text than the manner of its exposition. The arabesques were repetitions of what we had already read, yet they were also improvisations delivered with an energy and excitement which responded to the moment, inviting us to see things thought familiar in a different way. As David says at the beginning of one of his most familiar works: "If Christian wisdom is concerned to correspond thoughtfully, in many 'moods,' to God and God's purposes, the desire for this needs to be aroused; the heart and imagination must be moved as well as the mind."[1] The theologian's task is not just to distil a

1. Ford, *Christian Wisdom*, 12.

particular type of wisdom, that discerning perseverance in following the Word revealed in Christ, but to communicate it, to embed it in the heart, and make it live in ever-new contexts and cultures.

In this essay I want to reflect on this more holistic account of wisdom as the spirituality that undergirds all holy living. My initial premise is that theology is shaped as much by performance as it is by content. If I correctly remember the coda of David's variations on an inter-religious theme, it had less to do with the topics and ideas around which some sort of mutually acceptable convergence can be forged, than with the process of human interaction, with the learned skills which make communication possible and which point us, however tentatively, in the direction of the Spirit of God who leads us into all the truth. Any attempt to reflect on the joys and sorrows of Christian living begins, of course, with the text of Scripture and the story of God's dialogue with humanity that the Bible narrates. But, precisely because God's Word or Wisdom is made incarnate in the person of Christ, theology is always and already shaped by history and culture and social relations. Other ideas, concepts, and symbols soon get drawn in, some from the Christian tradition itself, some from cognate or connected disciplines of thought, some from very different worlds of religious discourse. In a multi-religious world the "mood" that moves heart and mind is formed not by Christians alone but by people from very different faith traditions struggling to understand each other and to articulate their faith in a sometimes difficult and fraught world of interpersonal and inter-communal relations. In short, if good theology is formed through the act of communication across and between persons, attention needs to be given not just to the text itself, the immediate focus of scrutiny and study, but to the context or "texture" which shapes that communication in a particular way.

It is that process of texturing, bringing the Word into dialogue with what Karl Barth in one of his more expansive moods called "other words,"[2] that must engage our attention. This is no straightforward addition of greater and lesser, as if the different religions are like variously sized packets of the same product on the supermarket shelves. Whatever we call them—ways of holy living, communities of conviction, or just variations of some sort of generic "religion"—the great religious traditions of the world differ in significant ways. Thinking them together raises a number of questions, phenomenological, philosophical, *and* theological. Christianity speaks its

2. Barth, *Church Dogmatics* IV/3. Barth's question is "whether there really are other words which in this sense are true in relation to the one Word of God" (ibid., 113).

own uniquely comprehensive vision of truth; indeed it *must* speak "in the name of Jesus," as Peter insists to the Sanhedrin, "for we cannot keep from speaking about what we have seen and heard" (Acts 4:20). Something similar can be said for other religious traditions—most obviously Islam and Buddhism; they offer a truth that is valid in some sense for the whole of humankind. If that is correct—if religions are less like interchangeable spiritual commodities than languages that attempt to speak of God *to each other*—then two points follow. The first is that there can in principle be no end to the forms in which religions present themselves; all are seeking new ways of communicating their particular visions of truth. The second is that the flux of interpretation provoked by the encounter challenges the integrity of faith. The wisdom intrinsic to faith must be spoken—or it dies. Yet there is always a risk that accommodation or adaptation to other sources of wisdom leads to that faith losing its own specificity and vital inner energy.

Theology of Religions

What in recent years has come to be called the theology of religions is an attempt to grapple with that dilemma. Some versions tend to be very much Christianity-centred and focus on theological principles for dialogue. Others are more concerned with the "results" of dialogue and their implications for Christian self-understanding. Jacques Dupuis' elegant excavations of the Catholic sacramental tradition provide a good example of the former;[3] Francis Clooney's "comparative theology," a Christian reading of Hindu texts, fits the latter pattern.[4] The former seeks to relate the practice of dialogue to a tradition based largely on proclamation and warns against simplistic attempts to limit the scope of inter-religious encounter to the exploration of some agreed or common agenda. The latter focuses on the results of practice—insights gained from study groups and seminars or from time spent in silent meditation or on pilgrimage with other persons of faith—and attends more to what is actually communicated and learnt in the encounter itself. Such practices are the stuff of theology of religions, what evokes the mood within which Christian participants are invited to

3. See especially Dupuis, *Toward*, and (a more condensed version of the same material) *Christianity and the Religions*.

4. For introduction and overview, see Clooney, *Comparative Theology*. Clooney's remarkable series of Christian commentaries on Hindu texts includes *Theology After Vedanta*; *Hindu God, Christian God*; and *Divine Mother, Blessed Mother*.

explore their own story as it interacts with other stories and other funds of sacred wisdom. However, they can only be understood within a particular context; that of the symbols and beliefs which underpin all Christian living and form the community of believers in a particular way. Thus, to invoke a principle often used by Dupuis, the two forms of theology of religions—in shorthand, a theology *for* dialogue and a theology *of* dialogue—can be distinguished but not separated. While in the former the emphasis is on theological content, in the latter it is on theology as performance.

What holds them together is the recognition that any attempt at communication across religious boundaries requires words and text, or a set of signs and symbols that act as some sort of guiding or heuristic concept. What distinguishes them is the relative value given to the quality of the encounter and the relations that it establishes. The theology *for* dialogue model tends to work with a straightforwardly bipolar model of dialogue. Two sets of words are made to structure a conversation in which some sort of resolution is sought; canonical and key commentarial texts are correlated with what other texts say about analogous topics. This can be fruitful and at the very least builds a wealth of common understanding from which genuine friendship and mutual regard can grow. It may also provoke reflection on the nature of Scripture itself, on what gives it a certain coherence, and on hermeneutical questions about the reading of formative texts in a fluid cross-religious context. But, if proper attention is not given to the experience of dialogue itself and to the effect that the interpersonal has on the personal, this approach to theology of religions risks being turned into a form of defensive apologetics.

The now familiar jargon of inter-religious relations distinguishes four types of dialogue: common life, common action, religious experience, and theological exchange.[5] Each describes a particular task, with distinguishable aims. But it would probably be more correct to see them as facets of a single process, dimensions of a growing relationship. Thus, the theology *of* dialogue model is more taken up with what the act of engagement teaches about the Christian self, about what it means to be persons-in-relation. The conviction here is that the activity of speaking and listening, learning through careful attention to what is vaguely sensed rather than clearly understood, often turns out to be more theologically significant than

5. The fourfold distinction is first noted in the 1984 document from the Secretariat for non-Christian Religions, "The Attitude of the Church towards the Followers of Other Religions." It is repeated in John Paul II's encyclical, *Redemptoris Missio*, para 57 (1990), and in the 1991 joint document from the Pontifical Council for Inter-Religious Dialogue and the Congregation for Evangelisation, "Dialogue and Proclamation."

any supposedly shared truth about the nature of things. Theology—and perhaps particularly theology of religions—is as inseparable from prayer and spirituality as it is from the everyday concerns which persons of faith share on the streets where they live. This is not to reduce theology to some vaguely spiritual extrapolation from shared hopes and values, but rather the opposite. Sometimes, when the anxiety to come up with answers has been overcome by a willingness to live with the questions, it is the impalpable touches and traces of transcendence in the mundane which resonate most powerfully with the Word revealed in Christ. But it takes real wisdom to discern them. Hence the question behind the title of this essay: what wisdom is contained in the "dust" which collects around our efforts to make sense of the other?

The Wisdom of God

There is more to the evocative image of dust than some dispensable epiphenomenon on the edges of the more rigorous oral communication that typifies the "dialogue of theological exchange." I will return to that point in my concluding section. Meanwhile let us open up the theme of inter-religious wisdom. That there are rich funds of wisdom in all the great religious traditions and that they overlap, covering similar themes and touching each other in various ways, is obvious. John Eaton's masterly study of contemplative wisdom in the world's religions neatly brings biblical themes into correlation with ancient Egyptian sources, on the one hand, and the likes of modern spiritual teachers like Thomas Merton and Bede Griffiths, on the other. Kabir, Lao Tzu, Denys the Areopagite, desert fathers, and Sufi mystics build up a contemplative sensitivity to the world of human experience that tempers the more aggressive side of human nature and human religiosity.[6] A rather different example of inter-religious wisdom is the work of the Sri Lankan theologian, Aloysius Pieris, who has spent a lifetime deeply engaged with the Theravada Buddhism of his native land. Pieris throws light on the Christian tradition of *sapientia* through a dialogue with an analogous pursuit in Buddhism. Just as the concepts of *prajña* and *karuna*, wisdom and compassion, are mutually co-inherent, dependent on each other, so in Christianity wisdom is to be understood not as some abstract *gnosis* but as the action of the Spirit which transforms

6. Eaton, *Contemplative Face of Old Testament Wisdom*; see especially 1–21.

both mind and heart.[7] Pieris' work moves easily from the contemplative to the practical and reminds us that a good deal of wisdom has grown up around inter-religious encounter as primarily a meeting of persons. From Leonard Swidler's "The Dialogue Decalogue"[8] and the concise guidelines prepared by the Inter Faith Network for the UK,[9] to the more theologically inspired "Handbook" for the practice of Scriptural Reasoning,[10] or the set of maxims which David Ford himself has suggested,[11] there is no shortage of clear and sophisticated advice on how to maintain the integrity of faith on both sides of the encounter and to grow intellectually and affectively as a result. More is at stake here than collecting together wise ways of speaking that transcend religious boundaries or setting out pragmatic ground rules and helpful hints on how to aid the interpersonal engagement. Theology of religions is not the ordering of the "results" of dialogue, still less of the "data of religion." More exactly, it is concerned with the narration of God's Word as it interacts with what "other words" have to say about God and ultimate reality. The distinction is crucial. The question is not whether human beings think similar ideas or say similar things or come up with the same sort of practical reflections on human experience. Clearly they do. It is rather about how God can be said to be at work in *this* particular encounter, in *this* particular context of inter-religious engagement.

In that regard Christians have learned, all too late, that an inter-religious element is built into the very foundations of their faith. Thanks to the welcome rapprochement between Jews and Christians, the Old—or First—Testament can no longer be patronized as an outdated set of obscure tribal memories. The words of Torah, Prophets, and Writings, witness to the vitality and diversity of a living tradition that, for the Jewish people, requires no further fulfilment beyond faithfulness to the covenantal promises. Christians may not, therefore, pick out a plausible "canon within the canon," which would smooth out the sheer "otherness" of the multiplicity of biblical narratives in order to balance the regrettably exclusivist instincts of the people of Israel with some latent openness to "the nations." Instead we have to learn how to read our own life-giving Scriptures within the

7. See Pieris, *An Asian Theology of Liberation*; Pieris, *Love Meets Wisdom*, especially 110–35.

8. See *Journal of Ecumenical Studies* 20.1, 1–4.

9. Available as a leaflet or online as *Building Good Relations with People of Different Faiths and Beliefs*. See http://www.interfaith.org.uk/publications/buildinggoodrelations.pdf.

10. Kepnes, "Handbook for Scriptural Reasoning," 367–69.

11. See Ford, "Inter-Faith Wisdom," 349–50.

broad context of our emergence from within a "Jewish matrix"; what we can be said to inherit from our Jewish "elder brothers."[12] This, however, is no straightforward process. It is one thing to insist that, in biblical terms, the divide between the chosen and the stranger can never be absolute, quite another to elide the two. While there is no neat schematic account of "other religions" in the pages of the Bible, we are nonetheless given the story (more exactly stories) of how God guides a fractious people towards a critical yet generous universalism. The Bible, Jonathan Sacks tells us, begins the story of Israel's call not with universal truths but with one individual, Abraham.[13] Sacks can thus extrapolate from Abraham's own experience to explain the paradox that a universality of moral concern comes from a very particular sense of being set apart and different. To apply the Deuteronomic principle to inter-religious relations: by accepting that at one point I was different, a stranger and an exile yet brought back to life by God's own merciful compassion, I learn not that differences are irrelevant or insignificant but, on the contrary, that it is only in experiencing for myself the "dignity of difference" that I can begin to see a reflection of that quality at work in other people. By learning virtues of empathy and compassion not in some abstract philosophical form but through practice, in relationship with these people in this place, here and now, we become properly persons, not "instances of a type."

The story of how God shapes created reality out of a formless void and brings unity and harmony into the chaos of human relations is depicted in terms of the creative power of Wisdom. In theology of religions this most richly textured of biblical concepts is sometimes given the status of an all-encompassing universal. Dupuis, for instance, speaks of Wisdom as "an essentially dynamic reality, closely associated with all the works of God in the world."[14] Wisdom dispenses all good things (Wis 7:11) and acts in the world as the source of right conduct (Prov 3:5–7; 8:13) and the source of salvation for all who bid her welcome (Wis 6:12–20). Personified as a popular preacher, as a gentle mother, as father-counsellor, Wisdom is the very manifestation of God "standing for the beauty, order, and wisdom

12. The term is associated with Pope John Paul II, who seems to have used it for the first time on his visit to the Rome Synagogue on 13th April, 1986: "The Jewish religion is not extrinsic to us, but in a certain way is 'intrinsic' to our own religion. With Judaism therefore we have a relationship which we do not have with any other religion. You are our dearly beloved brothers and in a certain way, it could be said that you are our elder brothers."

13. Sacks, *Dignity of Difference*, especially 45–66.

14. Dupuis, *Toward*, 43.

of the divine plan that unfolds in the history of salvation as a reflection of the harmony that exists in God's self."[15] Gerald O'Collins' scriptural survey of what he calls God's "other peoples" uses similar universalist language to speak about the theme of Wisdom as "international in character"; it is "general and non-specific in its religious approach, and so helps us to appreciate the one, long story in which no group or individual is forgotten by God."[16] Figures such as Melchisedek and Ruth, not to mention Job, take their place alongside "saints of the Old Testament" like Abraham, Noah, and the prophets as pointing the way to Christ. Certainly, such an approach is plausible if we are content to see in the Old Testament a prelude that foreshadows the fullness of Christian revelation. The problem, of course, is that too strong an emphasis on a biblical vision governed by the symbolic status of Wisdom risks leaving us with a theology of religions that remains at the level of vague generalities, a sort of universalizing supplement to the overarching story of God's engagement with the people of Israel. That the Old Testament includes non-Jewish sayings alongside the narrative of God's engagement with the people of Israel is clear, but does not in itself address our question: where precisely is God at work?

The possibility of a more adequate response arises when we forget about establishing universals and probe the specifically Jewish texture of the concept of Wisdom. Sacks' "dignity of difference" works as a principle of interpretation just as well with the last books of the Jewish Bible as it does with the first. The Wisdom of Solomon, for instance, is an immensely erudite engagement with Hellenistic thought, written most probably in Alexandria and intended to defend the Jewish faith of those now living in a very different religious milieu from their forebears. Sirach or Ecclesiasticus takes the form of the instruction of a young man. Rather like the book of Wisdom the author's object is to help his pupil make sense of the peculiar quality of Jewish wisdom in a world already suffused with wise teachings and wise ways of life. One passage stands out. After offering much moral exhortation, the author's mood changes and he turns to a direct address to God—"O Lord, Father and Master of my life"—and then has Wisdom praising herself:

> I came forth from the mouth of the Most High,
> and covered the earth like a mist.
> I dwelt in the highest heavens
> and my throne was in a pillar of cloud.

15. Ibid., 44.

16. O'Collins, *Salvation for All*, 54.

> Alone I compassed the vault of heaven
> and traversed the depths of the abyss. (Sir 24:3–5)

Wisdom as the manifestation of God's own creative power settles on Jerusalem, the "beloved city," where "I took root in an honoured people, in the portion of the Lord, his inheritance" (Sir 24:11). It is almost as if the author realizes that simply piling up the wise sayings only gets us so far. Proverbs and sage advice are valuable not because they are intellectually coherent, but because they are records of a sometimes painfully felt personal experience. If they are to move mind *and heart* they have to be anchored in a much deeper vision of what makes for the moral life. Both these great texts represent real dialogues with wider culture and a genuine effort to communicate to new generations and other audiences. But neither the author of Wisdom nor Jesus ben Sirach seems interested in making some sort of comparative presentation, arguing for the superiority of the Jewish version of a common possession, or just subsuming all forms of wisdom and learning into one undifferentiated generic "religion." However much they draw on a variety of religious sources, their main concern is to get their readers to value the God-given meaning that is to be discerned in the teachings of Jewish tradition.

In biblical terms Wisdom is not just the fruit of learning and experience, the collected customs and mores that make for personal happiness and the successful functioning of society. It is also a more speculative and deeply theological concept, which points beyond the mystery of creation itself to an inner meaning in God. These two dimensions are necessarily interlinked, but not because a purely human wisdom always proves unsatisfactory and remains in need of something more. Rather human beings are constantly searching for the former but find themselves drawn *by and into* the latter. This perhaps is what makes the biblical concept of Wisdom not just a fund of prudential advice for sound living but a source of delight and surprise which liberates and empowers. For who can say what is most valuable in human experience, what makes for human flourishing, let alone a more cosmic order and harmony? The corpus of Wisdom literature is not some neatly homogeneous collection of homely sayings: at one extreme is the sublime confidence of Proverbs; at the other the heartbreak of Job and the almost cynical realism of Qoheleth. Wisdom may represent the best of what it is to be human, but it is also a divine gift, especially to those who suffer and are not satisfied with convention and comfortable answers. Thus Job, in his anguish, asks: "Whence then comes wisdom? And where is the place of understanding? . . . God understands the way to it, and he knows its place" (Job 28:20, 23). It is this theological concept of Wisdom, a lesson learned in the tragedy and incompleteness of life, which challenges the more prudential version, a sort of universal collection of cross-religious moral truths.

There is more, in other words, to Wisdom than some form of "natural religion" that needs to be completed by "supernatural faith." Wisdom is a dialogical concept in the sense that, like so many common religious values, such as justice, peace, and tolerance, it lends itself to cross-religious understanding and, quite rightly, finds itself celebrated in all manner of inter-religious encounters. If, however, Sacks' argument for the "dignity of difference" is saying one thing, it is that dialogue is not about negotiating shared universals but about respecting and learning from the particular. It may seem plausible to set wisdom above the inter-religious fray and make it purely a facet or aspect of the *humanum* that is shared across Old and New Testaments alike, and indeed across religious traditions. However, as Walter Brueggemann points out, an account of Wisdom as some sort of secular guide to daily living that only subsequently attains to theological awareness is anachronistic in a faith-filled society.[17] Wisdom is theological through and through, ever pointing people in the direction of the creator God. It is precisely because life is filled with and guided by the sense of a God who promises to be *Emmanuel* that the ordinary routine processes of accommodation and adjustment by which life becomes manageable are given exemplary status. This is where God is to be found: not just in the practical wisdom that underpins human relations but in the creative and transformative action of God that graces the whole of life.

The Texture of Dialogue

What makes Wisdom such a powerful concept in inter-religious relations is not that it acts as shorthand for similar sources of consoling sayings and inspiring ideas, but that it implies careful and critical discernment of the ways of God in the world. The wise take their time; they know their limitations, how much they do not know and how much more they need to learn and understand. Wisdom is necessary for that generous and clear thinking without which theology risks becoming self-indulgent and

17. Brueggemann, *Introduction to the Old Testament*, 307. Brueggemann makes dialogue central to the concept of the God of the Old Testament; see especially his *Theology of the Old Testament*, 407–564, and in slightly adapted form in *Unsettling God*, especially 137–43.

defensive—repeating the familiar formulae whether or not anyone is listening. If Christian theology is to be faithful to its origins as performance, as the effort to find God's meaning through the act of communication with other human beings, then attention needs to be given to wisdom as the *virtue of a learned creativity*. Wisdom is, of course, vested in texts; in the words that encapsulate and pass on some timeless truth. But it is also at work in forming and building up context and texture—the wider span of relations, human and divine, which provokes imaginative reworking and variations on an "original theme." Together, the two forms of theology of religions described earlier involve more than a judicious analysis of the different languages and cultures with which Christians seek to dialogue; they are also attempts to reread our formative texts so that they go on speaking of the traces of the Spirit, which God places deep in God's own creation. This is where we begin—and, in a certain sense, where we must be content to end:

> The Lord created me at the beginning of his work, the first of his acts of old. Ages ago I was set up, at the first, before the beginning of the earth. When there were no depths I was brought forth, when there were no springs abounding with water. Before the mountains had been shaped, before the hills, I was brought forth; before he had made the earth with its fields, or the first of the dust of the world. (Prov 9:22–26)

Let me conclude with that last image and its most familiar occurrence in the book of Genesis. We human beings are created in the image of God, yet formed of dust; the beginning of wisdom lies with what the Wisdom texts call "the fear of the Lord," yet the revelation of "God with us" can never be separated from the vision of *this* world, with all its tragic frailty, as the site of God's life-giving action.

> In the day that the Lord God made the earth and the heavens, when no plant of the field was yet in the earth and no herb of the field had yet sprung up—for the Lord God had not caused it to rain upon the earth, and there was no man to till the ground; but a mist went up from the earth and watered the whole face of the ground—then the Lord God formed man of dust from the ground, and breathed into his nostrils the breath of life; and man became a living being. (Gen 2:4b–7)

This all but untranslatable sentence moves from a description of the earth as empty desert to the creation of humanity out of the very stuff of earth itself. In the Hebrew, man (*'ādām*) and earth (*'ădāmâ*) are made to echo each other. Creation of the earth is the necessary condition for the creation of humanity; the two are inseparable—made of the same raw material, the dust from which we are all taken and to which we all return (Gen 3:17b). But that is not all. Humanity is filled with life only when the breath of God enters the material body and transforms it. In these terms, human beings are not "body" and "soul" but, more exactly, matter and *life*, God's own life, which raises up and transforms the otherwise undifferentiated dust from which we are all formed. To do this particular text justice would require a lengthy exegesis, but my intention here is not to show how it supports a doctrine of creation. The point I want to make is this. Ancient biblical texts do not give us some universal notion of the human person, the "essence" of what it is to be human. They are to be recited before they are studied—and, as that wordplay between man and earth illustrates—they are full of echoes and resonances that stimulate the imagination. Wisdom lies not just in knowing how to read texts but also in savouring the texture of life, which is often infuriatingly hidden yet tantalizingly revealed in the sometimes frustrating attempts human beings make to communicate very ordinary things and very ordinary experiences —the "dust" which is generated by our life on *this* earth.

The God who creates all things goes on guiding the fruits of creation, both the magnificent and the prosaic, through God's own wise and benevolent action. Whatever their differences, my two forms of theology of religions would agree that, in principle, there can be nothing which is not open to the providential care of God; God remains, ever-creative, at work not just in the known and familiar dimensions of human experience but in what is different, strange, and quite other. In that sense theology of religions is, more exactly, a theology of creation—an account of God's continuing creative work in which all things, all peoples, and all human interaction in the pursuit of truth are brought together in God. Not that everything can be made to speak of God, for there is always that in the freedom of human endeavour that reflects a darkness and negativity, a sort of anti-wisdom, as Qoheleth knew. Thus the theologian celebrates and communicates that which is known, but is also called to discern that which is strictly unknown, the mystery of God revealed in unexpected ways and forms. It can—and indeed does—happen in inter-religious encounter that insights and ideas are generated that open up new vistas and promise an unexpected level of mutual understanding. Not everything, however, bears the imprint of a sacred wisdom. The resonances between faiths often remain just that—echoes of something familiar which yet remain impalpably strange and mysterious.

For the Christian theologian, therefore, dialogue is not about identifying, still less negotiating, some elusive textually inscribed wisdom but about learning *how to live wisely,* how to discern and speak responsibly about the dimly perceived signs of God in a pluralist world. This, of course, is more exactly the work of Word and Spirit who together generate a proper understanding of God's providential purposes and engage heart and soul in building humane learning and enterprise into a truly sacred Wisdom.

Bibliography

Barth, Karl. *Church Dogmatics* IV/3: *The Doctrine of Reconciliation.* 2 vols. Translated by G. W. Bromiley. Edited by G. W. Bromiley and Thomas F. Torrance. Edinburgh: T. & T. Clark, 1961.

Brueggemann, Walter. *An Introduction to the Old Testament: The Canon and Christian Imagination.* Louisville: Westminster John Knox, 2003.

———. *Theology of the Old Testament: Testimony, Dispute, Advocacy.* Minneapolis: Fortress, 1997.

———. *An Unsettling God: The Heart of the Hebrew Bible.* Minneapolis: Fortress, 2009.

Clooney, Francis X. *Comparative Theology: Deep Learning across Religious Borders.* Chichester, UK: Wiley-Blackwell, 2010.

———. *Divine Mother, Blessed Mother: Hindu Goddesses and the Virgin Mary.* Oxford: Oxford University Press, 2005.

———. *Hindu God, Christian God: How Reason Helps Break Down the Boundaries between Religions.* Oxford: Oxford University Press, 2001.

———. *Theology After Vedanta.* Albany: State University of New York Press, 1993.

Dupuis, Jacques. *Christianity and the Religions.* Maryknoll, NY: Orbis, 2002.

———. *Toward a Christian Theology of Religious Pluralism.* Maryknoll, NY: Orbis, 1997.

Eaton, John. *The Contemplative Face of Old Testament Wisdom—in the Context of World Religions.* London: SCM, 1989.

Ford, David F. *Christian Wisdom: Desiring God and Learning in Love.* Cambridge: Cambridge University Press, 2007.

———. "An Interfaith Wisdom." *Modern Theology* 22 (2006) 345–66.

John Paul II. *Redemptoris Missio* (1990). Online: http://www.vatican.va/holy_father/john_paul_ii/encyclicals/documents/hf_jp-ii_enc_07121990_redemptoris-missio_en.html.

Kepnes, Steven. "A Handbook for Scriptural Reasoning." *Modern Theology* 22 (2006) 367–83.

Pieris, Aloysius. *An Asian Theology of Liberation.* Edinburgh: T. & T. Clark, 1988.

———. *Love Meets Wisdom: A Christian Experience of Buddhism.* Maryknoll, NY: Orbis, 1988.

O'Collins, Gerald. *Salvation for All: God's Other Peoples*. Oxford: Oxford University Press, 2008.

Pontifical Council for Inter-Religious Dialogue and the Congregation for Evangelisation. "Dialogue and Proclamation: Reflections and Orientations on Inter-Religious Dialogue and the Proclamation of the Gospel of Jesus Christ." *Bulletin* 26.2 (1991).

Sacks, Jonathan. *The Dignity of Difference*. New York: Continuum, 2003.

Secretariat for Non-Christian Religions. "The Attitude of the Church towards the Followers of Other Religions." *Bulletin* 1.2 (1984).

PART FIVE

Speaking and Listening in Public

17

Tales of the Unexpected

Theology in Public Space

Rachel Muers

University of Leeds

Introduction: Postsecular Publics

Theologians in the United Kingdom and elsewhere in the West have increasingly to reckon with, and seek their vocation in, a "postsecular" context. The contemporary postsecular condition arises from a confluence of postsecular *discourse* (the theoretical articulation of religion's importance and of the weaknesses of secularist assumptions) and postsecular *practice* (the increased public and political visibility of religion, alongside developments in public policy that result in new interactions between "religious" and "secular" spheres and institutions).[1] Clearly many theologians, along with other scholars of religion, will want to argue, paralleling Bruno Latour, that "we have never been secular"—at least, not to the extent that some academic disciplines tended to assume. However, these scholars can still note, and respond to, a shift from the

1. The literature is large and complex. For some significant interdisciplinary collections focused on the term, see Molendijk, Beaumont, and Jedan, *Exploring the Postsecular*; Beaumont and Baker, *Postsecular Cities*; and for some theological treatments, see Ward, *Politics of Discipleship*, chapter 3; Baker, *Hybrid Church in the City*.

assumed theoretical irrelevance of religion (whatever its continuing practical relevance) to the explicit recognition, in a wide range of contexts, of the continuing power and salience of religious traditions. While many of us would argue that the practices and institutions now labelled as "postsecular" are nothing new, we can still recognize that their new public and theoretical visibility changes the context for theological work.

Discerning and negotiating the specific vocation of theology in this rapidly changing context is an important and fraught task. It can, of course, be said that theology's primary vocation is as it has always been: speaking—in communicative, critical, or celebratory mode—of God and of everything else in relation to God, for the sake of God, and for the sake of everything else.[2] Theology resists instrumentalization or spurious claims to relevance, in part, by remembering and reminding itself of this primary calling. And there is, for all modernity's learned forgetfulness of where we have been before, rather little new under the sun.

Furthermore, when we examine the details of theology's contemporary Western context, it is clearly not the case that the "old" modern arguments about the irrelevance of theology, or its lack of standing as a proper academic discipline, have disappeared. In certain circles, they are being put forward with equivalent vigour and added vitriol, as the emergence of postsecular awareness in the academy and the re-emergence of religion into political discourse in the UK is met by the mobilization of New Atheism. At the same time, theologians today do not face, as a primary challenge, the unquestioned hegemony of secular modes of practice and discourse. The postsecular—or, as David Ford puts it more often, the "religious and secular" moment—might offer new opportunities for unlikely collaborations in the seeking of wisdom.

In this essay, I explore some aspects of the vocation of theology in a public sphere constituted as postsecular, and, in particular, in a public sphere in which the social roles of "faith communities" receives increasing attention. In keeping with a key emphasis in David Ford's work, I conduct this exploration through a reading of a biblical text. My suggestion is that one possible vocation of theology is to undertake the critique of contemporary idolatries through a reflection on contemporary miracles—defined, following Nicholas Adams and Charles Elliott, as surprising events that Christians nonetheless expect.[3]

2. On "communicative, critical, and celebratory," see Williams, *On Christian Theology*, xii–xvi.

3. Adams and Elliott, "Ethnography is Dogmatics," 358.

The text on which I am focusing is Acts 3:1–13. It may seem obvious—though I am not aware that it has yet been done—to reflect on this passage in the context of asking questions about the contemporary public vocation of Christians in general and theologians in particular.

> [1]One day Peter and John were going up to the temple at the hour
> of prayer, at three o'clock in the afternoon. [2]And a man lame
> from birth was being carried in. People would lay him daily at
> the gate of the temple called the Beautiful Gate so that he could
> ask for alms from those entering the temple. [3]When he saw Peter
> and John about to go into the temple, he asked them for alms.
> [4]Peter looked intently at him, as did John, and said, "Look at us."
> [5]And he fixed his attention on them, expecting to receive some-
> thing from them. [6]But Peter said, "I have no silver or gold, but
> what I have I give you; in the name of Jesus Christ of Nazareth,
> stand up and walk." [7]And he took him by the right hand and
> raised him up; and immediately his feet and ankles were made
> strong. [8]Jumping up, he stood and began to walk, and he entered
> the temple with them, walking and leaping and praising God.
> [9]All the people saw him walking and praising God, [10]and they
> recognized him as the one who used to sit and ask for alms at
> the Beautiful Gate of the temple; and they were filled with won-
> der and amazement at what had happened to him. [11]While he
> clung to Peter and John, all the people ran together to them in
> the portico called Solomon's Portico, utterly astonished. [12]When
> Peter saw it, he addressed the people, "You Israelites, why do
> you wonder at this, or why do you stare at us, as though by our
> own power or piety we had made him walk? [13]The God of Abra-
> ham, the God of Isaac, and the God of Jacob, the God of our
> ancestors has glorified his servant Jesus, whom you handed over
> and rejected in the presence of Pilate, though he had decided to
> release him."

The Face in a Public Space

This story of an encounter in an ambiguous public space, in which a dramatic small-scale transformation occurs with a face-to-face gaze, the utterance of a name, and a grasp of the hand, begins the story of the apostolic ministry after Pentecost. In the remarkable moment in which the lame man and the two apostles look into each other's faces, a contemporary reader might well recall Emmanuel Lévinas' inauguration of ethics with the call to responsibility that meets us in the face of the other person.

It is noteworthy, for those concerned with the vocation of theology, that Lévinas is among those whose thought has recently been appropriated and developed in the quest for categories to describe and shape the landscape of "postsecular" ethics.[4] Like some of David Ford's other favoured tropes—wisdom, or the cry—the "face of the other" is neither simply a religious, nor simply a secular, starting point for ethics. Divisions of "religious" and "secular," and the modes of explanation and argumentation that belong to them, are subsequent to the response to the face of the other. As Charles Taylor emphasizes in his use of Ivan Illich's rereading of the Good Samaritan, the texts of religious traditions can overcome modernity's religious-secular divide, in part, by narrating and calling forth unsystematizable responses to a neighbour's need.[5]

Acts 3 locates the transformative moment of facing the other in a space at the boundaries of existing institutions—at the gate of the Temple. I can easily imagine, then, reading Acts 3 in the "postsecular" spaces of social action that Paul Cloke and others describe—say, in drop-in centres for homeless people in British cities, centres that occupy neither "religious" nor "secular" space and that engage Christians, adherents of other faiths and of none in the day-to-day work of responding to acute and chronic need.[6] The primacy of face-to-face encounter and the offer of one's embodied presence—the hand reached out to grasp—resonate with how both Christian and non-Christian volunteers describe their work.[7]

It is also easy to see the dangers of reading Acts 3 to discern Christian vocations in the complex public space we inhabit. Is this not—the vocal opponents of public welfare programmes might say—a text about the futility of systems of monetary support, the basis for a Christian critique of "dependency culture," and hence a mandate for withdrawing public funds from the kind of everyday support that the drop-in centres (for example) try to offer? And maybe also a text about the individual and hence non-political nature of the salvation with which theology is concerned? Is it, then, a text that withdraws theology from the public realm and separates it from all "secular" forms of public effectiveness?

And then, is it perhaps—I can hear (even) several of the volunteers at these drop-in centres saying—a text about the need to proclaim the gospel

4. See, for example, Cloke et al., "Ethical Citizenship."

5. Taylor, *Secular Age*, 737–43.

6. Cloke et al., *Swept-Up Lives?*

7. For more on this, see Muers with Britt, "Faithful Untidiness"; Cloke et al., "Ethical Citizenship."

over and above, and perhaps instead of, offering practical responses to society's ills? Or perhaps a text about the non-negotiability of the Christian "label," of making it clear in every situation that what is done is done in the name of Jesus Christ? Is it, then, about the need for theology's task to be exercised primarily in the interests of the maintenance of Christian identity?

And then, of course, isn't the very plurality of possible interpretations—the secularist opponent of "faith-based" organizations might say—an indication of how futile or even dangerous it is to allow religious traditions, their texts and reasonings, to have any kind of voice in the public sphere? Is it an indirect indication of the need to maintain a "secular" hegemony, and hence to keep theology as irrelevant as possible to public life? Particularly, of course, if theologians *will* insist on taking seriously, in the age of modern medicine, a very old book that talks about miraculous healings?

In order to respond to these challenges, we must first consider where the text might take us through and beyond the recognition of the face of the neighbour or the stranger. Recognizing the face of the neighbour or the stranger, after all, is not obviously and as such a theological vocation—which is one of the reasons why Lévinas, and (certain readings of) the Good Samaritan parable, appear to lend themselves to the formulation of a postsecular ethic. In this text, however, the face-to-face encounter is surrounded by traditions that make sense of what occurs, and that are read both by the apostles and by the narrator of Acts to render the encounter publicly effective. Not only does it take place at the gate of the Temple, but as the story progresses the "name of Jesus Christ of Nazareth" is juxtaposed with the names of Solomon, Abraham, Isaac, Jacob—and Pilate. The God who effects the transformation of the "man lame from birth" is named and discerned through the rereading and interweaving of the traditions that form the context for the man's story.

So a first and obvious contemporary public vocation for theology could be finding the words to speak about, and the stories to contextualize, what is going on in transitional and transformative spaces. I want to suggest that this is part of what is going on—but that the text and the contemporary context suggest a significant critical function for theological work. The story of the healing of the "man lame from birth" in the name of Jesus Christ of Nazareth is, after all, a story of opposition and reversal as well as a story of worthy social action. Examining the nature of this opposition brings us to a key area of contemporary theological vocation.

Theology as Anti-Idolatry: Denying Big Lies by Telling Small Stories

> Peter said, "I have no silver or gold, but what I have I give you; in the name of Jesus Christ of Nazareth, stand up and walk."

In Acts 3, the name of Jesus Christ of Nazareth appears in opposition, *not* to the Temple, but to "silver and gold." The name of Jesus Christ of Nazareth, like the possession of wisdom (Prov 8) or the words of Torah (Ps 19:10) is more valuable than silver and gold. The point, as I read it, is not that this text sets up an opposition between material help (silver and gold) and spiritual help (the name of Jesus Christ of Nazareth)—tempting though it may be to establish such a dichotomy. The point is, rather, that the *material* difference is made by or in the name of Jesus Christ of Nazareth. The meeting of glances, the reaching out of hands, and the act of standing and walking, can take place in the context of this name. The material difference is also, however, a "spiritual" difference. Surprisingly for Acts, this passage makes no direct reference to the Holy Spirit; but the power to call, and to make possible what is called for—"in the name of Jesus Christ of Nazareth, walk"—is, reading in context, the power of the Holy Spirit given at Pentecost.

Materially, in this story, it would seem that "silver and gold" as ordinarily used maintain the status quo. People can normally, it seems, give the lame man silver and gold without looking at him; it is probably, for at least some of them, a good way of avoiding having to look at him. Relationships based only on the exchange of "silver and gold" do allow the man and the passers-by to carry on with their lives—but not, it seems, to flourish, and probably not to change. Silver and gold buy the concealment of the man's particular suffering and need. As the paradigmatic "idols of the nations," the silver and gold coins bearing the ruler's face "have mouths, but do not speak; eyes, but do not see; . . . ears, but do not hear. . . . Those who make them are like them, so are all who trust in them" (Ps 115:4–8). The idols of the nations, which the "name of Jesus Christ of Nazareth" challenges, deal death, in part, by the indifference and ignorance they create.

How does this relate to the question of theology's contemporary vocation? It would be possible to develop a general argument about the theological task of anti-idolatry. Theology has the vocation to promote storied and traditioned resistance to taken-for-granted patterns of thought and behaviour, patterns that not only obstruct the worship of God, but prevent the recognition of suffering and need and impede human flourishing. This is an approach associated most strongly in the twentieth century with liberation theologies, but in different ways it recognizably shapes numerous theological responses to features of the public realm.

However, in the contemporary context it is also possible to read the text with more direct attention to the power of "silver and gold." Philip Goodchild has recently argued that the development of the autonomous "secular" sphere and the development of the modern system of money are intimately interconnected. Religion survived in the sphere—the private sphere—not given over to money; the cost of this withdrawal was that the power of money, as the value underlying all values, remained unchallenged. According to Goodchild's account of the modern settlement, Christian and other religious reasons and values, because they were not (as it were) common currency, circulated only in restricted spheres; the "bottom line" in any public debate or institution was, and is, financial. The very distinction between the material and the spiritual, as it has tended to operate in the modern context, is shaped by the illusion that only money is "material."[8]

The key insight presented in Goodchild's work is that money is a theological issue—not because theological insights can be applied to a subset of applied ethics that deals with business and finance, but because money, in ordering our time, care, and attention and determining the value of all other values, functions as god. The biblical writers, in denying that one could serve both God and Mammon, put this point sharply. Acts 3 read through this lens reveals, in miniature, the contrasting mobilizations of time, care, and attention, and the contrasting material effects, produced by "silver and gold" and by "the name of Jesus Christ of Nazareth."

Thinking about the contemporary meanings of "silver and gold" also helps us to uncover another dimension of theology's anti-idolatry. For "silver and gold" purport to offer a univocal, one-to-one, mapping of representations to facts—"we know where the bottom line is," "we know exactly what this can be traded for." Having no silver and gold is having nothing that will provide one with a fully predictable future or a fully exhaustive account of meaning. There is, it seems to me, an implication in Acts 3 (at least in the dramatic staging of the face-to-face gaze) that Peter takes a genuine risk when he calls the man to get up. He is risking an interpretation of the "name of Jesus Christ of Nazareth," in a context in which the meaning—the value, the capacity for material and spiritual effects—of that name is not fixed.

8. Goodchild, *Theology of Money*.

Moreover, the success of this first interpretation of Jesus' name—the moment of healing—provides, not a secure position of immediately comprehensible and communicable knowledge, but the need for a further and riskier reinterpretation in Peter's address to the crowd. And we can see particularly clearly, reading the latter reinterpretation today, how dangerous it is to halt the process here, extracting an exhaustive and universally applicable reading of Jesus' story (which would cause one, for example, to regard all "Israelites" as the agents of Jesus' death). Thinking back to my earlier discussion of the possibilities and difficulties of reading Acts 3 in a postsecular context, we might say that the commentator, whether secularist or fundamentalist, who wants religious texts to mean just one thing (and/or decides that they are useless when they do not mean just one thing) wants the equivalent of "silver and gold"; a completely predictable and accountable unit of meaning that can establish and maintain a status quo.

This line of interpretation also calls into question any reading of this text that is preoccupied with explaining, or explaining away, the healing miracle itself. Peter's account of the healing, after all, directly disavows control over the healing phenomenon ("Why do you stare at us, as though by our own power or piety we had made him walk?"). What he offers is not an *explanation* that would predict how this unexpected event could be reproduced under laboratory conditions, or turned into a standard service provided for everyone in similar circumstances, or traded for money.[9]

In fact, the story tends to disrupt the binary division between rich and poor—between a person who has needs and a person who has the means to address those needs, between the powerless recipient of help and the powerful helper. There are asymmetries of power and resources—seen in the contrast between the apostles walking into the Temple and the lame man being carried; but the apostles do not have in their possession anything that would fix the lame man's problem. Peter has no silver or gold. When he pledges to give the lame man what he (Peter) has, the "gift" turns out to be a summons to act: get up, and walk. He does not really "have" anything of his own to give to the lame man. So both the vocation and the lame man's capacity to fulfil it turn out to originate, not with the apostles, but in the "name of Jesus Christ of Nazareth" and with "the God of Abraham, the God of Isaac, and the God of Jacob." The apostles' call to heal and preach and the man's call to walk and praise God become, as we read

9. And, if space permitted, a reading of the story of Simon Magus (Acts 8:9–24) would enable the further development of this theme.

into the story, harder to distinguish from each other. Perhaps the apostles depend on the once-lame man—and on his remarkable act of placing his trust in two strangers and a strange name—as much as he depends on them.[10]

Anti-idolatry is always a proper dimension of theology's vocation, and it seems particularly urgent in our time to challenge the idolatry of "silver and gold." My modest proposal is that big lies, lies that dominate and reshape our social reality—such as the lie that money always knows best—are best challenged not (only) by propounding alternative grand narratives, but (also) by telling small stories. A big lie destroys—in theory, and then in fact—real lives, real values, and real relationships;[11] the big lie of monetary value is no exception.[12] Telling the stories of how and where that destruction happens is already a challenge to the big lie. Acting as if that destruction is not inevitable, and telling the stories of how lives, values, and relationships persist beyond and in the face of the big lie is an even more fundamental challenge. The big lie is not out-narrated by an even stronger single, universally applicable way of determining value in the world; it is out-narrated by multiple particular accounts of events, values, and lives for which it cannot account. It is out-narrated, in other words, by small stories that are also miracle stories.

The story of the life, death, and resurrection of Jesus Christ of Nazareth is, in this sense, a small story that resists any and every big lie. The story of one man healed at the doorway of the Temple is an even smaller story. One significant theological task for the Christian theologian is to allow the story of Jesus of Nazareth to establish the context within which other small and surprising stories can be heard, understood, and responded to. To return to the terms in which this discussion began—Christianity's liturgical

10. As a side comment on this, it is easy for questions about the *vocation* of theology today, asked of and to the relatively privileged possessors of academic jobs and salaries, to sound like questions about "how we can help" or "how we can fix the world's problems." Perhaps, also, the search for theology's vocation is not only a matter of walking around looking for problems to fix, but of remaining in place and being prepared to accept help from unexpected sources.

11. The relationship between the "big lie" and violence—between proclaiming that something does not exist and destroying it—is analysed as a component of totalitarianism by Arendt (*Origins of Totalitarianism*, 349). I would suggest, however, that there is no need for the "big lie" by which a society lives to be backed by recognizably totalitarian power in order for it to have destructive effects.

12. The remarkable durability of the ideology of money is being demonstrated as I write this; it is far from clear that any major changes in attitudes to the global financial system are likely to follow the "crash" of 2008.

and scriptural focus on the face of Jesus Christ does not detract from daily practices of facing neighbours or strangers, and from daily attention to the complexity of what is going on. In fact, it grounds such attention.

The small stories that challenge the big lie do not, of course, have to be "Christian" stories. In Acts 3, it is not obvious that the lame man joins the apostles' community. More helpful, as Nicholas Adams and Charles Elliott suggest, is the idea of offering theologically shaped descriptions of "anything in which God might be involved"—and, in particular, of miracles; that is, of surprising events that Christians nonetheless expect.[13]

But then, what contemporary stories should theologians be telling? There are clearly judgements to be made that would hold theology back from celebrating anything and everything that looks like "resistance," but would take us beyond speaking only about phenomena that fit neatly with predetermined Christian criteria or institutions.[14] Such judgments cannot, however, be made in the abstract. Theological work is done from a position of commitment, to places and people as well as to scriptures and traditions; it is done while walking some route, or sitting somewhere in particular, and the small stories we reread are the stories that come to us.[15]

A Small Story

What might the telling of contemporary "small stories," to resist big lies and to place the word and wisdom of God above silver and gold, look like? The example given here relates to a small-scale event in a British city, focused on extending welcome to asylum seekers and refugees.[16] The event

13. Adams and Elliott, "Ethnography is Dogmatics."

14. Adams and Elliott discuss the Chipko movement and the campaign against the Narmada Dam as examples of the overturning of entrenched and oppressive structures of privilege, occurring in largely non-Christian contexts.

15. Daniel W. Hardy's account of a "walking ecclesiology," patterned on Jesus' walking of the land, draws attention to the "step-by-step" character of the theological task: "Whoever and whatever turns up as they [theologians] walk, whatever they find as they go along, these become the found realities in response to which they think and act" (Hardy et al., *Wording a Radiance*, 86).

16. The practice of welcome to asylum seekers and refugees is a particularly important contemporary example of the re/construction of public space, for and with those who are not counted as part of the "public" of the modern state. It is also, of course, a practice in which churches have played a very significant public role. See the discussion in Bretherton, *Christianity and Contemporary Politics*, 126–74, in particular his account of the need of the person seeking sanctuary for a "new polity."

is a textbook case of the "postsecular," in that it fits neither within existing religious institutions nor within "secular" state or large-scale charitable institutions—while drawing in ad hoc fashion on the language, the categories, the people, and the resources of many such institutions. It has, at first glance, the spontaneity, the liminality, and the hybridity celebrated in several theological accounts of the postsecular;[17] but it is also an event that calls for links to be made to the past and the future through renarration and reinterpretation.[18]

> I'm at a gathering organised by the local City of Sanctuary movement.[19] The publicity states that it's run "on a shoestring," and asks for donations—of anything. It's in a community centre in a relatively poor area of the city, to which many asylum seekers are "dispersed." The central hall has tables and chairs, and stalls with hand-made signs, and a roughly-cleared stage area with a small band slightly over-amplified—for my taste anyway, but most people aren't put off, there's a buzz of conversation. Maybe a hundred people in this room. It's as multi-racial and multi-lingual, and as diverse in terms of class and culture, as I know this whole city is—but I don't often find the diversity gathered in one place. I see hugs of reunion, I see the nervous beginnings of conversations between people who have only just met but are determined to like each other. There's food, of course, and brightly-coloured squash in plastic jugs, and coffee in portable urns. There's a children's play space, with a motley collection of toys, and a crawling baby who with a baby's luck is avoiding being trodden on. And going through into the garden, there's a small bouncy castle, and a giant "Jenga" set that some girls are using to create a domino run, and many more people. I recognize a local Muslim youth worker, trying to gather teams for a game of cricket. I watch my seventy-odd-year-old Quaker friend demonstrating co-operative juggling with a seven-year-old boy she's just met. The dominoes fall and everyone cheers.
>
> I chat to a young woman; she's a regular volunteer with City of Sanctuary; she knows people I know. How did she get

17. For example in Baker, *Hybrid Church in the City.*

18. I am grateful to Rachael Loftus and Paul Magnus for assistance with City of Sanctuary material, and to Jemma Russell (whose work on the subject is as yet unpublished), Rhiannon Grant, Tiffy Allan, and people at PAFRAS for helpful conversations.

19. City of Sanctuary is a UK-wide movement to create a "culture of hospitality" towards people seeking sanctuary in UK cities, by drawing together local councils and public-sector bodies, voluntary organizations, faith groups, and businesses. See http://www.cityofsanctuary.org/about.

> involved? Through someone else—she mentions a name I recognize, he works for one of the big evangelical churches in the city centre. We pick up some toys, resolve a minor dispute between toddlers, talk about how the event's going. I wonder but don't ask how long her family have been in the UK; maybe a year or less, or maybe longer than parts of my family. She knows this city better than I do.
>
> It's a context where multiple languages and frameworks of interpretation overlap, and where unexpected shifts of category occur. Between the "religious" and the "secular," between one home-place and another, but also between the helpers and the helped, and between the necessary and the more-than-necessary.[20]
>
> Everyone's brought what they can. Not much silver or gold in evidence. A lot of faces, and a lot of helping hands. More food than could possibly be needed, so no distinction is made between the people who need it and the people who don't. (It'll be different at the drop-ins and the food parcel distributions, week by week; there's real and increasing destitution among asylum seekers and others in this city, and it's hard to keep the cupboards full.) This, today, isn't a "service" provided for cash or for free; it's a place where things can happen. And there's an enormous amount of work going on behind the scenes to establish and maintain the place—and, yes, to raise the necessary funds, using money to increase *this*, not this to increase money.
>
> Later in the day people gather around tables and discuss two questions: "What does sanctuary mean to you?" "What can we do in this city to move the story forward?" There are language barriers to overcome; some conversations are rapid and intense, some slow and difficult. Messages emerge piecemeal, making a different sense once they are set out on paper and separated from the faces and voices to which they belong.
>
> Sanctuary is home, family, people who listen. Sanctuary is freedom, having human rights, being able to speak without fear. Sanctuary is enough food, a roof over your head. Sanctuary is a holy place. Let's tell our stories to each other. Let's tell them to children. Let's write to our MPs. Let's watch football together. Let's do this more often.

This gathering, the various small encounters within it, and the wider process it exemplifies—the emergence of a "city of sanctuary" and a context

20. On God as "more than necessary," see Jüngel, *God as the Mystery*; Ford, *Self and Salvation*, 55–60.

of multiple hospitality—was in many respects a surprising event, of a kind that Christians venture to expect. It was both entirely explicable in terms of antecedent material and social conditions, and significantly unpredictable. An account of how it came about that focused solely on Christian traditions, habits, and practices as its antecedent conditions, and that made it a story about "what Christians do," would clearly not be truthful. The true story would pay attention to the multiple religious traditions present in that context—and to non-religious traditions, such as the tradition of speaking, campaigning, and legislating for human rights, alongside, of course, the venerable traditions of cricket and football.

And the true story, told thus, would still be a miracle, a tale of the unexpected. Interpreting it in the light of the story of Jesus Christ of Nazareth, the theologian might be able to speak about human life and flourishing in ways that at no point reduce to the misleading certainties "silver and gold," and hence at no point cut off the possibility of further and ongoing transformative encounter. As a small part of our vocation, theologians can interpret contemporary miracle stories in this way for participants and observers—including, but not only, those who identify themselves with the story of Jesus Christ of Nazareth.

Bibliography

Adams, Nicholas, and Charles Elliott. "Ethnography is Dogmatics: Making Description Central to Systematic Theology." *Scottish Journal of Theology* 53 (2000) 339–64.

Arendt, Hannah. *The Origins of Totalitarianism*. San Diego: Harcourt, 1968.

Baker, Christopher. *The Hybrid Church in the City: Third-Space Thinking*. Aldershot, UK: Ashgate, 2007.

Beaumont, Justin, and Christopher Baker, editors. *Postsecular Cities: Space, Theory and Practice*. Edinburgh: Continuum, 2011.

Bretherton, Luke. *Christianity and Contemporary Politics*. Oxford: Blackwell, 2010.

Cloke, Paul, et al. "Ethical Citizenship? Volunteers and the Ethics of Providing Service to Homeless People." *Geoforum* 38 (2007) 1089–1101.

———. *Swept-Up Lives? Re-Envisioning the Homeless City*. Oxford: Blackwell, 2010.

Ford, David F. *Self and Salvation: Being Transformed*. Cambridge: Cambridge University Press, 1999.

Goodchild, Philip. *A Theology of Money*. London: SCM, 2007.

Hardy, Daniel W., et al. *Wording a Radiance: Parting Conversations on God and the Church*. London: SCM, 2010.

Jüngel, Eberhard. *God as the Mystery of the World: On the Foundation of the Theology of the Crucified One: In the Dispute between Theism and Atheism*. Translated by Darrell L. Guder. Grand Rapids: Eerdmans, 1983.

Molendijk, Arie, Justin Beaumont, and Christoph Jedan, editors. *Exploring the Postsecular: The Religious, the Political and the Urban*. Leiden: Brill, 2010.

Muers, Rachel, with Thomas Britt. "Faithful Untidiness: Christian Social Action in a British City." *International Journal of Public Theology* 6.2 (2012) 205–27.

Taylor, Charles. *A Secular Age*. Cambridge, MA: Bellknap, 2007.

Ward, Graham. *The Politics of Discipleship: Becoming Postmaterial Citizens*. London: SCM, 2009.

Williams, Rowan. *On Christian Theology*. Oxford: Blackwell, 2000.

18

The Habitus of the Theologian

Thinking through Theological Vocation in Conversation with David Ford

Alistair I. McFadyen

University of Leeds

Conversation and friendship with David Ford have accompanied, shaped, and sustained my sense of theological vocation through the course of my theological life. I use that term "life" rather than "career" deliberately, since the best lesson I have learned from engaging with David and his work is that theology, above all else, is a venture that is lived.[1] Engaging with David Ford's theology, I believe, allows us to see the nature of theological vocation and of theological performance in a distinctive and attractive light; a light in which the traditionally identified coordinates of theological method appear somewhat differently. For that reason, I trust it will not appear overly self-indulgent to use the invitation

1. Of course, it will be true for an academic theologian that a significant part of that venture will find expression through the conventional markers of a career in academic institutions and through published academic outputs. Yet, it seems to me, we risk a fundamental misconstrual of the nature and vitality of theology done in the academy if we see it in isolation either from other contexts of life or from dynamics of living that are not reducible to those of an academic career.

to contribute to a *Festschrift* for David as a means of reflecting on and continuing my own conversation with him and his work concerning theological vocation.

Indeed, I hope this approach might rather appear especially fitting, since conversation and friendships are absolutely central to Ford's way of being a theologian. Hence, they might serve as significant initial signs pointing us towards something important that can be learned about theological vocation by engaging with his theology. Conversation and friendship are not the instrumental means taken up in order to pursue a task already independently identified. Rather, they are the highly particular, sometimes ad hoc and accidental (or graced?), lived and living human contexts of commitment in which theologians might simply find themselves or to which they may feel themselves called or drawn. One of the most refreshing aspects of Ford's theology is that (although seldom autobiographical) it is entirely unembarrassed about doing theology from within the positive embrace of the embracing particularities of his own life context—a nexus of conversations, commitments, institutions, encounters, and friendships. Consequently, his work is never delayed by excessively laboured methodological preamble or justification—whether of the approach being taken, of the conversation partners, or of key conceptual coordinates selected—nor yet by excessive autobiographical exposure. Instead, we are typically taken on a "journey of intensification"[2] through multiple layers of discernment which have often been brought together through the dynamics of multiple lived (and often recent or ongoing) involvements and encounters—engagement in academic institutions; the projects of research students; family; institutions such as L'Arche; learned societies and research projects; church bodies at many levels; active membership of a parish; deep friendships with people of other faiths; all of these contextualized in global culture and politics. It is these concrete contexts of living and working that have drawn attention to human realities, ways of thinking, key thinkers, interpretations of biblical texts, significant issues—the ingredients of his theology. In so many ways, Ford's theology is a deep thinking of things together that have already been brought together in a life, or are brought together precisely in order to fund the flourishing of that life, setting them into more deliberate and intensive conversation and sharing the fruits of the discernments that emerge.

2. Ford uses this phrase of David Tracy's several times. See, for example, Ford, *Theology*, 110ff.; Ford, *Self and Salvation*, 85ff.; Ford, "Salvation and the Nature of Theology," 564.

Hence, if we read Ford's work seeking some external, advance justification for the selection of these particular elements for inclusion in the discussion or of the significant role they play in it; if we expect the elements to be connected through the simple architecture of a single line of argument; if we look for the comprehensive set of dogmatic tropes associated with the doctrine under discussion: on all counts, we shall be disappointed.[3] Actually, not so much disappointed: we shall have missed the point. We would be looking in the wrong place for, and seeking an inappropriate form of, justification, coherence, and fidelity to the tradition. Thereby, we should have missed something significant about the situatedness of Ford's theology and the fundamental dynamics under which gravitational influence it is grounded and through which it is shaped. More important still, we shall have missed what Ford's theology is for and so missed out on the possibilities opened up by engaging with it. In what follows, I propose a way of understanding what is going on in Ford's theology as a means of more deeply coming to appreciate what it might mean to be a theologian, to live theologically, to engage in theology as comprehensive performance in multiple contexts of living and thinking.

What I have suggested so far is that the Ford corpus models, not a theology deliberately setting out to engage in multiple conversations or with "the world" for a specific (arbitrary) purpose; rather, a theologian already caught up in a web of lived conversations in "the world" which are allowed to "jazz"[4] together in ways that appear to promise richer and deeper understanding of God and of God's ways with the world. This is not a contextual theology in the sense more normally applied to, say, liberation, African, or feminist theologies. Yet it is a theology, I contend, which arises out of (and serves) deep immersion in the particularities of lived contexts, not least through conversations and friendships. It is theology that has a *habitus*. As a first approximation, we might say that that *habitus* is the theologian's own life. This is a helpful first approximation, since it draws attention to a way of doing theology that is not only deeply contextual, but also characterized by the dynamics of performance rather than the repetition of fixed contents.

3. Webster, "David F. Ford, *Self and Salvation*."

4. The metaphor of "jazz" constantly surfaces in Ford's writing, often riffing with or drawing more explicitly on its use in the poetry of long-standing friend and conversation-partner, Micheal O'Siadhail. See Hardy and Ford, *Jubilate*, 20–21, 142; Ford, *Self and Salvation*, 280ff.; Ford, *Christian Wisdom*, 139–42, 383f.; Ford, *Future of Christian Theology*, 93.

I realize that commending a style of theological performance as deeply embedded in the particularities of contexts of living is likely to suggest, not only that constructive conversations and conversation partners are highly particular, ad hoc, or represent a postmodern theological *bricolage*, but that they are accidental, random, or whimsical (which might occasion either suspicion or praise).[5] This is likely to be accompanied by a high sense of risk around the issues of order or of control in relation to the theological enterprise. Either the interconnections performed through the "jazzing together" of conversational partners and ingredients might appear to have no logic, being brought together by the mere random happenstance of life (the suggestiveness of otherwise random associations), or else the logic will appear to be external to Christian faith or the theological tradition and its established architecture, taken to be the only proper *habitus* of the theologian.[6] In place of the dependable, stabilized contents of Christian doctrine, such an approach is suspect as offering highly particularized, occasional, ad hoc "insights" which play fast and loose with the tradition; which begin and end not only in particularity but in the subjectivity of human experience and human life rather than with the prevenient, holy aseity of God—suspect, even if this is the human responsiveness of faith;[7] or, worse, which mould the contents of Christian faith to the contours of an independent context or world of meaning.

Such concerns helpfully illuminate a fundamental issue towards which Ford himself constantly draws attention in a variety of ways, and which is deeply instructive for understanding theological vocation: what is calling or shaping life?[8] If the *habitus* of theology is a life, it is highly likely to be populated by multiple events, encounters, and engagements, which fall under the rubric of accident or of serendipity, along with those more deliberately sought or actively desired. Yet, to the extent that these accidents subsequently prove to be formative for us, even to shape us in some way, they are drawn into and become part of our life-trajectory. Therefore, questions around the ordering and logic of theological performance, the *habitus* of which is a life, appear in the end to be questions concerning the direction of that life, as much through the way in which the accidentals are incorporated as through desire of what is actively sought.

5. Webster, "David F. Ford, *Self and Salvation*"; Ziegler, "The Many Faces of the Worshipping Self."

6. Webster, "David F. Ford, *Self and Salvation*," 548.

7. Ibid., 459.

8. See, for example, Ford, *Shape of Living*; Ford, *Shaping Theology*.

Fundamentally, this is not only a question of the shape and direction life actually takes, but what energizes and directs it and how it does so: what spirit animates this life? Unless we seek an answer to this question, there is serious risk, not only that we shall misunderstand Ford's theology and miss its distinctive ecology as a mode of coherence, but that we shall not respond to its invitation. We shall, perhaps, identify and appreciate its energy, but not ask what energizes it, from whence and towards what its ecology is fundamentally ordered and directed. We shall miss, therefore, the fact that the *habitus* of this theological performance is not simply a life, but living that is grounded in specifiable dynamics through identifiable material practices in particular contexts of living: to switch terminology, this is theology as calling, in the sense of being set in the dynamics of discerning, attending to, and responding to a call and the One who calls in specific contexts of habitation. There is not just *habitus*, therefore, but mode or spirit of habitation; not just living, but the shaping of lives in their most fundamental orientation in the world. And it is in the manner of this shaping, the animating spirit of this theological performance, that we are to look for reassuring evidence of continuity, coherence, and intimations of transcendence; for signs that this highly particular, creative, and contingent performance is grounded in the given contingencies of engagements, conversations, and realities of lived context. To express the matter in this way already suggests that we are looking for a spirit of habitation that is dynamic rather than static; that is to say, the spirit of habitation that is in living movement. To use a conventional ecclesiological and theological trope: living fully committed in and to this context ("world"), yet not of it in the sense of being overdetermined by its given realities. What I am suggesting is that the proper *habitus* of the theologian is not straightforwardly the contexts in which we live out a theological performance; it is, rather, that lived dynamic of movement in, to, and through the various habitats in which we live out and perform our theologies. Just as we might expect to find here a way of doing theology that is not overdetermined by place, so we also expect to find a form of theology that is not so overdetermined by the fixed contents of its theological inheritance (whether in doctrinal tradition or readings of Scripture) that it cannot be free to live in creative and mutually enriching conversation, encounter, and friendship—to *live* and to shape the living in this place. Rather, might one suggest that the mode of receptivity whereby this inheritance is received is itself dynamic, caught up already in the gravitational pull, the animating spirit, of this theological performance.

While, as intimated above, Ford tends not to engage in extensive methodological self-description, he does offer at least three distinct clue-constellations concerning the nature of his theological performance; in my terms, his theological *habitus*. First, from time to time, Ford offers accompanying, instructive commentary on his own theological performance, usually in response to direct question or challenge. It is revealing that such commentary often charts an association between the mode of theological performance and a core doctrinal locus, itself expressive of the heart of Christian faith. So, for instance, in response to John Webster's critique of *Self and Salvation*, Ford explicitly grounds the theological performance represented by that book in the incarnation. More frequently than explicit theological justification, however, we find Ford offering overlapping tropes by way of explanatory commentary on how his theological performance might fundamentally be characterized. For some time now, the dominant word-descriptor has been wisdom, possibly intended as a comprehensive, overall image, signalling precisely a performative mode of knowing, judging, discerning, and learning that is deeply immersed in its context; its habitats of living. The final constellation of clues concerns what might be considered, rather too flatly, the sources that he does not so much draw on, as permeate, feed, and nourish each note of his theological performance. There are key theological and philosophical interlocutors, of course. Yet among the most distinguishing characteristics of Ford's theology, in my view, is the place afforded to Scripture and to worship—primarily, these are not static fundaments, but living and shaping performative practices.

Considered together, these advance our understanding of the *habitus* of theological performance and its animating spirit in helpful ways. The first two clues strongly suggest the energized dynamics of movement that, in turn, provide grounds for a dynamic interpretation of the final set of coordinates indicated above. In his allusion to the incarnation as a theological warrant for modes of theological performance deeply immersed in the particularities of context (one might say, radically "in the world"), we are not being signed back towards a fixed, static, doctrinal content in propositional form. Rather, we are being issued an invitation. For doctrinal formulations sign us towards the reality of God, not locked up in a holy aseity, nor yet locked away within the innermost being of the human Jesus, but in the movement through Jesus towards the humanity of all. It is telling that, in Ford's brief allusion, he moves immediately from incarnation to worldliness, skipping over explicit reference to humanity altogether in favour of the lived contexts of humanity. In other words, explicitly following Bonhoeffer, he is here announcing principled theological resistance to performances of faith that hold God and world apart as though faced with a zero-sum choice between them. (And just as we do not have God without world, so we do not have human beings without worlds either—both affirmations are the marks of a fully incarnational theology.) Ford moves immediately to take up Bonhoeffer's understanding of the performativity of both theology and faith using musical metaphors of a *cantus firmus* amidst polyphony.[9] Before moving to note the connection Ford himself makes between this musical metaphor (and its dramatic analogues) and the character of wisdom, that overarching descriptor drawn from the second constellation of clues, we should pause to underline the significance of the dynamism of movement to the understanding of incarnation and of the trinitarian God which lies behind it. What Ford is flagging through this reference to incarnation (which he elsewhere takes up in pneumatological reference that more directly suggests both energy and movement as well as the agent behind such movement) is the movement of God through human being in, to, and for "the world." It is this movement which I suggest is the proper *habitus* of the theologian, oriented in, carrying, and committing her to the various lived habitats of her life—in other words, a movement not only of and in thought, but of and in living; a *habitus* that may lead us and with which we may immerse ourselves in multiple habitats of life, work, and thought. In this way, might we understand theology as performed discernment that enables and accompanies our following the movement of God towards the world and our own humanity in it: as answering God's call to follow and be present in the world.

It seems to me that this strong sense of theology being caught up in, called by, the movement of God in and to the world, which permeates the whole of Ford's theology, is a more basic and more important insight than the surface discussion of the methodological issues concerning the relationship between God, faith, and the world. This, it seems to me, is the animating spirit—the *cantus firmus*—of theological performance as Ford represents it, his *habitus*, and of the polyphony of theological performances that are invited through engaging with his theology and habituating ourselves to this same *habitus* in our own diverse habitats.

If we focus on this dynamic of movement, we might notice that the second set of clues also have a dynamic character. Not least amongst the

9. Ford, *Self and Salvation*, 255ff.; Ford, "Salvation and the Nature of Theology," 572.

various descriptive tropes, wisdom is not only performative and deeply contextual, representing not only a dynamic interaction with the contingencies of place, but an explicit means whereby the mechanisms of wise, contextualized, and contingent human discernment are responsive to divine Wisdom. Or, closer to the way Ford sometimes expresses himself, human wisdom caught up in the gravitational pull of, animated by, the Spirit of wisdom. This view is strengthened, not only by explicit avowal of dramatic categories of performance to characterize theology as a form of wisdom, but by the appearance of key terms in the verb form (facing, making habitable, offering hospitality, shaping, learning; hearing, and attending to cries), together with the dominance of grammatical moods indicating the dynamics of interaction (the interrogative, the vocative) or of transformation and new possibility (the optative and subjunctive).[10]

All of this strongly suggests a mode of theological performance caught up in the dynamics of God in movement towards the world. Yet what of our final set of clues? Surely, in relation to sources such as Scripture, we are dealing with a fixed and given reality and in worship we are dealing with practices withdrawn from the world. Not at all. Conversely, what becomes clear through Ford's theology is that Scripture is not a static source, the interpretation of which is somehow locked up in an authoritative past. Rather than Scripture appearing in Ford's theology as the imposition of set and rigidly overstabilized interpretation, values, or meanings, we are presented with extended readings of large portions of the Bible (often complete books) within the contingencies and particularities of specific contexts, generative of new discernments regarding both text and situation. In other words, not Scripture as a dead text, but the activity of reading Scripture, and doing so as simultaneously a mode of deep attentiveness to the text and to the habitats of life. Or, better still, what we witness time and again resulting from Ford's energetic immersion in Scripture is energized and directed immersion in the realities of world, which is profoundly disclosive. What is witnessed here is that in the reading of Scripture we encounter that same dynamic of God in movement towards the world and so are directed towards the world, our habitats, not with fixed contents of faith, but in the animating and energizing spirit of blessing and of transformation that allows for full immersion in the world as habitat: a movement "from God, to God, before

10. Ford, *Self and Salvation*, 257; Ford, *Christian Wisdom*, 45ff., 63, 78, 103, 11ff., 22, 42, 247, 63.

God and for God's sake."[11] That our being caught up in this movement from God, to God involves an orientation towards the world and its full flourishing is, for Ford, closely correlated with being caught up in God's constantly overflowing abundance and generosity.[12]

Yet there is something profoundly misleading in this presentation so far of the reading of Scripture in the various habitats of life as resourcing the *cantus firmus*, of energizing and shaping the spirit of living theologically which is the *habitus* of the theologian. So far, perhaps, the impression is given of the solitary theologian reading Scripture in the study or in the world. What we find modelled in Ford's theology, however, is something quite different. Here, reading Scripture, while not exclusively a church activity, is nonetheless grounded in the realities of church—and not church as some abstract, doctrinal ideal type of the academic theologian, but church as specific material institution and organizational structure at many levels, not least the congregational, constituted through concrete material practices existing in specific times and places. That the primary locus for the reading of Scripture is participation in the concrete realities of an actual church, is further indicated by the significant place afforded worship, prayer, praise, thanksgiving, and lament in Ford's theology. While, again, these are all activities that may be conducted extra-ecclesially, their primary and grounding locus is in the constitutive performance of the gathered community.

Perhaps this latest move appears to be backtracking somewhat on the trajectory of the discussion thus far, which has emphasized the performative and dynamic nature of theology, practised in contexts in which the theologian may already be embedded; animated, energized, and oriented by spirit directed towards the reality of the world (the proper *habitus* of the theologian); itself nourished through practices that might easily appear to involve a withdrawal from the world into a form of "churchiness." It would certainly be in keeping with the evangelical spirit of Ford's theology to offer here a missiological definition of church, which makes orientation towards the world constitutive of its reality. I wish, however, to pose, not an alternative, but a parallel suggestion. One, I think, that might do justice to the characteristics I have drawn attention to and help explain the attractiveness of Ford's way of doing theology to Christians not trained in academic theology (and not, perhaps, inclined to take it

11. Ford, *Future of Christian Theology*, 189.

12. Ford, "Epilogue," 721.

too seriously), especially those who—while not being ordained—sense they have a specific vocation to be lay, to discern more clearly how their life and work in the world relates to the movement of God.

I began this chapter by noting how deeply my own sense of theological vocation has been shaped through a professional lifetime of conversational engagement with Ford's theology. One of the most treasured fruits of that conversation, for me, has been a strong sense of the centrality of the lay condition, in both ecclesial and theological life. This is not a view I necessarily wish to saddle Ford with. I mean merely to indicate the way in which one (not terribly significant) interlocutor has come to make sense of his own theological vocation by trying to understand what is suggested in Ford's way of doing theology. That suggestion centres on making the "*laos* of God" central to our understanding equally of church and of the nature and responsibility of theology. This, I think, casts light both on the underlying dynamic that animates Ford's theology in ways that may be helpful in establishing one's own theological *habitus* and the operative assumption that faith and world are already conjoined performatively (I would say, paradigmatically, in the life of the laity). Thus responsible theology can begin, not so much in the world where the laity already find themselves, as in the dynamics of movement between world and church that is the lay condition.

Much changes our understanding of both church and theology if we centre it on the *laos* of God. Most importantly, we cannot make laity central and have our gaze rest within the confines of church building or congregation. Rather, we are caught in the movement between church and world that reflects, serves, and is caught up in the dynamics of God in movement through church into the world and, through the world, back again.

To say that the dynamics of the *laos* of God are the primary and defining reality of church, which theology serves, is not to devalue the Monday to Saturday conditions of lay dispersal into the world over the Sunday gathering. Rather, it is to suggest that the *movement* whereby the laity disperse into the world, subsequently to gather again to be and to do church together, defines and is present in the positions at both poles (and that these positions are not points of rest). Hence, it must be no less true to say that the laity are church and are engaged in a performance of church in their being in and making the world, than it is to say that we are in the world and worldly where we gather as church. Our capacity to be church in the worldly pole of this movement will be nourished, shaped, and vitalized by the dynamic orientation of our gathered ecclesial performance: if our focused attentiveness to God in movement towards the world sends us out into the world in and shaped by that same spirit—not only in the closing words of the dismissal, but through every constitutive act of our worshipping together, not exclusively (but certainly not least) through the prayer and preaching which can hold all the other elements together and orient them towards our life in the world (but which also runs the risk of the whole turning into a form of Christian ghetto-talk where it is not itself caught up in the directionality of this movement towards and for the world).[13]

We might perhaps go further here and make the corresponding suggestion that our capacity to be worldly in the pole of this movement represented by the gathering of church (so that we are not disconnecting from the world and entering the Christian ghetto) will depend upon the directionality and shaping power of constitutive ecclesial practices performed in the gathering, combined with our own performance of such practices under the conditions of lay dispersal in the world: reading Scripture, praying, praising, worshipping, lamenting. This is, in fact, what I think Ford's theology models and is at least part of what he means when he speaks of the church as "a school of desire and wisdom."[14] Offering us, consequently, not only substantive theological positions with which we might engage, but a way of reading God and world together that is already embedded in the dynamics of lay dispersal, which reflect and follow the movement of God in and to and for the world. In this, theology—including doctrinal theology—is an essential accompaniment. This is what I see Ford doing—reading Scripture, praying, worshipping in the gathered community in a way oriented towards the worldly habitats of lay dispersal; being in those habitats engaged in exactly those practices shaping not only being in the world with and before God, but equipping us for the return movement to the gathered community. Above all else, his is a theology set within this movement where God and world, church and world are already come together in the living and being lay in the multiple habitats of the world and the church. Just as is the case in relation to the church pole of this movement, where a primary task is the servicing of preaching, formal theology is to be done in a way that

13. This possibly accounts for the significant place he affords (afFords?) to preaching and theology's service of preaching. See, for example, Ford, *Future of Christian Theology*, 190.

14. Ford, *Christian Wisdom*, 58, 191ff., 225, 59, 349, 81, 471.

accompanies and serves the immersion of the laity in worldly habitats at the other pole of the dynamic. This, I think, is what Ford means when he speaks of theology as an open and exploratory attempt to find forms of theological and doctrinal expression which are "habitable":[15] not that they are entirely and without remainder habituated to, conform to, and reflect the worldly context or habitat of the theologian; rather, that they be living vehicles, serving and a part of the movement of God in, to, and for the world, in which the oscillation between church and world of lay dispersal is caught up. This is incarnational theology as a form of faithful living in the world and what is sought in a habitable theology is no more one that serves a static positioning in the world than it does in the church. Instead, what is sought are forms of doctrinal expression that may be vehicles which might transport in this movement, the dynamic *habitus* of the theologian.

In this frame, we might more easily see the logic of incarnation played out in daily lives, not only in the world but in the world as a way of being and doing church and in church as a moment in the performance of true worldliness. We might also see what it might mean to read Scripture, to worship, to pray, to praise, to lament already caught up in this movement of the *laos* of God already living for and before God in various worldly habitats, which I have come to see through Ford's theology as my own lived theological *habitus*.

It has become commonplace in discussions of theological method to characterize ways in which the three primary spheres of theological accountability (church, world, and academy)[16] might appropriately be ordered in the practice of theology. Once we come to see theology in terms of its *habitus* in a theological life, I suggest we are invited to see the ordering of the relationship between academy, church, and world as something that is first lived out and only secondarily reflected on and thought through in formal methodological terms. In other words, this is not only, and not primarily, a question to be approached externally, prior to theological work, nor subsequently as a question concerning external communication of theological knowledge; it is an answer in some sense already being given and being sought in the calling of a theological life

15. Ford, *Self and Salvation*, 6–7; Ford, "Salvation and the Nature of Theology," 563, 65; Ford, *Theology*, 28–29; Ford, *Future of Christian Theology*, 14.

16. See the discussion in Tracy, *Analogical Imagination*, 28–38; Ford, *Shaping Theology*.

which is already living in and living out of the interconnection between these distinct spheres or habitats.

Approaching issues of theological method from the perspective afforded by recognition of the fact that the three "publics" are, in fact, distinct habitats already brought into interrelation in the performed *habitus* of each theologian draws attention to two further significant features that might otherwise be missed. First, thinking of the three spheres or publics, as habitats performatively brought into interrelation through living, suggests strongly that these are not virtual places of merely noetic, disembodied mentation or interpersonal exchange. These are not metaphorical spaces where theologians think. These are concrete material, historical, institutional, and therefore highly specific, varied, and particular locations. This is where our bodies are, alongside other bodies. And our bodies are only "in" the generic spheres of academy, church, and world by virtue of the fact that we actually do live, work, and participate in specific, determinate, and highly particular institutions, processes, and exchanges that have material and not only ideational form.

Second, to think of theology as performed vocation lived out in the *habitus* of an embodied life—the course of which forges an interconnection between at least these three distinct habitats in which the (academic) theologian places herself and finds herself placed—we are forced to think of having *habitus*, of habitation, as dynamic. Hence, we are faced, not only with questions of *where*, as theologians, we place our bodies (which institutions, processes, conversations), but *how* we place them and how they are placed there; not only, then, with what the proper habitat of a theologian might be, but what the proper mode of habitation might be. If the *habitus* is a life lived in multiple habitats, we are seeking the identity of this mode of habitation, its ecology and economy, by asking what animates, energizes, and orients it. In what dynamic is this theological performance caught? What drives and energizes this mode of habitation, a distinctive *habitus*, which accounts for the way in which one lives in and relates together the three habitats of academy, church and world?

Bibliography

Ford, David F. *Christian Wisdom: Desiring God and Learning in Love*. Cambridge: Cambridge University Press, 2007.

———. "Epilogue." In *The Modern Theologians*, edited by David F. Ford, 760–61. Oxford: Blackwell, 1997.

———. *The Future of Christian Theology*. Chichester, UK: Wiley-Blackwell, 2011.

———. "Salvation and the Nature of Theology: A Response to John Webster's Review of *Self and Salvation: Being Transformed*." *Scottish Journal of Theology* 54 (2001) 560–75.

———. *Self and Salvation: Being Transformed.* Cambridge: Cambridge University Press, 1999.

———. *The Shape of Living.* London: Fount, 1997.

———. *Shaping Theology: Engagements in a Religious and Secular World.* Oxford: Blackwell, 2007.

———. *Theology: A Very Short Introduction.* Oxford: Oxford University Press, 1999.

Hardy, Daniel W., and David F. Ford. *Jubilate: Theology in Praise.* London: Darton, Longman & Todd, 1984.

Tracy, David. *The Analogical Imagination: Christian Theology and the Culture of Pluralism.* London: SCM, 1981.

Webster, John. "David F. Ford, *Self and Salvation*." *Scottish Journal of Theology* 54 (2001) 548–59.

Ziegler, Luther. "The Many Faces of the Worshipping Self: David Ford's Anglican Vision of Christian Transformation." *Anglican Theological Review* 89 (2007) 267–85.

19

Between the Constraints of Freedom and the Aspirations of Love

On Bergson, Levinas, and Theology in the Service of Politics

Paul D. Janz

King's College London

Through an exchange with the work of Henri Bergson, and secondarily also with Emmanuel Levinas, this essay locates and amplifies a certain incommensurability or breach that can be shown to open up between the demands of a politics grounded in freedom and the demands of an ethics grounded in love. Inspired by David Ford's "hospitable wisdom seeking" the theme of theology's "vocation" today is taken up by pointing to a certain opportunity this breach affords for expanding theological orientations to hospitable interdisciplinarity.

In an echo of an almost identical statement by Chancellor Angela Merkel six months earlier about the situation in Germany, British Prime Minister David Cameron, at a recent international security conference in Munich (February 2011), pronounced that state multiculturalism in Britain had failed. What was meant by this was not that ethnic and cultural diversity had not been allowed to flourish, but that state policy had failed to engender along with this a reciprocal commitment across all such communities to an underlying social cohesion or consensus, by which again was meant, as stated explicitly by Cameron, a commitment to certain British way of embracing and expressing the liberal democratic values of freedom and equality, and the rights and duties associated with this.

Now what is tacitly assumed here is that the ideals of freedom, equality, human rights, and so on, which underlie liberal democratic values, have a basic and universal human appeal and resonance. For these ideals are taken not only to be self-evident and sacrosanct as moral absolutes, but also as supported by the full apodictic weight of reason as expressed paradigmatically in Rousseau, Kant, and others of the so-called Age of Enlightenment, around a rigorous logic by which the quintessentially modern philosophical ideals of liberty, equality, and fraternity are linked together.

According to this logic, everything begins and ends in the liberty or freedom of the human being as a reasoning and willing being, where freedom or the will is defined initially in the most basic way, as simply the ability of the self-conscious reasoning subject to deviate from the necessities of instinct.[1] Now freedom as such not only comprises the individual human being's special dignity, but, as an inviolable endowment and not an achievement of human beings, it (by definition) also entails the equality of free subjects. In its logical corollary of equality, therefore, freedom actually entails something that contradicts or constrains freedom; for as a free subject among equals I am not entitled to any liberty but only those liberties that do not violate the liberty of these equals. Fraternity, as we know, is then what resolves this contradiction, and it is here that we see the real beauty of the Enlightenment logic coming to its full force, which is why fraternity is sometimes exalted above the other two.

For in the fraternity of the social contract, the freedom of the reasoning subject is in fact raised to a new level of resilience in that it is preserved fully intact despite the constraints of equality. Or as Levinas puts it, in fraternity, freedom is able to be constrained without constraint.[2] Rousseau's own logic captures this exactly. If the social contract limiting freedom in light of equality is consensual—i.e., if it is a genuine contract or rational consensus—then the very acceptance of the limitation of freedom is itself an exercise of freedom, and therefore a constraint without constraint. This constraining without constraint occurs with even greater

1. Rousseau, *Discourse on the Origin of Inequality,* 207–8.

2. Levinas, "Uniqueness," 163.

logical apodicticity in Kant's deduction of the categorical imperative. It is thus not only through an assumption of their self evidence but also to this whole tradition of a special rigor of reason that liberal democratic ideals can appeal in laying claim to their universality as a basis for intercultural agreement.

Yet in the recent multiculturalism debates in Europe, it has become clear that it is precisely these liberal democratic ideals that have not been as readily embraced as the basis of a common social agreement as had been assumed they should be. There are doubtless many different reasons for this. Some see these ideals as merely a euphemistic cover for a deeper underlying commitment to consumer capitalism; others as contributors to what is viewed as a moral decay in the West. But other factors appear to be rooted in a more fundamental kind of impasse, or an incommensurability of outlook, which might suggest that deeper philosophically anthropological and cultural issues may be at work here.

In what follows, I want to use aspects of the work of Henri Bergson to work toward a certain destination that challenges the simple assumption that liberal democratic ideals should be easily and self-evidently translatable onto the values and norms of any particular social and cultural community. Or I want to suggest that this assumption may rest on a basic misdiagnosis of the nature of morality as grounded in freedom. However, the conclusions reached through conversations with Bergson will themselves leave us at an impasse or quandary, and it is onto this quandary that I then wish to bring certain theological orientations to bear.

In his book *Two Sources of Morality and Religion*, Bergson's general approach to obligation and morality is evolutionary, which is to say etiological or causal rather than philosophically analytical; and in the broadest sense of the term it is biological, which is to say it is centrally concerned with life, or more exactly with living organisms. In tracing the origins of human obligation Bergson focuses initially on the evolutionary emergence of intellectual societies from instinctual societies and thus on human societies in an early or rudimentary stage; and the basic logic here (in highly condensed form) runs roughly as follows.[3]

All living organisms are comprised of living elements (cells, tissues), which are united by imperceptible links and which work for the general good or flourishing of the whole. Now in an individual body, it would be a stretch to construe the harmony between the cells and tissues comprising

3. I follow the argument only, or mainly, as developed in Part One of the book (pages 9–101).

the body as the harmony of a community, or even as relating through a social instinct, still less by any sort of obligation to behave in the harmonious way that they do. The relations here are rather governed by necessity, that is, by inexorable biological and genetic laws.

However, we do observe some instances of living communities—for example, the beehive or anthill—to which the term "social instinct" can be applied and yet which behave exactly like organisms. For "the social instinct of an ant," as Bergson says, "cannot differ radically from the cause, whatever it be, by virtue of which every tissue, every cell of a living body, toils for the greatest good of the whole."[4] Now granted, the constraint, or submission to the discipline of the instinctual society in this latter case is no more yet a matter of obligation than in the former (i.e., in the individual body), but rather still of necessity. Yet Bergson will want to show that an importantly effectual residue of the necessities of instinctual society remains in the intellectual, and that the deeper we look even into full grown moral obligation the more inexorably we will find the necessities of our instinctual past informing it.

To be sure, it is one thing to speak of an organism subject to inexorable laws, and quite another of an intellectual society composed of free wills. But the comparison holds nonetheless, and not merely analogically; for once these wills are organized "they will assume the guise of an organism" and in this virtual organism it is *habit* that will come to play "the same role as necessity in the work of nature."[5] Most of these are habits of obedience and command, whether obedience to a person through social mandate or a more vaguely felt conformity to society itself. Crucially, however, all such social habits will condition the individual to conformity through the exertion of a *pressure* or *constraint* on the will, such that it is in the character of a pressure on the will that the awareness of obligation first emerges.

Now the number of such habits, even in a primitive society, let alone an advanced intellectual society, will of course be myriad. But over the course of time and experience as these become stored up and internalized, they will tend to link together to form a kind of unified social bond so as to comprise what Bergson calls a "totality of social obligation" which is only vaguely felt but still powerfully present; and this totality of obligation will have a force comparable to that of necessity in instinct. We ourselves will see clear evidence of this in the fact that in the vast majority of

4. Bergson, *Two Sources*, 29.

5. Ibid., 9–10.

daily activities we find ourselves simply conforming instinctually to social obligations rather than thinking of them. Almost every waking minute of every day, in the most mundane activities, we are obeying certain internalized rules and submitting to obligations that have become virtually instinctive through habit.

It will be obvious that what we have been dealing with thus far in a rudimentary society of wills is a society that is essentially closed. This is the natural state of social obligation and cohesion, just as it is the natural state of enclosed physical organisms. And although the civilized societies we inhabit today are much more complex and interpenetrating, nevertheless, as the vexing problems of multiculturalism with associated problems of extremism provide ample evidence, the basic and natural closedness of social communities around cultural norms and obligations remains intact even today. In Bergson's words, in the rudimentary instinct, social cohesion "is largely due to the necessity of the community to protect itself against others. . . . [I]t is primarily as against all other men that we love the men with whom we live";[6] and this rudimentary instinct remains largely unaltered today, even though it can be largely "hidden under the accretions of civilization." But this brings us to the critical question. If social communities are naturally enclosed, how then do we move from the closed to the open? Or how, out of this natural closedness, has the language of love of humanity, of peace and accord with humanity in general, arisen? What has moved us from the fraternity or peace of the city to envisioning the brotherhood of man, from the relative justice of social solidarity to the universal justice of what Levinas will call the "interhuman" per se?

The more usual approach here has been to jump directly to the universal resolutions available through appeals to the abstract ideals of reason, which are seen as able to be glimpsed through an inferential expansion of reason. An evolutionary approach, however, which seeks to observe the actual causal history of human development, tells a different story. Through tracing this along various lines, Bergson is able to claim that wherever the move from the closed to the open has occurred, it has not come through an expansion in the power of inference opening up to increasingly higher, more general and all inclusive ideas of the understanding. It has come rather through the lives and actions of exceptional individual persons, though pioneers of morality whom he also calls "mystic souls," in whom the move from closed to open expresses itself as an unpredictable kind of novelty, or what Bergson calls a "leap" out of evolutionary uniformity, the

6. Ibid., 29–30, 32.

possibility of which evolution has provided for but the exact character and outcome of which it cannot predict and does not determine.

But what is the source or impetus for the particular kind of leap or novelty of which Bergson speaks? Here again it is not at its origin a new idea of reason which has opened up through rational inference, but rather, as he puts it, "a new emotion" which motivates to new and open kinds of action, although the meaning of "emotion" here is to be distinguished from that of the normal usage of the word. The usual way we experience and refer to emotion—the emotion that is of interest to psychology—is as something infra-intellectual: i.e., not an idea but a feeling or sentiment which is at best the vague reflection of an idea. But the new emotion of which Bergson speaks is supra-intellectual: i.e., it is not derivative of any prior idea but rather, and to the contrary, is itself generative of a host of new ideas. Indeed, emotion in this sense can be seen as the catalyst for all truly creative endeavour. In Bergson's words, "that a new emotion is the source of the great creations of art, of science, and of civilization in general there seems to be no doubt."[7] As the impetus for creative novelty or a leap out of evolutionary uniformity, it can be compared to what Thomas Nagel speaks of as inferentially inexplicable flashes of inspiration or intuition in cognitive geniuses by which genuinely progressive rather than merely cumulative advances in knowledge come about.[8]

But here we come to the decisive point. Just as there is a genius of the cognitive intellect, so also, says Bergson, we can speak of a genius of the will, which is to say a genius of the practical intellect. This is the genius exemplified by pioneers of morality or mystic souls who find themselves drawn through an entirely gratuitous and unconstrained impetus of an attraction of a superior order, to move from the fraternity of social solidarity to the brotherhood of man; from the socially enclosed and still conditional love of family and love of country (nourished by patriotism and the divisions this entails), to the unconditional love of humanity; in short, from the social to the supra-social, or to the genuinely interhuman. But it is important to see that the move from the one to the other, from the social to the supra-social or from the love of country to the love of humanity per se, is not simply an expansion of the love and obligation of the former, as if the difference between the two were essentially one of degree. What we find here (in a recurring Bergsonian theme) is not merely a difference of *degree* but rather a fundamental difference in *kind*, and this is most clearly

7. Ibid., 43.

8. Nagel, *View From Nowhere*, 75–76.

manifest through the difference in the essential character of obligation in each. In the social, as we have seen, obligation is encountered always as some sort of *pressure* or *constraint*. In the latter, however, in the love at the supra-social level, the source of obligation is encountered by such pioneers of morality not as pressure or constraint, but rather as an *attraction* and *aspiration* under the impetus of the new and original emotion of a superior order.

Let me offer a further comparative observation that may be helpful in understanding the logic at work here. The genius of the cognitive intellect, as the faculty of reasoned *thought*, does not merely add a new insight—however profound—to an existing paradigm of knowing; it rather transfigures or surpasses the intellectual paradigm itself under which even the genius mind had hitherto been operating. The genius of the will, however, as the faculty of reasoned *action*, transforms the very *life* of the pioneer through a radical transformation of ethical action and orientation to action. And it spreads or is communicated as this same higher-order emotion, by the same attraction, generates transformative action in the lives of others, such that the impetus and attraction of the higher generative emotion spreads not as a paradigm-changing idea but as a life-changing kind of flame.

But where has all of this led us, especially with regard to our initial concerns with intercultural consensus? To begin with, my intention here has not been to try to convince the reader of the merits of Bergsonism per se (although I think there is much to speak for it), and in any case it is not crucial to the argument that all aspects of Bergson's evolutionary narrative be met without criticism. I limit myself to some reflections on just one influential insight that has received wide acknowledgement: the distinction in kind between the social obligation of pressure or constraint and the supra-social obligation of attraction and aspiration.

We noted to begin with that what is implied in putting forward liberal democratic ideals as the basis for multicultural harmony or peace is that these ideals, grounded in moral absolutes, are seen as having a universal resonance across all human communities. And in light of the foregoing discussions we can now add to this by saying that what is tacitly assumed here as such is that these ideas are supra-social; for they are seen as able to transcend or surpass the natural enclosedness of social communities and to provide a basis for genuinely interhuman relationality. But this is a false assumption; and here we come to the crux of the misdiagnosis alluded to at the beginning. For as we have seen, the moral and political philosophy based on the ideals of freedom and equality, and the liberal democratic values derived from it, remains entirely within the obligations of pressure and constraint and thus within the natural conflict of the social order defined by constraint. Indeed it presides over this order of constraint, even when freedom can surpass itself by theoretically preserving itself in the language of constraint without constraint. It is hardly surprising, therefore, that these ideals based on freedom have been unable to generate the intercultural harmony imputed to them if, as the ethical gatekeepers of the obligation of pressure and constraint, they watch over and indeed are integral to precisely the social conflict they aspire to overcome.

But if the pure ideals of reason based on the constraints of freedom cannot provide the basis for intercultural harmony or peace, does Bergson's model based on attraction, aspiration, and unconditional love of Everyman fare any better with regard to political realities? Not obviously. For just as the Enlightenment ideals in which liberal democratic values are rooted do not and cannot be expected to rise above the social obligation defined by pressure and constraint; so also it is hard to see how the suprasocial of Bergson could relate to politics and to questions of a normative grounding for a social contract or intercultural consensus. For the realm of the political is, of course, intrinsically the social, and it is nothing if not social, even at a cosmopolitan or intercultural level, or even if extended to the level of the "global society." There seems to be a fundamental tension or disconnect here then between the obligations derived from freedom and the obligations motivated by love, one that allows for no easy resolution but points instead to a thoroughgoing incommensurability.

We can see the problem of this disconnect arising in an especially pronounced or radical form in the work of Emmanuel Levinas, for whom (as he himself is repeatedly at pains to stress) the work of Bergson is an indispensable impetus for putting forward of a new kind of ethics no longer grounded in the freedom of the individual but in responsibility to the call of the other; a responsibility that, especially for the later Levinas, is the hallmark of love at the interhuman level, which he refers to variously as "love without Eros" or (following Pascal) "love without concupiscence." Levinas writes with great rhetorical beauty and, for many, with great persuasive power. But as rightly emphasized by many of his critics, and in keeping with the breach already evident in Bergson, his work remains doggedly resistant to yielding normative principles for conduct or political judgment (and this remains the case even after the entry of the "third party" and the more qualified justice flowing out of this). Leora Batnitzky, for example, argues correctly that Levinas's work is "politically dangerous," precisely because "it provides no criteria for [political] judgment"[9]—to which we must immediately add, however, that this is to be expected, for any such principles, as normative, would again precisely be constraining principles, whereas as Kant rightly says, "what is done from constraint is not done from love."[10] One of the clearest outworkings and, in a way, "proofs" of this breach—starkly evident precisely at the political level—is that the social or constraining obligations of freedom can be legislated and enforced, whereas the supra-social and attracting obligations of love obviously cannot.

But while the critique about absence of criteria for political judgment in Levinas is a correct assessment (for to make love the basis of a politics grounded in freedom is indeed a dangerous idea), nevertheless this absence, as the above shows, is not so much a failing on Levinas's part as it is testimony to the uncompromising philosophical rigor underlying his often rhetorical style. Indeed, Levinas draws the line of incommensurability more sharply still, even to the extent of offering a whole new account of the meaning of "proximity" at the supra-social or what Levinas calls the interhuman level—which is to say, at the level of the Levinasian "face to face" encounter—as opposed to proximity on the social level of "the state of Nature of civil society."[11] On our normal understanding of the term, "proximity" denotes a relation of closeness or distance based on spatial and temporal factors in common, or also conceptual factors in common. In other words, proximity in this usual sense defines precisely the social relation as we normally understand it, and as we have been tracing it through Bergson—a proximity defined essentially by what is shared in common, or by the common frontiers around which social and cultural groupings are formed and cohere. By contrast, the proximity that for Levinas defines the interhuman order of the face-to-face relation is precisely devoid of every "common frontier."[12] It is a "phenomenological" proximity mediated by the idea of infinity, a proximity which yields a relation between "the Same

9. Batnitzky, *Leo Strauss and Emmanuel Levinas*, 90.

10. Kant, *Metaphysics of Morals*, 6:402.

11. Levinas, "Useless Suffering," 86–87. It is true that Levinas himself still uses the term "sociality" (although designated as the "excellence of sociality") and not "supra-sociality" to denote the interhuman relation. But as is the case with so much of his terminology, its meaning as such differs quite radically from its usual denotation, and as the "excellence of sociality" it corresponds in Levinas precisely to the relationality of love which for Bergson occurs at the supra-social level.

12. Levinas, *Totality and Infinity*, 39.

and the Other . . . where nothing is in common," or a relation of difference "behind which no commonality arises in the guise of an entity."[13]

Through the rigor and consistency that Levinas brings to bear on Bergson's distinction between the two sources of morality, therefore—the social and constraining obligations of freedom and the supra-social and attracting or aspiring obligations of love—we are brought with even greater finality to the incommensurability of the breach between the two. Levinas himself grants that his ethical position as such is "hard" or severe, acknowledging also that he has "no illusions" as to its actual efficacy in history, or that he has "no optimistic philosophy for the end of history," and adding that he "leave[s] the whole consoling side of this ethics to religion."[14]

Is there then any possibility of making any headway at this impasse—not only in a "consoling" way, but in a genuinely constructive way? In light of the opening discussions it would seem vital that we be able to do so—regardless of whether one's view of the end of history is optimistic or not. If there is any such possibility, it will likely need to come in searching out new kinds of exchange between the social domain of the political, and—in the best sense of the term as that form of life concerned quintessentially with what Pascal calls "love without concupiscence"—the supra-social or genuinely inter-human domain of true religion.

For at least two reasons, theology, both theoretical and practical, is uniquely placed to play an important role in exploring such an exchange for political purposes—that is, an exchange at the impasse between the constraining obligations of freedom that can be legislated and the attracting or aspiring obligations of love that cannot. The first reason is the more obvious one, and concerns the place or vocation of theology traditionally. Throughout much of its history, Christian theology has understood its place as both within religion and within the academy; or as we might say, more precisely for our purposes, its place between religion—which again in virtually all of its various true expressions comes together quintessentially around the common denominator of "love without concupiscence"—and the Western traditions of philosophy which, as Levinas correctly notes, have predominantly taken freedom as their ground.

Secondly, the problem we face at the impasse between the constraining obligations of freedom and the attracting obligations of love is reflected structurally with remarkable similarity in one of the most basic

13. Levinas, "New Rationality," 55.

14. Levinas, "Philosophy, Justice and Love," 93, 98.

and defining problems of "fundamental" theology: i.e., the relation of transcendence and immanence. Let us look at this briefly. In its most rationally rigorous and uncompromisingly consistent apophatic or negative expressions, theology has always sought to avoid the error of orienting itself to the transcendence of God through spatial and temporal (or indeed conceptual or ideal) qualifiers of what is "beyond" or "outside" the immanent reality in which we find ourselves alive. Such language can at best be only metaphorical, for it approaches transcendence by precisely those spatial and temporal (or also conceptual) quantifiers and qualifiers—in short, those *creaturely* quantifiers and qualifiers—which the uncreated divine transcendence transcends. This is why we see Augustine saying that because God's transcends the extensive magnitudes of distance and time, God can be closer to us than we are to ourselves; the same kind of orientation at work in Luther's well known dictum of *simul justus et peccator;* or again in Bonhoeffer's assertion that divine transcendence is not what is infinitely remote but what is nearest at hand.

Now we see a similar "simultaneity yet incommensurability" occurring in Bergson's evolutionary account of the two sources of morality and religion—the one, social; and the other, supra-social. The point is that the "supra" in supra-sociality precisely does *not* imply an order "beyond" the social or "outside" the necessary constraints and strictures of the social. The supra-social does indeed "transcend" the social to the point of a breach of it; but to "transcend" here must not be understood in the pseudo-sense of the term, either as a flight from the natural limitations and constraints of the social, or as that which is beyond or outside it in the abstract perfection of an idealized or utopian society. For the "love without concupiscence" that characterizes the supra-social or the genuinely interhuman order *is nothing apart from the acts of love themselves,* acts which cannot be enacted anywhere else than within the constraints of embodied sociality. In Bergson, remember, it is first the *action and life* of the pioneers of morality or mystic souls—and not first various teachings they may have been able to derive or infer from some new idea—that breaks through to the genuinely interhuman order of the supra-social and that thus paves the way for others to engage in similar action. And yet while the one is enacted indispensably within the other—and never the one without the other—we are nevertheless, for any reflective or normative purposes, left with the breach with which this whole essay has been concerned, between the aspiring or attracting obligations of the one and the constraining obligations of the other. And it is through theology's grappling with this problem over centuries—productively and imaginatively and in myriad ways on both theoretical and practical levels—that makes it especially well placed to contribute interdisciplinarily to the understanding of the meeting of the two.

Such an interdisciplinary engagement would seek to participate in and contribute to what David Ford lays out as the "hospitable wisdom-seeking" aspired to by "partners of difference." However, its participation would be somewhat different than what Ford documents as occurring in the many "theology and . . ." endeavours which, as he shows, have played the largest role in making the last century "the most theologically prolific in Christian history,"[15] and have thereby also contributed importantly to expanding theological self-understanding and thus the vocation of theology. It seems clear, however, from Ford's own surveys, that these "theology and . . ." endeavours have tended to move mainly in one direction, that is, mainly or at least ultimately to serve theological ends and purposes. By comparison, the interdisciplinary engagement suggested here would move in the other direction. We might say it would not be a "theology and . . ." endeavour but rather an example of an ". . . and theology" endeavour. It would suggest a project between political science and philosophical ethics, on the one hand, and religion, on the other—which is to say again, a project between the constraining obligations of freedom that can be legislated and the aspiring obligations of love that cannot; or using Levinasian terms, between the social proximities of the city and the supra-social proximity of the interhuman—a project mediated by theology, although not for theological ends but for thoroughly social and political ends, thus expanding to an even fuller partnership, the kind of hospitality for which Ford's work provides the quintessential theological model today.

Bibliography

Batnitzky, Leora. *Leo Strauss and Emmanuel Levinas: Philosophy and the Politics of Revelation*. Cambridge: Cambridge University Press, 2006.

Bergson, Henri. *Two Sources of Morality and Religion*. Translated by R. Ashley Audra and Cloudesley Brereton. Notre Dame: University of Notre Dame Press, 1977.

Ford, David F. *The Future of Christian Theology*. Oxford: Wiley-Blackwell, 2011.

Kant, Immanuel. *The Metaphysics of Morals*. In *Immanuel Kant, Practical Philosophy*, translated and edited by Mary J. Gregor, 353–603. Cambridge: Cambridge University Press, 1996.

Levinas, Emmanuel. "A New Rationality: On Gabriel Marcel." In *Entre Nous*, translated by Michael B. Smith and Barbara Harshav, 53–55. New York: Continuum, 2006.

15. Ford, *Future of Christian Theology*, xi, 11.

———. "Nonintentional Consciousness." In *Entre Nous*, translated by Michael B. Smith and Barbara Harshav, 105–13. New York: Continuum, 2006.

———. "Philosophy, Justice and Love." In *Entre Nous*, translated by Michael B. Smith and Barbara Harshav, 88–104. New York: Continuum, 2006.

———. *Totality and Infinity*. 1969. Reprint, New York: Continuum, 2006.

———. "Uniqueness." In *Entre Nous*, translated by Michael B. Smith and Barbara Harshav, 162–68. New York: Continuum, 2006.

———. "Useless Suffering." In *Entre Nous*, translated by Michael B. Smith and Barbara Harshav, 78–87. New York: Continuum, 2006.

Nagel, Thomas. *The View from Nowhere*. Oxford: Oxford University Press, 1986.

Rousseau, Jean-Jacques. *A Discourse on the Origin of Inequality*. In *The Social Contract and Discourses*. Translated by G. D. H. Cole. New York: Dutton, 1950.

PART SIX

Theology and the University

20

For Its Own Sake, For God's Sake

Wisdom and Delight in the University

Mike Higton

University of Cambridge and University of Exeter

Introduction: The Two Sakes

At a Scriptural Reasoning conference in the summer of 2011, my small group studied a Mishnaic passage from *Avot* 6:

> Rabbi Meir would say: Whoever studies Torah for its own sake [*Torah l'shma*], merits many things; not only that, but [the creation of] the entire world is worthwhile for him alone.[1]

As we explored the passage, we tried out—sometimes only briefly—fourteen distinct interpretations of the phrase "for its own sake."

1. Is to study Torah for its own sake a matter of giving the highest priority to this activity when one arranges one's time and energy?
2. Is it to study Torah simply for the joy of the activity—to revel in it or bathe in it?

1. *Pirkei Avot* 6:1, translation slightly altered from that cited in the bibliography.

3. Is it studying simply in order to know more about Torah, to increase in Torah-knowledge—and to regard that growth as requiring no further justification?
4. Is it to study for the sake of one's growth in wisdom—the wisdom that *is* Torah?
5. Is it to study Torah with no thought of reward?
6. Is it to study Torah using methods wholly determined by their object: to study Torah the Torah way?
7. Is it to study Torah in order to keep the study of Torah alive—to keep the conversation, the tradition, the transmission going?
8. Is it to study for the sake of Torah's adornment: to uncover its secrets, display its beauties, explore its possibilities?
9. Is it to study Torah in order to take on the characteristics of Torah oneself—to become clothed in it, to embody it?
10. Is it to study for the sake of God, whose word Torah is—in the sense that one does it simply because it is what God, in Torah, has commanded?
11. Is it to study for God's sake in the sense that one does it for the love of God, whose loving communication it is?
12. Is it to study for God's sake in the sense that it brings joy to God (or "rejoices God," in the words of the translation of *Avot* 6:9 that we had in front of us)?
13. Is it to study for God's sake in the sense that it brings union with God, makes one alive in the Godhead?
14. Is it to study for God's sake in the sense that it fits one to do God's will, to be God's agent in the world, to carry out his word, his Torah?

In other words, the idea of studying Torah for its own sake is not a straightforward one—and our attempts to make sense of it veered between interpretations in which *l'shma* ("for its own sake") was a way of saying "for God's sake" and interpretations in which it was a way of saying "for its own sake," via interpretations in which it was a way of saying, in effect, "for God's sake *and therefore* for its own sake."

The same sort of mixing of "for God's sake" and "for its own sake" that we generated in our discussion of *Avot* 6:1 is a characteristic feature of David Ford's recent writings. Early in his 2011 John Paul II Lecture on

Interreligious Understanding, for instance, he offered this maxim in relation to Scriptural Reasoning:

> *This practice of shared reading could be done for its own sake—or, better, for God's sake.* Each of the three traditions has its own ways of valuing the study of its Scriptures as something worth doing quite apart from any ulterior motive. Scriptural Reasoning might of course have all sorts of practical implications, but to do it above all for God's sake—as Jews say, *l'shma*—encourages purity of intention and discourages the mere instrumentalizing of inter-faith engagement . . .[2]

Here as elsewhere, David can slip from "for its own sake" to "for God's sake" with barely a pause, confident that each supports or feeds into the other, or even that they are two ways of saying nearly the same thing. And here, as elsewhere, he indicates by his explicit use of the term *l'shma* that the thought-world in which he is moving is not very distant from that of *Avot* 6:1.[3]

One of the contexts in which the two "sakes" appear in this intimate relationship is in David's recent writings about universities. In *Christian Wisdom* (2007), he notes that reflective Christian participants in universities can, as one of the gifts they bring to those institutions, reflect upon "The wisdom of loving God for God's sake, which in universities might provide a Christian rationale to inspire the love of truth and knowledge for their own sake."[4]

Placing discussion of the two sakes in this context, however, creates an interesting question of interpretation. When one proposes that university study should be undertaken "for its own sake," the most obvious connotations for most readers are likely not to be those established by Jewish accounts of Torah-study but those established by John Henry

2. Ford, "Jews, Christians and Muslims Meet around Their Scriptures," section 4.

3. Ford tends to attach *l'shma* primarily to the "for God's sake" side of the connection. Literally, it means "for the name" or "for its name"—and it can therefore be taken to be a way of saying "for the sake of the *divine* name—that is, for God's sake" as well as, more typically, as a way of saying "for its own sake." For the possibility of reading *l'shma* as "for God's sake" or "for its own sake," see Jacobs, "Aspects of Scholem's Study of Hasidism," 102—or, more simply, see the contrasting titles of Sidney Askelrad with Elaine Berman, *Lishma: For His Name's Sake* and Norman Lamm, *Torah Lishmah: Torah for Torah's Sake*. Ford tends to favour the former interpretation; Peter Ochs the latter—as in his "Coda" to the January 2008 edition of *The Journal of Scriptural Reasoning*.

4. Ford, *Christian Wisdom*, 349.

Newman's *Idea of a University*, and by the tradition of thinking about the nature and purpose of university life that Newman's book helped spawn. Yet in *that* world of thought, as we shall see, the connection between the two sakes—between "for God's sake" and "for its own sake"—is very far from obvious. In order to pursue the kind of theological reflection about universities and the two sakes that David recommends, therefore, we will need to learn to distinguish his insistence upon *l'shma* from Newman's on "learning as an end in itself." In this chapter, therefore, I will argue that Newman's account of education as an end in itself is problematic, unless his "for its own sake" can be connected more directly than he does to "for God's sake"—and that when the two sakes are more intimately connected, as they are in David's work, they offer a fresh and enticing way of thinking about the purpose of university life.

Gordon Graham on the Value of Knowledge

I'm going to begin not with Newman himself but with a recent attempt to champion Newman's ideas by Gordon Graham, Henry Luce III Professor of Philosophy and the Arts at Princeton Theological Seminary. I have chosen Graham simply because he offers a clear example of recent Newmanesque thinking about universities, and because his account is a plausible representative of the more widespread recourse to Newman in recent discussions. Graham's book *Universities* is subtitled *The Recovery of an Idea* and a picture of Newman dominates the cover. He acknowledges that his account of the value of university education and research is deeply influenced by Newman,[5] and shows that indebtedness most fully in his attempt to demonstrate that university education and research are valuable for their own sake. Unlike Newman's book, however, but like most of Newman's recent followers, Graham's contains no reference at all to the idea of studying for *God's* sake.

Graham's most detailed account of learning for learning's sake comes in his discussion of university research, where he asks what claim such

5. Of course, Newman might not have approved of the focus on research. Even though, in practice, research was part of the picture he painted of the university, and part of the Catholic University of Ireland in its actual functioning, he insisted that the University is not *in its essence* a context for research: "its object is . . . the diffusion and extension of knowledge rather than the advancement" (*Idea of a University* 5 [ix]; Ker's critical edition gives the 1889 text. I follow his text, giving his edition's page number first, followed by the 1889 page number in brackets).

research can have to public support.[6] He begins with the standard differentiation between applied and pure research, and argues to begin with that this should be understood as a differentiation between research undertaken for the sake of its contribution to human welfare and research undertaken for the sake of the knowledge gained itself.[7] He then further explains, however, that undertaking the pursuit of "knowledge for its own sake"[8] is itself the pursuit of a significant aspect of human flourishing. For "[t]he mind flourishes, we might say, in so far as it understands, and academic research is to be valued, therefore, in so far as it contributes to this understanding."[9] And since "the life of the mind is as much a part of the nature of human beings as the life of the body or the emotions . . . there is just as much reason to value the full development of mind as of body or personality."[10] It is not that "applied" research serves the advancement of the human race while "pure" research leaves humanity as it was; rather "pure" research seeks "to ameliorate the human condition from the point of view of ignorance and misunderstanding,"[11] and to enrich the stock of human understanding, while "applied" research pursues such amelioration and enrichment in regard to other aspects of human life.

Pure research is, for Graham, not at all research that has to seek to remain behind closed doors, locked safe away in the researcher's study or lab—but the wider impact it has upon society does not happen when its results are put to use to serve some other goal, but when the knowledge and understanding gained by research are themselves diffused to a wider public, "reducing ignorance, confusion and misconception."[12]

Despite its clarity and plausibility, however, there is a problem with Graham's account—and specifically with its dependence upon a distinction between trivial knowledge and genuine knowledge. "There is a fact of the matter," he says, "as to how many people listed in a telephone directory between, say, pages 171 and 294 have surnames beginning with the same letter as the street in which they live, and quite some time could be spent ascertaining this fact." He regards it as obvious, however, that "the knowledge that we came to possess . . . would be quite worthless and

6. Graham, *Universities*, 81.

7. Ibid., 82–84.

8. Ibid., 87.

9. Ibid., 98.

10. Ibid., 94.

11. Ibid., 95.

12. Ibid.

the time spent in gaining it completely wasted."[13] On the other hand, he has earlier suggested that it is "a good thing if, for example, somebody somewhere discovers how the Abbey at Bury St Edmunds was run in the time of the Abbot Samson."[14] To explain this distinction, he simply argues that valuable knowledge, unlike trivial knowledge, contributes to and enriches human understanding. Yet, since this is in a context where he has already isolated his justification of the value of knowledge for its own sake from any contribution that this knowledge might make to other aspects of human welfare, it is still not clear what tool he is using to separate the valuable from the trivial.

I suspect that the thinness of Graham's account at this point is not accidental, but systemic. Rhetorically, his argument is presented as a plea to any reasonable reader, asking them to recognize the entailments and connections of common claims about knowledge and understanding. It is an attempt to clear up regrettable confusions by means of clear argument and sound common sense. Any attempt to specify more closely the nature of the distinction between valuable and trivial knowledge would risk upsetting this rhetorical apple-cart, however, by introducing—of necessity—debatable construals of the human good that might *not* be shared by all Graham's readers. To put this criticism another way, the problem with Graham's account is that it relies upon our ability to recognize value without acknowledging that such an ability is formed within particular traditions of moral reasoning. It is not clear *who* will make the judgments of value that are needed to power Graham's account, nor what formation they might need if they are to be able to make those judgments.

Newman's Idea

We might expect Graham's illustrious predecessor, John Henry Newman, to be far clearer about this question. In the lectures that became *The Idea of a University*, he was, after all, advocating the establishment of an explicitly Catholic university in Ireland—and he was quick to insist that a specifically Catholic moral formation was necessary to steady and to guard the university's intellectual life. In Newman's account, however, there is a rather complex relationship between the university and the church, and therefore between learning as an end in itself and a moral

13. Ibid., 88.

14. Ibid., 81.

formation undertaken strictly for God's sake—and it is not in the end very much more satisfactory than Graham's.

Newman certainly insists that knowledge is an end in itself, and a "very tangible, real and sufficient end"[15] at that. Like Graham, he makes it clear that this is true even if we discount all the extrinsic ends that knowledge might serve: "physical comfort and enjoyment . . . health . . . conjugal and family union . . . the social tie and civil security."[16] "Knowledge . . . is valuable for what its very presence in us does for us after the manner of a habit, even though it be turned to no further account, nor subserve any direct end."[17] This claim about knowledge as an end in itself does not stand in isolation, however, but at the top of a hierarchy of claims about knowledge's value. Newman insisted that "though the useful is not always good, the good is always useful"; it "communicates itself" with an "intrinsic fecundity."[18] "If then the intellect is so excellent a portion of us, and its cultivation so excellent, it is not only beautiful, perfect, admirable, and noble in itself, but in a true and high sense it must be useful to the possessor and to all around him; not useful in any low, mechanical, mercantile sense, but as diffusing good, or as a blessing, or a gift, or power, or a treasure, first to the owner, then through him to the world."[19] Of course, this simply means that seeking knowledge for its own sake is not necessarily the same as seeking knowledge for *my* own sake. One might seek a diffusion and growth of knowledge more broadly in society without thereby making knowledge a means to some end extrinsic to knowledge. Yet Newman's fullest description of this diffusive social value of university education goes further than this. He claims that "it aims at raising the intellectual tone of society, at cultivating the public mind, at purifying the national taste, at supplying true principles to popular enthusiasm and fixed aims to popular aspiration, at giving enlargement and sobriety to the ideas of the age, at facilitating the exercise of political power, and refining the discourse of private life."[20] Here, "facilitating the exercise of political power" at least certainly sounds like an end external to knowledge itself—and elsewhere Newman makes it

15. Newman, *Idea*, 97 [103].

16. Ibid., 98 [105].

17. Ibid., 97–98 [104].

18. Ibid., 143–44 [164]; 103 [111].

19. Ibid., 144 [164].

20. Ibid., 154 [177–78].

clear that a life securely rooted in the apprehension of truth is not simply a life more knowledgeable, but one more stable, more peaceful, and more harmonious. To pursue the sound formation of the mind is, therefore, *ipso facto* to contribute to well-ordered individual and social life more generally—and the university therefore can properly be expected to turn out students who will further this good order. Hence Newman can say, "If then a practical end must be assigned to a University course, I say it is that of training good members of society. Its art is the art of social life, and its end is fitness for the world."[21] Regard for truth for its own sake must come first, because the other benefits that Newman sees university education producing are benefits *of* the truth—but those other benefits are still important.

Newman's clearest presentation of the broader utility of pursuit of knowledge for its own sake is found in his description of the liberally educated man who "will be placed in that state of intellect in which he can take up . . . any [calling] for which he has a taste or special talent, with an ease, a grace, a versatility, *and a success* to which another is stranger."[22] Such education will teach students to "fill any post with credit"[23] and provide them with "a faculty of . . . taking up with aptitude any science or profession."[24] It should therefore be no surprise to find that the plans Newman set out for the Catholic University begin with two years of liberal education from sixteen to eighteen which could then be followed by two years of professional training from eighteen to twenty.[25]

So, there is a complex picture here, which does not trade on as simple distinction between "pure" and "applied" learning as we found in Graham. Nevertheless, nothing I have expounded so far shows where religious formation and the "for God's sake" come into the picture, even though *The Idea of a University* is designed above all to supply precisely that lack. Newman held that the human mind "may be regarded from two principal points of view"—intellectual and moral. The perfection of the intellectual aspect of human life is the cultivation of the mind that we have been discussing so far, and much of what Newman says about it *can* stand on its own. The perfection of the moral aspect of the mind,

21. Ibid., 154 [177].

22. Ibid., 145 [166], emphasis added.

23. Ibid., 154 [178].

24. Ibid., 11 [xviii].

25. See Newman, *Report to Their Lordships*, 31–32.

however, is found in religion—and the religious perfection of humanity is incomparably higher and greater than its intellectual perfection. Yet knowledge and religion are not entirely independent. Properly steadied by the church, university education can be a service to it, and the pursuit of that knowledge which is a good in itself can become a component in the formation of human beings who have been perfected harmoniously both in that intellectual aspect of their being, and in the still more important moral aspect of their being. Unsteadied by the church, however, intellectual development can become positively injurious to religion. Intellectual excellence, if not held in its proper position—a position of inherent but limited dignity—can run amok and damage both its own intellectual sphere and the religious sphere that should be its proper context.

Nevertheless, despite these connections, there is an uneasy gap between the "for its own sake" of sound intellectual formation, and the "for God's sake" of religious formation. The religious steadying and perfecting of intellectual development can appear all too easily as interference or imposition—as the control of something that already has its own independent vigour. It should be no surprise that so many recent appropriations of Newman have been able to extract his account of intellectual formation from the context of religious formation within which he places it. No more than Graham does Newman provide us with a clear account of the inseparability of "for God's sake" and "for its own sake" that we find in David's work.

The Two Sakes in Christian Wisdom

In stark contrast to Graham, and even in contrast to Newman, David's work places the emphasis very firmly on the "for God's sake" throughout. His fullest exploration of this theme is in *Christian Wisdom*, which declares that "love and worship of God for God's sake" is one of its key topics, that "loving God for God's sake" is the "core practice" to emerge in the book, and that the idea that "God is to be loved for God's sake" is the "core insight into the nature of wisdom" that the book discovers "in Old Testament, New Testament, and the Christian tradition," the summit of Christian wisdom.[26] And alongside *loving* God for God's sake, the book speaks of acknowledging, clinging to, desiring, focusing on, praising,

26. Ford, *Christian Wisdom*, cover blurb, 193, 225, 389.

loving, and blessing God for God's sake.[27] It rings with calls to live for God's sake and to hallow, fear, love, praise, and glorify God's name "simply because God is God," "for nothing, for the sake of God's name, for God's own sake," "letting God be God, acknowledging who God is, and living from that acknowledgement whatever the circumstances and whatever the circumstances."[28]

That last quotation comes from a description of Job, who provides one of David's central examples of the love of God for God's own sake.[29] The whole of *Christian Wisdom*, he says, could be taken as a commentary on Satan's question, "Does Job fear God for nothing?"[30] David's account explains the way in which, through the traumas that afflict him, Job is "offered the possibility of blessing God for God's sake," and so awoken to a "'for nothing' relationship with God for God's sake," his eyes opened to see "who [God] is for his own sake."[31]

Significantly for my purposes, Job's journey to this relationship involves a changed relationship to creation.[32] When God speaks to Job from the whirlwind "the wisdom of fearing God for God's sake is . . . transposed into wondering at and celebrating creation for creation's sake," because in those speeches "God celebrates creation for its own sake" and "rules out seeing creation in terms of human utility, control, or even comprehensibility."[33] Job is enabled to see that "God generates and celebrates creation 'for naught,' for its own sake."[34] The movement is complex—by learning to see creation for creation's sake (how richly it exceeds human use, control, and comprehension), Job is drawn towards an understanding of God as standing still further beyond human use, control, and comprehension—and so to see God for God's sake.[35] But at the same time, it is by leaning of God's gratuitous and incomprehensible generation of creation for its own sake that Job is taught to see creation differently, as loved by God for its own sake. "[F]earing and adoring God for God's sake . . . in turn frees us to acknowledge the preciousness of

27. Ibid., 208, 260; 81, 150, 152, 214, 229, 232.

28. Ibid., 172, 188, 225, 100, 5.

29. Ibid., 133.

30. Ibid., 99.

31. Ibid., 104, 119, 115.

32. Ibid., 134.

33. Ibid., 103, 113.

34. Ibid., 114.

35. Ibid., 229.

creatures, human and non-human, for their own sake." A fuller summary of the message of Job therefore is as a call to "celebrate God for God's sake and creation for creation's sake."[36]

Alongside Job, the other central example in the book is Jesus, who "embodies the love of God for God's sake."[37] David sketches a "christological drama of desire" in which "loving God for God's sake" is the central note.[38] Whereas with Job, this love of God for God's sake is accompanied by a love of creation for creation's sake, with Jesus we see it accompanied by a love of God's kingdom. Jesus gives up everything "for the sake of the Kingdom of God and for the sake of the Father."[39] If loving God for God's own sake is a matter of loving the One who loves creation for its own sake, it is also a matter of loving the one who redeems creation for its own sake—drawing it into the peaceable kingdom for its own sake. Since God is the one who "hears the cries of the world and is compassionately committed to it," to love God for God's sake "also involves discernment of cries and living according to what is discerned"; it involves being "committed, for God's sake, to being part of God's response."[40] David therefore repeatedly places together love of God and love of God's kingdom or "loving God and loving other people for God's sake," or "learning to love God, neighbours, and enemies."[41] To love God for God's sake involves "seeking the public good for the sake of God and God's peaceful purposes"[42]—or, less impersonally, it involves loving for their own sake "[t]he poor, the despised, the disfigured"[43] in whom God delights (an idea that David explores most of all in relation to the L'Arche communities of those with disabilities).[44] Loving God for God's sake involves "learn[ing] together to live in the Spirit for the sake of God, of other people and of the world."[45]

David sees biblical hermeneutics in general, and Scriptural Reasoning in particular, through this lens. We should learn to read together "for

36. Ford, *Christian Wisdom*, 284.

37. Ibid., 381.

38. Ibid., 191.

39. Ibid., 33, cf. 226.

40. Ibid., 5, 303.

41. Ibid., 234, 68–69.

42. Ibid., 301.

43. Ibid., 369.

44. Ibid., 359.

45. Ibid., 194.

the sake of God,"[46] but that means more fully that we learn to "read in the Spirit for the sake of the kingdom of God."[47] "Read and reread Scripture above all for the sake of God and God's purposes; hear it as God the Creator, Judge, and Saviour crying out to humanity; respond to it . . . with love for God and for the world God loves."[48]

It is this very same lens through which David looks at universities. His discussions of the love of "understanding and truth for their own sake"[49] present them as inseparable from the love of God for God's own sake—and he argues that the love of truth and understanding for their own sake can lead towards, and even more can flow from, the love of God for God's own sake.[50] David's account of learning for learning's sake is inextricably embedded in the whole book's account of "God's love of creation for its own sake and a responsive human love of God for God's sake and of other people for their own sake."[51]

Delight and Wisdom in the University

We are in a position, finally, to see how, for David, the two "sakes" are connected in a university context. To undertake study for the love of God is not like studying for the sake of some particular object or end amongst others; rather it is study undertaken for the love of the one who creates and redeems all things—for the love of the one who freely loves the world into being, and who loves the world into redemption, and does so entirely freely, which is to say for its own sake.

To study for God's sake is to study as a form of participation in the love of God who loves creation for its own sake. But that means that to study creation for God's sake simply *is* to study creation for its own sake—and that studying it for its own sake is a matter both of delighting in its sheer existence beyond all use and control and final comprehension (studying for the sake of the Creator), *and* a matter of studying it for the sake of fuller creaturely flourishing (studying for the sake of the Redeemer).

46. Ford, *Christian Wisdom*, 68, 203, 280, 302.

47. Ibid., 88.

48. Ibid., 81.

49. Ibid., 308, cf. 322.

50. Ibid., 349.

51. Ibid., 380.

To study for God's sake is therefore to study for the sake of wisdom: to study for the sake of that understanding that enables graceful living with our fellow-creatures. And, at the same time, it is to study for the sake of that delight which marvels at the ways in which creatures exceed all the plans, programmes, and frames of comprehension by which we shape our life with them. And this wisdom and delight are co-inherent: to live graciously with a fellow-creature is, in part, to live in delighted acknowledgement of its otherness; to delight in the otherness of a fellow-creature is to hear its call to live graciously (rather than rapaciously) with it. The proper end of university study is delightful wisdom and wise delight.

To study for God's sake is study for the sake of delightful wisdom and wise delight; but to study for the sake of delightful wisdom and wise delight must also be to study for God's sake. God is the one who teaches wisdom and delight—because to learn wisdom and delight is inescapably to enter on a process of the purification of desire—and, for a Christian theologian, God is the one who purifies desire, who makes holy. The fear of the Lord is the beginning of wisdom.

David makes no pretence that a God-centred account of the purpose of university study will be justifiable to all rational people regardless of the traditions of their intellectual formation, nor that the particular shape of his God-centred account will be justifiable to all religious people regardless of the particular traditions of their religious life. His account is unashamedly theological, and unashamedly Christian. And yet he celebrates academic institutions that enable partial but real pursuit of this end not just despite the fact, but *in and through* the fact that they are made up of a complex collegiality of religious and secular voices. He presents his account of Christian wisdom concerning universities not as an attempt at a master discourse, but as a delighted invitation to others to understand this tradition more deeply, and to be driven in response deeper into their own traditions of thinking and judgment in regard to universities. After all, it is a vision that calls him to delighted acknowledgement and exploration of the difference of his colleagues from him, and to a search for wise institutional settlements by which those who differ in these ways can live and work graciously with each other. And that is why it makes sense for the proponent of such an unashamedly Christian theological account of the nature and purpose of university study to have laboured for the sake of the Cambridge Inter-faith Programme with its promotion of engagements with and between multiple religious traditions, for the sake of the Divinity Faculty with its intellectual life shaped by an even wider range of religious and non-religious traditions, and for the sake of the University of Cambridge with all the complexity and diversity of its religious and secular settlement. For David, labour for God's sake and labour for the good of these institutions for their own sake have rightly been inseparable.

Bibliography

Askelrad, Sidney, with Elaine Berman. *Lishma: For His Name's Sake*. Lincoln, NE: iUniverse, 2005.

Ford, David F. *Christian Wisdom: Desiring God and Learning in Love*. Cambridge: Cambridge University Press, 2007.

———. "Jews, Christians and Muslims Meet around Their Scriptures: An Inter-Faith Practice for the 21st Century." 2011. Online: http://www.interfaith.cam.ac.uk/en/resources/papers/jpii-lecture.

Graham, Gordon. *Universities: The Recovery of an Idea*. 2nd ed. Exeter, UK: Imprint Academic, 2008.

Jacobs, Louis. "Aspects of Scholem's Study of Hasidism." *Modern Judaism* 5.1 (1985) 95–104.

Lamm, Norman. *Torah Lishmah: Torah for Torah's Sake*. Hoboken, NJ: Ktav, 1989.

Newman, John Henry. *The Idea of a University Defined and Illustrated*. Edited by Ian Ker. Oxford: Clarendon, 1976.

———. *Report to Their Lordships, the Archbishops and Bishops of Ireland, 1854–55*. In *My Campaign in Ireland* 1: *Catholic University Reports and Other Papers*, edited by W. Neville, 3–56. Aberdeen: King, 1896.

Ochs, Peter. "Coda." *The Journal of Scriptural Reasoning* 7.1 (2008). Online: http://etext.lib.virginia.edu/journals/ssr/issues/volume7/number1/ssr07_01_e09.html.

Pirkei Avot: The Ethics of the Fathers. Online: http://www.chabad.org/library/article_cdo/aid/5708/jewish/Ethics-of-the-Fathers-Translated-Text.htm.

21

The Place and Significance of Theology in the Contemporary University

Joseph D. Galgalo

St. Paul's University, Limuru

Universities the world over are research-oriented, with ever-increasing emphasis on the need to integrate research and teaching. University rankings are often based on their specific contribution to innovation and new technologies. With this in mind, there is a certain expectation and a level of accountability that demands the justification for inclusion of each discipline or subject on the university syllabus. This is more so where funding of public university education dictates prioritizing with the aim of achieving a well-considered allocation of ever-limited resources. Such prioritizing is done on the basis of "importance," where subjects or disciplines are considered based on their perceived or real contribution to the national economy, human progress, welfare, health, technology, and generally, the advancement of knowledge. Competition for funding often pits arts and humanities against physical or social sciences. In the circumstances, universities live by the unwritten code: "every subject must earn its place on the university syllabus."

In this chapter, I address the question of the place and significance of theology in the contemporary university. A simple conceptual framework is adopted. I examine theology's basic nature and employ this in my attempt to answer the questions of theology's public vocation and why it should be taught and studied as part of a university program. There are numerous assumptions (unfortunately negative) about the subject of theology that lend urgency to our topic. First, I briefly make a note of and quickly dispense with some of these assumptions as a way of setting the stage for the discussion. Secondly, the nature of theology is explored to contend for theology's importance. David F. Ford, in whose honour this festschrift is prepared, has made substantial contributions to the topic of the study of theology and religious studies in university settings.[1] While I choose not to engage with his works for the purpose of this chapter, nevertheless, in my effort to set aside the assumptions mentioned here, I find very helpful David Ford's account of "common academic prejudices and *idées fixes*," including:

> a modern parochialism that cannot take the pre-modern seriously in matters of truth; an incapacity to appreciate the intellectual achievement in the area of religious thought; a failure to respect the large numbers of religious academics who are at least as intelligent, well-educated, sophisticated and critically alert as their secular colleagues; an insistence on religious and theological positions meeting standards of rationality that are by no means accepted throughout the university; or a blindness to the complexly religious and secular character of our world.[2]

These prejudices shape public perceptions and carry great potential in influencing the prioritization and allocation of funding, and can determine what most universities around the world include or exclude in their curricula.[3]

1. Numerous of his published works on this subject can be mentioned: Ford, *Theology: A Very Short Introduction*, especially chapters 1 and 2; Ford, *Fields of Faith*; Ford, "Faith and Universities in a Religious and Secular World (1)"; Ford, "Faith and Universities in a Religious and Secular World (2)"; Ford, *Christian Wisdom*, especially chapter 9, 304–49.

2. Ford, *Christian Wisdom*, 290–91.

3. For detailed accounts of the history of the modern university, including shifts in the position of theology within it, see Pedersen, *The First Universities*; Ridder-Symoens, *Universities in the Middle Ages*; Riché, *Education and Culture in the Barbarian West*; Johnson, *The Renaissance*; Brubacher, *Higher Education in Transition*.

In today's universities, generally speaking, theology as an academic discipline often finds itself in a rather unfamiliar territory. Theology often tops the list of those subjects struggling to gain inclusion on a university syllabus, continuously competing for a place on the priority list for funding. There are various general assumptions that contribute to theology's struggle. These assumptions may not always determine official decisions but such assumptions powerfully shape perceptions and can influence a university's choice of disciplines to be taught. Among the most common of such views is that theology's core concerns are rather parochial and it is best if theological education is left to the private sphere and not imposed on public arena such as a university. This view's best contention is that the right place for the study of theology is not in a university but in other tertiary level institutions such as Bible schools and seminaries. The view, all things considered, fails to appreciate theology's wider public vocation, which I will endeavour to assert in this paper. Let it suffice for now that such a rather myopic view of the subject uncritically assumes "certain unity" of theology and some singular purpose of all religious traditions, an assumption that makes no sense.

Another rather uncritical assumption is one that holds theology and generally every religious tradition as totally concerned with the "subjective matter" of faith. Theology is dismissed, often cursorily and without proper scrutiny, as advancing unsubstantiated truth claims about what people should believe in order to purportedly secure eternity with God. The assumption is fueled by the belief that theology lacks concrete scientific grounding in terms of sound methodology and procedures that can produce and convincingly sustain a logical conclusion of any of its arguments. Summarily this assumption holds that theology is uncritical. That is, theology is not "academic" enough, or as David Ford puts it, it lacks "standards of rationality"[4] to meet the academic rigor and accountability to which all academic disciplines must be subjected. If it is subjected, like all other academic disciples to "ruthless critique," this assumption holds, none of theology's claims can pass the searching test of any "objective" verification principle.[5]

4. Ford, *Christian Wisdom*, 291.

5. I do not intend to discuss such complex issues as "religious faith and psychological limit," religious language, or "theology and falsification," but one could refer to such basic texts as Flew and MacIntyre, *New Essays in Philosophical Theology*, or works of a more general nature including Peacock, *The Sciences and Theology in the Twentieth Century*, and Griffin and Hough, *Theology and the University*.

Such a view of theology merely hinges on the support of unexamined popular beliefs and cannot be taken seriously. It is faulty not least for the failure to appreciate the scientific and historical nature of academic theology. The view also simply overlooks the fact that comparative religions, their distinctive theologies, and for that matter, the "subjective matter" of faith could be studied in their own right—if only for interest's sake, but more importantly for the knowledge of religious traditions and their enduring power of influence on societies world over. We might also consider theology's role and contribution to our understanding of religious and cultural dynamics of communities of faith, interfaith matters, as well as its appreciation and appraisal of both the secular and the religious' complex contestations and convergences in today's world.

Another popular assumption is the claim that theology is primarily concerned with religious and ministerial formation and therefore should not be taught in the universities but be left to particular denominations and private institutions, where matters of religious faith should rightly be placed. Arguably there is strength in denominationally based theological education. The benefits of having theology in a university, however, far outweigh any such benefit that a denominational seminary may afford. Whereas denominational seminaries do have a place and significant role in theological formation, they lose out on the enriching but also challenging diversity of theological views, mutually shared theological space, mutual interrogation of cherished practices and dogmas, a critique of the same, the continuous negotiation and renegotiation and setting of "objective" criteria (compare: "standards of rationality") or appropriate procedure—all of which the university context affords better than denominational seminaries can ever do. Denominational theology also tends to be overly apologetic in its efforts to preserve and perpetuate a particular theological heritage and traditions. In this case, matters of hermeneutics and interpretations of meaning are tightly controlled and perpetuated. Doing theology in the context of a university, on the contrary, can afford exposure to and greater interaction with multiple faiths, religious traditions, and theological orientations. On that account, theological study in the university carries the greater potential for being not only informative but also helpfully corrective. This can keep in check negative tendencies that often arise as a result of denominational parochialism and can aid the clarification and a better appreciation of the universal vocation of theology.

Many more such popular assumptions, prejudices, and misconceptions could be mentioned: "religious faith is dangerous and delusional," "religion is generally oppressive," "religious beliefs are irrational," or "mythological and manifestly false." These and such other stereotypes could be discussed, but that is not my concern here. I note, however, that these and other such assumptions, and generally the popular critique of theology are not without some benefit. Theology as an academic discipline is strengthened if challenged to strive for greater and continual improvement of its methodology, clarification of its subject matter, and of its relevance and role in public life. Theology rightly appreciated has great contributions to make, which I now discuss.

D. W. D. Shaw, citing Douglas Young, tells the story of Thomas Jackson, a professor of divinity in Glasgow. On his retirement, this elderly divine purposed to accomplish his lifetime dream: to write his greatest work of theology. When Jackson died after four years of labour, it was only this single sentence that was found left behind: "Theology is everything, and everything is theology."[6] This is a simple thesis—yet so profound. The claim for theology's all-encompassing character is not a matter of opinion, nor subjective feeling. It is rather because theology is primarily "the science about truth," a matter that in and of its nature is of "ultimate significance." In the words of the Reformer, John Calvin, "true and sound wisdom consists of two parts: the knowledge of God and of ourselves," and according to Calvin, "Without knowledge of self there is no knowledge of God, and without knowledge of God there is no knowledge of self."[7] Calvin's thesis touches on the ultimate import of theology—the truth about the self, which is impossible without the knowledge of God. This makes theology relevant to the general public, not just a concern of individual believers or followers of a particular faith.

A key point to consider here is theology's contextual nature. Theological reflection always takes place in the specificity of a context and thereby necessarily adopts a "conversational mode" of engagement between received texts (and traditions), on the one hand, and the recipient's context, on the other. It is this conversational model, basic to the nature of theology, that has influenced key theological trends. A worthy example here is the theologies of liberation, which generally have proved influential in engaging with and shaping public discourses on critical matters of social justice, political accountability, economic justice, relational nature of societies, sensibilities of religious teachings and traditions, value

6. Shaw, "Theology in the University," 217.

7. Calvin, *Institutes of the Christian Religion*, 1.1.1–2.

of theological imperatives (such as Christian discipleship), and their relevance for productive living.

These theologies assume certain criteria, standards, and methods of engagement. The general public (not just specific communities of faith) has become the context and the proper arena of such engagements. Their import and significant impact in shaping theological discourses, individual and by extension social choices, and even political engagements, cannot be ignored. These theologies force questions of certain immediacy and particular contextual relevance, and influence critical reflection and appropriation of such universal themes as responsibility, power, commitment, freedom, human dignity and empowerment, transformation, and social vision. This public role of theology is of particular import to the university. Its critical nature calls for sustained academic research, accountability, intellectual scrutiny, continuous critique of its methods and conclusions, and in effect is capable of shaping communities by way of "theological conversations" that envision possibilities of a better social order of things and human existence. "Surely the university—the community of knowledge—is impoverished if it settles for a naiveté that excludes such possibilities."[8]

In today's university, theology as an academic discipline has become highly specialized with regard to areas of its study. I do not refer here simply to the traditional divisions of theology such as biblical, doctrinal, historical, and pastoral—but more to the specialties that continue to evolve within particular divisions. With regard to Christian theology, for example, the contributions of the "theology of hope," itself a type of political (or public) theology, and for that matter, a type of liberation theology, cannot be ignored. One aspect of the impact of the theology of hope arises from its critical engagement and "conversations" in context. Particular emphasis and attention is given to issues of pressing societal concerns. These are then brought to bear on and to act as "midwife" (so to speak) for creative ways of appropriating biblical teachings, especially the values of the kingdom of God, in the most practical ways possible. This has produced an integrative influence of sorts—where beliefs and teachings can be integrated with decisions, choices, and practices. Theology's attempt at integrating "professional practice" with beliefs, which in turn is constantly enriched, influenced, and informed by sustained research is basic to its great public vocation, making a valuable contribution to realistic ways

8. Farley, *Fragility of Knowledge*, 27.

of envisioning the realization of human desires for good life and fruitful living.

We need not belabour the relevance of theology and its place in the contemporary university, but perhaps a specific example of how theology may do this is in order. I have worked in the same university for close to eleven years now. My university, St. Paul's in Limuru, Kenya, has over the years continued to support the integration of research and teaching, but has also evolved a method of reflective practice in an effort to adopt an appropriate model for doing a contextual theology. Reflective practice seeks deliberately to integrate academic research and teaching, on the one hand, and professional practice, on the other. It typically adopts a participatory approach to the study and practice of theology. Structured and sustained discourses on critical issues of a theological nature, and on major social concerns such as gender-based violence, interfaith dialogue and relations, economic justice, HIV/AIDS, and disability studies, are mainstreamed in the curriculum and conducted in the setting of a specific community of faith. Such subject communities have become defined pedagogical partners and participants with the university. The objective is to map dominant understandings, interpretations, theological considerations, and practices among grassroots faith communities. This is not just for the sake of achieving rigor in research, as is required by the university, but is done so that theology may serve some practical purpose: mainly to evolve a hermeneutic that does not only discover or construct meaning, but can also guide and inform discernment of a fruitful theological way of living. The conclusions of the partner-participants are usually not considered complete until they are introduced to a wider public, that is, the community of faith who formed the initial setting/partner for the study.

The input from the external publics, mainly composed of the critique of the church's teachings (dominant views and interpretations) is then taken back to the initial community (partner-participants) for critical analysis and response. This has not only continued to enrich theological reflection among the primary communities of faith and the university publics who together form the "partner-participants," but has also proved extremely challenging in many ways. Often theological positions have been clarified, even wholly abandoned and reformulated as a result of this reflective method and the accompanying theological practice. Examples include, but are not limited to, the questions of the place and role of HIV positive persons at the communion table sharing the "common" cup, believing polygamists who seek baptism, and the ordination of severely disabled persons. In this regard, university theology continues to influence in a very practical way specific moral and ethical choices, judgment between right and wrong, and helpful interpretations and appropriation of meanings of such subjects as *imago dei*, human dignity, community and communion, individual responsibility and social orientations, inclusion and exclusion, mutuality and hospitality.

This particular methodology shows how theology is a highly cognitive and a highly practical enterprise, as opposed to being simply abstract and imaginative. The result has often proved invaluable not only in aiding the "discernment" of human potentials and possibilities for fruitful living, but also in shaping attitudes, knowledge, and particular life choices and ways of life that reflect the gospel vision for the "abundant life" in a real and practical ways. For any institution of higher learning to compromise or overlook this key contribution of theology is to forfeit real possibilities for shaping a rewarding social vision and providing a point of reference for a meaningful engagement and growth in the world.

Theology is by nature not only contextual but also "historical." By this we mean that Christian traditions and canonical Scripture form the core concern of Christian theology. In this respect, theology is an enterprise engaged primarily in the "retrieval of wisdom"—by which we mean the critical reading, interpretation, and study of patterns of appropriation of wisdom (and the sources of such wisdom) that over the centuries have been central to the lives of believers. Theology's task of "retrieval," to be clear, is not about the simple repetition or rehearsal of wisdom from the past, but rather the critical reinterpretation and recovery of the significance of such wisdom for the present. It is this noble vocation of theology that ironically underlies the erroneous assumption that "theology is uncritical" as we noted above. The commonplace argument thus runs: how is it that theology so uncritically concerned with the furtherance of religious faith is at all relevant to the university? Edward Farley helpfully describes the sum of this argument: "The University's formal critical principle was hard won, and the battle left the conviction that knowledge can be freely pursued only if the university does not subject itself to tradition, religious or otherwise."[9]

Such argument against theology is mistaken in equating "critical retrieval" with "uncritical acceptance" of the said traditions and wisdom. To quote Farley again, "When the tradition-oriented hermeneutic is not suppressed, there can take place a retrieval of wisdom from the various

9. Ibid.

ages, cultures, and literatures of the past."[10] Of particular importance here is the nature of Christian wisdom as a *living* tradition, which on this basis alone is worth its keep and deserving of a place among university taught subjects, and on equal standing (at least) with the study of secular history, literature, music, fine art, archaeology, classical philosophy, or ancient languages. To quote Farley again, "modern students can . . . be shaped by East and West, by Isaiah and Homer, by Thomas Aquinas and Sigmund Freud."[11] Where can this be done better than in a university?

We now revisit the claim, "theology is everything and everything is theology." Critically analyzed the statement runs into some logical difficulties, especially on account of the second part. However, the claim that "theology is everything," makes great sense. The central concern of theology is the knowledge of God, which is intricately connected, as noted above, with the knowledge of self. In this regard, the subject of theology deals with matters of "ultimate concern," of human destinies, meaning, and the purpose of all things. These are ultimate questions of life, which are a concern of every human being regardless of their religious faith or lack of it. This reminds me of what Paul Tillich, in his short treatise, *The Irrelevance and Relevance of the Christian Message*, called "the anxiety of finitude," where as he puts it, "Real human beings [without exception] . . . ask passionately and sometimes cynically the question of the meaning of life."[12] Theology in this sense "becomes everything" because it concerns everyone and addresses everything that ultimately matter; the meaning of life. On this account, the study of theology is a discourse that naturally belongs to the "public" square. Technical and professional expertise is required to guide such a discourse. Theology's import and relevance is indispensible in this regard. In a practical sense, this is how theology serves this role; as D. W. D. Shaw puts it, in answering "the big questions" theology provides proper tools and language that are required for this purpose.[13] Theology's task in this regard is to provide conceptual and linguistic tools needed for the articulation of answers to the "big questions" of life, a task that forms theology's most valuable public vocation and justifies its role and place in the highest place of learning, the university.

Closely related to the point just made in this last paragraph, is theology's hermeneutical and exegetical task. In this regard theology makes

10. Ibid.

11. Ibid.

12. Tillich, *Irrelevance and Relevance*, 44.

13. Shaw, "Theology in the University," 224.

"connections" between faith and reason, history and context, secular and the sacred, ephemeral and the eternal, past and the present, the beginning and end of things, humanity and divinity, the spiritual and the corporal, the visible and the invisible, thereby holding in a creative tension a whole host of antithetical truths while constructing meanings in the most rational way possible. Equally, Christian theology can provide a "connecting" element in resourcing an inter- and multi-disciplinary task of mutually critical engagements in the university. In making such connections theology has a lot to offer to, as well as to learn from, the fields of psychology, sociology, philosophy, ethics, anthropology, history, and others. In doing this, theology must carefully negotiate our complexly pluralistic world by constantly reviewing its vocation, re-examining its role and relevance, reinvigorating its methodology, and keeping alive its vigour for the service of both the academy and the wider society.

In conclusion then, theology's "elastic" dimensionality and particular contributions cannot be ignored. Theology's hermeneutical, didactic, and practical influence is proof of theology's objectivity and its capacity to add value to the critical, academic, and "progressive" aims of any university. That billions of people around the world are adherents of one form of religion or another, and most are ardent students of some sacred texts—and that secularism itself is arguably a sort of "religiosity," and takes cognizance (however lightly) of religious phenomena of the world—lends urgency to the study of theology. As Keith Ward observes, "Religions are such an important and vital force in the modern world that it would be a dereliction of intellectual duty if its [*sc.* religion's] claims were not taken seriously, investigated carefully, and evaluated with reasoned criticism."[14] Theology is well placed to lead the way in this regard, and surely, this can be done nowhere better than in a university.

I have attempted to examine the contextual, historical, and hermeneutical nature of theology and to demonstrate theology's capacity adequately to provide critical tools and ways necessary for our appraisal of faith claims, our evaluation of faith claims' practical value, our comprehension and expression of truth, and especially our understanding of God and self. Theology can provide ways of perceiving the world, and is able to "name" concerns of specific matters of faith in a constructive, communicative, dynamic, and conversational model of engagement that lifts the "standards of rationality," where matters of religious faith are concerned, in ways other disciples are comparatively ill-equipped to do. Theology's

14. Ward, "Why Theology Should be Taught at Secular Universities," 26.

place on any university's syllabus is justified, indeed should even be indisputable.

Bibliography

Brubacher, John S., and Willis Rudy. *Higher Education in Transition: A History of American Colleges and Universities*, 1636–1968. New York: Harper & Row, 1968.

Calvin, Jean. *Institutes of the Christian Religion*. Vol. 1. Translated and edited by John T. McNeill. Philadelphia: Westminster, 1960.

Farley, Edward. *The Fragility of Knowledge: Theological Education in the Church and the University*. Philadelphia: Fortress, 1988.

Flew, A. N. G., and Alasdair MacIntyre, editors. *New Essays in Philosophical Theology*. London: SCM, 1955.

Ford, David F. *Christian Wisdom: Desiring God and Learning in Love*. Cambridge, Cambridge University Press, 2007.

———. "Faith and Universities in a Religious and Secular World (1)." *Svensk Teologisk Kvartalskrift* 81.2 (2005) 83–91.

———. "Faith and Universities in a Religious and Secular World (2)." *Svensk Teologisk Kvartalskrift* 81.3 (2005) 97–106.

———. *Theology: A Very Short Introduction*. New ed. Oxford: Oxford University Press, 2000.

Ford, David F., Ben Quash, and Janet Martin Soskice, editors. *Fields of Faith: Theology and Religious Studies in the Twenty-first Century*. Cambridge: Cambridge University Press, 2005.

Griffin, David Ray, and Joseph C. Hough, editors. *Theology and the University: Essays in Honour of John B. Cobb, Jr.* Albany: State University of New York Press, 1991.

Johnson, Paul. *The Renaissance: A Short History*. New York: Modern Library, 2000.

Peacock, A. R. *The Sciences and Theology in the Twentieth Century*. Oxford: Oxford University Press, 1981.

Pedersen, Olaf. *The First Universities: Studium Generale and the Origins of University Education in Europe*. Cambridge: Cambridge University Press, 1997.

Riché, Pierre. *Education and Culture in the Barbarian West: From the Sixth through the Eighth Century*. Columbia: University of South Carolina Press, 1978.

Ridder-Symoens, Hilde de, editor. *A History of the University in Europe*. Vol. 1, *Universities in the Middle Ages*. Cambridge: Cambridge University Press, 1992.

Shaw, D. W. D. "Theology in the University—A Contemporary Scottish Perspective." *Scottish Journal of Theology* 41 (1988) 217–31.

Tillich, Paul. *The Irrelevance and Relevance of the Christian Message*. Edited by Durwood Foster. Cleveland, OH: Pilgrim, 1996.

Ward, Keith. "Why Theology Should be Taught at Secular Universities." *Discourse* 4.1 (2011) 22–37.

22

Ecclesial Theology in the University

C. C. Pecknold

The Catholic University of America

The Great Reversal

From the advent of the medieval university, the theologian's task and mission has been tethered to the church. Why, then, should there be any question of "ecclesial theology in the university" today? The historical, philosophical, and theological reasons why this has become an intelligible question are complex, and multiple accounts of "the great reversal" can be given.[1] At the very least, we can agree with Charles Taylor that "the conditions of belief" have changed so dramatically that one now "naturally" questions the place of theology in the university in a way that would have been unthinkable prior to the Enlightenment.[2] From the beginning, there were defensive and offensive responses to the upheaval. Friedrich Schleiermacher's *On Religion: Speeches to its Culture Despisers*

1. Hans Frei, one of David Ford's esteemed teachers at Yale, understood the importance of this "great reversal" in his landmark book, *The Eclipse of Biblical Narrative.* Frei saw the founding of the University of Berlin (1810) as an exemplary shift away from an ecclesial context for theology towards a "scientific" context that ironically excluded theology as a science (and certainly excluded theology as queen of sciences).

2. Taylor, *Secular Age*, 1.

provides the archetypal defensive account, and Karl Barth's work exemplifies the offensive strategy: "the best apologetics is a good dogmatics." David Ford's dulcet continuation of Hans Frei's work on "the eclipse of biblical narrative"—and the role of theology at the University of Berlin in the nineteenth century—belongs to these oscillating responses to the epistemic challenge besetting the ecclesial theologian in the university today. Such developments have not, however, only troubled Protestant theologians.

Amongst Catholics, there have been numerous theologians analogous in this respect to Schleiermacher, seeking to reconcile the patristic and medieval intellectual patrimony with the Enlightenment challenge to the place of theology in the university.[3] Karl Barth has no Catholic analogue, though arguably Hans Urs von Balthasar and Pope Benedict XVI represent more dogmatically demanding responses that resisted the challenge. Like Protestant theological responses to the challenge of the Enlightenment, the alternative strategies attracted labels that opposed them to each other, as "accommodationist" or "reactionary." Instead of high-quality theological distinction-making (concerning God, Christ, and Us), theologians became concerned to categorize "types of theology."[4] Admittedly, for medieval theologians, distinction-making produced theological "schools"—but schools were not camps that divided the church catholic. The modern bifurcation of ecclesial theology—into defensive or offensive, accommodationist or reactionary, liberal or conservative—has made theological formation difficult. It raises the question: what is the nature of "ecclesial theology"? It is not the same as monastic or scholastic theology, but should it not have real continuity with those earlier forms of ecclesial theology? How does a university context contribute negatively or positively to the formation of theologians? What obstacles does it present, and

3. For a fascinating account of how seventeenth- and eighteenth-century Benedictine communities either flourished or failed depending on their response to the Enlightenment, see Lehner, *Enlightened Monks*.

4. There has been endless such categorizing of theology into types in modernity, such as H. Richard Niebuhr's *Christ and Culture*, or Hans Frei's *Types of Christian Theology*, yet I observe that modern theological typologies seem to be separated by hermeneutical or epistemic differences whereas medieval "schools" were always separated by philosophical and theological distinctions. Instead of thinking of theological disagreement in terms of doctrinal distinctions in an ecclesial context in which we are all in communion, our modern theological typologies fit "theologies" into different hermeneutical frames entirely, enforcing the habits of ecclesial division forged in the early modern period. This goes to the very heart of the great reversal that so concerned Hans Frei (and by extension, David Ford).

who presents the obstacles? This essay examines how "the great reversal" shaped twentieth-century conversations about Catholic higher education in America. Though not perfectly analogous to the Protestant experience, the essay shows that Catholics still have much to learn if we seek full recovery for the ecclesial vocation of theology in the university today.

First, though, we must confront the claim that theology in the service to the church is counter to the demands of academic freedom, precisely to the extent that it is tied to tradition and authority. It is not at all surprising, for example, that John Henry Newman writes, in his *Apologia Pro Vita Sua*, that he believes "the whole revealed dogma as taught by the Apostles, as committed by the Apostles to the Church, and as declared by the Church to me. I receive it, as it is infallibly interpreted by the authority to whom it is thus committed, and (implicitly) as it shall be, in like manner, further interpreted by that same authority till the end of time."[5] Yet if such words were uttered in the academic senate of any modern university today, they would invite, at best, blank stares. To claim that a science would be accountable to such an authoritative body of teaching seems inimical to academic freedom itself.[6] Recalling Pontius Pilate, here we can see that the sceptical questioning of transcendent truth—a question that finally paralyzed the Third Academy—invariably puts theologians either on the defensive or the offensive.

One might expect that theologians at Catholic universities would never have to face such a question. Yet this problem was acutely felt in a different way by American Catholic theologians in the years immediately following the Second Vatican Council. There arose a contestable interpretation of Vatican II, which Joseph Ratzinger has called "the hermeneutic of discontinuity." Tied to that hermeneutic of discontinuity was a program of theology as a revision of Catholic faith and morals—often inspired by the same transcendental Thomists highlighted at the outset under the unhappy label of "accommodationist." The project of theological "revision" according to post-Kantian Christian accounts of reality quite easily became a project of theological "dissent," because such resistance to the received tradition of authoritative teaching was (wrongly) taken to be a sign of intellectual legitimacy in the university. This shift is clearly illustrated by the *Land O'Lakes* statement, issued soon after the close of

5. Newman, *Apologia Pro Vita Sua*, 389.

6. The great reversal also entailed defining "religion" as irrational, which greatly contributes to the problem of our academic senate refusing any traditional authority. For a devastating critique of these constructions of "religion" see Cavanaugh, *The Myth of Religious Violence*.

the Second Vatican Council, which treated specifically the nature of the Catholic university, and by implication, theology itself, as a discipline that was to be emphatically independent from the Catholic Church, and in service of the university as an enterprise of inquiry free from the claims of any body of teaching.

Land O'Lakes

Signed by twenty-six presidents, theologians, and other higher education officials, the Land O'Lakes statement on "The Nature of the Contemporary Catholic University" was issued in 1967.[7] It was immediately celebrated in the media as consistent with "the reform of the Council." As Philip Gleason notes, "What made Land O'Lakes news were its radically novel claims for 'institutional autonomy and academic freedom.'"[8] The statement was seen as a "declaration of independence from the hierarchy and a symbolic turning point" that had its centre of gravity in theological dissent and the student unrest of the late 1960s.[9] Underlining institutional independence from the Church, the drafters of the document pronounced, "the Catholic University participates in the total university life of our time" (LL 1). The cultural context trumped the place of the Church in relation to the university.

Notice that the drafters of the document make a distinction between the Catholic or ecclesial university and "the total university life of our time." What could that distinction mean? What is "the total university life of our time"? Is that "total university" a more comprehensive view of the nature of the university (or truth itself), while "Catholic" (which simply means "universal") means something a bit less comprehensive? What did the drafters think made a university distinctively Catholic? The answer in the statement is that a university is "Catholic" because of the "perceptible presence" and the "effective operation" of Catholicism within it—in other words, the only thing that makes a university Catholic is that there are Catholics on campus! But on that tautological premise, doesn't any university with a perceptible presence of Catholics count as "a Catholic University"? What is clear is that the drafters want to minimize the difference the adjective "Catholic" makes for the normal work of "the total

7. The full text of the Land O'Lakes document is reproduced in McCluskey, *The Catholic University*. All references are parenthetically indicated in the text below as LL.

8. Gleason, *Contending with Modernity*, 317.

9. Ibid.

university." In an odd way, they seem to think that the Church is accidental, and has no substantial relationship to the university that has described itself as Catholic. This universal claim ironically challenges the universality claimed by the Church in relation to the university. It is an odd repetition of the Enlightenment reversals of earlier centuries (and even more oddly repeats the complex reversals between political and ecclesial authority in mediaeval centuries).

While the drafters should be given credit for seeing the discipline of theology as integral to the work of the Catholic university, they had a highly programmatic vision of how theology should be done in such a context. According to the authors of the statement, theology must be "diverse," "plural," and it must attend to "the total religious heritage of the world" and serve "the ecumenical goals of collaboration and unity." Would this require theology departments to become "religious studies" departments, or would it mean that theology and religious studies would coexist as equal partners? They never considered such concrete institutional questions. Interestingly, the key words of the document are not dissent and revision, as I highlighted above. But they do carefully circumscribe how theology is to be *unified*. The inter-religious and the ecumenical were particularly prominent, but the key criterion for theology in such a university was that it should be "inter-disciplinary." Yet refusing any sense of theology as "queen of the sciences"—"there must be no theological . . . imperialism" (LL 4)—the document expressed little if any clarity about the purpose and ends to which such "creative dialogue" with other disciplines should be put. Nor does the document ever indicate that such theological labour should ever be held accountable to the teaching of the Church, or seen as an extension of the work of bishops to preserve and proclaim the received deposit of the faith. At best, theology was envisioned contextually as a discipline about *everything relevant to the total university life of our time*. At worst, ecclesial theology is discarded as no discipline at all—any account of theology held accountable to the teaching of the Church is dismissed as "catechesis."

One can sense in the Land O'Lakes statement an enthusiastic embrace of the so-called spirit of Vatican II, a hermeneutic of discontinuity (again, contestable) which was usually a good deal less about the traditional, doctrinally rich Council documents and a good deal more about the spirit of what would become the 1970s. The statement further encouraged students to express their Christianity "in a variety of ways and live it experientially and experimentally . . ." (LL 9). Even liturgically, the students were encouraged to be "contemporary and experimental" (LL 9). The drafters added, presumably for the benefit of faculty and staff, that "the total organization should reflect this same Christian spirit" (LL 10). But what Christian spirit is that? Replacing the word "liberal" for the word "Christian" in fact gives the document a much greater coherence.

The Land O'Lakes statement unfortunately lacked self-reflexive awareness of how, in asserting its independence from the Church, it had recourse to a radical dependence on (quite temporary) cultural norms. It was exchanging one court of public accountability (the Church) for another. This made it incapable of speaking "uncomfortable truths" to the culture, precisely because it had declared its independence from those truths proclaimed by the Church that might challenge the culture. It is hardly surprising that those Catholic colleges and universities that followed this "extra-Magisterial" teaching began to lose their distinctive Catholic identity at an alarming rate. But in their rush to be free from the Church, they soon discovered that the only freedom they had was the freedom of dissent—which is really no freedom at all—and that in dissenting from one authority, they had only embraced another which was, in fact, foreign to the nature of a Catholic institution. The strategy, which was also an interpretation of the Second Vatican Council as an "embrace of the world," entailed an unfortunate forgetfulness of history, which meant that it was not really an embrace of *the* world, but only *a* world constructed at a particular moment in time. The Land O'Lakes statement represented an "identity crisis" for ecclesial theology in the university that lacked wisdom and piety.

Sapientia Christiana

In response, the Vatican began a patient dialogue with leaders in Catholic higher education. Two documents by Pope John Paul II stand out as particularly good expressions of *an ecclesial correction* to the culturally well-intentioned, but largely mistaken Land O'Lakes statement. The first is the apostolic constitution *Sapientia Christiania* (1979) and the second the famous encyclical *Ex Corde Ecclesiae* (1990). These statements of magisterial teaching seek to define the relationship between the Church and the university, and, by implication, the vocation of the ecclesial theologian working in any university. I draw on both to direct our thinking about the task of ecclesial theology in the twenty-first century.

The Land O'Lakes statement cannot have been far from the mind of Pope John Paul II when he opened *Sapientia Christiana* by affirming that "the Church carries out her mission of evangelizing also by advancing human culture" (SC 3). He also must have thought that a certain forgetfulness about history needed correction, for he opened his encyclical with a reminder that the university arose from within the Church: "there arose within the Church, from her earliest period, *didascaleia* for imparting instruction in Christian wisdom so that people's lives and conduct might be formed. . . . With the passing of centuries schools were established in the neighborhood of cathedrals and monasteries, thanks especially to the zealous initiatives of bishops and monks. *These schools imparted both ecclesiastical doctrine and secular culture, forming them into one whole.* From these schools arose the universities, those glorious institutions of the Middle Ages which, from their beginning, had the Church as their most bountiful mother and patroness" (SC 3, emphasis mine).

Restoring the memory of the Church as mother and patron of "the total university" is crucial to the pope's response to the identity crisis well underway in the 1970s. Equally important to John Paul II is a reminder of what the distinctive task and mission of the ecclesial theologian is today as always. The pope writes that

> those Faculties which treat of matters that are close to Christian revelation should also be mindful of the orders which Christ, the Supreme Teacher, gave to His Church regarding this ministry: "Go therefore and make disciples of all nations, baptizing them in the name of the Father and of the Son and of the Holy Spirit, teaching them to observe all that I have commanded you" (Matt. 28:19–20). It is fitting to recall the serious words of Pope Paul VI: "*The task of the theologian is carried out with a view to building up ecclesial communion . . .*" (SC 12, emphasis mine)

In great contradistinction to the Land O'Lakes statement, John Paul II stresses the way in which the Church has a stake in universities "to collaborate intensely, in accordance with their own nature and in close communion with the Hierarchy, with the local and universal Church the whole work of evangelization" (SC Section III, n.3). He also uses the language of the "common good" (curiously missing from the Land O'Lakes statement), especially "safeguarding . . . the common good of the Church," keenly aware that theology contributes first and foremost to the common good of the Church. While this is explicitly stated with respect to the complex relation of Ecclesiastical Faculties to the Church, it has a transferable meaning to which we will return—namely, that there need to be institutional ways of safeguarding ecclesial theology in any university context, perhaps even at universities that can have no explicit interest in the common good of the Church.

Importantly, the encyclical does not avoid the question of academic freedom that so animated the Land O'Lakes statement. The pope states that "(a) true freedom in teaching is necessarily contained within the limits of God's Word, as this is constantly taught by the Church's Magisterium, [and] (b) likewise, true freedom in research is necessarily based upon firm adherence to God's Word and deference to the Church's Magisterium, whose duty it is to interpret authentically the Word of God" (SC Sect. IV, Art. 39, n. 1.2). As a consequence, the encyclical emphasizes the importance of the "canonical mission" of theologians working in Ecclesiastical Faculties, establishing an important precedent that was followed up in *Ex Corde Ecclesiae* with the apparently controversial institution of the *mandatum*.

Ex Corde Ecclesiae

In *Ex Corde Ecclesiae*, more than a decade after *Sapientia Christiana*, we see an even more decisive statement. It sought to heal at the root the identity crisis that has had an enormous influence on Catholic higher education, and has not entirely abated even two decades later. From the outset, the encyclical makes the positive historical and theological claims that (a) the university itself is an institution "born from the heart of the church," (b) every university shares in "the joy of truth," and finally (c) every Catholic university has the privileged task "to unite existentially by intellectual effort two orders of reality that too frequently tend to be placed in opposition as though they were antithetical: the search for truth, and the certainty of already knowing the fount of truth" (ECE 3). It comes as no surprise that the question of truth is foremost on the mind of the pope when it comes to the nature and mission of the Catholic university.

> It is the honour and responsibility of a Catholic University to consecrate itself without reserve to *the cause of truth*. This is its way of serving at one and the same time both the dignity of man and the good of the Church, which has "an intimate conviction that truth is (its) real ally . . . and that knowledge and reason are sure ministers to faith" . . . The present age is in urgent need of this kind of disinterested service, namely of *proclaiming the*

> *meaning of truth,* that fundamental value without which freedom, justice and human dignity are extinguished. (EC 4)

What is remarkable here, especially in contrast to the Land O'Lakes statement, is that it is the Catholic university that has the "disinterested" task of proclaiming the truth. It is not the "total university" that is the disinterested servant of truth, and the Catholic university that is somehow "partial." Rather, the pope clearly states the inverse, that "by its Catholic character, a University is made more capable of conducting an *impartial* search for truth, a search that is neither subordinated to nor conditioned by particular interests of any kind" (EC 7).

Yet how could the encyclical make such a claim, and also insist that the Catholic university is intimately tied to the mission of the Church? How could it claim disinterestedness for the Catholic university, or by extension, for the ecclesial theologian? The encyclical's first part deals precisely with this question concerning the mission and identity of Catholic institutions of higher learning. In certain respects, it actually echoes the Land O'Lakes document, stating that "the objective of a Catholic University is to assure in an institutional manner a Christian presence in the university world confronting the great problems of society and culture" (EC13). But here "in an institutional manner" greatly qualifies what is meant by "a Christian presence in the university."

The pope goes on to give content to what are the essential marks of a Catholic university:

1. a Christian inspiration not only of individuals but of the university community *as such*;
2. a continuing reflection in the light of the Catholic faith upon the growing treasury of human knowledge, to which it seeks to contribute by its own research;
3. fidelity to the Christian message as it comes to us through the Church;
4. an institutional commitment to the service of the people of God and of the human family in their pilgrimage to the transcendent goal which gives meaning to life. (EC 13)

On first glance, that all sounds communal and evangelical, not "disinterested and impartial." References to "the growing treasury of human knowledge" seen "in the light of the Catholic faith," suggest a happy relation between human reason and the light of revealed truth. Furthermore, "in the light of these four characteristics, it is evident that besides the teaching, research, and services common to all Universities, a Catholic University, by *institutional commitment*, brings to its task the inspiration and light of the *Christian message*" (EC 14). The institutional commitment of the total university, in other words, is to be found in the relation of reason and revelation, not in their separation. This is the most impartial approach because it has not excluded the universal claims of revealed truth.[10]

This is also to say that what makes a university Catholic is its institutional commitment to the gospel that comes to us through the Church. As the encyclical later states, "Every Catholic University, without ceasing to be a University, has a relationship to the Church that is essential to its institutional identity" (EC 27). This stress upon institutional commitment takes its most characteristic, practical, and local form in the relationship between the Catholic university and *the local Bishop*, directly and concretely challenging the Land O'Lakes claims to autonomy.

> Bishops have a particular responsibility to promote Catholic Universities, and especially to promote and assist in the preservation and strengthening of their Catholic identity, including the protection of their Catholic identity in relation to civil authorities. . . . Even when they do not enter directly into the internal governance of the University, Bishops "should be seen not as external agents but as participants in the life of the Catholic University." (EC 28)

Most importantly, the encyclical insists on a special relationship between the Bishop and the theologian:

> [S]ince theology seeks an understanding of revealed truth whose authentic interpretation is entrusted to the Bishops of the Church, it is intrinsic to the principles and methods of their research and teaching in their academic discipline that theologians respect the authority of the Bishops, and assent to Catholic doctrine according to the degree of authority with which it is taught. Because of their interrelated roles, *dialogue between Bishops and theologians is essential* . . . (EC 29, emphasis mine)

In addition to making communion with the Bishop central to the University and the theologian, the encyclical advocates also on a wide range of topics, particularly around the dialogue of cultures, and the

10. In a different way, David Ford has been making a similar argument in the rapidly changing context of the University of Cambridge. See his "Responsibilities of Universities in a Religious and Secular World."

pressing public need for study on a whole range of issues. However, aside from the crucial issue of Bishops, the dominant theme of the encyclical is probably the one that most worried our advocates of university autonomy: *evangelization*. John Paul II writes: "By its very nature, each Catholic University makes an important contribution to the Church's work of evangelization. It is a living *institutional* witness to Christ and his message, so vitally important in cultures marked by secularism, or where Christ and his message are still virtually unknown. Moreover, *all the basic academic activities of a Catholic University are connected with and in harmony with the evangelizing mission of the Church* . . ." (EC 49, emphasis mine). Those who advocated the Land O'Lakes approach wanted Catholic universities to look like "total university life," which sounded very much like "secular university life." The pope teaches the opposite. He teaches that it is crucial that the Catholic university itself be in harmony not with cultures marked by secularism but *in harmony with the evangelical mission of the Church*. It is not just theology, but "all the basic academic activities of a Catholic university" are connected to "the evangelizing mission of the Church." This clearly would not have gone over well at the University of Berlin, and it could not have been well received by the drafters of the Land O'Lakes statement.

Though the encyclical says very little about the non-Catholic university, the pope does not deny the goodness or integrity of secular universities, and affirms that all universities delight in the search for truth, delight in its discovery and communication. The pope does not attempt a critique of the "multiversity," nor does he engage in a polemic against relativism as he does in many other encyclicals of the same period. He does, however, think very carefully about the intimate bond between the Church and the Catholic university, especially through the gift of the Bishop, and by extension between the Church and the ecclesial theologian in the university today. To think analogously about what wisdom could be gleaned from this encyclical for theologians not working in a Catholic university is an intellectual task we need to attend to. But for now it is enough to notice that the encyclical concludes with very pragmatic directives that were controversial at the time, and remain so now.

One of the most important pragmatic counsels of the encyclical was to have encouraged theologians to seek the *mandatum* from their local Bishop, following the logic promulgated in *Sapientia Christiana* concerning the canonical mission for theologians working in Ecclesiastical Faculties. It is a small but symbolically important requirement that was immediately taken up as a point of debate amongst Catholic theologians. Many refused to seek the *mandatum* from their Bishop on principle. Other theologians embraced the *mandatum*, and hoped it would provide an easy solution to the identity crisis that had faced Catholic theologians in America. For all Catholic theologians, the *mandatum* became a marker of a choice that had been made about academic freedom, and this single sentence of the encyclical concerning the expectation of a "mandate" became a hot button for competing accounts of the vocation of the (ecclesial) theologian.

Rival Accounts of Intellectual Freedom and the Formation of Conscience

By now it should be clear that I think Catholic theologians have a clear choice between Land O'Lakes and *Ex Corde Ecclesia*. It is a choice that oddly mirrors "the great reversal" that Frei talked about with regard to the University of Berlin. For some, it sounds like the choice between freedom and obedience to an external authority; but, in fact, it is simply two forms of obedience to authorities that are both internal and external to the discipline in complex ways. While the modern university has not been inclined to see itself as accountable to the Church, it has been surprisingly willing to see itself in service of the rapidly advancing nation-state, or the needs of the market and consumer culture.[11] Autonomy from "external authority" is a chimera.

Strong claims for the nature of the Catholic university does not mean that other universities cannot conceive of "universality" differently; it only means that any university that describes itself as Catholic must see that it is first of all committed to the common good of the Church, its evangelical mission, and its vision of the whole. There are certainly other courts of public accountability, but none are as *institutionally* crucial to the Catholic university as the Church—not because the university is partial, but because the university is impartial, and judges impartiality according to a tradition that makes universal claims on how parts are ordered to the truth as a coherent, organic whole (*universitas*). This holds, *a fortieriori*, for the Catholic theologian—and it is with the theologian that we can see what is personally at stake: namely, the conscience. Through a consideration of conscience that we can clearly see two accounts of intellectual freedom at work, one which is genuinely Catholic and one which is not.

11. See D'Costa, *Theology in the Public Square*.

Here our Land O'Lakes drafter would ask about the troubled conscience of the Catholic theologian who believes that magisterial teaching is wrong on some point relating to faith and morals. What if the conscience—which Thomas Aquinas tells us must always be followed, even if it turns out to be wrong—directs the theologian to oppose Church teaching? Such a question already presupposes a non-ecclesial context, and a supposedly individual set of norms and judgments; the context which has formed those norms and judgments is usually not acknowledged. To borrow from Augustine's *De Magistro*, the appeal to "the inner teacher" is not really an appeal to Christ, the Truth, but simply an appeal to some external authority other than Christ that has been internalized. The key for the theologian is to ask which external authorities they have interiorized as crucial for the formation of their conscience.[12] John Paul II states the matter clearly, "The cause of the human person will only be served if knowledge is joined to conscience" (EC 18). This is why magisterial Catholic teaching does not simply talk about the individual conscience, but about the well-formed and informed conscience. The question of the theologian's personal conscience, then, is inseparable from questions of which communion will form and inform the conscience.

In 2011, these issues came to public attention in the case of Sr. Elizabeth Johnson, a Catholic feminist theologian whose work was severely criticized by the United States Council of Catholic Bishops' Committee on Doctrine. In many ways, the Committee on Doctrine simply critiqued Johnson's book *The Quest for the Living God*, in the same way as a colleague might critique her work in the context of academic debate.[13] But, at the same time, the Bishops are not like other external critics (not least because they insist that they are not external!). For Johnson, their theological critiques are not welcome precisely because they are wielded with an authority that does not respect her creative freedom and intellectual autonomy. She rejects the legitimacy of this authority to form (or re-form) her theological judgments. Even though her intellectual labour is unthinkable apart from the Church, she refuses the Church the power to speak correctively to her. This is both ironic and sad; this should have been an

12. For a discussion of the migrations of conscience, and the political and theological importance of attending to its formation in relation to external authorities, see Pecknold, *Christianity and Politics*.

13. See the analysis of Johnson and Bauerschmidt, "Censure or Critique?" Bauerschmidt's analysis is especially good because he fruitfully implies that critique can look very much like censure rather than pastoral correction if it does not happen within a sustained dialogue in the context of ecclesial communion.

opportunity for a dialogue between bishops and theologians, to speak about theology together in a serious way that concerns the common good of the Church. Instead, it became a lightening rod of controversy in which the Catholic Theological Society of America (CTSA) stood in solidarity with Johnson and against the Bishops, intensifying a crisis within Catholic theology that mirrors the problems that Protestant theology has faced at least since the nineteenth century.

In reflecting on the controversy, the head of the Committee on Doctrine, Fr. Thomas Weinandy, Cap., lamented that "much of what passes for contemporary Catholic theology often is not founded upon an assent of faith in the divine deposit of revelation as proclaimed in the sacred scriptures and developed within the living doctrinal and moral tradition of the church." Rather, for some, Catholic theology has become "an attempt by reason to pass judgment on the content of the faith as if it were of human origin," with theologians as "judges who stand above the faith and arbitrate what is to be believed and what is not."[14]

What can be done? For Weinandy, the issue returns to the *mandatum*, not as an infringement of intellectual freedom, or as an affront to the autonomy of "Catholic theology," but as a warm endorsement of the ecclesial vocation of the theologian. The mandate should be something that honours the theologian, an "authoritative expression and endorsement of their vocation as truly ecclesial." It should be an invitation to a privileged conversation. He concludes: "Such a mandate does not demean the vocation of Catholic theologians but rather confers upon it a dignity and gravity that it truly deserves. I would argue that the mandate testifies to the church and to the academic community that to be a teacher of Catholic theology is indeed to enjoy a distinctive and valued vocation within the ecclesial community."[15]

The Ecclesial Vocation of the Theologian

There are many similarities between this particular account of Catholic universities and theologians in crisis, and the crisis that theology faced in the university during "the great reversal" that Hans Frei narrated, and that David Ford has responded to in concrete, institutional ways at the University of Cambridge. Yet the crisis is far from over. We are just becoming fully aware of the problem, and the next generation seems poised to go in a

14. Weinandy, "Faith."

15. Ibid.

new direction. The question concerns the epistemic norms for the kind of *scientia* that a theologian is called to understand and explain with clarity, precision, and beauty. Every theologian must submit—wittingly or unwittingly—to courts of public accountability, but the ecclesial theologian in the university must give pride of place to the common good of the church, especially through its most authoritative expressions in the great creeds and ecumenical councils. If we belong to a tradition of inquiry, then it is essential to ask ourselves how we are to be held accountable to that tradition in ways that the tradition has recognized as good. Otherwise we have nothing to offer other traditions of inquiry.

If we are not Catholic, we still must ask, "Is there any authoritative body of teaching that we would allow to correct us?" We each have to answer that question for ourselves. Perhaps we would say only Christ the inner teacher, or only Holy Scripture, or Holy Scripture as interpreted by the creeds or ecumenical councils, or reason, or local ecclesial communities or the academy. But we *must* answer that question concretely. Furthermore, if we want to be ecclesial theologians, we must venture to conform ourselves to the intellectual tasks of evangelization. This festschrift honours one ecclesial theologian who is not only personally committed to the intellectual tasks of evangelization, but he has done the hard work of forming the next generation of ecclesial theologians. Perhaps most importantly, he has attended to the concrete, institutional frameworks of the modern university, and sought to make them hospitable, rather than hostile, to theology as a science. In this way, David Ford has continued the vision of Hans Frei in the university. Many more hands will be needed to untie all the knots that "the great reversal" tied, but we will know how to do this work better because of him.

Bibliography

Cavanaugh, William T. *The Myth of Religious Violence*. Oxford: Oxford University Press, 2009.

D'Costa, Gavin. *Theology in the Public Square: Church, Academy and Nation*. Oxford: Blackwell, 2006.

Ford, David F. "Responsibilities of Universities in a Religious and Secular World." *Studies in Christian Ethics* 17.1 (2004) 22–37.

Frei, Hans. *The Eclipse of Biblical Narrative: A Study in Eighteenth and Nineteenth Century Hermeneutics*. New Haven: Yale University Press, 1974.

———. *Types of Christian Theology*. New Haven: Yale University Press, 1992.

Gleason, Philip. *Contending with Modernity: Catholic Higher Education in the Twentieth Century*. Oxford: Oxford University Press, 1995.

Johnson, Elizabeth A. *Quest of the Living God: Mapping Frontiers in the Theology of God.* New York: Continuum, 2007.

Johnson, Luke Timothy, and Frederick Christian Bauerschmidt. "Censure or Critique? The Bishops and Elizabeth Johnson." *Commonweal*, June 3, 2011. Online: http://www.readperiodicals.com/201106/2361288511.html#b.

Lehner, Ulrich. *Enlightened Monks: The German Benedictines, 1750–1803*. Oxford: Oxford University Press, 2011.

McCluskey, Neil G., editor. *The Catholic University*. Notre Dame: University of Notre Dame Press, 1970.

Newman, John Henry. *Apologia Pro Vita Sua*. London: Longman, Green, 1865.

Niebuhr, H. Richard. *Christ and Culture*. New York: Harper & Row, 1956.

Pecknold, C. C. *Christianity and Politics: A Brief Guide to the History.* Eugene, OR: Cascade Books, 2010.

Taylor, Charles. *A Secular Age*. Cambridge: Harvard University Press, 2007.

Weinandy, Thomas. "Faith and the Ecclesial Vocation of the Catholic Theologian." *Origins CNS Documentary News Service* 41.10 (July 2011).

23

The Shaping of Catholic Theology in the UK Public Academy

Paul D. Murray

University of Durham

Introduction

As detailed in the introduction to this volume and many of its essays and as befits the great teacher of systematic theology he is, David Ford's theological *oeuvre* covers a remarkable range: stretching from his groundbreaking doctoral studies on Barth, through constructive scriptural exegesis and major fresh treatments of theological anthropology, soteriology, wisdom, and praise, to an unparalleled textbook project that has shaped and defined the field whose evolution it was itself devoted to charting in three markedly different editions. In some respects these varied interests and more culminate in the decisive co-role he has played in the formulation and global spread of the practice of Scriptural Reasoning.

Alongside, however, these more traditionally academic modes of contribution through text and teaching, David Ford is distinguished amongst his contemporaries by an unparalleled commitment to the institutional shaping of the field as itself a profoundly theological activity. Central to the literal rebuilding of the Faculty of Divinity at Cambridge, he has invested tirelessly in the wider institutional health of the subject and of the guilds, structures, and contexts that promote the flourishing of theological vocation, with his writings pertaining to this constellation of concerns representing one of the most significant extant contributions in this regard.[1]

In turn, this essay is written from the perspective of one who has been generously encouraged by David—as also by David's fellow Anglicans, Ann Loades, Stephen Sykes, and Dan Hardy before him—to find his own voice as a lay Catholic theologian, to grow into the specificities and possibilities of this vocation; and who after many years working in various explicitly Catholic institutional contexts has been situated for the past decade in the UK public academy. From this perspective, this essay pays tribute by, in part, reflecting on the relevance of David's work to the *Shaping of Catholic Theology in the UK Public Academy* and, in greater part, by offering something of a manifesto in this regard that resonates with, plays upon, develops and re-performs key notes within David's own programmatic contribution.

As a way in to this we can take John Coulson's opening words to the 1964 collection, *Theology and the University*, representing papers from the 1963 Downside symposium on the need for Catholic theology in the British university: "Theology can choose; it can remain dead and neglected, or take the pressure of the times and live; but if it chooses life it has need of three things: a university setting, lay participation and the ecumenical dialogue."[2]

Leaving aside theology's supposedly "dead and neglected" status, the argument sketched in this essay is that *Theology and the University*'s advocacy for an explicit Catholic theological presence in the public academy remains as relevant today as it was forty-five years ago. With that, the proposal is that the unique ecology of Theology and Religion in the UK—so prized by David[3]—presents a remarkable opportunity for the flourishing of explicitly Catholic theology in the UK academy in a manner that is for the good of church, society, and academy alike, as illustrated by recent developments at Durham University.[4]

1. See Ford, *Shaping Theology*; Ford, *Christian Wisdom*, 304–49; Ford, *Future of Christian Theology*.

2. Coulson, *Theology and the University*, 1.

3. See, for example, Ford, *Future of Christian Theology*, 148–67.

4. After some years of informal related activity, in October 2007 and May 2008 respectively Durham University's Department of Theology and Religion established the UK's first permanent Centre for Catholic Studies within the public academy and the first endowed chair of Catholic theology (the "Bede Chair") since the Reformation.

From the outset it should be noted that in advocating the need for Catholic theology in the public academy, I am in no way denigrating *per se* either the various more explicitly ecclesial contexts in which theology is pursued (and in which I have been privileged to work) or the orientation of such theology relative to a supposedly more objective, tradition-neutral, academic theology. On the contrary, I am arguing that the postmodern public academy provides a distinctive home precisely for genuinely rooted, ecclesial theology of an appropriately exploratory kind not always easy to maintain in church-run institutions; a home where there is no question that cannot be asked, nor any line of enquiry that cannot be tested. That is, lying behind developments in Durham is both a strong sense of the authentically ecclesial nature of theology and of the need for an institutional space in which there is, in Newman's terms, sufficient "elbow room" for theology to be pursued in its properly critical and constructive dimensions.[5] The Centre for Catholic Studies and the Bede Chair of Catholic Theology at Durham are together geared towards securing just such an institutional space.

The essay proceeds in three steps. First, the Durham developments are situated in proximate historical perspective. Second, comparison is drawn between two differing visions of the prospects for Catholic theology in the public academy: that of the lay Catholic, Gavin D'Costa, and that implied by David Ford's work. Finally, inspired more by David Ford than by Gavin D'Costa in this regard—although profoundly sympathetic to some aspects of D'Costa's constructive agenda—brief, manifesto-like articulation is given to what the dual establishment of the Centre for Catholic Studies and the Bede Chair jointly represent and the vision into which they seek to grow.

Catholic Theology and the Public Academy: The UK Context

When I began my theological studies in 1983, individual Catholic scholars and even more so Catholic theology as a collective entity were a somewhat marginal, underrepresented phenomenon within the UK theological establishment. A combination of historic factors contributed here. On the one hand was the tail-end legacy of the established church allegiances of the older universities and their faculties of divinity. To be Catholic was to be *other* to the assumed norm and more awkwardly *other* than the Protestant

5. For Newman on "elbow-room," see "Letter to Emily Bowles," 20:447; "Letter to W. J. O'Neill Daunt," 20:476.

free churches. On the other hand, as inverted reflection of this and perhaps even more significant in terms of serving to keep Catholic theology out of the public academy, was the deeply habituated inclination within UK Catholicism to forms of separatism, wherein the Catholic minority would do its own Catholic thing. This was an instinct bred of centuries of counter-Reformation exclusivism, combined more locally with a dual history of either recusancy or mass immigration and social disadvantage. In turn, further complicating this historic instinct for Catholic parallelism and pertaining specifically to the appropriate location of Catholic theology was the ingrained assumption that such scholarship must come under direct hierarchical authority if its Catholicity were to be ensured.

Notwithstanding the still relatively low-profile of Catholic theology in the UK in the early 1980s, the period from the late 1970s through the early 1990s was also one of significant transition during which the hopes of the Downside symposiasts began to come to maturity. In 1966 John Coulson, together with Bishop Christopher Butler, launched the Downside Centre for Religious Studies within Bristol's Department of Theology, the first, relatively short-lived, attempt to found a Catholic theological research centre in the UK, with Coulson initially filling the role of an externally funded Research Fellow. When, after a few years, he was appointed to a publicly funded lectureship in theology within the same department, he was the first Catholic to hold such a post in the UK. This initiated a tradition of Catholic scholarship at Bristol that continues to the present day.

Similar stories were repeated elsewhere. In 1977 Hamish Swanston was, at Canterbury, the first Catholic to be appointed to a UK chair in theology since the Reformation, as was Nicholas Lash in 1978 the first to achieve an Oxbridge chair in theology throughout that time. Over subsequent years, Lash was joined at Cambridge by a remarkable team of other lay Catholic theologians. Similarly, in the very bastion of non-confessional religious studies at Lancaster University, Ninian Smart established a lectureship in Catholic thought to which Patrick Sherry was appointed. For its own part, at Oxford hugely influential figures such as Herbert McCabe, OP, and Fergus Kerr, OP, and Edward Yarnold, SJ, and Norman Tanner, SJ, operating out of the Dominican and Jesuit private halls respectively, established a lasting tradition of Catholic scholarship.

It was also during this period, in 1984, that the Catholic Theological Association of Great Britain was established, an initiative flowing in part from the increased numbers of lay Catholic theologians in the secular universities and providing decisive support and space for further development. By so doing the founding fathers and mothers nurtured an entire younger generation of lay Catholic theologians. As one looks around the UK academy today, far from Catholics being a marginal presence, they are a clearly visible, highly respected, and now standard feature of departmental life. So much so that Dan Hardy notably referred to the UK having become a leading centre for lay Catholic theology;[6] one, we might add, largely free of the polarized acrimony marking Catholic theology in some other contexts. This is a situation deriving in part, I suggest, from the way in which various of the founding grandees, McCabe, Lash, and Kerr in particular, served helpfully to muddy the waters around overly neatly drawn boundaries between liberal or progressivist, and conservative instincts.

In common theological parlance, "liberal" refers not simply to theological creativity but to the dissolution of core doctrinal commitments, and embrace of prevailing secular norms as an uncriticized "foundation." In contrast, with McCabe, Lash, and Kerr we have theologians of avowedly, if richly and creatively, orthodox doctrinal persuasion; theologians committed to mining the tradition in its depth and breadth for that tradition's own healing and re-expression, and in service of transformative engagement with contemporary society. The conviction is that it is the tradition that is creative; the tradition that is radical. The point is neither to reject nor to foreclose the tradition but to be, we might say, radically traditional. In this, Lash and McCabe might be thought of as exemplifying a form of Catholic "postliberalism" before George Lindbeck gave such influential articulation to the notion. In turn, their writings provide a model of good practice; a certain tone and attitude of mind that in varying ways continues to characterise the broad mainstream of contemporary UK Catholic theology.

In some ways related to this muddying of the waters and holding together of the virtues of theological creativity and theological robustness—the supposedly opposed instincts of the progressivist and the conservative—is the fact that UK Catholic theology does not split neatly down clear theo-political divides of Rahnerians and Balthasarians. There is a not uncommon concern to pursue what we might call "whole-church Catholicism"; to be open to the need both to renew Catholicism in the light of what can be learned from resources outside the Church and to offer back a richer understanding than the world can achieve simply on the basis of such resources. Two values must be held together here. First there is a clear ecclesial commitment: loving appreciation of a richness to be conserved in

6. See Hardy, "Theology through Philosophy," 284, n.114.

its fullness and communicated in its appeal. Second there is humble, honest, self-criticism: loving acknowledgement that individually, collectively, and institutionally we fall short of that which we are called to be; of that which by grace we already are, in part, sign and sacrament. Such a stance requires both the most refined critical expertise to be acquired through academic training and for these skills to be resituated, reorientated, redeemed, in the context of convicted ecclesial passion.

In closing this section, it is perhaps worth noting that, other than in the case of the Catholic Theological Association of Great Britain, the developments reviewed here occurred largely without planning. They are, we might say, graced happenings, fortuitous events. Be that as it may, they are, nevertheless, happenings that bring with them responsibilities for their nurture, long-term stability, and furtherance. Before turning to engage in planning for this, however, it is first necessary to engage the question as to whether it is in fact possible to pursue explicitly ecclesial theology in the secular academy without detriment both to the character of such theology and the integrity of the academy and the freedom of students.

Is Catholic Theology in the Public Academy a Non Sequitur? Two Perspectives Compared

Gavin D'Costa and the Need for a Catholic University

D'Costa's early-career critique of John Hick's pluralist theology of religions as collapsing radical differences between traditions to superficially differing expressions of a common underlying reality has remained fundamental to his theological vision. For D'Costa we can only sustain genuine pluralism if we take real differences between religious traditions with full seriousness. He has consequently vigorously maintained the need for an explicitly ecclesial theology rooted in the particularity of Christian tradition.

This might rightly appear to accord with one of the central assumptions in this essay. Things begin to look different, however, when we turn to his 2005 work, *Theology in the Public Square: Church, Academy and Nation*, where D'Costa turns to reflect on the possibility of ecclesial theology in the secular university. His provocative argument is that it is utterly impossible to pursue a genuinely Catholic theology in this context, for which task it would be necessary newly to construct a thoroughgoing Catholic university. In D'Costa's analysis, the secular university simply cannot tolerate theology unless it abandons its tradition-specific ways of understanding and becomes a tradition-neutral religious studies; that is, no more than the history of Christian thought and practice. If correct, he pulls the rug from under the present case for Catholic theology in the public academy.

In reality, D'Costa weaves together two sets of agenda that are best kept separate. One relates to the need to recover a properly ecclesial theology;[7] the other to what D'Costa perceives to be the need, for the sake of a genuine pluralism, to develop a diversity of faith-based universities guided by an integrating theological vision throughout all their activities.[8] Whilst each aspect is worth arguing for in its own right, it remains unclear, *pace* D'Costa, that the first can only be satisfied by the second.

By way of illustration, let us explore his argument in the fourth chapter, "Why Theologians Must Pray for Release from Exile," where the focus is on the role of prayer in all genuinely theological activity, understood as *fides quaerens intellectum*.[9] His point is that prayer and the commitment it entails is, by definition, precisely what cannot be required of students within the secular university and that, as such, it is impossible to teach and study theology properly in this context.[10] Whilst, however, it is refreshing to find the irreplaceable role of prayer in constructive theological work being so strongly emphasized, there is something of a sleight of hand going on. Three points are significant.

First, staff and student bodies in secular departments are mixed affairs. Whilst many do come not out of personal commitment but with a desire simply to develop the skills of understanding religious beliefs and practices (the theological equivalent of musicologists rather than performing musicians), many others pursue theology from a living faith commitment—as means not simply of interpreting what Christian tradition has been but of discerning what it might be today in their lives, in the church and in the world.

Second, whilst it would clearly be inappropriate to require public theology students to pray or to adopt religious practice as a condition of study, there is nothing whatsoever inappropriate about emphasizing that the texts and practices under study presuppose prayer and faith commitment as their originating context. Indeed, even on purely phenomenological

7. D'Costa, *Theology in the Public Square*, 17, 19, 69–76 et passim.

8. Ibid., 48.

9. Ibid., 112, 114–15.

10. Ibid., 1.

or historical grounds, anything less would be to provide an inadequate interpretation of the material. Through empathy students of theology, like cultural anthropologists, are required to develop a sensitive appreciation for beliefs and practices that may be alien to them. So, while it is inappropriate to require students to pray, there is nothing inappropriate about encouraging them to develop a sensitive appreciation for what prayer is and the role it plays in a believing theologian's thinking.

Third, in emphasizing the role of prayer in a believing theologian's work, too much should not be expected of academic theological studies themselves. While believing students will indeed find their academic studies feeding into their spiritual and pastoral sensitivities and *vice versa*, the immediate purpose of such studies is to form not the theologian's prayer life but their critical-constructive faculties in relation to the material under examination. Academic studies are but part of a full theological-spiritual formation. This is not to debase the valid academic components of theological formation. Nor does it mean that theology in the secular context cannot properly be pursued by those seeking to become praying, playing theologians; that is, creative performers rather than just sophisticated critics and interpreters.

D'Costa is right. There *is* a challenge here both for ecclesial theologians operating in the public academy and for the church institutionally in recognizing that a full theological-spiritual formation requires elements that cannot properly be promoted in the secular *aula*. But the character of this challenge lies not in its suggesting that believing practitioners cannot appropriately train in the university; nor again in its requiring the construction of entire new institutions. Rather, the challenge consists in its indicating an urgent need for the church to devise appropriate strategies of pastoral formation for the considerable numbers of committed lay students and teachers of theology now located in the secular university system; strategies aimed at nurturing and modelling the ecclesial vocation of the academic theologian. Properly resourced chaplaincies have a vital role to play here.

Leaving aside, then, D'Costa's stimulating if somewhat utopian vision of what a thoroughly Catholic university might look like, his argument simply does not follow that a properly ecclesial theology cannot be pursued in the secular academy. With this, neither does he attend to the ways in which his desired ecclesial confinement of theology might carry its own potential pathologies, nor the ways in which the secular academy might in fact—at least when functioning well—provide a privileged place for ecclesial theology that can help it be itself. A different vision is called for.

David Ford and the Public University as Providing Necessary Space for Self-Critical Encounter between Radically Differing Commitments

Ford shares the assumption that postmodern critiques of objectivism have shown the claim of an unreconstructed Religious Studies to displace theology to be misguided. For Ford, as for D'Costa, postmodernity reopens the way to modes of committed knowing. He also accepts that the postmodern pluralist university cannot have one integrating narrative or framework. However, whereas this is a cause of lament for D'Costa, pushing him to argue for the rebuilding of the Catholic university, for Ford it is a moment of unique opportunity that allows us to take seriously the genuinely traditioned nature of knowledge while holding such traditions together in mutual challenge and accountability rather than as hermetically sealed. As he puts it, "In place of the Enlightenment's 'neutral ground,' it activates the 'mutual ground' of particular traditions in deep engagement with each other."[11] Ford usefully plays upon David Tracy's well known image of there being three different publics for theology—the academy, the church, and society—not as three different kinds of theology situated in three different contexts, but as three interwoven responsibilities pertaining to all theologians regardless of context: to be rigorous in critical analysis; to be truthful to the religious traditions in view; to be in service of the common good.

For present purposes, the implications of Ford's vision are that in the public university Catholic theology can indeed be pursued alongside other traditions, other academic disciplines, and the total range of modes of analysis that rightly needs to be brought to bear on the critically constructive study of theology. As such, the pluralist, public academy, somewhat ironically, allows much-needed space for a theology that can be pursued with ecclesial passion in service of the church, but free from the narrowing of possibility and imagination that can, too easily, arise in church-controlled institutions. There is a paradox here: the postmodern public academy that is presumed to paralyse commitment can help preserve within a properly ecclesial theology the critical and creative functions authentic to it in mutually critical engagement with other traditions.

11. Ford, "Introduction," xvii.

Catholic Theology in the UK Public Academy: A Durham Manifesto

Given both that the Centre for Catholic Studies (CCS) was informally operational long before it was formally established in October 2007 and that there is a very considerable prehistory out of which the CCS and the Bede Chair emerged, it would be inappropriate to speak of their establishment as a birthing *de nuovo*. Equally, any talk of a *coming of age* might seem premature, particularly so if we lose sight of the long process of growing into the challenges, freedom, and responsibilities of adulthood that necessarily follows any coming of age. But we can at least properly speak of these developments as marking a significant process of maturation, and do this in a sixfold manner.

First, it marked the maturing of immediate developments at Durham University and the range and depth of partnerships that have made this possible—with Ushaw College, stretching back to the late nineteenth century; with the sponsors of the Bede Chair (the Diocese of Hexham and Newcastle, the Oaklea Sisters of Mercy, the Sisters of La Retraite (Britain and Ireland), and the Martin Ballinger Trust); with various professional associations, most notably the Catholic Theological Association of Great Britain and the Society for the Study of Theology; and with various funding bodies.

Second, beyond the specifically Durham scene, we are dealing here with a more general maturing of Catholic theology in the UK, and of lay Catholic theology in particular. Account was earlier given of the remarkable transformation that has occurred in the relationship between Catholic theology and the public universities over the past forty years and more. The CCS builds upon these achievements and provides an explicit focus and stable platform for taking them forward.

Third, these developments mark a correlative longer-term and even more general process of maturation in UK theology across the board, whereby a scene that was once the almost exclusive preserve of the Anglican establishment has hospitably opened space for real mutually critical conversation across and within diverse traditions. With this also has occurred the welcome turn from tending to view theology in somewhat abstract, tradition-neutral terms to reclaiming a much clearer sense of theology as grounded in the life and practice of diverse communities of faith; communities which should be to departments of theology and religion as industry is to engineering. This has opened the way, in Ford-like style, to overcoming any unnecessary dichotomies between academic and ecclesial theology, on the one hand, or between theology and the further range of critical, analytical resources that sail under the study of religions, on the other.

Fourth, also intertwined with this maturation of UK theology is the broader societal transition that has occurred to a multipolar world of insurmountable cultural and religious plurality. As such, developments at Durham represent one small further step in the maturing of UK society as regards recognition of the need to work towards a full and proper pluralism that does not reduce all to the same and that seeks to allow space for the challenges and possibilities of unabrogable traditioned difference to be put at the service of mutual well-being and flourishing rather than mutually assured destruction. When set against that greater ecumenism, the development of the CCS, while certainly significant, is but one relatively small step along the way, and one certainly requiring extension in relation to the other great religious traditions.

Fifth, perhaps these developments also suggest something of a maturing of the contemporary UK public academy whereby it begins to take seriously its responsibility to be a laboratory of full and proper pluralism and the negotiation of difference in service of society's good. This goes beyond viewing departments of theology and religion as just dealing in particular additional if somewhat strange domains of knowledge about religious exotica, or as just additional lucrative income streams, to viewing them as dealing in a particularly clear and sophisticated way with the embeddedness of all knowledge, practice, and evaluation in context, commitment, perspective, and presupposition. As such, these developments might even be suggestive of the maturation in some small way of the university precisely as a university—as that place wherein all disciplines require to be held in critical conversation with each other for the sake of their own appropriate furtherance.

Sixth, as noted, these developments also represent a further indication of the maturation of the UK Catholic community as a whole and its willingness now to enter into the mainstream to play its part alongside other traditions and voices in the complex, pluralist context of the contemporary UK. Whilst acknowledging the many historic gains that flowed from the erstwhile default strategy of Catholic parallelism, recent developments at Durham deliberately represent a somewhat different strategy: that of the Catholic community having the confidence to take its place at the common table, contributing to the shaping of church, academy, and society by participating in the process of conversation, challenge, and mutual accountability in the public square.

So, developments at Durham can be seen to mark a sixfold process of maturation. The historical, theological, sociocultural, and institutional ecology within which these developments are situated is itself highly suggestive of the kind of space and structuring ethos that is here being opened up, as also of the kind of activities that will unfold within it. First, in being located in the secular, public, pluralist academy alongside myriad other traditions of thought, practice, and commitment and the total range of critical resources and analytical perspectives that operate within this context, the CCS is rightly going to be a space marked by challenge, criticism, and mutual accountability. This is the distinctive gift that the secular academy offers to religious communities: to provide space for sustained critical enquiry; a space that religious communities themselves desperately need but which they find most difficult to sustain; a problem from which Catholicism is clearly not immune. Equally, in being a space for explicitly Catholic theology in clear relationship with the Catholic community, it will be a space where far from criticism and commitment and constructive articulation being seen as intrinsically alien, they are rightly viewed as necessary correlates. So yes, as situated in the public academy, the CCS is to be a space for appropriate freedom but it is the mature freedom of adult responsibility, creative fidelity, and dynamic integrity in constructive service of the diagnosing and healing of ills rather than the merely negative freedom of adolescent rebellion.

By Way of Conclusion

The temptation for theologians, as for all intellectuals, is to think that the hard labour of conceptual reimagining, testing, and scholarly exploration is all. Christian theologians, however, must constantly recall that we are in a tradition focused not upon an idea, a theory; nor even, simply, upon a word spoken; but upon a "deed," a life lived, an act performed. Within this perspective, the institutional responsibility that seeks to nurture contexts in which the health of the church can be served through appropriate critical constructive theological exploration is not merely ancillary to the work of theology proper. Such responsibility is itself already a performance of theology in its ministerial mode; in service, at once, of the good of the church, the aims of the academy, and the well-being of society. It is this that David Ford has grasped and acted upon in exemplary fashion.

The emergence of the CCS at Durham—this explicitly Catholic space with immense potential at the heart of the UK public academy—has, in no small part, been enabled by the generosity of heart that David Ford showed in encouraging this particular Catholic *other* to grow into his distinctively lay Catholic theological vocation; similarly by the cogent vision he has articulated for multiply-traditioned theologies properly belonging within the secular academy in critical-constructive conversation with each other, with the range of analytical resources and methodologies that require to be brought to bear on their understanding, and with the entire range of other disciplinary specialisms to be found in a leading broad-subject university; and, by no means least, enabled also by the infectious charisma and graced energy with which he has himself turned vision into practice on so many fronts. It was for all these reasons that David, an Anglican, was fittingly invited to present the keynote opening address at the May 2008 conference marking the formal dual establishment of the CCS and the Bede Chair of Catholic Theology at Durham.[12]

Bibliography

Coulson, John, editor. *Theology and the University: An Ecumenical Investigation*. London: Darton, Longman & Todd, 1964.

D'Costa, Gavin. *Theology in the Public Square: Church, Academy and Nation*. Oxford: Blackwell, 2005.

Ford, David F. *Christian Wisdom: Desiring God and Learning in Love*. Cambridge: Cambridge University Press, 2007.

———. *The Future of Christian Theology*. Oxford: Blackwell, 2011.

———. "Introduction." In *Fields of Faith: Theology and Religious Studies for the Twenty-first Century*, edited by David F. Ford et al., xiii–xvii. Cambridge: Cambridge University Press, 2005.

———. *Shaping Theology: Engagements in a Religious and Secular World*. Oxford: Blackwell, 2007.

Hardy, Daniel W. "Theology through Philosophy." In *The Modern Theologians: An Introduction to Christian Theology in the Twentieth Century*, edited by David F. Ford, 252–85. 2nd ed. Oxford: Blackwell, 1997.

Newman, John Henry. "Letter to Emily Bowles (May 19, 1863)." In *The Letters and Diaries of John Henry Newman*, edited by Charles Stephen Dessain, 20:445–48. London: Nelson, 1970.

———. "Letter to W. J. O'Neill Daunt (June 17, 1863)." In *The Letters and Diaries of John Henry Newman*, edited by Charles Stephen Dessain, 20:475–76. London: Nelson, 1970.

12. The papers deriving from this event, together with some commissioned essays, are to be published as Paul D. Murray and Marcus J. P. Pound (eds.), *Catholic Theology in the Public Academy* (in preparation).

PART SEVEN

Theology and the Face

24

The Transforming Power of People with Disabilities

Jean Vanier

Introduction

IN GENESIS, THE FIRST recorded words of Adam in response to God who was looking for him are: "I was afraid because I was naked and I hid myself" (Gen 3:10). Fear, nakedness, hiding. Fear is a terrible thing, yet we all burn with fear. Every human being has some experience of the fear of not being loved, the fear of loss and failure, the fear of rejection and loneliness, the fear of pain or of being with people in pain, the fear of feeling powerless.

People with disabilities experience all these fears, and are also frequently a source of fear. We see this every year when some 150 young people from different schools near our community come to visit us in little groups and meet people with disabilities in our workshops and homes. At the end of their visit each one writes down an evaluation of their stay. Nearly all of these evaluations begin with: "I was terribly frightened to come to L'Arche to meet people with disabilities." There is an immense fear of the different; a fear of not knowing how to communicate.

In this chapter I shall explore how we can begin to make sense of and face our fear of people who are different, and in particular people with disabilities, and thereby be set free to enter into relationships based on what we share—our common humanity. Not only do we discover that we are all in almost every way alike, but also that we are all beautiful people, even in our vulnerability. In some mysterious way disabilities—vulnerability and pain in ourselves and others—can help us to become more human and to grow into greater maturity. At a very deep level people who live openly with their disabilities can heal others of their fearful needs for success and power. They are messengers of peace for our world.

Basic Trust

In L'Arche we want to *live with* people with disabilities and not just *do things for* them. Many assistants who come to L'Arche stay because of a relationship that they have formed with one of the people with disabilities. They talk about how that particular relationship has transformed them and how they have been enabled to look at the world, themselves and other people in a new way. Their friends and family notice the change in them and they become a sign that change is possible. It is perhaps a small sign in our world, but it spreads like ripples on a pond.

I would like to describe what we mean by living with and not just doing for, and to explore more deeply how transformation takes place. My hope is not to present definite answers but to open doors to further reflection.

L'Arche is not alone in speaking about the transforming power of people who are weak and vulnerable. The mother of Juanito told me the other day that her little son, who lives with Down's syndrome, has transformed her family. She has three other older children who are wonderfully successful at school and in sports. Juanito, who is not successful either at school or in sports, has brought something entirely new to the family: a simplicity, a spirit of celebration, relationships of deep affection. Juanito lives in a different culture, a culture of relationship and of celebration where the joy of being together is central, and into which he draws his family. What is this power hidden in Juanito? Many years ago at a meeting of theologians held in my community of L'Arche in France David Ford told us "you in L'Arche have a good spirituality but if you do not have a good theology this spirituality will wither out." David has helped us immensely to discover a theology of people with disabilities that sustains our spirituality.

Erol

We met Erol in the psychiatric hospital in 1978. He was sixteen, blind, deaf, and living with a very severe intellectual disability. He was unable to walk. He had been admitted to the hospital when he was four years old. Never before had I met a young person so agitated and in so much anguish.

His mother felt lost in front of her little son. She had three other children and did not know what to do with this little one who was so very handicapped. She, like many such parents, asked herself those terrible questions, "Why me? What have I done wrong to have a child like this?" Parents can feel guilty, not just because they do not know how to care for and bring up their child with a severe disability, but also because they fear that a bad fruit reveals a bad tree.

Parents may feel anguish for many reasons. They may feel angry with God, or angry with their children who do not develop as their other children or do not meet their expectations. Mothers sometimes wonder if they could have done something different during the pregnancy and so prevented the disability. Parents can be frustrated by the screaming of their children. When friends and family turn away from them they may feel horribly alone in front of all the pain. Parents frequently have broken hearts.

What about Erol? Did he know that he had a handicap? Born blind, did he know he was blind? In order to welcome and care for Erol when he came to our community we had to become aware of his fundamental needs and desires.

One thing is certain, a little baby, who has just been born, knows whether he is loved or not. Babies are so weak and vulnerable, and without any defence mechanisms. They can only grow humanly if they are certain that they are loved with tenderness and seen as precious. This love is made manifest in the way the mother and child play with each other, laugh and smile together, and by the way the mother responds to the baby's needs. This communion between the mother and the child is beautiful, and a sacred celebration. The bonding between the child and the mother opens them out to other relationships. The mother experiences joy as the child relates to his father, siblings, and others. The child sensing the love of his mother feels lovable, important, and precious. When children are loved they develop trust and because of this first experience are able to love and trust others. At the heart of the growth to adulthood there must be a basic trust in self: "I am lovable, I am someone."

What happens when a child feels that he or she is a source of pain, tears, and anguish? What happens when a child is abused physically, verbally, or even sexually? The child will not necessarily die if he is not loved. Biological life is stronger than emotional life, and in spite of the pain he has ways of surviving. The child, however, will be deeply wounded in his capacity to trust. "If I'm not loved, cherished, and seen as a source of joy, I am no good: nobody can love me. I am dirty, even evil." Then the child, with all his vulnerability, will begin to hide behind protective walls.

A psychiatrist, who works in a psychiatric hospital prison for men and women who have committed serious crimes and have deep personality disorders, told me that all her patients suffered horribly as little children. If people are not cared for tenderly and seen as important as children, how, when they grow up, can they see others as important? If they have spent all their time protecting their vulnerability, learning to be strong and cunning so as to avoid pain and abuse, then they will grow up seeking to be strong and aggressive, and frequently violent. In order to be someone, they had to be tough, tougher than others, keeping people away and so creating a protective barrier of fear around themselves. To risk opening up lovingly to others was impossible.

The Erols of this world do not have in their infancy the same capacity to react to the pain of rejection as some of these criminals. Instead their response was to fall into despair and to hide behind walls of depression and silence, or to flee into the imagination. Because they experience themselves as a source of anguish, fear, and pain for others, reality is unbearable and even dangerous.

Welcoming Erol in L'Arche

What did Erol, closed up behind protective walls, need when he came to L'Arche? In order to grow and to develop, to do more than merely exist, he needed people who believed in him and believed that he was capable of giving joy and life to others. Such a belief is not the privilege of those with religious faith. The belief that we are all part of the human family, and that we are all important whatever our culture, our religion, our origins, our abilities, or our disabilities is basic to all humans.

To believe that Erol can be a source of joy and life to others often requires a personal experience. Many parents of children with learning disabilities can tell you about this paradoxical joy. It is also our experience in L'Arche. Many assistants have experienced life-giving and life-transforming relationships with men and women with disabilities. It is a mystery that people who are so disabled have so much to give. However, for their gifts to be revealed there have to be people who are ready to enter into a relationship with and receive from them. Unless another believes deeply in Erol as a person who can bring life to others, then he will only be seen as someone of no value, a non-person, a vegetable, a waste of time, and maybe an object of charity. He will be unable to come out from behind the walls that have been built around his sensitive and wounded heart. Nothing is worse than becoming an eternal object of charity, never having anything to give to others.

Erol obviously needed the support of professionals such as doctors, psychotherapists, and child psychiatrists. But Erol also needed people who liked being with him, living with him, enjoying his presence, having fun with him; people who sought to communicate with him through touch and through his body.

Our bodies speak in our tears and smiles, through expressions of violence and tenderness. Erol needed to be with people who would learn to be present to him and to listen with respect to his needs, to his fundamental cry to be seen as worthy. The pedagogy of L'Arche is to reveal to the other, "I am happy you exist. I'm happy to live with you."

Creating a relationship of trust with Erol took a lot of time. He had spent so many lonely years in anguish and without meaningful relationships. It takes time to create trust. It takes time for the protective barriers around the heart to begin to melt away. It takes time to enter into real friendship. It is a very long road for many people with disabilities to discover that they are a joy for others, that they are a source of life.

Breaking Down the Barriers of Self-Hatred

Marie Elizabeth Alacoque, a psychotherapist in Quebec describes how in her work with people with learning disabilities she had observed how many of her clients wanted more than anything to be appreciated and loved by those with whom they lived, and so they would conform to what they understood the other wanted of them.[1] Therefore, even in their relationship with her very few came to the point of trust, where they could dare to speak of the pain of rejection, of being a disappointment to the family, and even the cause of conflict in the family. Marie Elizabeth quickly found it was impossible to work therapeutically with these clients in her office. They either closed up, fooled around, did stupid things, or said what they thought was expected of them. They were not free to say what they really felt and, of course, many did not have the words that would express what they felt. Others were so locked into patterns of behaviour and being that they did not really know what they felt.

Marie Elizabeth did not understand her task to be simply that of behaviour modification. She wanted to help each person discover his or her inner person and so to be free to speak. In order to enable this she chose to work therapeutically with her clients in diverse contexts, in swimming pools, in a car, or in another apparently inappropriate place. Because she was so convinced of their value, and respected their fears and blockages, little by little they began to trust her and to speak.

Here we can see a difference between Marie Elizabeth and many of the assistants when they first arrive at L'Arche. Unlike Marie Elizabeth, new assistants may not be convinced of the value of people with disabilities and their place in society. Many of them have never met a person with disabilities. They come to help in a spirit of generosity. They are open, and often gentle and kind. They try to follow the culture of the community but still they come to do something, to do good things. They do their best to enter into communication with the people of their home. All this is good. However, gradually they can begin to use the language of "them and us"; they can begin to talk about work and holidays, holidays being when they are away from L'Arche. The physical "living with" is there but it becomes "doing for." What are the factors or events that help assistants to discover they are not in L'Arche just to help people with disabilities but to enter a relationship of trust and to allow themselves to be transformed?

The Difficulties for Assistants

It can be difficult for assistants to create relationships of trust with people with disabilities because of their own childhood wounds. These wounds of fear and rejection are common to every human heart. Furthermore,

1. Alacoque, Jane et le boxeur offensé.

we live in a culture of competition. Children learn at home and at school to do well and to be congratulated for good marks, for winning in sports. Competition can be a good thing because through it we can learn to exercise our gifts to the full and to extend ourselves. But there is a difference between doing things well, and wanting to win or to prove we are better than others.

If we do not win or are not at the top we fear that we might be considered "no good." Those who are strong and healthy with beautiful bodies and great capacities are honoured in our society. The weak are more easily put aside and even despised; they can become an object of charity but are not seen as having gifts to bring to our world. In a society based on competition there is the real fear that we are nobody unless we succeed. We must prove we are someone. Assistants carry these social attitudes, and likewise fear that they may become a nobody, or be humiliated or fail in work, in exams or in relationships.

We all belong to some group, whether political, religious, or social, which gives us security, establishes norms, and encourages us to obtain more power and better situations. A cultural pattern based on success, promotion, and social recognition can become tyrannical. Competitiveness in such a culture tends to close us off from others. The "other" quickly becomes a rival, the one who prevents our success. In order to eliminate this threat those who are different—whether through their abilities, origin, culture, ways of being and of thinking—are seen as having no value, and excluded. In order to sustain this dissociation we create divisive and protective walls around our hearts.

From Generosity to Communion

This drive to succeed extends beyond the realm of sports or finance. It reaches into our charitable and religious aspirations and activities. Assistants who come to L'Arche have been formed by the society in which they live. They may be admired for their generosity, and yet be wary of entering into a real friendship with a person with a handicap. It is good to be generous, to give money, wealth, and knowledge in order to help people who are weaker and poorer, but to be generous is also to have a certain power. We give what we want, when we want, and to whom we want.

This generosity can become a protective wall, behind which we hide. It feels good to do good things and to be admired. It is important for the assistants to be generous, and to be competent but if they remain in an attitude of needing to be *for* people, and to feel that they should help the other behave correctly, they will be unable to take time to be *with* and so to become friends. The attitude of friendship is something quite different.

Generosity can be a good starting place. As we live, work, and eat together, waste time, have fun, and pray together, generosity can become a place of meeting between those who seem to be strong and those who seem to be weak. The doing for can little by little become being with. As we look into each others' eyes something happens. There is a flow of life, of trust, of mutual recognition. Love flows from one to the other. A bond of friendship begins to grow and this friendship becomes a place of celebration and a source of joy.

The Transforming Power of People with Disabilities

To meet at the level of the heart—heart to heart, person to person—implies a shift of attitudes. Instead of living from the certitude of knowing what needs to be done and from a position of power, the assistants begin to understand that the person in front of them wants something else, that he desires a friendship built on trust. They begin to sense the need to put relationship first. Their focus shifts from the head, with all its ideas and certitudes, to the heart.

The hearts of the assistants are moved by the cry for mutual trust and love. It may be that in recognising this cry and trying to respond they are met with aggression and resistance from the person with disabilities who may be unsure about wanting to enter into a new relationship and so may need to refuse or to test out the waters. In front of this seeming rejection the assistants may feel insecure and lost, and sometimes even angry. The road to a real encounter between a person who has been affirmed by society and a person who is experienced as different and who is vulnerable passes through many moments of darkness and of pain.

As the relationship matures, each can relax, no longer having to hide their fears, to cover up all that is not strong and beautiful and wonderful. They become free to be who they are with all their strengths and weaknesses. In this experience of wholeness they discover that they are loved and appreciated. In being transparent and vulnerable they know they are truly loved and accepted. For some this experience brings an awareness that this is how they are loved by God, a love that liberates them, unifies them, and brings them to a new wholeness.

Our greatest fear is to lose, to live failure, to be humiliated. We are frightened that our powerlessness will be revealed. Who are we if we are powerless? As little vulnerable children we learned to survive in front of pain and feelings of rejection. We hid behind protective systems. We learned to succeed in multiple ways and to develop a positive image of ourselves. As we enter into real relationships some of these protective systems and prejudices begin to drop. We discover a new life in the mutuality of our relationship. We realize that we do not have to win and be the best. It is enough to love one another, and to help each other be.

The other day I asked Suzanne, a person with a disability, if she had won any prizes at some games or sports events. She said "It doesn't matter if I win or not. What is important is to have fun together." At the Special Olympics meeting some years ago, Francis, a young man living with a disability, wanted very much to win the 100 meter race. He got into the finals. During the race, another young man in the next lane slipped and fell. Francis stopped, helped the fallen man to his feet, and hand in hand they continued the race. . . . Both were last. Francis sacrificed the medal for togetherness and solidarity.

This is the beginning of transformation for the assistants. It is the beginning of a very human and a very spiritual journey. Assistants begin to see in a new light people of whom they had been consciously or unconsciously afraid, whom they had considered to be "no persons." Community members with learning disabilities begin to see as friends those who had frightened them, and furthermore to see themselves as people able to give life and joy to others. Each discovers himself as a blessing in the world. It is then that they begin to sense a new vision for humanity.

We do not have to be strong, powerful, and clever all the time! Together we can celebrate our common humanity. Witnessing the inner freedom and spontaneity of the people with disabilities many assistants are led into the presence of God. They begin to discover prayer and inner silence. The very simple attitudes of love for Jesus as a person, as shared by the people living with intellectual disabilities, reveal to the assistants that to have faith is to trust in a loving and personal God.

This transformation within the assistants comes as a surprise. It is as if a new life, which brings a new joy and peace, has been set free within them. It is not something sought after. It is something given that opens them up to all people, to all of creation, and to God. This friendship does not suppress the need for the competent caring of people with disabilities. On the contrary it strengthens this need.

Assistants come and go. During their stay many live such a transforming experience, an experience that will remain with them all their lives hidden in their innermost being. No matter what they do, most will never forget that every person is of unique value and that the cry of the weak is above all other things the cry for real relationship. They will never forget the fundamental experience of a relationship in which they could be themselves. They will bring that experience into all their other relationships, with their husband or wife, with their children, with their colleagues at work. It will allow them to live richer lives.

Friendship with People with an Intellectual Disability

A true encounter, a true relationship, takes a lot of time, and a lot of listening with more than our ears. It involves the welcoming of another into our lives. Learning how to receive from others, especially from those who appear to have nothing to give, is one of the most important things that we can do. True friendship between people who are different teaches us how to be faithful, sensitive, and forgiving of both the other and oneself. We long to be honest and vulnerable in our relationships but in order to be so we have to overcome our fears and our desire to control.

An encounter with a person with a disability often leads us into a world of relationship that many of us never suspected existed; a world of receiving from and being enriched by those whose gifts were hidden from us; a world of relationship in which we learn how to really give in a way that does not belittle the other or makes him an object of charity, but which values the other person and creates communion.

This friendship challenges some of our assumptions about friendship. We may have assumed that friends have to have similar aspirations, interests, and activities. Yet this new friendship between a person living with a learning disability and a person living without such a disability is one between people who are equally human but who have different abilities and possibilities. The bond of this friendship is not grounded in the accomplishment of great activities together, but at the level of the heart and of the body. These friends are present one to another in laughter and in sorrow. It is a relationship of mutual presence. Often without words, it can be like a moment of contemplation, or silent prayer. The gentlest moments I had in my friendship with Erol were when I gave him his bath. He was totally abandoned and trusting, and my heart was filled with a new peace and a deeper silence. We were present one to another.

Dangers in These Friendships and the Need for a Community

Daily life in L'Arche is shaped by the constant encounter with people who are vulnerable. If we are present in a spirit of generosity, then we can protect ourselves from being touched by the other. If, however, we dare to enter into mutual relationship with the other, then we too are vulnerable. We welcome the other person as he is. We listen to his story, his pain, and his needs. We try to understand his language, his cry, and his needs. We do not always know how to respond or what to do. We begin to experience our own limitations, weaknesses, powerlessness, and our deepest selfishness. At the same time we also discover that part of our being which is deeper than our "ego" and our need to be affirmed and acclaimed.

There are real dangers in this friendship. When the person who is stronger touches his own limitations, he may seek to compensate by assuming power over the weaker person. An assistant may seek to use a weaker person to fill his or her own affective needs in a fusional way, using the other to forge an identity of power and of superiority. Assistants may become bored, tired, and fed up with the people with disabilities, and with their sometimes difficult or depressive attitudes and behaviour. The energies and motivations of the assistants may slacken. They can be there but not really present.

A relationship that is only "one to one" can deteriorate or even disappear. It is for this reason that all such relationships should normally be lived in community where there is understanding of the gifts and dangers of life lived together, and the possibility for supervision. The community becomes a guarantor of the authenticity of relationships; a guarantor that the organization and the style of life are in fact of real benefit to the people with disabilities. In a true friendship neither person is "used." Each is helped to become mature and to discover their value and particular mission in this world. It implies a real presence, and a listening that not only understands the needs of the other but also glimpses their true identity and value as seen in the eyes of God. Such encounters and friendships happen more easily and more frequently in a supportive and encouraging context where they are valued and honoured.

What are the essential characteristics of a community that will favour the transformation of people with disabilities and assistants? The first and most obvious characteristic is that it be a community, not created essentially for the visible results of healing, autonomy, and integration, or good administration, but for the real happiness and growth of each person, both assistants and people with disabilities. In order to be a community where "people come first," it is necessary that all the members work together in unity, and that there is good communication between the different people serving the community, and that they value one another and enable each other to exercise their specific role. Without this unity, division can enter into the hearts of the community members.

The community needs to be a place of celebration where unity is sung, a place where each one feels accepted and has a place. A celebration is a cry of thanksgiving, and an opportunity to rejoice in our common humanity, and our love for one another. Celebrations are a sign of our unity and at the same time help foster and create this unity. Communities may begin in a beautifully prophetic way, filled with enthusiasm and joy, but if authority is not exercised with wisdom in a spirit of cooperation, service, and communion, seeds of conflict can arise and finally the administrative aspects take precedence over the vision of "people first."

The Journey of Assistants: Stages of Transformation

A community can only be really living if each person and in particular each assistant is determined and motivated to "work upon" themselves, so that they are not governed by fear, egoism, depression, revolt, and the need to prove that they are better than others, but by love and a desire to be artisans of peace and of unity. When assistants first come to a community of L'Arche they often have experience of encounter and relationship with the members with learning disabilities. Thier first transformation fills them with joy and real happiness. When this initial joy wears off they may begin to discover their own conflicts within, while at the same time be confronted by the difficult decision of whether to continue with or leave the community. This is the time that they need to start working on their own growth and spiritual journey.

As assistants deepen their spiritual journey in L'Arche they become more fully aware of the message and vision of Jesus, which invites them into a particular way of life. This way of life, if lived out in the light of the Spirit, can bring fundamental change to our societies. This vision brings about a social renewal that puts people first, and relationships with the rejected and the downtrodden at the centre. It is a call not to create a society which is like a pyramid with the rich and the powerful at the top, but a society which is like a body—a body filled with the wisdom of love and of compassion, and one in which every one has a place. In this body the weak and the less honourable are indispensable.

Gradually assistants open up in a new way not only to people with disabilities, but to other members of the wider community, to neighbours, to their own family, to all people. They become aware that every person is important and has value, is a brother or sister in the vast family of humanity, and has a history of love, pain, and rejection. They recognize that every one has a gift to offer. The transformation that began in particular friendships with people with disabilities continues to develop as assistants seek to live without judgment or condemnation of the other but in ways that liberate the other so that they too can discover their deeper self and the meaning of their existence in this world. This implies that community members are growing in a spirit of prayer, and in union with Jesus. It means that fear and egoism are being purified.

This vision of community can appear as utopian, yet it is what so many people really desire and long for. It gives them hope and motivation, especially in moments of difficulty. I believe that this type of community is possible. I believe also that communities that today seem to be closing in on themselves and becoming institutional in their mode of functioning can be renewed. Nonetheless, this vision is not static, and needs constantly to be reflected upon and worked at by people who are themselves on a road of transformation and who see community living as a transforming power in our world.

Communities: A Source of Hope for Our World

Communities like L'Arche and Faith and Light are a source of hope for our world, a world where life is too quickly enclosed in systems of hierarchy and power, while the unique value and importance of each person is forgotten. In January 2004, Pope John Paul II addressed the Symposium for the Rights and Dignity of People with Disabilities, saying: "disabled people are humanity's privileged witnesses. They can teach everybody about the love that saves us; they can become heralds of a new world, no longer dominated by force, violence, and aggression, but by love, solidarity, and acceptance, a new world transfigured by the light of Christ, the Son of God who became incarnate, who was crucified and rose for us." Our world encourages people to become powerful, but Jesus came to be with those who are rejected. The "Logos" emptied himself and took the last place so that he might be with all the downtrodden of this world. This is not a vision confined to the Christian tradition. The Brothers of Taizé organized a pilgrimage in Bangladesh for people with disabilities coming from different faith traditions with the invitation: "Our weak and vulnerable brothers and sisters . . . open a way of peace and unity: welcoming each other in the rich diversity of religions and cultures, . . . preparing a future of peace."[2] If the strong, the clever, and the powerful, instead of fighting amongst themselves for the best place, turn towards the rejected to live a relationship of trust and friendship together, a new peace and a new unity can be born in our world. Those whom society rejects can become its healers and transformers.

Bibliography

Alacoque, Marie-Elizabeth. *Jane et le boxeur offensé*. Molsheim, France: Zénith, 2010.

Communauté de Taizé, *Letter from Taizé*, December 2005. Ateliers et Presses de Taizé, Communauté de Taizé, F-71250 Taizé.

2. *Letter from Taizé*.

25

Facing Each Other

Friendship, Meaning, and Shaping a World

Micheal O'Siadhail

Face to Face

David Ford and I have faced one another as best friends for forty-six years. I want here to pay tribute to an extraordinarily generous, loyal, and wise friend. We have been deeply involved in sharing and shaping one another's lives. As always in friendships, I feel a dissymmetry, a sense that David has given more than I could ever return. Yet symmetry is a bad image for friendship, where there is no bookkeeping or need for a reconciled account. We have faced each other in trust, allowing the flow of conversation, the passing on of insights and discoveries, the sharing of friends and the back and forth of advice, comfort, or support as suited our changing circumstances and the different times of life. I offer this *homage* in delight and gratitude.

David Ford and I first came face to face in the rooms of a common friend when we were both students at Trinity College Dublin. This friend, Leslie Webb, who drowned in Brunei a few years after graduation, was then a student of the Classics and devoted much time to socializing and in particular to introducing his friends to one another. I was in my third year and David was two years behind me. David was a freshman reading Classics while I was studying Celtic Languages. As the years pass and the canvas of life widens, it seems so appropriate, almost prophetic, that we met through a friend who we remember as a great student host. Hospitality would later become, like the face, another *leitmotif* in David Ford's work.

The sociological mix of Trinity College Dublin at the time was unique. The college was still banned for Catholics, and the then less than three thousand student body was comprised largely of students from Irish Protestant schools, Northern Irish Unionists, English students who chose Trinity College Dublin in preference to what they would have termed "redbrick" universities in Britain, a small number of foreign students, and some Irish Catholics who had got special permission or simply defied the ban. Leslie Webb's introduction was also symbolic in another sense as he was the product of a "mixed" marriage, a Catholic mother and Protestant father. David had grown up in the Church of Ireland (as an Anglican) while I was reared as a Catholic. In the mid-sixties in Dublin our face to face as students, which was to become such a significant lifelong friendship, would hardly have been possible anywhere except in Trinity College Dublin.

Social Background and Childhood

Although Dubliners, both our religious upbringing and our socio-economic background differed. I was from a comfortably-off, professional, middle-class Catholic background, but David had a somewhat less well-off, middle-class Protestant background. His father and mother met in a subsidiary of Imperial Tobacco where they worked in administration. On his father's side, David comes from steady family-oriented people, originating in Yorkshire and Lancashire, and his grandfather came to work in Guinness's Brewery. His mother had an English father and a Dutch mother. Up to the 1960s, if not longer, both Guinness and Imperial Tobacco would have been "Protestant" firms, in the sense that the upper echelons would have been largely Protestant. Even in a city the size of Dublin of those years such small class differences were reflected linguistically in minor ways. To this day what David would call a flannel, for me is a facecloth.

During the Second World War it was expected of Dublin Protestants in a British company that they join the British Army. David's father George took a decision that because he lived and earned his living in what was then the Irish Free State (which remained neutral throughout the war, though that was not predictable at the beginning), he should instead join the Local Defence Force. This decision, it seems, meant he was passed over for promotion for many years after the war. Later, shortly after he was eventually promoted, he died tragically of a heart attack on St. Stephen's Day (Boxing Day) 1960.

The sudden death of his father was undoubtedly the crucial and formative experience of David's childhood. It threw David, aged twelve, into the role of man of the house, consoling his mother, sister, and brother. This event was profoundly to affect him and the directions his life would take. I am certain that because of this David could no longer take life for granted, and it opened him up from this young age to ask the bigger questions about life and meaning. This need to make sense of the world and to see ourselves in some greater context would always be a deep bond between us. There was also here a parallel as my own mother had been unwell throughout my childhood and this, combined with a serious illness I suffered, ensured that I too had a similar cast of mind.

Schooling and Student Days

David Ford was educated at the High School Dublin where he was an extraordinary all-rounder. He was not only outstanding academically but also head of school, captain of rugby and cricket, and founder and head of the school's first debating society. He entered Trinity College in 1966 as an entrance scholar and with a Dublin Corporation scholarship to read classics. I, on the other hand, had attended the Jesuit Clongowes Wood College and also been something of an all-rounder, though not quite to the same degree! We have often reflected how that sense of achievement at school affected our outlook and perhaps freed us somewhat from certain types of ambition and cravings for the symbols of conventional material success.

David showed an extraordinary energy as a student. He not only got first class honours in each of the four years and was elected a Foundation Scholar but was highly involved in college life. He was auditor of the major college debating society, the thousand-member College Historical Society that had been founded by Edmund Burke and was run along the lines of the English parliament.

Our lives here both parallel and differ. I had been active in the College Historical Society but resigned as I felt that debating and arguing only one side of a case that you might not fully support separated heart and mind in a way that was unhealthy for a poet. David typically respected the institution and tried from within to be on the side of the heart. In those days women were not allowed as members of the Society. Again David eschewed the extremes of the conservative males who wanted no truck with women and those who wanted to bring women in by protest and disruption. He wanted women as members and to achieve this according to the laws of the Society—and he succeeded after much struggle and some knife-edge votes. For him Burke's club represented something fundamentally constitutional and democratic. David was also an active member of the Archaeology and Folklife Society. In addition, in his final year he successfully took on the demanding role of editor of the lively student weekly Trinity News. Also this year he did the round of interviews and was offered jobs with, among others, both British Steel and Rolls Royce, before deciding to opt for a scholarship to study Theology at St John's College Cambridge.

Our friendship throughout our common student days was literally face to face. We would meet for what we called "conversation tennis." This consisted of knocking up unhurriedly on a tennis court with no point scoring, no element of rivalry or facing the other down. We simply concentrated on our conversation! In some ways these gentle non-competitive rallies, kept going by shots that didn't try to outwit the other but by bouncing something back and forth across the disciplining net, were a metaphor for how we would face each other for life.

The One Less Travelled By: Theology, Poetry, and Vocation

Robert Frost's most famous poem "The Road Not Taken" begins "Two roads diverged" and ends with the decision to take "the one less travelled by."[1] For all his brilliance as an undergraduate, I never felt that David really ever had his sights on an academic career as a classicist. I know in later years when asked what he would have been if he hadn't been a theologian, he replied: a businessman. The roads that diverged were the way of business and the way of theology. David chose theology, the road less travelled. The again successful years as an undergraduate in theology at St. John's College, Cambridge, would lead on to a masters at Yale Divinity School, and back to complete a doctorate on Karl Barth at Cambridge, with time in Tübingen.

But I began here with Robert Frost for two reasons. Firstly, apart from our shared need from childhood to consider questions of meaning,

1. Frost, "The Road Not Taken."

David and I faced each other through our love of poetry. Secondly, I too left a post as a lecturer in Trinity College Dublin and subsequently as a research professor at the Dublin Institute for Advanced Studies to devote my life to poetry, to take the road less travelled. We both, along two quite different trajectories, chose to follow our first love.

So often our connection was poetry. One favourite quotation was from the poet Patrick Kavanagh in his "Self-Portrait": "Any poet worth his salt is a theologian." To put it another way, the best poetry is like theology in facing up to the larger questions about our lives. Both are a ministry of meaning. One of the great gifts we gave each other was to swap two favourite poets. I encouraged David to read Patrick Kavanagh and he got me to focus on George Herbert.

I still have in my copy of Herbert's poems a list of those which David loved and sent me in a letter. David told me recently that he still had a list of the Kavanagh poems I had drawn his attention to. It seems to me in hindsight that this exchange was symbolic of our facing together both our different backgrounds and our passion for understanding and living life to the full. In some way the thoughtful propriety and the elaborate rigorous form of Herbert's poems catch something of the spirit of Anglicanism:

> How fresh, O Lord, how sweet and clean
> Are thy returns! Ev'n as the flowers in spring;
> To which, besides their own demean,
> The late-frosts tributes of pleasure bring.
> Grief melts away
> Like snow in May,
> As if there were no such cold thing.
> (Herbert, "The Flower")

Some three centuries later, Patrick Kavanagh, whose poetry was to feature in the book *Jubilate* that David co-wrote with Daniel Hardy, has an earthier, almost premodern Irish Catholic ebullience:

> Green, blue, yellow and red—
> God is down in the swamps and marshes,
> Sensational as April and almost incred-
> ible the flowering of our catharsis.
> (Kavanagh, "The One")

Just look at how both Herbert and Kavanagh refer to the face in their very different ways. Firstly Herbert:

> Therefore my sudden soul caught at the place,
> And made her youth and fiercenesse seek thy face.
> (Herbert, "The Affliction" 1, from "The Temple")

Then Kavanagh:

> The tracks of cattle to a drinking-place,
> A green stone lying sideways in a ditch,
> Or any common sight the transfigured face,
> Of a beauty that the world did not touch.
> (Kavanagh, "A Christmas Childhood")

The poetry lover in David Ford plays a large part in his gift as a theologian. He delights in tropes, which become the lens through which he focuses his theology. In *Self and Salvation*, in an inspired and brilliant move, he connected the constant use of God's face in the Bible with the philosophy of Emmanuel Lévinas. For Lévinas, the face of the other was the asymmetrical command to be seen and respected, which demands an ethical stance to the world.

Like our conversation tennis, our thoughts and inspiration are tapped back and forth. No sooner had David discovered Lévinas (through the teaching of Henri Nouwen in Yale) than he passed on the word to me. I was fascinated and the face later became a pivotal metaphor in my own *A Fragile City*. A poem called "Delight" from that collection would appear in David's *The Shape of Living*. The last verse is:

> Wine sinks its ease to the nerve-ends.
> Here are my roots. I feast on faces.
> Boundless laughter. A radiance of friends.

And so on through the years the tap and pat and volley of conversation, of things discovered, shared, appropriated and echoed as we became each other's first readers.

I know no one who reads a poem with the same delight, respect, and absolute attention as David. He brings a laser-like concentration to the poem, which picks up the nuances of both content and form in a loving close-reading. I read immediately all he writes with fascination and pleasure, though I often feel my comments are inadequate to match the depth and range of his work. But on both sides there is the realization that what we "pass" will one day be in print open to many other readers, so there can be no indulgent lack of criticism, and we have had many moments of painful truth to the effect: "I do not think this will do."

Shared Friendships and Conversations

Another of David Ford's gifts is the pleasure he takes in sharing his friendships. His enthusiasm in introducing friends, and the way no sooner has he met someone new than he mentions others, makes you feel he lives in a "radiance of faces." When I think of the number of close and trusting friends of mine who I met through David, I am both astounded and deeply grateful. Daniel Hardy, Tom Greggs, Robert Kruger, Peter Ochs, Paul Murray, Gavin Flood, Peter Scott—on and on the list goes. I do not know whether this was an ability I too had or whether I have fed off my friend's gift. I find I too soon want to feel new friends as part of a meshwork of trust. David's vocation as a theologian by its nature is more social and less individual than the artistic lifestyle. That is not to say that theology cannot be individualistic and competitive—there is a history to *odium theologicum*—but it never is for David Ford.

One of the hallmarks of David's theology has been his conversation and collaborations with other theologians. Conversations are intricately woven into the Ford theology. In *Self and Salvation*, which in my opinion is a pivotal book in David Ford's oeuvre, he finds his own very distinctive voice. He, as author, hosts conversations with Emmanuel Lévinas, Eberhard Jüngel, Paul Ricoeur, Dietrich Bonhoeffer, and Thérèse of Lisieux. I think the reason that in this book he acquires a distinct mode and tone which is both individual and characteristic is that he finds here the style that best reflects his own personality. He achieves the most daring thing of all: to be himself. He is doing in theology what he has always done in life, hosting others with magnanimity and discretion, bringing out what's best in all, mediating, attending to detail without losing the big picture, allowing thinkers to meet as friends and to grow in the light of each other.

In some ways this approach is Ricoeurian, though the Fordian voice is distinctive. They both have a range and sweep alongside a generosity and respect for others and their viewpoints. But in the case of Ford there is both a lightness of touch and a groundedness that reflects his daily involvement with the cut and thrust of institutions, the practicalities of ordinary living. I think David Ford's method is best summed up as seeking through multiple engagements with texts, Scripture, and friends a worldview characterised by wisdom and love.

In all David's and my face-to-face meetings as friends down through the years we dared to be ourselves. Perhaps once the decision is made to take the road less travelled, any false gravitas, self-importance, or concealment is unnecessary. Throughout David's journey through Cambridge, Yale, Tübingen, Birmingham, and back to Cambridge we have shared friends, thoughts, books, and experience as together we shaped a common worldview.

Shaping a Worldview

In hindsight it is clear that David Ford's outlook on the world was formed over the years by a series of expanding and deepening engagements. Through all this there are certain continuities, what I am sure he himself would describe in a favourite trope as a *cantus firmus*, or perhaps in later years as "a grammar" or a "DNA."

In his time as a student at Trinity College Dublin he combined reading the great Classics of Greek and Latin with an energetic and committed involvement in institutions and contemporary and institutional politics. It is not difficult to see how this period foreshadows his later lifestyle.

As a student at Cambridge he trained in theology. This was followed by his time at Yale, which was a contemplative period of initiation and apprenticeship with such teachers as Hans Frei, David Kelsey, Henri Nouwen, and George Lindbeck. He returned to Cambridge to complete his doctorate on Karl Barth under the guidance of Stephen Sykes and Donald MacKinnon. Another influential figure from his Cambridge student days was the New Testament scholar C. F. D. Moule.

From 1976 to 1991 Ford was a lecturer (later senior lecturer) at the University of Birmingham. In many ways this was an extraordinarily formative time in his life. It was here that the social and institutional commitment and his contemplative theological gifts combined. These fifteen years laid down patterns of engagement simultaneously with God, the church, and the world. At Birmingham he grew into the role of collegial teacher and was particularly close to his senior colleagues Daniel W. Hardy and Frances Young. During his time in Birmingham he wrote books with both of them.

On a personal level the most significant event of these years was his marriage to Deborah Hardy, daughter of his colleague Daniel Hardy. Their three surviving children Rebecca, Rachel, and Daniel were born in Birmingham. Their second child, Grace, tragically died at birth. Clearly fatherhood and family life affected David deeply, particularly in the light of the loss of his own father when he was so young. His marriage would also deepen his bond to his colleague and father-in-law Daniel (or "Dan" as he was known to his friends) Hardy.

Beyond the university he was living in a multi-ethnic inner-city parish where he was churchwarden for five years. He was active in his church and engaged in other areas of life including a housing association. This intense time of local involvement played an important role in arriving at his worldview. I know that his father before him had been warden of his local church in Dublin, and I see his wide-ranging engagement with his neighbourhood as a reflex of his father's commitment to his community, even when it cost him dearly.

Also during the Birmingham years, the friendship that he had with Frances Young would lead him simultaneously in another direction. In her book *Face to Face: A Narrative Essay in the Theology of Suffering*, Frances Young, whose son Arthur was born with profound physical and mental disabilities, wrestles in Jacob-like fashion with the brutal reality of impairment. Through Frances, David would come in contact with Jean Vanier and the L'Arche movement, which is an international federation to promote homes and support networks with people who have intellectual disabilities. David Ford and Jean Vanier became friends and David has regularly visited the original home at Trosly-Breuil in northern France. The work of Jean Vanier would later form one of the three case studies in David Ford's book *Christian Wisdom*, alongside the future of the university as an institution and the interfaith movement.

It is worth noting that during the Birmingham period David's focus remained a mix of Christian and secular. The question of interfaith engagement had not yet gripped him. He once told me that at that time there had not been anything of an interfaith nature that had excited him. All that would come later.

Regius Professor at Cambridge: Institutions and Global Aspect

In 1991 David moved with his family to Cambridge to become the first non-ordained Regius Professor of Divinity at Cambridge University. Here he and Deborah oversaw the building of a new house, which they had planned and designed with their architect, Nicholas Ray. This building in some ways was emblematic of another turning point in his career. As the mantle of his professorship fell on him, David took on a new role of leadership at this globally connected university. This period has been characterised to date by two shifts in emphasis. Firstly, the word "intergenerational" occurred frequently in conversations with David. He was in the position and at the age when the questions of the renewal and the founding of institutions became an important part of how he would contribute to the world around him. Secondly the word "global" started to feature in his conversations.

Clearly, the question of the future of the university itself as an institution was greatly on his mind, as can be seen in his Gomes lecture in 2003, "Knowledge, Meaning and the World's Great Challenges: Reinventing Cambridge University in the Twenty-first Century," and in his case study chapter, "An Interdisciplinary Wisdom: Knowledge, Formation and Collegiality in the Negotiable University," in *Christian Wisdom.*

Since David Ford came as professor to Cambridge, when the Faculty of Divinity concentrated mostly on Christianity, an ambitious new development plan for the faculty has been largely implemented. David oversaw, among much else, the fundraising and erection of a new building to house the faculty and the founding of a new Centre for Advanced Religious and Theological Studies. There have also been several new endowed posts, including one in theology and science, one in Jewish Studies, and two in Islamic Studies.

There is now too a global aspect to David Ford's work. There is a global Christian aspect through the wider outreach of Anglicanism, and he acted as an adviser to the Anglican primates during the Lambeth Conference in 1998. From 2000 to 2004 he led the primates in Bible study sessions. There is also now both a Chinese and Indian dimension to his work. He spent three weeks in China in 2000 and has visited India three times. Recently in Rome he gave the fourth Pope John Paul II Lecture on Interreligious Understanding: "Jews, Christians and Muslims Meet around their Scriptures: An Inter-Faith Practice for the Twenty-first Century."

Although interfaith matters had not featured during the Birmingham phase, in the early 1990s, David was introduced by Daniel Hardy to Peter Ochs. One of the great conversations that David Ford, alongside Peter Ochs and Daniel Hardy, founded is Scriptural Reasoning. Others have told the background to this movement in Textual Reasoning, which involved Jewish philosophers reading Talmud in conversation with scholars of rabbinics in what might be called a rereading of Judaism after modernity. Scriptural Reasoning has participants from multiple religious traditions meeting, very often in small groups, to read and discuss passages from their sacred texts, usually choosing a common theme. While it grew out of an attempt by scholars trained in modern philosophy to approach their sacred texts, it has developed into a broader movement. There is no seeking after "consensus" but rather an attempt to learn openly and honestly from others in a way that increases self-awareness. At its core this is face-to-face friendship where participants of different traditions are both hosts and guests in a "tent of meeting."

The Future

It is fascinating to speculate how David Ford will continue to grow both in his theology and in the range of his contribution to what he would no doubt sum up as to "God, church, and the world."

The major theological work that he has been thinking about for some years now is a commentary on John's Gospel. Already there have been tantalising pieces, which I'm sure will fall into the greater jigsaw. But I have known his style of working so well over the years that I know it will percolate, brew, and mature over many years. I am continually astonished at how books get written. Major books can take a decade. They seem to accumulate as he turns constantly aside to give lectures, write sermons, even write shorter books. His list of publications is astonishing. Yet the major books arrive.

I am sure that the coming years will see all sorts of growth in the institutions that he cares so deeply for. David Ford is director of the Cambridge Inter-Faith Programme with its two-pronged approach involved with both academic work and public education, dialogue, and civic work. A part of this is the Cambridge Coexist Programme, which is in partnership with the Coexist Foundation, and I assume that he will work to develop this civic domain. David has a boundless energy, an infectious enthusiasm, and a palpable integrity that galvanises others and nudges forward project after project. I am sure also that he has thoughts about contributing to Cambridge University itself and can imagine a whole new combination, even a new college, where the study of theology, interfaith engagement, and ecology could address the most significant issues of the twenty-first century.

Undoubtedly David Ford will continue to grow and his horizons will inevitably expand. Whatever he undertakes or whatever direction he goes in, his capacity for work, conversation, cooperation, and leadership will certainly continue to contribute and transform the institutions that he has helped to shape. The most extraordinary thing is that the various parts of his life, his family and his friends, his church and university, his academic and his civic pursuits all seem to fuse and enrich each other so that his life is all of a piece. I suspect that the richest fruits are yet to come.

Cross-Fertilization

I have been deliberately focusing on David's career and work. Yet I want to return just a little to the theme of facing each other. All through those various phases of David Ford's life and career our friendship, our long exchange, has continued. We are still lobbing and starting our rallies with underarm serves, still playing conversation tennis. The poet Robert Frost once famously said that writing poetry without the tools of metre, rhyme, stanzas, and so forth was "like playing tennis without a net." We always knocked up back and forth over a net. For both of us the net was to face questions of meaning, truth, beauty, and practice. Or to put in a briefer form at the centre of our play was a search for meaning and a little wisdom. For David this was done through theology, for me it was in poetry.

I have dared to call this brief section cross-fertilization; I have to trust that our conversation was, at least to some degree, that. From my perspective it mostly seemed like fertilization. There is always a risk as a poet of being self-absorbed and a lyric poet could so easily slide into solipsism. I work alone day by day and could become isolated. Yet our conversations never allowed this to happen. David had always just discovered a new book, met someone whom he wanted me to know about, or was cooking up a new trope, a new lens to view things through. There was always a new ball lobbed somewhat unexpectedly to my backhand and I had to stretch to keep the rally going.

Let me give just a few hints of how our respective journeys paralleled. I have already mentioned how David introduced me to the philosophy of Emmanuel Lévinas and how the face would became a core image in *A Fragile City*. In a similar way our endeavours to try to come to terms with the Holocaust ran parallel and I threw myself for four years into writing *The Gossamer Wall: Poems in Witness to the Holocaust*. As the range of David's connections gradually became worldwide, I too had begun to meditate on the meaning of history and the pace of change in our world and I published a collection called *Globe*. Of course, not only are we in constant conversation but, as we are almost the same age, we are also reflecting both our shared concerns and the changing environment that we are both experiencing from a similar perspective.

The examples I have given are broad themes. I want to mention just one case of what I might call micro-cross-fertilization. David came on a newly published book by Stephen Toulmin called *Cosmopolis* and passed the word on to me. As far as I can now recall in 1990, by some peculiar process I will never really understand, some of the inspiration of that book filtered into a poem in the last section of *The Chosen Garden* entitled *Motet.* It happens that a few years before I had studied harmony for a while and had been fascinated by the historical implications of the shift from polyphony to the foregrounding of melody. I also remembered David's image of the *cantus firmus.* Then David in turn took an interest in the poem *Motet* and was to use it in his inaugural lecture as Regius Professor of Divinity in Cambridge. The phrase *a long rumour of wisdom* from *Motet* was the title of his lecture, which was later published as *A Long Rumour of Wisdom: Redescribing Theology.*

Our experiences of life continue to parallel in strange ways. As I write this David is coping with the pain of watching his ninety-two-year-old mother growing feebler. Although, of course, in some ways it's a very different experience, I am struggling with seeing my wife, Bríd, suffering from the heartbreaking mental and physical debilitation of Parkinson's disease.

Conclusion: Wonder and Gratitude

Looking back on the years David Ford and I have faced each other, mutually shaping our lives and our views of the world, I am filled with amazement that such a friendship is possible and that we have managed to sustain it even though we have not lived in the same country since our student days together. I know that this has in no small way been made possible by David's gifts of loyalty, trust, and care. I'm so thankful that we faced each decade and each phase of life as best friends. My wonder spills over into an endless gratitude that I tried to capture in a poem called "Oak," which first appeared in *Our Double Time.*

> How can I describe my friend for you?
> Gentle, strong, playful, innocent, wise?
> Does that seem a paradox?
> I want like a child to fetch my crayon box—
> Red and yellow, green and blue—
> And sketch a great, broad, hunching man,
> Big brow, a smile and stars for eyes.

Or maybe I'll draw an oak with limbs that bend
Over a boy and say "This will be my friend"!

That vast and deep rooted system of an oak.
The sturdy entry of a twelve-year-old boy:
Today, my Daddy died.
He was the best daddy in the whole wide . . .
Almost as though at one stroke
Grief and pride of all in each
Hollows an anguished heart for plunges of joy.
Ein süßes Schrecken geht durch mein Gebein
"A sweet shudder travels this body of mine."

Then I sit down beside a tall young man.
There we are, our backs against the furrowed bark,
Our early side-by-sideness.
A sweet travelling shudder? O yes! O yes!
A ramifying joy? We promise. We plan.
Our scheme of years cupped on a swaying stalk.
Things to do. How we'd make our mark.
The split-openness of an acorn, naked and new.
Our daring to say "Love me as I love you."

And plans unfold in ways we'd never planned.
Overtaken by surprise, caught again unawares,
As all the expected unravels.
Still and always a sweet shudder travels
The bones, our stretching to understand,
To desire according to the desire of another
As stage by stage we climb the decades' stairs.
Dreams, tasks, troubles, secrets we confide,
Double openness of growing side by side.

Who are we? Springs, falls, branchings out,
By turns Telemachus or Mentor, father and brother,
That loyal reassuring voice
At every change or fork of choice
Steadying my obsessions, recalling in nights of doubt:
Ein süßes Schrecken geht durch mein Gebein,
That first promise we keep for one another.
An acorn rooted and ovate leaves unfurled.
My friend. An oak for all the world.

Bibliography

Herbert, George. "The Flower" (1633) and "Affliction 1" (1633).

Frost, Robert. "The Road Not Taken." In *Mountain Interval*. New York: Holt, 1920.

Kavanagh, Patrick. "The One" (1958) and "A Christmas Childhood" (1947). Reprinted in *Collected Poems*, edited by Antoinette Quinn. London: Penguin, 2005.[2]

O'Siadhail, Micheal. "Delight." In *A Fragile City*. Newcastle-upon-Tyne, UK: Bloodaxe, 1995.

———. "Oak." In *Our Double Time*. Newcastle-upon-Tyne, UK: Bloodaxe, 1998.

Toulmin, Stephen. *Cosmopolis: The Hidden Agenda of Modernity*. Chicago: University of Chicago Press, 1992.

Young, Frances. *Face to Face: A Narrative Essay in the Theology of Suffering*. Edinburgh: T. & T. Clark, 1990.

2. Extracts reproduced by kind permission of the Trustees of the Estate of the late Katherine B. Kavanagh, through the Jonathan Williams Literary Agency.

26

"Playing Face to Face"[1]

Deborah Hardy Ford

"Engrossed in each other's chance"

IT WAS SUPPERTIME IN the Hardy house when David F. Ford first entered my consciousness. We were gathered around the kitchen table on an otherwise very ordinary school evening. My father was late home from work, so the rest of us had already tucked in. I have no memory of at what stage he finally arrived, but what I can still hear as if it were yesterday is the smile in his voice as he walked in announcing: "We've just appointed a bright young spark from Dublin! His name is David Ford." (My father was a lecturer in theology at the University of Birmingham).

At some level, I wasn't all that bothered: at fifteen, I was much more captivated by adolescence than whatever it was that went on in his faculty. And although I was quite intrigued by "God," I had no interest yet in this thing called "theology" that took so much of my father's time and attention.

So what really struck me was the energy and delight in my father's voice (known more for his critical comments than for spontaneous outbursts of joy): he wanted us to realize and share in his excitement and wonder that something deeply significant had begun: something very

1. I am indebted to Micheal O'Siadhail and his poem "Session" for the title and many of the subtitles of this essay. O'Siadhail, *Globe*, 115–16.

good. He was being given a companion with whom to share and develop his interest in modern theological thought.

But it took many years for theology to begin to come alive for me. I first dipped my toe in on a subsidiary university course ("An Introduction to Theology") with David Jenkins (later bishop of Durham), but it followed the "via negativa" so uncompromisingly that I was left with not the slightest notion of who or what God or theology might be about. In desperation (exams looming) I turned to my father for help: "What *is* theology?" and he answered simply: "Theology is 'Who is God?' and 'What are God's purposes here?'"

The next stage in getting to know David was through his voice. From time to time he would phone the house and, in contrast to other members of the faculty (who would immediately ask, "Is Dan there?"), David would ask: "Who's that I'm speaking to? Oh, Deborah! How are you?" I found it slightly disconcerting, but was also moved by his warmth and the soft lilt in his voice (which I couldn't quite place, but put somewhere "mid-Atlantic").

When we finally "met" face to face, years later, this was what I first loved about him: David was always so interested in what I (and others) thought or felt about things; he made it seem as if it (whoever or whatever "it" was) really mattered.

We were each as surprised as the other to find ourselves rapidly swept up into marriage and saying "yes" to going deeper into the "who" of God and God's purposes together for the future.

It is impossible here to do justice to the many people and scenes that have made up our lives since: the places; homes; buildings; gardens; children; animals; friends; family; jobs; games; colleagues; communities; meals; conversations; churches; travels; cultures; books; writings; hopes; fears; deaths and births. Rich years filled with hope, joy, and fulfilment, as well as times of deep barrenness, loss, and pain. Hospitality has been central and we have a flow of fascinating people through our house, enabling the overlap and sharing of friends, as well as keeping space for us to develop intense conversations and relationships independently with others.

Although theology was already in each of our "bones," it took some years for us to find a language with which to share and let it grow between us.

The death of our second child, Grace, marked a crossroads in our life together and was the beginning of years of grappling and not-knowing, which were hard to share and sustain together. David often seemed to be in a very different place to me: partly, perhaps, because he had already faced some of the big questions of theodicy and providence (his father died very suddenly when he was twelve years old), but he was also much more into "praise" and trusting and celebrating the goodness, abundance, and generosity of God than I was able to be.[2]

As we left Birmingham for Cambridge (David had said, "Oh don't worry—I haven't got a hope of getting *that* job"), David had special bookmarks made by Chip Coakley, printed with his favourite biblical verse, which he gave as a farewell to our friends:

> *hoti ho theos ho eipōn Ek skotous phōs lampsai hos elampsen en tais kardiais hēmōn pros phōtismon tēs gnōseōs tēs doxēs tou theou en prosōpō Iēsou Christou.* (2 Cor 4:6)[3]

Meanwhile I was crying, "Oh God, where *is* your face?" And no matter how hard I (or they) tried, the theological answers/explanations people offered did not really help. One of the few things we found did help was a little book by Nicholas Wolterstorff, *Lament for a Son.* It helped because it didn't offer any easy answers or solutions; it simply grappled very honestly with the stark questions and feelings of grief and loss in relation to the person(s) of God. We found the friendship and work of Frances Young, Jean Vanier, and the L'Arche communities deeply resonant, too. But theology was still something I saw as "David's" and/or "my father's" (although it was so exhilarating, all-absorbing, and life-giving that I often secretly wished that I could be part of it too).

Out of the depths of these years, I had a very clear call to priesthood. It was simultaneously a complete shock and a "coming home," that suddenly made such sense. Again, until then (partly because it had not been an option for women in the Church of England, but partly because it was the *last* thing I was ever going to do) it had been "my father's" vocation—and possibly David's too (although when David was offered the chair as Regius Professor of Divinity at Cambridge, he was clear that

2. He spent much of our extended honeymoon/sabbatical writing *Jubilate*, the book which he and my father had conceived together over many years. I was astonished to meet a theologian who could write so easily and fluently; when he said "I'm going to write x today"—he did!

3. "For it is the God who said, 'Let light shine out of darkness' who has shone in our hearts to give the knowledge of the glory of God in the face of Jesus Christ."

ordination was not his calling and that he would be much freer to speak to the Church as a layman).

"Listening as never before"

This opened up a whole new joint world. Despite initial dreads, I soon found that (in spite of myself) I, too, *loved* theology; I relished rapidly and repeatedly being out of my depth and struggling to find new categories within which to do justice to the God who says "I am who I am and I shall be who I shall be" (Exod 3:14).

The Anglican Franciscans (in St. Bene't's Church, Cambridge) introduced us to the art of "intertextuality" in preaching: letting the lectionary texts "read each other." At the same time, "SR" (Scriptural Reasoning) was finding its form, so David and I (often on our own, but often with others—Peter Ochs, Vanessa Ochs, Steve Kepnes, and Aref Nayed) began to look at texts together. The spirit in which it was done was all-important: letting the texts read us and our lives as we tried to let them read and open up the other(s) in a serious, yet playful and imaginative mood of enquiry (primarily in David's "interrogative," "subjunctive," and "optative" moods of faith/theology[4]).

There was a coming together of our backgrounds: literature (Classics and English), as well as language, and we delighted in the etymology, translation, and intricacy of words, metaphors, and images. We began to study and do theology through other texts too, with long hours listening to and reading Dante's *Divine Comedy*, Milton's *Paradise Lost*, Homer's *Odyssey* and *Iliad*—sometimes sitting in deckchairs, interspersed with cream teas at the Orchard in Grantchester; sometimes at the Lake (the Hardy summer home in Connecticut), but mostly at home in Cambridge.

I have become more and more convinced that the "split" implied by the notion of "practical" or "pastoral" theology is false. Doing theology with my father and with David has shown that good theology is always accessible and "applicable," however abstract or conceptual it might be. The issues and questions we have brought to different texts have often grown out of my work as a psychotherapist, spiritual director, and chaplain in acute and forensic mental health. They are often sermon-oriented as one (or both) of us prepares to preach, and again, the key thing is for us to try to remain as open as we can to the texts with their tensions and obscurities, and to resist the temptation to find premature resolution or closure.

4. Ford, *Christian Wisdom*, 45–51.

Till We Have Faces

One of the texts David and I have read and been gripped by in recent months is C. S. Lewis' last novel *Till We Have Faces*. It is a book I have found particularly interesting in terms of its genre and themes of imagination, loving, seeing, hearing, and believing in relation to God.[5]

This is partly thanks to Murray Cox, who first introduced me to the book, and whose work on the transformative potential and nature of metaphor has been formative in my own thinking and practice. His friendship and conversation with David and me opened up vast new areas and overlaps in our thinking and doing theology together.[6]

Cox (with his co-author the neuroscientist Alice Theilgaard) describes how, through containing elements of the "known" and the "unknown," metaphor helps to "bridge the gulf" between that which can be understood and that which is beyond understanding. Appealing simultaneously to both sides of the brain (the "rational" and the "feeling/sensing") and to different levels of psychic functioning, it facilitates the linking of different psychic experiences, while also enlarging the reflective capacity of both therapist and patient to recognize that they are part of a much bigger story. In its rich and uninhibited use of metaphor and association, the "Aeolian mode" of therapy (resting on *poiesis*: "making/creating," rather than logical/rational analysis) is "catalytic, spontaneous, and enabling, rather than predetermined and reductive."[7]

Sadly, Murray's death stopped him taking this further ("beyond" Shakespeare), through exploring the "amending imagination"[8] of the Bible (he had begun to work on a book on "Secrets" with David). But Coleridge had already done so. For Coleridge, it is imagination in its fullest, most "primary" sense that takes us deeper into reality: beyond the realm of the intellect, deeper into the "who" of the infinite "I am" of God. Lewis was on to this, too, in understanding myth (along with his friend Tolkien) as something of divine origin, expressing a deep, universal dimension of reality, through "a real though unfocussed gleam of divine truth falling on human imagination. . . . Myth hits us at a deeper level than our thoughts or even our passion, troubles oldest certainties till all questions are reopened,

5. For a sensitive and thorough reading of this text, see Schakel, *Reason and Imagination in C. S. Lewis*.

6. Cox, *Mutative Metaphors*, 98–123.

7. Pfafflin, *In Memoriam*.

8. The subtitle of Cox and Theilgaard's book: *Shakespeare as Prompter*.

and in general shocks us more fully awake than we are for most of our lives."[9] And this is the form that he chooses for *Till We Have Faces.*

Both Lewis and Coleridge were concerned not simply with the creative process itself, but with its source—its Author.[10] In 1894 Rankin preached:

> It is not the book, but the Author who finds Coleridge in the depths of his being. It is the ethical revelation of God in the Bible that gives its grip upon man's nature and its life and power in us is partly owing to our own attitude to its Author; to the moral hurt of our nature. . . . The conscience is man's deepest part. No thoughtful man can read the Bible indifferently; can read it intellectually, even. He must read it ethically . . . so that he is compelled to say with the Psalmist "O Lord, thou hast searched me out and known me." It is the eye of the Omniscient One penetrating into the very depths of the soul. . . . This ethical character of both the Bible and of Shakespeare appeal only to our moral sense. Knowledge of God is neither intellectual nor ethical; . . . they are both preparatory to something higher and better . . . that God is. Is what? Is Love![11]

David says, "I discover what I think when I write."[12] Writing was vital for Lewis, too, and his writings mirror the "mutative" and "therapeutic" process of metaphor and imagination as the tension between rationality and imagination gradually become reconciled within him—from a position where the two stances are very "split," to their increasing juxtaposition (in *Till We Have Faces*) and eventual integration (in his final work *Letters to Malcolm*). Lewis also wrote "in conversation" with others; Joy Davidman (whom he went on to marry the following year), was the pivotal partner in *Till we have Faces* (which he finally wrote in just three months, only a few days after "kicking ideas around" with her).[13]

9. Schakel, "Till We Have Faces," 288.

10. Otherwise, as in the current flurry and popularity of the neuro-scientific research/understanding in relation to the mind and human being (for example, Iain McGilchrist's *The Master and His Emissary*), the true "source" of meaning and purpose is missed, leaving those seeking (and whose instinct is perhaps very sound) "thirsty."

11. Rankin, "Knowing God by Love," 416. Rankin adds: "Coleridge writes that the 'great speculative differences' involved in the inspiration of the scriptures fade into nothing—if taken as all religion ought be practically thus-inspired."

12. In conversation together.

13. Schakel, "Till We Have Faces," 281.

The main shift in Lewis' writing seems to have coincided with his conversion to Christianity—a time when he was getting into the "who" of God: firstly as simply "God" and then as the God revealed in the person of Jesus Christ: "I was driven to Whipsnade one sunny morning. When we set out I did not believe that Jesus Christ is the Son of God, and when we reached the zoo I did. Yet I had not exactly spent the journey in thought. Nor in great emotion. . . . It was more like when a man, after long sleep, lying motionless in bed, becomes aware that he is now awake."[14] He continued to write in an "apologetic" form of dialectic for a number of years (perhaps because rationality had played such a part in his conversion) until he began to grow in confidence about the role of the "subjective" in humans' perception of reality (and God) and the need for "imagination" to help bridge the "gap that reason cannot fill."[15]

I would like to now explore some faces that have captivated me while thinking about this essay: three are "contemporary" faces and the others are some of the more "universal" faces described in Lewis' final novel. I consider how they might each "read" and enlighten the other, and what they might have to say to us about the dynamics of self and God in the Spirit.

Overview

Lewis' version of the myth of Psyche is set about 200 years B.C. in an imaginary land called "Glome": a pagan city and culture, bordering on one side with the "Greeklands" (the world of rationality, causality, and clarity) and on the other with the Grey Mountain, the home of the goddess Ungit and her son (the world of imagination, the gods, and dark mystery).

The main character (the writer and "I" of the story) is Orual, who begins with her complaint against the gods. In Part 1 she tells her story, as she understands it so far, with an account of her passionate and overwhelming love for her half-sister Psyche, to whom she assumes the role of "mother." When Psyche is sacrificed on behalf of Glome in an attempt to appease the gods, Orual cannot bear to let her go. She refuses to believe that Psyche could find happiness in someone else (Psyche's new husband, the god of the Grey Mountain). When her father dies, Orual becomes Queen of Glome for many years, but goes on blaming the gods for "tantalising" her, taking Psyche away, and feeling that they have been completely

14. Lewis, *Surprised by Joy*, 184.

15. Schakel, *Reason and Imagination in C. S. Lewis*, 88–182.

unjust: "I say the gods deal very unrightly with us. For they will neither (which would be best for us all) go away and leave us to live our own short days to ourselves, nor will they show themselves openly and tell us what they would have us do . . ."[16]

In the second part of the novel Orual reinterprets her story in the light of a growing self- awareness and insight about herself (including how possessive and controlling her love for Psyche and others has become) in a series of significant events and encounters. She begins to own and "face" her self, becoming more and more open to the perspectives and opinions of others and the reality of her deeper fears, motives, and distortions, and is finally able to remove the veil with which she has tried to conceal her "ugliness." The more the unconscious becomes conscious in her, the more she is able to perceive the realm of the spiritual and the gods and discovers the answer for which she has been looking—initially, through voicing and hearing the inadequacy of her own judgment in the presence of others. Then her ultimate moment of revelation is through meeting her true Judge in person: "the most dreadful, the most beautiful, the only dread and beauty there is, was coming. . . . I cast down my eyes."[17] As she looks down, she sees herself reflected in a pool standing next to Psyche and realizes and hears for the first time that she, too, is loved: "I ended my first book with *no answer.* I know now, Lord, why you utter no answer. You yourself are the answer. Before your face questions die away. What other answer would suffice?"[18]

Three Faces

"Leila"[19]

Leila is a young woman (in her early twenties) whom I have come to know in my role as chaplain in a medium secure psychiatric hospital. Her face is always covered by a large grey "hoodie" and for many months she gave me a very wide berth, as she weighed me up: watching and listening to my encounters with others. But over time she has gradually begun to relate, wanting me to see the deep and extensive scars that cover her face and body, and hear how she set fire to herself a few years ago. She says she thoroughly intended to kill herself, but could not help crying out because

16. Lewis, *Till We Have Faces,* 258.
17. Ibid., 319.
18. Ibid.
19. I have changed her name.

of the pain (which she had completely underestimated) and staff immediately came to her rescue and put out the flames. She suffered severe sexual abuse as a child and, although she has occasional contact with her father and stepmother, the person she most longs for is her mother, who has refused to have any contact with her since the fire. Leila says: "She thinks I'm too repulsive now."

What I see is the light in her clear blue eyes and the beauty of her smile, but that seems to be of little comfort to Leila. Like Orual, after betraying Psyche's trust, (through manipulating her into betraying her husband and into revealing his face before he chooses to do so freely), Leila is convinced that she is ugly "inside" and is filled with self-hatred, guilt and shame, unable to live with the consequences of her betrayal and deception of herself and of God's image in her.

When Psyche agrees to betray her husband, she says she does so, "not for any doubt of my husband or his love. It will only be because I think better of him than you. He cannot be cruel like you. I'll not believe it. He will know how I was tortured into my disobedience. He will forgive me . . ."[20]

Leila, however, is unable to conceive that either she or anyone else could find her forgivable. When we talk of a God whose love goes even deeper (and that physical beauty is not all that beauty is about), she listens and seems to raise hope fleetingly, before retorting dismissively: "If God loves me, why did he make me set fire to myself, then?" Some part of her believes that God is responsible for making her "ugly" and for not waving a magic wand to make her "beautiful" again. She cannot (yet) hear what's at the heart of her complaint or hold onto the "Good" being strong enough for her to work through the pain, anger, and loss of her grief and shame. Like Orual, she is unable (yet) to hold together the good and the bad: "You won't understand the wonder and glory unless you listen to the bad part. It wasn't very bad you know" (Psyche says later, to Orual, who replies, "It's so bad I can hardly bear to listen").

For years Orual, too, lives behind a veil, trapped in a similar refrain against the gods: "I was my own and Psyche was mine and no one else had any right to her. . . . You stole her to make you happy, did you?"[21] When Psyche is exiled, it is as if a part of Orual is lost, too. Like Leila, she defends against her grief and vulnerability by burying it: "I did and did and did . . . the Queen of Glome had more and more part in me and Orual had less and less. I locked her up and laid her asleep as best I could somewhere deep down inside me; she lay curled there. It was like being with child but

20. Ibid., 175–76.

21. Ibid., 235.

reversed, the thing I carried in me grew slowly smaller and less alive. . . . I became something very mysterious and awful."[22]

At times, Leila's dread of being deceived in raising hope in a better reality is echoed in moments in Psyche's journey, too. Psyche has been able to imagine and trust in the Good since her early childhood, but even in her times of intense joy (such as meeting her lover) she experiences fear of disappointment: "All the time I was afraid there might be some bitter mockery in it and that at any moment terrible laughter might break out . . . but I was wrong, sister. Utterly wrong. That's part of the mortal shame."[23]

Despite this fear, Psyche's stronger capacity to imagine and to wonder enables her to recognize and welcome the truth of what happens to her. Faced with Orual's deep resistance to her story, she exclaims "Have you no wonder?"[24] Like Orual, Leila seems to lack wonder; her thinking is literal and concrete; it is almost impossible for her to imagine, dream, or conceive of an alternative hope or reality. Within a medical management model, and its tendency to "pathologize" and idealize individuality, rationality, and materiality, Leila is trapped and unable (as yet) to find a language and story within which she might make sense of the dark places within her. Orual confronts the same limits; she struggles to believe and hold on to what she has seen with her own eyes, but despite Psyche's warnings, the voice of rationality—personified in "the Fox"—is still more powerful in her.

At this point in the stories of both Leila and Orual, there is a sense of the presence of Job's "false comforters"—very plausible in their own (clear, logical) terms, but also very limited by their inability to be open to the otherness and mystery of God.[25] As the Priest puts it: "Holy places are dark places. It is life and strength, not knowledge and words, that we get in them. Holy wisdom is not clear and thin like water, but thick and dark like blood."[26]

At some level, Leila is perhaps beginning to face what she has done ("I was very ill when I set fire to myself, you know") but at other levels it is too unbearable. She still has a long way to go in the process of remorse Cox describes in his work.[27] Perhaps she still needs to veil and protect her sense and image of her self, with her hoodie. Neither therapy nor "the gods" are

22. Ibid., 237.

23. Ibid., 123.

24. Ibid., 114.

25. Barth, *Church Dogmatics* IV/3.1, 457–61.

26. Lewis, *Till We Have Faces*, 58.

27. Cox, *Remorse and Reparation*, 27

about the ruthless stripping away of our defences: as Jesus says tenderly to his disciples "I have still many things to tell you, but you cannot bear them now" (John 16:12–13). As Orual is all too aware: "human kind cannot bear much reality";[28] but Orual has a growing sense of openness to "but what if I had been wrong. . . . A real god? . . . was it impossible?"

A Mother and Her Baby

The second contemporary image of the face that I want to bring into play is the face-to-face relationship between a mother and her baby, captured in a film documentary "Help Me Love My Baby."[29] In an opening scene, Izzy (six months) is shown lying alone on her back in the middle of the living room floor while her mother, Zoe, stands at a distance keeping a vague, but instrumental, watch. Izzy's face and head are constantly on the move, searching, as if to engage with someone or something; but Zoe's face is anxious, drawn, and looks rather "dead." Izzy is Zoe's second baby, and although there were no problems after the birth of her first child (now about six years, and with whom she has a good relationship), this time round Zoe is depressed, feeling angry and resentful towards Izzy, and is struggling to love and care her.

She describes how, when Izzy was born six weeks prematurely (with jaundice), she felt an overwhelming sense of guilt. When asked "What was it like when you first saw Izzy?" She says "I felt numb. . . . There was no connection between us." Zoe was terrified of picking her baby up: partly for fear of hurting her (because she was so small), but also because she felt so guilty—feeling so responsible for her prematurity and jaundice, that it somehow confirmed that she was a bad ("ugly") person.

At the beginning of the film (six months later), Zoe has sought the help of a parent-infant therapist to help her face herself and her relationship with Izzy, and so has already begun to take responsibility about her failures ("ugliness").

Over a period of a year, the therapist works with Zoe and Izzy together, trying to understand who and what of Zoe's own story might be being replayed and contributing to the present difficulties between them. At the same time, she encourages Zoe to hold Izzy in her arms and to cuddle and look at her face (rather than keeping her at a distance). At the beginning it is almost unbearable: even when their faces are "in range," Izzy

28. Eliot, "Burnt Norton," in *Four Quartets*, 190.

29. Channel 4, first shown in 2009.

avoids her mother's face and look at all costs and this perpetuates a vicious circle where both mother and baby perceive their (and the other's) love as rejected, and themselves as a disappointment or "failure." It is hugely costly for Zoe to keep turning her face towards her baby, and only possible through the patient understanding, acceptance, and encouragement of the therapist. Zoe both longs for intimacy with Izzy and dreads what Izzy might need and demand of her if she lets her get close. Her greatest fear is that she will end up having to raise a "clingy, dependent child."

"Clingy, dependent child" seems an apt description for Orual at points in her story. Her early descriptions of her love for Psyche (and the Fox) have a carefree innocence about them, but there is a radical change when it is threatened by Psyche's sacrifice. Her love becomes more demanding, controlling, and possessive of those objects she loves and depends on for her sense of herself. She is no longer able to see Psyche for who she is: she can only see her in terms of her own needs. Her economy of love is thoroughly competitive.

One of the things that is most transformative in the relationship between Zoe and her baby is Zoe's recognition and acceptance that parts of her still need "mothering" too. As these are gradually understood, met, and held by the therapist, she is increasingly able to contain, accept, and forgive herself and to tolerate Izzy's needs. And as the therapist helps her to reinterpret and reflect on her own story and dynamics, she is increasingly able to see and let Izzy be fully her self.[30]

Orual chooses to "begin my writing with the day my mother died"; she wants her readers to know the significance this has held in her life and in the shaping of her "complaint" ("You lure and entice. . . . Those we love best, whatever's most worth loving—those are the very ones you'll pick out").[31] And although Psyche's mother has also died, Psyche has been the subject of Orual's "maternal reverie"[32] since the day of her birth. She

30. Compare how, when Orual sees and then finally meets Psyche face to face at the end of the book, Psyche has/is not suffering nearly as much as Orual has feared:

"'But how could she—did she not really—do such things and go to such places—and not . . . ? But Grandfather, she was all but unscathed. She was almost happy.'

[Fox replies:] 'Another bore nearly all the anguish.'

'I? Is it possible?'

'That was one of the true things I used to say to you. Don't you remember? We're all limbs and parts of one Whole. Hence, of each other. Men, and the gods, flow in and out and mingle.'

'Oh, I give thanks. I bless the gods . . .'" Lewis, *Till We Have Faces*, 311–12

31. Ibid., 301. It is worth noting that Lewis's own mother died when he was a child.

32. Bion, *Second Thoughts*, 116.

knows she is loved and is secure enough to sustain her sense of self when they are separated, and to trust that the god to whom she is being sacrificed is good. But Orual has not had that experience of being utterly loved, and it is still too soon for her to be able to let go and trust others to be free in their response.

By the end of the film, Zoe and Izzy have fallen in love. Beauty and intimacy grows between them, as they trust and delight in the to and fro of light and love in each other's faces. Izzy (now eighteen months) is still anxious when she is separated from Zoe, and needs to cling tight when they are reunited, but Zoe is now able to embrace and even welcome this, knowing that Izzy will gradually grow in a sense of her presence, which will one day sustain her even when she is absent.

In a pivotal moment, Orual (now Queen and almost in spite of herself) decides to set her close friend and mentor, the slave Fox, free. The full potential of this moment only dawns on her as she hears others describing what it will be like without him: "'Grandfather!' I cried, no queen now; all Orual, even all child. 'Do they mean you'll leave me? Go away?' . . . And now this game of queenship . . . failed me utterly . . . I might have to live without Fox. . . . [H]e had been the central pillar of my whole life, something (I thought) as sure and established, and indeed as little thanked, as the mere earth."[33]

In her panic, she begins to doubt; but Fox has compassion and sacrifices his freedom out of his love for her. The effect is a radical change in Orual: "The freeing of the fox, though I had done it myself, felt to me like another impossible change; . . . the whole world—all the world I knew—had fallen to pieces. It was so new and strange, that I could not that night, even feel my great sorrow. One part of me tried to snatch it back . . ."[34]

Choosing to risk and trust rather than possess and control, Orual can begin to discover the meaning of "chosen." As the Fox turns his face to her freely in love (just as Zoe does to Izzy), Orual finally begins to trust and let go. As Orual follows in Psyche's footsteps and gives up her self in service of another, her spiritual senses are awakened; and although for a long time she is still tormented over what she has done to Psyche, she is increasingly open and able to hear and see things in new ways. And the more she can face the parts of herself that she is ashamed of, the more they can be transformed by the gods: "How can they meet us face to face until we have faces?"[35]As she risks going deeper into the "Psyche" part of her

33. Lewis, *Till We Have Faces*, 216.

34. Ibid., 219.

35. Ibid., 305.

self, Orual discovers that the answer to her rational "how's and whys" are met in a "who": "And then at last, for a moment, I saw him. Now I knew it was he, not it, I wasn't the least afraid . . ."[36]

"Mathias"[37]

The last contemporary face I want to explore briefly is the face of the son of one of the Chilean miners (trapped underground for sixty-nine days), eagerly awaiting his father's reappearance. Grinning from ear to ear at the prospect of the sight of his father, Mathias' face was broadcast around the world. About seven years old, he is hardly able to contain his excitement (much less stand still), his whole body quivering as the rescue "cage" inches its way towards the surface. Then suddenly his face crumples and he turns away. He is overwhelmed.

I know no more of this boy's story, but even in this glimpse, there are resonances with moments in *Till We Have Faces.* When Psyche first sees her husband, she experiences a sense of deep and unbearable shame at her own mortal nature. Then, after betraying Psyche's trust in her (and hearing the dreadful sound of her weeping) Orual too, is filled with a sense of shame that is so deep she cannot yet bear it:

> I was not left free. There came as if it were a lightning that endured; . . . this great light stood over me as still as a candle burning in a curtained and shuttered room. In the centre of the light was something like a man, . . . though this light stood motionless, my glimpse of the face was as true as a flash of lightning. I could not bear it for longer. Not my eyes only, but my heart and blood and very brain were too weak for that. A monster—the Shadowbrute that I and all Glome had imagined—would have subdued me less than the beauty this face wore. And I think anger would have been more supportable than the passionless and measureless rejection with which it looked upon me . . .[38]

Orual cannot bear the beauty, goodness, or truth on his face in the light of what she has done. She sees only the rejection she feels she deserves: and it is a total rejection of herself, rather than a rejection of what she has done. She cannot yet see the "Who" of his face.

This moment is in sharp contrast with her encounter with her ultimate Judge at the end of her journey. Having faced and been honest about

36. Ibid., 121.

37. I have given him a name.

38. Lewis, *Till We Have Faces*, 181.

her inadequacies (which she now describes as her "wounds" rather than "ugliness"[39]), and, as she prepares to meet her true judges, she is now able to say, "I cannot hope for mercy." Fox replies, "Infinite hopes—and fears—may both be yours. Be sure that, whatever else you get, you will not get justice."[40] As she lets herself be seen, Orual discovers that the mercy and compassion of her judge ("the most dreadful, the most beautiful, the only dread and beauty there is," in whose light she casts down her eyes) goes far deeper than her even her imagination could have prepared her for. What she sees are "Two figures, reflections, their feet to Psyche's feet and mine, stood head downward in the water. But whose were they? Two Psyches, the one clothed, the other naked? Yes, both Psyches, both beautiful (if that mattered now) beyond all imagining, yet not exactly the same. 'You also are Psyche,' came a great voice. I looked up then, and it's strange that I dared." Orual sees the true "who" of herself and of Psyche, who embodies the face and the "Who" of a god who is love: "I know now, Lord, why you utter no answer. You yourself are the answer. Before your face questions die away. What other answer would suffice? Only words, words, words; to be led out to battle against other words . . ."[41]

"For nothing but the music's sake"

I return to David's favourite verse:

> For it is the God who said, "Let light shine out of darkness" who has shone in our hearts to give the knowledge of the glory of God in the face of Jesus Christ. (2 Cor 4:6)

Although David would probably now add to this a Johannine exegesis (in light of his current immersion writing a commentary on the Gospel of John), I shall simply add one of my own favourites:

> I pray that you may have the power to comprehend, with all the saints, what is the breadth and length and height and depth, and to know the love of Christ that surpasses knowledge, so that you may be filled with all the glory of God. (Eph 3:18–19)

39. Ibid., 254. Rankin describes how, in letting the "moral hurt" of our own nature be seen, "we feel as though a surgeon were dressing a wound, which we dread to have disturbed." Rankin, "Knowing God by Love," 416.

40. Lewis, *Till We Have Faces*, 307.

41. Ibid., 319. "When God sees his image in us, then it is that we are known." Rankin, "Knowing God by Love," 418.

With these Scriptures at the heart of our relationship and vocations, living and keeping up with David can be quite a challenge! His capacity and passionate enthusiasm for "abundance" and "excess" can be exhausting to the point when certain words have been temporarily banished from the household: the "O" word (overwhelmed); "Wisdom"; "core" and (as I write, soon) "left brain" and "right brain." But, of course, it is also deeply exhilarating and energizing and an utter privilege and delight to be met again and again by the light and warmth in David's face. His deeply patient, joyful, and grateful spirit overflows again and again in his huge generosity and sense of delight. Quite often he comes home from work saying, "Deb, I simply cannot get over the fact that I'm paid to do something that I love! Just imagine!"

The invitation is to be swept more and more fully into the infinite imagination and creativity of the "Who" of the "I am" of God together: the playful energy and delight at the heart of all that is.[42] Playing jazz together is the best way I can find to describe it; where the only imperative is a commitment to improvising together, "for nothing but the music's sake."

Somewhere
Against the grain, again the flair
Among a jazz's daring few

Some new
Delight in playing face to face
Grace notes
For a line that steadies as it floats,
Without a theory or a base,

Shared space
Holding what we hold and not to fear
Those bars
Where our history clashes or jars
And in lines unsymmetrical to the ear

Still hear
Deep reasonings of a different lore.
No map
Of any middle ground or overlap
Yet listening as never before—

42. Ellen Davis translates Proverbs 8:30b–31 as "And I was delights daily, playing before him continually, playing in his inhabited world, and my delights were with human beings." Davis, *Proverbs, Ecclesiastes and the Song of Songs*, 67.

No more—
Just hunched jazzmen so engrossed
In each
Other's chance outleap and reach
Of friendship at its utmost.

No host
And no one owns the chorus or break.
Guests all
At Madam Jazz's beck and call.
For nothing but the music's sake.[43]

43. O'Siadhail, "Session," from *Globe*, 116. David is the singer and I am an alto sax.

Bibliography

Barth, Karl. *Church Dogmatics* IV/3.1: *The Doctrine of Reconciliation*. Translated by G. W. Bromiley. Edited by G. W. Bromiley and T. F. Torrance. Edinburgh: T. & T. Clark, 1961.

Bion, W. R. *Second Thoughts: Selected Papers on Psychoanalysis*. Reprint, London: Karnac, 2007.

Coleridge, Samuel T. *Biographia Literaria*. Edited by W. Jackson Bate and J. Engle. Princeton: Princeton University Press, 1983.

———. *Confessions of an Inquiring Spirit*. Edited by A. Hart and C. Black. London: Black, 1956.

Cox, Murray. *Mutative Metaphors in Psychotherapy: The Aeolian Mode*. London: Tavistock, 1987.

———. *Remorse and Reparation*. London: Kingsley, 1999.

Cox, Murray, and Alice Theilgaard. *Shakespeare as Prompter: The Amending Imagination and the Therapeutic Process*. London: Kingsley, 1974.

Davis, Ellen F. *Proverbs, Ecclesiastes and the Song of Songs*. Louisville: Westminster John Knox, 2000.

Eliot, T. S. "Four Quartets." In *Collected Poems* 1909–1962, London: Faber & Faber, 1963.

Ford, David F. *Christian Wisdom: Desiring God and Learning in Love*. Cambridge: Cambridge University Press, 2007.

Lewis, C. S. *Letters to Malcolm: Chiefly on Prayer*. London: Collins, 1963

———. *Surprised by Joy*. 3rd ed. London: Fount, 1998.

———. *Till We Have Faces: A Myth Retold*. London: Collins, 1979.

Lossky, Vladimir. *The Mystical Theology of the Eastern Church*. Crestwood, NY: St Vladimir's Seminary Press, 1976.

McGilchrist, Iain. *The Master and His Emissary*. New Haven: Yale, 2009.

O'Siadhail, Micheal. *Globe*. Newcastle-upon-Tyne, UK: Bloodaxe, 2007.

Pfafflin, F. *In Memoriam: In Honour of Murray Cox*. Paper presented at IAPF Conference, Ulm, Germany, 1997.

Rankin, J. "Knowing God by Love." *The Homiletic Review* 27 (1894) 416–20.

Schakel, Peter. *Reason and Imagination in C. S. Lewis: A Study of* Till We Have Faces. Grand Rapids: Eerdmans, 1984.

———. "Till We Have Faces." In *The Cambridge Companion to C. S. Lewis*, edited by R. MacSwain and M. Ward, 281–93. Cambridge: Cambridge University Press, 2010.

Wolterstorff, Nicholas. *Lament for a Son*. Grand Rapids: Eerdmans, 1987.

Young, Frances M. *Face to Face: A Narrative Essay in the Theology of Suffering*. Edinburgh: T. & T. Clark, 1990.

Publications by David F. Ford

Listed in order of publication

Books

Barth and God's Story: Biblical Narrative and the Theological Method of Karl Barth in the "Church Dogmatics." Studies in the Intercultural History of Christianity. Frankfurt am Main: Lang, 1981. Reprint, Eugene, OR: Wipf & Stock, 2008.

Jubilate: Theology in Praise. With Daniel W. Hardy. London: Darton, Longman & Todd, 1984. US edition: *Praising and Knowing God*. Philadelphia: Westminster, 1985. Revised and updated as *Living in Praise: Worshipping and Knowing God*. London: Darton, Longman & Todd, 2005.

Meaning and Truth in 2 Corinthians. With Frances M. Young. London: SPCK, 1987. US edition: Grand Rapids: Eerdmans, 1988. Reprint, Eugene, OR: Wipf & Stock, 2008.

Essentials of Christian Community. Edited with Dennis Stamps. Edinburgh: T. & T. Clark, 1996.

The Modern Theologians: An Introduction to Christian Theology in the Twentieth Century. Edited. 1st ed. 2 vols. "Preface" and "Introduction to Modern Christian Theology," vol. I, vii–ix, 1–19; "Preface" and "Epilogue: Postmodernism and Postscript," vol. II, vii–viii, 291–97. Oxford: Blackwell, 1989. German edition: Paderborn: Schöningh, 1993. 2nd ed. in a single vol. "Introduction to Modern Christian Theology" and "Epilogue: Christian Theology at the Turn of the Millennium," 1–15 and 720–28. Oxford: Blackwell, 1997. Chinese edition: Hong Kong: Logos & Pneuma, 2000.

The Shape of Living. London: Fount, 1997. US edition: Grand Rapids: Baker, 1997. Reprint, Grand Rapids: Zondervan, 2002. Italian edition: Magnano: Edizioni Qiqajon, 2003. Reprint (with a new preface), London: Canterbury, 2012.

Self and Salvation: Being Transformed. Cambridge Studies in Christian Doctrine. Cambridge: Cambridge University Press, 1999.

Theology: A Very Short Introduction. Oxford: Oxford University Press, 1999 and 2000. Chinese edition: Hong Kong: Oxford University Press, 2000. Korean edition: Seoul: Imprima Korea Agency, 2003. Romanian edition: Bucharest: Editura Allfa, 2004.

Jesus. Edited with Mike Higton. Oxford Readers. Oxford: Oxford University Press, 2002.

Reading Texts, Seeking Wisdom: Scripture and Theology. Edited with Graham Stanton. "Introduction" (with Graham Stanton) and "Jesus Christ, the Wisdom of God (1)," 1–3 and 4–21. London: SCM, 2003.

Being Human: A Christian Understanding of Personhood, Illustrated with Reference to Power, Money, Sex and Time. As part of the Doctrine Commission of the General Synod of the Church of England. London: Church House, 2003.

Fields of Faith: Theology and Religious Studies for the Twenty-First Century. Edited with Ben Quash and Janet Martin Soskice. "Introduction," xiii–xvii. Cambridge: Cambridge University Press, 2005.

The Modern Theologians: An Introduction to Christian Theology since 1918. 3rd ed. Edited with Rachel Muers. "Introduction to Modern Christian Theology" and "Epilogue: Twelve Theses for Christian Theology in the Twenty-First Century," 1–15 and 760–761. Oxford: Blackwell, 2005. Korean edition: Seoul: Christian Literature Crusade, 2005.

The Promise of Scriptural Reasoning. Edited with C. C. Pecknold. "An Interfaith Wisdom: Scriptural Reasoning between Jews, Christians and Muslims," 1–22. Oxford: Blackwell, 2006. Also published in *Modern Theology* 22.3 (2006) 345–66.

Musics of Belonging: The Poetry of Micheal O'Siadhail. Edited with Marc Caball. "Life, Work, and Reception," 1–24. Dublin: Carysfort, 2006.

Christian Wisdom: Desiring God and Learning in Love. Cambridge Studies in Christian Doctrine. Cambridge: Cambridge University Press, 2007.

Shaping Theology: Engagements in a Religious and Secular World. Challenges in Contemporary Theology. Oxford: Blackwell, 2007.

Wording a Radiance: Parting Conversations on God and the Church. With Daniel W. Hardy, Deborah Hardy Ford, and Peter Ochs. London: SCM, 2010.

The Future of Christian Theology. Blackwell Manifestos. Oxford: Wiley-Blackwell, 2011.

The Modern Theologians Reader. Edited with Mike Higton and Simeon Zahl. Malden, MA: Wiley-Blackwell, 2012.

Articles, Book Chapters, Lectures, and Addresses

"Barth's Interpretation of the Bible." In *Karl Barth: Studies of His Theological Methods*, edited by S. W. Sykes, 55–87. Oxford: Oxford University Press, 1980.

"Narrative in Theology." *British Journal of Religious Education* 4.3 (1982) 115–19.

"The Best Apologetics is Good Systematics: A Proposal about the Place of Narrative in Christian Systematic Theology." *Anglican Theological Review* 68.3 (1985) 232–54.

"Prayer and Righteous Action: Exploring Bonhoeffer's Suggestion." *New Blackfriars* 66 (1985) 336–47.

"Faith in the Cities. Corinth and the Modern City." In *On Being the Church: Essays on the Christian Community*, edited by Colin E. Gunton and Daniel W. Hardy, 225–56. Edinburgh: T. & T. Clark, 1989.

"Tragedy and Atonement." In *Christ, Ethics and Tragedy: Essays in Honour of Donald MacKinnon*, edited by Kenneth Surin, 117–30. Cambridge: Cambridge University Press, 1989.

"System, Story, Performance. A Proposal about the Place of Narrative in Christian Systematic Theology." In *Why Narrative? Readings in Narrative Theology*, edited by Stanley Hauerwas and L. Gregory Jones, 191–215. Grand Rapids: Eerdmans, 1989.

"Hans Frei and the Future of Theology." *Modern Theology* 8.2 (1992) 203–14.

A Long Rumour of Wisdom: Redescribing Theology—Inaugural Lecture as Regius Professor of Divinity. Cambridge: Cambridge University Press, 1992.

"George Herbert: The Centrality of God." *Theology* 96.773 (1993) 357–64.

"Hosting a Dialogue: Jüngel and Lévinas on God, Self and Language." In *The Possibilities of Theology: Studies in the Theology of Eberhard Jüngel*, edited by John Webster, 23–59. Edinburgh: T. & T. Clark, 1994.

"Response to 'The Problem of the Starting Point of Theological Thinking.'" *Hermathena* 156 (1994) 28–39.

"Constructing a Public Theology." In *Dare We Speak of God in Public? The Edward Cadbury Lectures 1993–94*, edited by Frances Young, 151–61. London: Mowbray, 1995.

"On Being Theologically Hospitable to Jesus Christ: Hans Frei's Achievement." *Journal of Theological Studies* 46.2 (1995) 532–46.

"What Happens in the Eucharist?" *Scottish Journal of Theology* 8.3 (1995) 359–81.

"Transformation," and (with Alistair I. McFadyen) "Praise." In *God in the City: Essays and Reflections from the Archbishop of Canterbury's Urban Theology Group*, edited by Peter Sedgwick, 95–104, 199–209. London: Mowbray, 1995.

"On Substitution." In *Facing the Other: The Ethics of Emmanuel Lévinas*, edited by Sean Hand, 21–43. Richmond, UK: Curzon, 1996.

"L'Arche and Jesus: What Is the Theology?" In *Encounter with Mystery: Reflections on L'Arche and Living with Disability*, edited by Frances M. Young, 77–88. London: Darton, Longman & Todd, 1997.

"Before the Face of Christ. Thérèse of Lisieux and Two Interpreters." In *The Way* 37.3 (1997) 254–62.

"Theology and Religious Studies at the Turn of the Millennium." *Teaching Theology and Religion* 1.1 (1998) 4–12.

Remarks at Final Plenary Session, Lambeth Conference, 8 August 1998. LC112. Online: http://www.lambethconference.org/1998/news/lc112.cfm.

"A Messiah for the Third Millennium." *Modern Theology* 16.1 (2000) 75–90; also in *Theology and Eschatology at the Turn of the Millennium*, edited by James Buckley and L. Gregory Jones, 73–88. Oxford: Blackwell, 2001.

"Theological Wisdom, British Style." *The Christian Century* 117.11 (April 5, 2000) 388–91.

"British Theology after a Trauma: Divisions and Conversations." *The Christian Century* 117.12 (April 12, 2000) 425–31.

"British Theology: Movements and Churches." *The Christian Century* 117.13 (April 19, 2000) 465–73

"Why Church? A Presidential Address given to the Society for the Study of Theology at the University of Manchester, April 1998." *Scottish Journal of Theology* 53.1 (2000) 50–71.

"Christology." In *The Oxford Companion to Christian Thought: Intellectual, Spiritual and Moral Horizons of Christianity*, edited by Adrian Hastings et al., 114–18. Oxford: Oxford University Press, 2000.

"Christian Wisdom for the New Millennium." In *Plurality, Power and Mission: Intercontextual Theological Explorations on the Role of Religion in the New Millennium*, edited by Philip Wickeri et al., 111–34. London: Council for World Mission, 2000.

"Radical Orthodoxy and the Future of British Theology," and "A Response to Catherine Pickstock." *Scottish Journal of Theology* 54.3 (2001) 385–40, 423–25. Translated in *Logos & Pneuma: Chinese Journal of Theology* 23 (2005) 123–42.

"Salvation and the Nature of Theology. Response to John Webster's Review of *Self and Salvation.*" *Scottish Journal of Theology* 54.4 (2001) 560–75.

"'He is our peace': The Letter to the Ephesians and the Theology of Fulfilment—A Dialogue with Peter Ochs." *The Journal of Scriptural Reasoning* 1.1 (2001). Online: http://etext.lib.virginia.edu/journals/ssr/issues/volume1/number1/ssr01-01-a01.html.

The Future of Cambridge University. Lady Margaret's Sermon, Commemoration of Benefactors. Preached in the University Church, Great St Mary's, on Sunday, 4 November 2001. Cambridge: Cambridge University Press, 2001.

"Apophasis and the Shoah: Where was Jesus Christ at Auschwitz?" In *Silence and the Word: Negative Theology and Incarnation*, edited by Oliver Davies and Denys Turner, 185–200. Cambridge: Cambridge University Press, 2002.

"Dramatic Theology: York, Lambeth and Cambridge." In *Sounding the Depths: Theology through the Arts*, edited by Jeremy Begbie, 71–91. London: SCM, 2002.

"Responding to Textual Reasoning: What Might Christians Learn?" In *Textual Reasonings: Jewish Philosophy and Text Study at the End of the Twentieth Century*, edited by Peter Ochs and Nancy Levene, 259–68. London: SCM, 2002.

"Faith and Change: A Christian Understanding." In *The Road Ahead: A Christian-Muslim Dialogue*, 70–80. London: Church House, 2002.

"Jesus Christ in Scripture, Community and Mission: The Wisdom of John 1:1–18." In *Scripture, Community, and Mission: Essays in Honor of D. Preman Niles*, edited by Philip L. Wickeri, 300–11. London and Hong Kong: Council for World Mission and the Christian Conference of Asia, 2002.

"A Few Thoughts in Response to Peter Ochs." *The Journal of Scriptural Reasoning* 2.1 (2002). Online: http://etext.lib.virginia.edu/journals/ssr/issues/volume2/number1/ssr02-01-r05.html.

"Response to Magid, Hauerwas, and Koshul." *The Journal of Scriptural Reasoning* 2.2 (2002). Online: http://etext.lib.virginia.edu/journals/ssr/issues/volume2/number2/ssr02-02-r13.html.

"Knowledge, Meaning and the World's Great Challenges: Reinventing Cambridge University in the Twenty-first Century." The Gomes Lecture, delivered at Emmanuel College on Friday, 14 February 2003. *Emmanuel College Magazine* 85 (2002–3) 38–63; and *Scottish Journal of Theology* 57.2 (2004) 182–202.

"Bonhoeffer, Holiness and Ethics." In *Holiness Past and Present*, edited by Stephen C. Barton, 361–80. London: T. & T. Clark, 2003.

"The Way of Wisdom—The Practical Theology of David Ford." Interview by David S. Cunningham in *The Christian Century* 120.9 (May 3, 2003) 30–37.

"The Wisdom of Love for God's Sake: Interpreting the Papers, and Our Scriptures, Together." *The Journal of Scriptural Reasoning* 3.2 (2003). Online: http://etext.lib.virginia.edu/journals/ssr/issues/volume3/number2/ssr03-02-r06.html.

"Holy Spirit and Christian Spirituality." In *The Cambridge Companion to Postmodern Theology*, edited by Kevin J. Vanhoozer, 269–90. Cambridge: Cambridge University Press, 2003.

"Learning from Lambeth 1998 and Primates' Meetings 2000–2003." Submission to Lambeth Commission on Communion. Online: http://www.anglicancommunion.org/commission/process/lc_commission/doc3indExod.cfm.

"The God of Blessing Who Loves in Wisdom." In *Denkwürdiges Geheimnis—Beiträge zur Gotteslehre: Festschrift für Eberhard* Jüngel *zum 70 Geburtstag*, edited by Ingolf

U. Dalferth, Johannes Fischer, and Hans-Peter Großhans, 113–26. Tübingen: Mohr Siebeck, 2004.

"The Responsibilities of Universities in a Religious and Secular World." *Studies in Christian Ethics* 17.1 (2004) 22–37.

"An Easter Sermon: The Third Day He Rose Again from the Dead." In *Exploring and Proclaiming the Apostles' Creed*, edited by Roger E. Van Harn, 154–60. Grand Rapids: Eerdmans, 2004.

"The Qur'an: A New Translation." Speech given at the launch of *The Qur'an: A New Translation* by M. A. S. Abdel Haleem, School of Oriental and African Studies, University of London, 13 May 2004. Online: http://www.interfaith.cam.ac.uk/en/resources/papers/the-quran-a-new-translation.

"Response to the Papers by Kepnes, Richardson and Umar." *The Journal of Scriptural Reasoning* 4.2 (2004). Online: http://etext.lib.virginia.edu/journals/ssr/issues/volume4/number2/ssr04_02_r01.html.

"A Theology of Church Leadership—Response to Steven Croft." In *Focus on Leadership—Papers, Commentary and Reflections on a Seminar Launching the Foundation for Church Leadership*, 42–45. York: Foundation for Church Leadership, 2005.

"Wilderness Wisdom for the Twenty-First Century: Arthur, L'Arche and the Culmination of Christian History." In *Wilderness: Essays in Honour of Frances Young*, edited by R. S. Sugirtharajah, 153–66. London: T. & T. Clark, 2005.

"Reading Scripture with Intensity: Academic, Ecclesial, Interfaith, and Divine." *The Princeton Seminary Bulletin* 26.1 (2005) 22–35.

"Incarnation, Rationality, and Transformative Practices." In *Truth, Religious Dialogue and Dynamic Orthodoxy: Essays in Honour of Brian Hebblethwaite*, edited by Julius J. Lipner, 187–202. London: SCM, 2005.

"Faith in the Third Millennium. Reading Scriptures Together." Address at the inauguration of Iain Torrance as President of Princeton Theological Seminary and Professor of Patristics, 10 March 2005. Online: http://etext.lib.virginia.edu/journals/jsrforum/writings.html.

"Theology." In *The Routledge Companion to the Study of Religion*, edited by John R. Hinnells, 61–79. Abingdon: Routledge, 2005.

"Faith and Universities in a Religious and Secular World (1)." *Svensk Teologisk Kvartalskrift* 81.2 (2005) 83–91.

"Faith and Universities in a Religious and Secular World (2)." *Svensk Teologisk Kvartalskrift* 81.3 (2005) 97–106.

"Foreword." In *Diverse Gifts: Varieties of Lay and Ordained Ministries in the Church and Community*, edited by Malcolm Torry, vii–ix. Norwich, UK: Canterbury, 2006.

"A Third Epoch: The Future of Discourse in Jewish-Christian Relations," with Peter Ochs. In *Challenges in Jewish-Christian Relations*, edited by James K. Aitken and Edward Kessler, 153–70. New York: Paulist, 2006.

"Gospel in Context: Among Many Faiths." Lecture at the Fulcrum Conference, Islington, 28 April 2006. Online: http://www.fulcrum-anglican.org.uk/news/2006/20060428ford.cfm?doc=101.

"A Wisdom for Anglican Life: Lambeth 1998 to Lambeth 2008 and Beyond." *Journal of Anglican Studies* 4.2 (2006) 137–56.

"God and Our Public Life: A Scriptural Wisdom." *International Journal of Public Theology* 1.1 (2007) 63–81.

"Gospel in Context: Among Many Faiths." *Pilgrim: Magazine of the Friends of the Church in India* 30 (2007) 3–7.

"Developing Scriptural Reasoning Further." In *Scripture, Reason, and the Contemporary Islam-West Encounter: Studying the "Other," Understanding the "Self,"* edited by Basit Bilal Koshul and Steven Kepnes, 201–19. New York: Palgrave Macmillan, 2007.

"Professor David Ford's Response to *A Common Word*." 2007. Online: http://www.interfaith.cam.ac.uk/en/resources/papers/professor-david-ford-response-to-a-common-word.

"Foreword." In *A Bicentenary History of the Anglican Church of the Diocese of West Malaysia (1805–2005)*, by Archdeacon Sadayandy Batumalai, 1–2. Malacca, Malaysia: Diocese of West Malaysia, Church of the Province of South East Asia, 2007.

"God and Our Public Life: A Scriptural Wisdom." In *Liberating Texts? Sacred Scriptures in Public Life*, edited by Sebastian C. H. Kim and Jonathan Draper, 29–56. London: SPCK, 2008.

"Foreword." In *The Irish School of Ecumenics (1970–2007)*, edited by Michael Hurley, 15–26. Blackrock, Dublin: Columba, 2008. Abridged version printed in *Irish Times*, April 1, 2008, 11.

"God's Power and Human Flourishing: A Biblical Inquiry after Charles Taylor's *A Secular Age*." Paper at the 2008 God and Human Flourishing Consultation, Yale Center for Faith and Culture. Online: http://www.yale.edu/faith/rc/rc-ghf-cons-2008.htm.

"Comment on 'A Common Word for the Common Good.'" 2008. Online: http://www.acommonword.com/comment-on-a-common-word-for-the-common-good/.

"Foreword." In *Wanting Like a God: Desire and Freedom in Thomas Traherne*, by Denise Inge, xi–xii. London: SCM, 2009.

"Paul Ricoeur: A Biblical Philosopher on Jesus." In *Jesus and Philosophy: New Essays*, edited by Paul K. Moser, 169–93. Cambridge: Cambridge University Press, 2009.

A Muscat Manifesto: Seeking Inter-Faith Wisdom. Cambridge and Dubai: The Cambridge Inter-faith Programme and Kalam Research & Media, 2009. First delivered as "Seeking Muslim, Christian and Jewish Wisdom in the Fifteenth, Twenty-First and Fifty-Eighth Centuries: A Muscat Manifesto," Sultan Qaboos Grand Mosque, Muscat, Oman, Monday, 20 April 2009; "What is Required of a Religious Leader Today?" Institute of Shariah Studies, Muscat, Oman, Monday, 20 April 2009.

"The Christian Code." Sermon preached at the Ordination and Consecration of Graham Kings to be Bishop of Sherborne, Westminster Abbey, 24 June 2009. Online: http://www.fulcrum-anglican.org.uk/page.cfm?ID=435.

"Theology and Religious Studies for a Multifaith and Secular Society." In *Theology and Religious Studies in Higher Education: Global Perspectives*, edited by Darlene L. Bird and Simon G. Smith, 31–43. London: Continuum, 2009.

"Responsive Reading: Texts that Make Us Tick." *The Christian Century* 126.16 (August 11, 2009) 10–11.

"Foreword." In *New Perspectives for Evangelical Theology: Engaging God, Scripture, and the World*, edited by Tom Greggs, xiv–xvi. Abingdon, UK: Routledge, 2010.

"Where is Wise Theological Creativity to be Found? Thoughts on 25 Years of *Modern Theology* and the Twenty-First Century Prospect." *Modern Theology* 26.1 (2010) 67–75.

"Dante as Inspiration for Twenty-First-Century Theology." In *Dante's* Commedia: *Theology as Poetry*, edited by Vittorio Montemaggi and Matthew Treherne, 318–28. The William and Katherine Devers Series in Dante and Medieval Italian Literature. Notre Dame: University of Notre Dame Press, 2010.

"Foreword." In *Christus Victor: An Historical Study of the Three Main Types of the Idea of the Atonement*, by Gustaf Aulén, ix–xi. London: SPCK, 2010.

"The What, How and Who of Humanity before God: Theological Anthropology and the Bible in the Twenty-First Century." *Modern Theology* 27.1 (2011) 41–54.

"In the Spirit: Learning Wisdom, Giving Signs." In *The Holy Spirit in the World Today*, edited by Jane Williams, 42–63. London: Alpha, 2011.

"Reading Texts, Seeking Wisdom: A Gospel, a System and a Poem." *Theology* 114.3 (2011) 173–80.

"Jews, Christians and Muslims Meet around their Scriptures: An Inter-faith Practice for the 21st Century." The Fourth Pope John Paul II Annual Lecture on Interreligious Understanding, delivered at The Pontifical University of St Thomas Aquinas, Angelicum, with The Russell Berrie Foundation, Rome, 5 April 2011. Online: http://www.interfaith.cam.ac.uk/en/resources/papers/jpii-lecture.

"The Challenge of Inter-Faith Relations and the University as an Institution: A Response to *Christianity and Contemporary Politics*." *Political Theology* 12.3 (2011) 448–53.

"Faith Seeking Wisdom: How My Mind Has Changed." *The Christian Century* 127.24 (November 18, 2010) 30.

"Foreword." In *The 50 Years' Pilgrimage of a Malaysian Christian: An Autobiography*, by the Rt. Rev. Datuk S. Batumalai, i. Malacca, Malaysia: private publication, 2011.

"Conclusion: Tragedy, Theology and the Discernment of Cries." In *Christian Theology and Tragedy: Theologians, Tragic Literature and Tragic Theory*, edited by Kevin Taylor and Giles Waller, 233–40. Farnham, UK: Ashgate, 2011.

"Christianity and Universities Today: A Double Manifesto." The Third Lord Dearing Memorial Lecture, delivered to The Cathedrals Group at Church House, London, 1 November 2011. Online: http://cathedralsgroup.org.uk/Dearing.aspx.

"Equal before God." In *Islam in English Law: Rights, Responsibilities and the Place of Sharia*, edited by Robin Griffith-Jones. Cambridge: Cambridge University Press, forthcoming.

Index

Abbot Samson, 294
Abravanel, Don Isaac, 14, 194–209
Adams, Nicholas, 13, 74, 92–107, 246, 254, 257
Alacoque, Marie Elizabeth, 349–50, 358
Al-Ghazali, 196, 203, 208
Allan, Tiffy, 255
Alston, William P., 133–40, 144–45
Ambrose, 142
American Revolution, 164
Anglicanism, 150, 152, 157–58, 172, 193, 339, 363, 368
anthropology, 8, 144, 162, 312, 330
anti-Semitism, 196
Aphrahat, 25
Aphrodite, 219
apocalypticism, 196, 208
Apollo, 219
apophatism, 282–83
Apphou, 115, 119–20
Aquinas, Thomas, 21, 25, 144–45, 283, 311, 326, 397
Arendt, Hannah, 253, 257
Aristotle, 193, 203
Arius, 27, 34
Asad, Talal, 132, 144, 167, 176
Ashkenazi, Saul ha-Kohen, 201
Askelrad, Sidney, 291, 302
atonement, 62–63, 67, 73–74, 393, 397
Augustine, 21, 25, 93, 96–117, 159, 161, 184, 208–9, 283, 326
Austin, J. L., 134, 144
Avot, Pirke, 200, 289–81, 302
Baker, Christopher, 245, 255, 257
Bakhtin, Mikhail, 178–80, 189
Barnes, Michael, 14, 228–41
Barrett, C. K., 62–63, 69, 71, 73
Barth, Karl, 2, 6, 7, 12, 17, 21–23, 26–27, 29–34, 37, 46–47, 49–60, 182, 229, 240, 315, 330, 362, 366, 383, 390–92
Basil the Great, 116
Batnitzky, Leora, 280, 284
Bauckham, Richard, 126, 128
Bauer, Walter, 73
Bayer, Oswald, 64, 73
Beaumont, Justin, 245, 257
Bell, Catherine, 132, 145
Bell, Richard, 80–84, 91
Ben-Sasson, H., 195, 197, 209
Berger, Peter, 170, 176
Bergson, Henri, 15, 273–85
Berman, Elaine, 291, 302
Bhaskar, Roy, 179
Bible. *See* Scripture
Bion, W. R., 386, 390
Blake, William, 157
Blondel, 29
Blumhardt, Christopher, 25
Bonaventure, 25
Bonhoeffer, Dietrich, 21, 265, 283, 311, 365, 392, 394
Borodowski, Alfredo Fabio, 195, 201, 203, 209
Bourdieu, Pierre, 132, 145
Braaten, Carl E., 185, 189
Bretherton, Luke, 254, 257
Brichto, H. C., 31, 34
Bringhurst, Robert, 185–87, 189

Britt, Thomas, 248, 257
Bromiley, Geoffrey W., 34, 46, 60, 240, 390
Brown, Callum, 163, 170–77
Brubacher, John S., 304, 313
Brueggemann, Walter, 237, 240
Brunner, Emil, 37, 46
Buddhism, 230, 232, 241
Burke, Edmund, 361–62
Butler, Bishop Christopher, 333

Calvin, John, 25, 30–31, 34, 93, 96, 101–7, 140, 185, 189, 307
Cameron, David, 273–74
Canlis, Julie, 185, 189
Cappadocian Fathers, 115, 119
Cavanaugh, William T., 316, 328
Chalmers, Thomas, 171–73, 175
Christensen, Michael J., 74
Christian ethics, 46, 206, 219, 328, 370
Christology, 8, 36, 43, 393
Chrysostom, John, 142, 144–45
church, 1–3, 8, 13, 18, 22–34, 38, 41, 59, 88, 92, 101, 108, 110, 114–29, 132, 145, 150, 158, 160–65, 171–76, 183, 190, 221, 229, 231, 240, 241, 245, 254–57, 260, 267–71, 294, 297, 309, 313–42, 360, 366–70, 375–77, 383, 390–97
Cloke, Paul, 248, 257
Clooney, Francis, 230, 240
Coakley, Sarah, 13, 131–45, 185, 189
Code, Lorraine, 138–40, 145
Cognition, 13, 27, 133, 135, 138, 182, 188, 202
Coleridge, Samuel Taylor, 25, 146–8, 158, 378–79, 390
Communion of Saints, 12, 22–34
compassion, 9, 82, 111, 186, 232, 234, 239, 357, 386, 388
Comte, Auguste, 153, 162
Coulson, John, 331, 333, 342
Cox, Murray, 378, 383–84, 390
creation, 4–5, 34, 39, 41–42, 46, 49, 53, 55, 59–60, 78, 84–87, 113–17, 120–21, 125–26, 151, 157–58, 168, 175, 183–84, 200, 203, 209, 223, 225, 236, 238–39, 289, 298–300
cries, 8–9, 42, 46, 52–53, 223, 266, 299, 397
cross, 42–44, 110–12, 127, 135, 156, 231, 237
crucifixion, 43, 358
Cunningham, Conor, 184, 189, 394
Cunningham, David S., 2, 17, 184, 189, 394

D'Costa, Gavin, 325, 328, 332, 335–42
Danker, Frederick William, 73
Dante, 25, 377, 396
Darwin, Charles, 184, 189
Davey, Francis Noel, 74
Davidman, Joy, 379
Davie, Grace, 68, 70, 77
Davies, Oliver, 17, 394
Davis, Ellen, 389–90
de Lubac, Henri, 190
de Tocqueville, Alexis, 165
del Medigo, Elijah, 199, 201
Descartes, René, 159–61
Diodorus of Sicily, 156
Dionysius the Areopagite, 185, 189, 232
disabilities, 16, 111–12, 119, 299, 309, 345–58, 367, 393
discipleship, 127, 245, 258
Duke, James, 47
Dunn, James, 61–62, 73, 80, 91
Dupuis, Jacques, 230–31, 234, 240

Eastern Orthodoxy, 185
Eaton, John, 232, 240
Ebeling, Gerhard, 185

Edwards, Jonathan, 25
Election, 30–31, 50, 56, 77, 79, 82, 89
Eliot, George, 148, 153–56, 161, 384
Eliot, T. S., 148, 153–54, 156, 161, 384, 390
Elliott, Charles, 246, 254, 257
Enlightenment, 24, 151, 159, 162, 274, 280, 314–15
Ephrem, 25, 117
epistemology, 133, 136, 138, 140, 145, 214
Erasmus, 25
eschatology, 8, 24, 31, 34, 71–72, 81, 87, 121
ethnography, 33, 166, 173, 175, 246, 254, 257,
Eucharist, 115–19, 132, 144–45, 158, 393
Euclid, 215
evangelism, 73, 96, 99, 101–2, 107, 110, 172, 231, 241
Ezra, Ibn, 202

facing, 16, 112, 140, 160, 225–27 247–58, 266, 281–82, 343, 359–93
Farley, Edward, 308, 310–11, 313
Feldman, Seymour, 195–96, 201–3, 209
Finlan, Stephen, 63, 67, 73
Fiorenza, Francis, 47
Fishbane, Michael, 183, 189
Flew, A. N. G., 305, 313
Flood, Gavin, 365
Florovsky, Georges, 185, 190
Fodor, James, 5, 17
Ford, Deborah Hardy, 2, 3, 16, 18, 374–90, 392
forgiveness, 61–63
Fout, Jason, 12, 48–60
Frank, Georgia, 142, 144–45
Frei, Hans, 5, 6, 18, 21, 24, 34, 64, 67, 74, 314–15, 325, 327–29, 366, 392–93
French Revolution, 163
Freud, Sigmund, 311
friendship, 2–3, 11, 16, 28, 193, 260–63, 349–59, 365, 369
Frost, Robert, 362, 370, 373

Gadenz, Pablo, 81, 91
Galgalo, Joseph, 15, 303–13
Gallaher, Brandon, 185, 190
Gaon, Saadya, 208
Gaon, Vilna, 208
Gersonides, 196, 202–6
Gleason, Philip, 317, 329
God
- aseity of, 53, 262, 264
- attributes of, 35–44, 51, 203
- cries of, 42
- embodiment of, 154, 186
- essence of, 36, 39, 40, 43
- freedom of, 51, 58, 88, 182–183
- glory of, 59–60, 110, 155, 161, 376, 388–89
- hiddeness of, 109–10, 112
- infinitude of, 24–25, 40, 59, 79, 89, 378, 389
- kingdom of, 24, 124–28, 299, 300, 308
- love of, 12, 35–47, 119, 128, 187, 225, 290, 298–300
- otherness of, 186, 283, 383
- pre-eminence, of 49
- revelation of, 12, 48–60, 182, 235, 238, 320, 323, 327, 379
- sovereignty of, 86

Goodchild, Philip, 251, 257
grace, 37–38, 43, 49, 51, 62, 65, 80, 90, 146, 148, 170, 177, 227, 296, 335, 366, 375
Graham, Gordon, 292–97, 302
Grant, Rhiannon, 255
Green, S. J. D., 177

Greggs, Tom, 1–18, 21–34, 396
Gregory of Nyssa, 24, 117, 141–45
Griffiths, Bede, 232

Habermas, Jürgen, 168
Hailer, M., 65, 73
Hansen, Walter A., 74
Harding, Susan, 173, 177
Hardy, Daniel W., 2, 3, 11, 18, 34, 109, 121–22, 131, 145, 150–51, 157, 193, 211, 212, 254, 257, 261, 272, 331, 333, 342, 363, 365–68, 374, 377, 391–92
Harrison, Frederic, 153
Harvey, Susan, 114, 117, 121, 142, 145
Harvey, Susan Ashbrook, 117, 121, 145
Healy, Nicholas, 26, 34
Hegel, G. W. F., 167, 169
Herbert, George, 158, 363–64, 373, 394
Hermeneutics, 7, 18, 32, 44, 54–55, 60, 84–85, 135, 140, 190, 206–7, 231, 299, 306, 309–12, 315–16, 329
Higton, Mike, 4, 15, 289
Hinduism, 230, 240
Hollenweger, Walter, 10

Holton, Phil, 211
Holy Spirit, 10, 17, 22, 24, 39, 55–57, 64, 100, 102, 113, 149, 152, 160, 250, 320, 394, 397
Homer, 311, 377
Hooker, Richard, 25, 158
Hopkins, Gerard Manley, 116, 149, 149, 155–59, 161
Hoskyns, E. C., 74
Hovey, Craig, 48
Howard, Thomas, 163, 165, 176–77
human agency, 60, 65–66, 69–70, 73, 90
Hume, David, 203
hymnody, 132, 137

idolatry, 83–85, 250–51
Iggers, George G., 30, 34
Ignatius of Loyola, 25
Illich, Ivan, 248
incarnation, 17, 39, 42–43, 55, 110, 118, 120, 142, 154, 182, 264–65, 270, 394
interdisciplinarity, 15, 245, 273, 284, 368
Irenaeus, 116
Islam, 3, 6, 11, 14, 17, 33, 93, 131, 176, 181, 184, 200, 203–4, 212–13, 222, 230, 255, 291, 302, 368, 392, 394, 396–97
Israel, 31, 34, 57, 77–91, 126, 128, 236, 233–35, 247, 252

Jackson, Thomas, 307
Jacobs, Alan, 179, 190
Jacobs, Louis, 291, 302
Janz, Paul D., 15, 273–85,
Jefferson, Thomas, 151, 155, 161
Jenkins, Tim, 13, 163–77
Jensen, Robert W., 189
Jesus Christ
  face of, 160, 254, 393
  genealogy of, 94, 97, 102–5
  lordship of, 59, 60, 84, 97, 110, 127
  as Messiah, 94, 102–5, 125
  name of, 247–52
Joest, Wilfried, 64, 67, 74
John of the Cross, 135
Johnson, Elizabeth, 326–29
Jones, David, 46–48, 156–57, 161
Judaism, 6, 11, 14, 18, 33, 78–81, 90–93, 125–7, 131, 162, 181, 183–84, 189, 193–200,

204–13, 222–23, 233–6, 291, 302, 368, 392, 395–97
Jüngel, Eberhard, 256, 365, 393–94
justice, 9, 40, 91, 199, 237, 277, 280, 282, 307, 309, 322, 388

Kabir, 232
Kadushin, Max, 206, 209
Kant, Immanueal, 24, 135, 214, 274, 281, 284
Kavanagh, Patrick, 363–64, 373
Keener, Craig, 69, 74
Kelly, J. N. D., 23, 34
Kepnes, Steven, 17, 233, 240, 377, 395–96
Kerr, Fergus, 132, 145, 332–34
Koshul, Basit, 14, 17, 211–27, 394, 396
Kretzmann, Norman, 136, 145
Kruger, Robert, 365

Laato, T, 65, 74
Lamm, Julia A., 41, 46, 291, 302
Lamm, Norman, 41, 46, 291, 302
Lash, Nicholas, 333–34
Latour, Bruno, 245
Lectio divina, 32
Léon, Judah Messer, 199
Levinas, Emmanuel, 15, 247–49, 273–75, 277, 280–84, 364–65, 370, 393
Lewis, C. S., 16, 378–90
liberalism, 167, 221, 274–75, 279–80, 296, 315, 319, 334,
Lindbeck, George, 5, 209, 324, 366
Lindbeck, Kris, 209
liturgy, 13, 109, 114–15, 119–20, 126, 131–45, 253, 319
Loades, Ann, 331
Locke, John, 139
Lodge, David, 180, 190
Loftus, Rachel, 255
Lossky, 29, 182, 185, 190, 390
Louth, Andrew, 70, 74
Luther, Martin, 12, 21, 25, 61–75, 185, 189, 283,

MacCulloch, Diarmaid, 185, 190
Macintyre, Alasdair, 313
MacKinnon, Donald, 2, 366, 392
Mackintosh, H. R., 47
Magus, Simon, 252
Maimonedes, 196, 200–203, 208
Mannermaa, Tuomo, 65
Margolis, Joseph, 179, 190
Martin, David, 132, 145
martyrdom, 42, 117–18
materialism, 114, 116, 118–21, 154, 200
Maximus the Confessor, 25
McCluskey, Neil G., 317, 329
McCormack, Bruce, 31, 34, 37, 47,
McFadyen, Alistair I., 5, 15, 259–72, 393
McGilchrist, Iain, 379, 390
McGrath, Alister E., 64–65, 74
McInroy, Mark J., 65, 74, 141, 145
McLeod, Hugh, 174, 177
Melanchthon, 65
Merkel, Angela, 273
Merleau-Ponty, Maurice, 159, 162, 180, 190
Merton, Thomas, 232
Messianism, 200–208
Methodism, 110, 114–15, 121
Milton, John, 25, 377
miracles, 14, 119, 201, 203, 208–9, 246, 249, 252–54, 257
missiology, 267
Molendijk, Arie, 245, 257
Morris, Jeremy, 175, 177
Mother Teresa, 125
Moule, C. F. D., 366
Muers, Rachel, 1–18, 34, 209, 245–58
multiculturalism, 273, 275, 277
Murray, Paul D., 16, 330–42

Muscat Manifesto, 212–13, 222–27, 396
music, 106, 113, 116, 122, 132, 152, 265, 311, 336, 388–89, 392
mysticism, 62, 135–36, 145, 182, 190, 196, 200–201, 209, 219, 232, 277–78, 283, 390

Nachmanides, 202
Nagel, Thomas, 278, 285
Nanos, Mark, 81, 91
nature, 103, 151–57, 203, 276,
Nayed, Aref, 377
Neoplatonism, 199
Newman, John Henry, 31–32, 34, 292–97, 302, 316, 329, 332, 342
Nexon, Daniel H., 168, 177
Nietzsche, Friedrich, 189, 215, 227
Nimmo, Paul, 12, 35–48
nonconformity, 172
nouvelle theologie, 185
Nouwen, Henri, 364, 366
Nowak, Kurt, 41, 47

O'Siadhail, Micheal, 9, 16, 18, 261, 359–74, 389–90, 392,
Ochs, Peter, 3, 5, 10, 11, 14, 18, 122, 150–52, 157, 162, 193–210, 211–12, 291, 302, 365, 368, 377, 392, 394, 395
Ochs, Vanessa, 377
Ogren, Brian, 195, 210
Origen, 25, 84, 141–43
Ortiger, Stephen, 126
Otto, Rudolph, 223, 227

parables, 57, 249
paradox, 88–89, 109–10, 118, 185, 188, 221, 227, 234, 371
Pattison, George, 74
Paul Althaus, 64, 73
Peacock A. R., 305, 313
Pechey, Graham, 148, 162
Pecknold, C. C., 11, 15, 17, 131, 145, 314–29, 392
Pedersen, Olaf, 304, 313
Peels, H. G. L., 84
Peirce, Charles, 209, 215, 227
Pelikan, Jaroslav, 74
Pfafflin, F., 378, 390
philosophy of religion, 132–33, 138, 140, 143–44
Pickstock, Catherine, 159, 162, 393
Pieris, Aloysius, 232, 240
Plato, 117, 141, 199, 215
pneumatology, 10, 12–13, 146–49, 158, 161–62
poetry, 6, 9, 18, 33, 36, 49, 54, 58, 73, 111, 116–17, 122, 132, 146–48, 156–57, 161–62, 185, 187, 261, 361–64, 370–74, 390, 392, 396–97
polytheism, 126, 219
Pope Benedict XVI, 315
Pope John Paul II, 231, 234, 240, 290, 319–20, 324, 326, 357, 368, 397
postliberalism, 5–6, 17–18, 150, 152, 157, 162, 193, 209, 334
postmodernism, 16–17, 28, 34 332, 338, 394
postsecularism, 245–46, 248–49, 252, 255, 257
Potano, Giovanni, 199
Pound, Marcus, 342
pragmatism, 10, 208–9
praise, 3, 5, 10, 18, 60, 121, 125, 131, 145, 160, 252, 262, 267, 270, 272, 298, 330, 376, 391, 393
preaching, 5, 13, 36, 72, 81, 105, 107, 109–10, 114, 116–17, 120–24, 126, 219, 230–34, 241, 252, 269, 369, 377, 379, 394–96
predestination, 154
Prochaska, Frank, 175, 177

providence, 33, 39, 80, 102

Qu'ran, 395
Quash, Ben, 6, 13, 18, 146–62, 167–68, 177, 255, 313, 392

Radcliffe, Timothy, 88
Radical Orthodoxy, 26, 393
Rahner, Karl, 334
Rankin, J., 379, 380, 388, 390
Ray, Nicholas, 367
Redeker, Martin, 41, 47
redemption, 37–41, 46, 105, 142, 169, 174, 200, 225–26
Reformation, 26, 30, 63, 65, 115, 150, 157, 162, 182, 185, 331, 333
Reid, Thomas, 135–39, 145
religious experience, 133, 135, 140, 231
religious studies, 3–4, 15, 212, 304, 313, 318, 333, 336, 338, 342, 392–93, 396
resurrection, 57, 99, 116–17, 141–45
Riché, Pierre, 304, 313
Ricoeur, Paul, 8, 49, 54, 60, 122, 365, 396
righteousness, 61–74, 85, 90, 100
Ritschl, Dietrich, 46
Rogers, Eugene, 149, 162
Roman Catholicism, 16, 23, 29, 164, 169, 198, 221, 230, 292, 294, 296, 315–42, 360, 363
Rousseau, Jean-Jacques, 274, 285
Rudy, Willis, 313
Rüegg, Walter, 210
Ruskin, John, 152–58, 162
Russell, Jemma, 255

Sacks, Jonathan, 234–34, 237, 241
salvation, 5, 8, 17, 51, 59, 61–66, 71–72, 77–82, 84–89, 93, 114–16, 119, 121, 145, 160–61, 193, 200, 216–19, 225, 234–35, 241, 248, 256–57, 260–66, 270, 272, 364–65, 391, 393
Schakel, Peter, 378–80, 390
Schellong, Dieter, 96, 107
Schleiermacher, Friedrich, 12, 21, 35–47, 314–15
Schluchter, Wolfgang, 221, 227
scholasticism, 32, 162
Scott, Peter, 365
Scotus, Duns, 155–56
Scriptural Reasoning, 2, 3, 11, 17, 41, 79, 93, 122, 131, 145, 193–94, 196, 204, 208–9, 212, 233, 240, 289, 291, 299, 302, 330, 368, 377, 392, 394–95
Scripture
- exegesis of, 25, 27, 29–30, 42, 78, 84, 91, 109, 113, 184, 198–201, 239, 330, 389
- interpretation of, 11–13, 21, 27, 41, 44–45, 48, 57–58, 79, 93, 106, 108–9, 122, 184, 188, 204, 233, 266–70, 291, 300, 365, 368
- nature of, 184, 231, 266, 291, 300, 328
- and theology, 7–8, 41, 44–47, 108, 118, 120, 229, 231, 263–64, 266–67, 300, 328
- and tradition, 2, 3, 17, 32, 35–37, 79, 120

secularization, 163–78, 312, 314
self, 5, 8, 15, 17, 38–39, 43, 40–41, 54, 80, 84, 88, 93, 112, 138, 145, 160–61, 164–67, 173–75, 182–89, 195, 206, 224, 230–31, 256–57, 261–62, 264–66, 270, 272, 284, 307, 311–12, 319, 348–49, 357, 364–65, 369–70, 380–87, 391, 393

sex, 98, 119–20, 169–70, 174, 176, 218, 348, 382, 392
Shaffer, E. S., 153–54, 162
Shakespeare, William, 155, 378–79, 390
Shaw, D. W. D., 307, 311, 313
Shoah (Holocaust), 9, 17–18, 42, 209, 370, 394
sin, 37–40, 62–65, 97–100, 105, 110
Smart, Ninian, 333
social theory, 165, 167
Soskice, Janet, 122–28, 313, 392
soteriology, 8, 36, 36, 62–65, 73, 193, 330
Spencer, Jennifer, 159
Stang, Charles, M., 185, 189
Stephen Westerholm, 61, 64, 74
Stewart, J. S., 47
Stowers, Stanley K., 80, 91
Strabo, 156
subjectivity, 138–39, 145, 167–69, 182, 262, 305–7, 380
suffering, 9, 43, 57, 113, 118, 124, 186, 216, 226, 250, 281, 285, 367, 371, 373, 385, 390
Sufism, 232
Swanston, Hamish, 333
Swidler, Leonard, 233, 250, 289–91, 302
Swinburne, Richard, 136, 145
Sykes, Stephen, 2, 331, 366, 392
Symeon the Translator, 143
syncretism, 223

Talmud, 184–84, 205, 368
Tanakh, 184
Tatian, 117
Taylor, Charles, 169–70, 175, 177, 248, 257, 314, 329, 396
Teresa of Avila, 135, 145
Theilgaard, Alice, 378, 390
Theodore of Mopsuestia, 142
Theology
  and academy, 1, 2, 13, 16, 25, 41, 108, 120–21, 181, 189, 194, 246, 270–71, 282, 312, 316, 328, 330–42
  apprenticeship of, 21–34
  as conversation, 2–3, 11–12, 15–16, 18, 21–22, 28–34, 35–36, 41, 48, 58–64, 148, 158, 178, 185, 225, 255–57, 259–72, 290, 307–8, 312, 339–42, 359–73, 375, 378–79, 392–93
  and drama, 6–7, 9–10, 18, 73, 78, 110, 159, 160–62, 167–69, 176–77, 251, 265–66, 299, 394
  ecclesial, 5, 8, 13–16, 23, 25, 109, 267–69, 314–29, 332–39, 395
  feminist, 32, 119, 133, 138, 145, 174, 261, 326
  historical, 12, 22–24, 30, 32–33
  liberation, 232, 240, 251, 261, 307–8
  and narrative, 15, 17–18, 34, 168–69, 174, 184–88, 233–35, 253, 314–15, 329, 338, 391–92
  natural, 38
  Pentecostal, 10
  and politics, 15, 32, 164–69, 176–77, 193–201, 205–8, 217–18, 225, 245–48, 254, 257–58, 260, 273–88, 396
  practical, 2, 17, 394
  public vocation of, 3, 14–15, 247, 249, 304–5, 308, 311
  and science, 178–84, 188–90, 196, 205, 208 213–27, 278, 284, 296, 305, 307, 313–16, 318, 328, 368
Therese of Lisieux, 365, 393
Thompson, E. P., 172

Thoreau, Henry David, 152
Ticciati, Susannah, 12, 77–91
Tice, Terrence N., 47
Tolkien, J. R. R., 378
Tönnies, Ferdinand, 221
Torah, 195, 206, 209, 233, 250, 289–91, 302
Torrance, Thomas F., 34, 60, 107, 182, 184, 190, 240, 390
Toulmin, Stephen, 371, 373
Tracy, David, 260, 270, 272, 338,
Traherne, 25, 158, 396
Trinity, 49, 53–55, 60, 62, 182, 359–63, 366
Turner, Denys, 17, 394
Tzu, Lao, 232

VanGemeren, Willem, 84, 91
Vanhoozer, Kevin J., 17, 394
Vanier, Jean, 16, 111, 121, 160, 345–58, 367, 376
Vaughan, Henry, 160, 162
von Balthasar, Hans Urs, 6, 155–57, 161, 167, 315, 334
von Lowenich, 185

Ward, Graham, 74, 245, 258
Ward, Keith, 312
Watson, Francis, 64, 74
Webb, Leslie, 359–60
Weber, Max, 14, 211–27
Webster, John, 183–84, 190, 261–62, 264, 272, 393
Weil, Simone, 188
Weinandy, Thomas, 327, 329
Wesley, John, 34, 110
Whitman, Walt, 152
Wickham, E. R., 172
Williams, Jane, 17, 397
Williams, Robert R., 47
Williams, Rowan, 12, 14, 27, 29–30, 34, 49, 53–60, 84–85, 88, 91, 178–90, 246, 258
Williams, Sarah, 173, 175, 177
Williamson, Corrine, 158
wisdom, 3–4, 7–12, 14–15, 17–18, 22–23, 26, 31–48, 51–53, 57–60, 62, 68, 93, 122–28, 157–58, 161, 187, 189, 193, 203, 209, 212, 222–41, 246, 248, 250, 254, 261, 264–66, 269, 271, 284, 289–302, 304–5, 307, 310–13, 319–20, 324, 330–31, 342, 356–57, 365, 367–68, 371, 377, 383, 389–90, 392–97
Wittgenstein, Ludwig, 135–37, 143, 145
Wittung, Jeffrey A., 74
Wolsterstorff, Nicholas, 138–40, 144–45, 376, 390
Wood, William, 44–45
Word of God, 27, 34, 50, 57, 118–19, 229
Wright, T. R., 153, 162
Wynn, Mark, 134, 145

Yarnold, Edward, 333
Young, Douglas, 307
Young, Frances, 7, 13, 17, 108–21, 366–77, 373, 376, 390–91, 393, 395

Zahl, Simeon, 1–18, 61–74, 392
Ziegler, Luther, 262, 272

www.ingramcontent.com/pod-product-compliance
Lightning Source LLC
LaVergne TN
LVHW041057080826
845145LV00007B/1612

* 9 7 8 1 6 1 0 9 7 6 2 5 1 *